environmental
finance

Founded in 1807, John Wiley & Sons is the oldest independent publishing company in the United States. With offices in North America, Europe, Australia, and Asia, Wiley is globally committed to developing and marketing print and electronic products and services for our customers' professional and personal knowledge and understanding.

The Wiley Finance series contains books written specifically for finance and investment professionals as well as sophisticated individual investors and their financial advisors. Book topics range from portfolio management to e-commerce, risk management, financial engineering, valuation and financial instrument analysis, as well as much more.

For a list of available titles, please visit our Web site at www.WileyFinance.com.

environmental
finance

*A Guide to Environmental Risk
Assessment and Financial Products*

SONIA LABATT
RODNEY R. WHITE

John Wiley & Sons, Inc.

Copyright © 2002 by Sonia Labatt and Rodney R. White. All rights reserved.

Published by John Wiley & Sons, Inc., Hoboken, New Jersey.
Published simultaneously in Canada.

For general information on our other products and services, or technical support, please
contact our Customer Care Department within the United States at 800-762-2974, outside
the United States at 317-572-3993 or fax 317-572-4002.

Wiley also publishes its books in a variety of electronic formats. Some content that appears
in print may not be available in electronic books.

Designations used by companies to distinguish their products are often claimed by
trademarks. In all instances where the author or publisher is aware of a claim, the product
names appear in Initial Capital letters. Readers, however, should contact the appropriate
companies for more complete information regarding trademarks and registration.

Library of Congress Cataloging-in-Publication Data:

Labatt, Sonia.
    Environmental finance: a guide to environmental risk assessment and
financial products/Sonia Labatt, Rodney R. White.
    p. cm.—(Wiley finance series)
    ISBN 978-0-471-12362-0
    1. Environmental economics. 2. Environmental management. 3.
Environmental protection. I. White, Rodney R. II. Title. III. Series.
    HC79.E5 L32 2002
    363.73'5—dc21   2002008984

10 9 8 7 6 5 4 3 2 1

Hundreds of the world's largest companies now issue environmental reports alongside their financial reports and accounts every year.

Increasingly, these publications contain quantitative data on such issues as the company's water consumption, the volumes of waste it produces, its emissions to the atmosphere, and how much of its electricity comes from renewable sources.

In most cases, these initiatives are voluntary, although pressure is mounting in some countries for such reporting to be made mandatory. The reason many companies consider it worth their while to devote considerable time and effort to compile this data is that they see value in monitoring and measuring their environmental assets and liabilities just as they do for their financial counterparts.

These businesses—and many more each year—feel a need to record their performance against a "triple bottom line" of environmental, social, and financial criteria rather than just the conventional economic benchmarks that remain the norm. While some are acting in response to stakeholder pressure, a growing number believe that good environmental policies will translate into a strong financial performance.

Regulation of environmental issues is clearly growing, however, in response to disasters such as the asbestos-related deaths and associated lawsuits of the 1970s, major oil spills, contaminated land problems, acid rain, climate change, and mounting concern about the depletion of natural resources.

Just as important is the dramatic rise in public anxiety about the state of the environment. Well-funded nongovernmental organizations (NGOs) are now capable of organizing global campaigns on a range of issues and mobilizing opinion around the world against companies that they perceive to be damaging the environment. Just as globalization has boosted the influence and revenues of multinationals, so, too, it has helped environmental pressure groups to campaign more effectively on a global basis.

A striking measure of the shift in public opinion is the rapid growth of investment funds whose asset allocation decisions are determined by environmental and social criteria. The money under management by such funds now exceeds $2 trillion, by some estimates, and is growing far faster than investments in conventional, unscreened equity funds.

In the past five years, leading providers of equity indexes such as FTSE International in the United Kingdom and Dow Jones of the United States have launched families of indexes specifically targeted at the socially responsible investment community. These influential stock market institutions recognize the possibility of a positive relationship between good environmental performance and superior share price performance. Companies selected for these indexes are required to demonstrate that they meet certain minimum standards of environmental performance.

These indexes have attracted considerable media coverage and brought unwelcome attention to companies that failed to make the grade. The index compilers report many cases of excluded companies contacting them for advice about what they need to do to be admitted. In the three years since its launch, some $2 billion has been invested in products linked to the Dow Jones Sustainability Index.

But it is not just companies' shareholders that are paying more attention to their environmental records. Such issues are of increasing concern to banks and insurance groups. Environmental risks facing prospective borrowers are important considerations in many bank-lending decisions. More than 60 percent of banks now have written policies setting out how environmental factors should be considered in their lending and project finance decisions.

As property is frequently used as collateral against corporate loans, banks have been hard hit when defaulting companies have left the lender owning land that was later found to be contaminated. Cleaning up such properties ready for sale so that the bank can recoup its losses is costly and time-consuming.

Insurance companies also have painful memories of industry's environmental disasters. The slew of asbestos claims, which began in the 1970s and continues to this day, is a prime example. It led to the demise of many insurers and contributed to the painful root and branch reform of Lloyd's of London, the 300-year-old insurance market.

Natural environmental disasters, too, are causing insurers and reinsurers to rethink decisions on corporate coverage. The frequency of major floods, typhoons, and hurricanes seems to be increasing, with 16 of the 20 most costly natural events of the recent century occurring in the past 10 years. Hurricane Andrew, which hit Florida in 1992, remains one of the most costly natural disasters of all time, causing more than $15 billion of insured losses. It led to many insurers failing and prompted a fundamental rethink of how such risks could best be handled.

Insurers realized that they lacked the resources to deal with losses on such a scale on their own. One imaginative response, to enable them to continue offering protection against such extreme events, was to attract extra funding from the capital markets by securitizing some of the risks in bonds, which could then be sold to high-yield investors. Such "catastrophe bonds" typically pay a relatively high coupon unless a specific event occurs—a hurricane striking Florida, for example, or an earthquake within a certain distance of Tokyo—in which case the coupon payments may cease and, in some cases, the whole capital invested may be lost.

This is one example of a range of innovative financial products that have been developed in recent years to deal specifically with environmental problems. A more recent example is weather derivatives—contracts designed to help companies protect their earnings against the impact of adverse (but not catastrophic) conditions—unseasonably hot/cold/dry/wet weather, for example. Such products have proved particularly popular with power companies in the United States and are now finding buyers in agriculture, leisure, retail, and transport sectors. As it is estimated that some $1 trillion of the U.S. economy is weather-sensitive, these new hedging instruments appear to have an enormous potential market. In the five years since its birth, the market in weather derivatives has transferred an estimated $12 billion in underlying risk.

Perhaps the best known of the new family of environmental financial products are emission allowances. The most celebrated example was created by the U.S. Acid Rain Program, which in 1995 imposed emissions limits on major sources of sulfur dioxide (SO_2)—the main cause of acid rain. Each of these sources—mainly power plants—was allocated a limited number of emission allowances, each representing one ton of SO_2. Companies that emit more than the number of allowances they hold face financial penalties. Those that can reduce their SO_2 output relatively cheaply and easily are allowed to sell their excess allowances to those that find it more costly to curb their emissions.

This traded market in emission allowances confounded initial skepticism by achieving the targeted reduction in SO_2 emissions much faster and at a far lower cost than had been expected. It is generally regarded by regulators, industry, and environmentalists as an outstanding success. It raises the cost of doing business for those companies that remain heavy polluters while presenting new opportunities to those that adopt clean production methods.

As a consequence, the same approach is being applied to other environmental problems. The United States itself has introduced regional markets in nitrogen oxide allowances to combat local smog problems, and the

European Union is planning an international market in carbon dioxide (CO_2) emissions as part of its efforts to tackle global warming.

In early 2002, the United Kingdom jumped the gun on its European Union partners by launching a domestic market in CO_2 allowances, to help it meet its goal under the terms of the Kyoto Protocol to reduce its greenhouse gases (GHG) emissions to 12.5 percent below their 1990 level by 2012. This single-country market is open to more than 6,000 U.K. companies and, within the first six months of its existence, several foreign businesses had also bought allowances in the scheme to help them comply with restrictions that they expect to face in future.

The controversial Kyoto agreement—signed in 1997—is intended to help combat global warming by reducing emissions of CO_2 and other greenhouse gases from industrialized nations. Although the United States has turned its back on the Protocol, it is expected to enter into force early in 2003, thus paving the way for a global market in CO_2 emission allowances or "carbon credits." An international emissions trading scheme is at the heart of this agreement, as it is seen as the best way to ensure that the desired reductions are achieved as cheaply as possible.

The Protocol also introduces two other market-based approaches to tackle global warming. These schemes—known as Joint Implementation and the Clean Development Mechanism—are designed to promote energy efficiency and CO_2 reduction projects in industrialized and developing nations respectively. Several national governments and private-sector companies are already investing in such projects in the expectation that they will receive carbon credits in return.

As stressed by the authors of this impressive book, climate change is a global problem and is irreversible in the short term. It threatens to be one of the most important drivers of economic change over the next 50 years and will have far-reaching implications. Some leading companies are convinced it already poses a threat to their traditional businesses and are adapting their corporate strategies accordingly. Others see it creating promising new business opportunities. These varied responses are starting to attract the attention of far-sighted equity analysts who are attempting to include companies' carbon intensity in their stock valuation methods.

Meanwhile, many national governments are responding to the Kyoto challenge by attempting to boost the supply of electricity from renewable sources. Several of them, along with some U.S. states, are pinning their faith on another new financial product—renewable energy certificates—to help them achieve their goal.

Market-based solutions are also being considered to help combat very different environmental problems, such as landfill capacity, watershed damage, and loss of biodiversity.

All these initiatives are in their infancy, however, and it is still a small minority of companies that have used weather derivatives, emissions permits, or any of the other new financial products linked to the environment. But more are doing so each day. Some are acting simply for public relations benefits, and some in anticipation of regulation, but many have a genuine belief in the need to embed environmental issues at the heart of their approach to business.

Sonia Labatt and Rodney White are to be praised for this bold attempt to map out the many various developments that are contributing to what they suggest is a fundamental paradigm shift. Whereas, until recently, environmental damage was seen as an inevitable consequence of economic growth, a new scenario is emerging in which economic growth and a healthy environment are mutually reinforcing.

GRAHAM COOPER
Publisher
Environmental Finance magazine
August 2002

acknowledgments

In order to write a book that covers such a broad sweep of subject matter we have had to call on the advice of many people, and we are happy to acknowledge their contributions to the final product. Our first thank-you goes to our friend and colleague, Virginia Maclaren of the Department of Geography and the Institute for Environmental Studies at the University of Toronto. It was Virginia who suggested that we pool our various ideas and work on the book together.

We also benefited from the advice of the following people, many of whom are the pioneers in the emerging field of environmental finance:

Dominic Barton (McKinsey & Company), Gerhard Berz, Angelika Wirtz, and Thomas Loster (Munich Re), Ian Burton (Professor Emeritus, University of Toronto), Amy Casey (Chicago Board of Trade), Jack Crane (South Shore Bank), Andrew Dlugolecki (formerly of CGNU), Wendy Dobson (Rotman School of Management, University of Toronto), David Etkin (Environment Canada), Jamie Evans, the late John Gray, and Tom Fowles (all of Royal Bank of Canada), Scott Henshaw (UBS Warburg), Carlos Joly (Storebrand), Yan Kermode, Bettina Furrer (UBS), Kimberly Gluck (State Street Global Advisors), Odette Goodall (AIM Funds Management), Julie Gorte (Calvert Group), Stanley Griffin (Insurance Bureau of Canada), Kenneth Hague (Aon Re), Robert Harrison (INVESCO), Richard Ilomaki (Factory Mutual), Charles Kennedy (McDougall, McDougall, McTier), Michael Jantzi (Michael Jantzi Research Associates), Paul Kovacs (Insurance Bureau of Canada), Christine Little (AIG Environmental of Canada), Helen Lup (The Economical Insurance Group), Lawrence McGrath (Fondelec), Robert Merrick (Canadian Bankers Association), Michael Millette and Andrew Kaiser (both of Goldman Sachs Risk Management Group), Jeremy Leggett (Solar Century), Andrei Marcu (International Emissions Trading Association), Naimh O'Sullivan (United Nations Environment Program—Financial Initiative), Alan Pang (Insurers' Advisory Organization), Bernhard Raberger (formerly of the Environmental Change Institute, University of Oxford), Darrell Riley (T. Rowe Price), Janice Reiner (The Cooperators Insurance/Financial Services), Angus Ross (formerly with Sorema), Eric Urbani (Emerald Group), Michael Walsh (Environmental Financial Products

LLC), Don Wharton (TransAlta), Martin Whittaker, Matthew Kiernan, and Peter Wilkes (all with Innovest SVA), and Alan Willis (Alan Willis and Associates).

To Graham Cooper, publisher of the magazine *Environmental Finance*, we owe special thanks for several reasons. First, by founding the magazine he demonstrated that the field of environmental finance was indeed emerging and was not just a figment of our imagination. Second, he took our proposal forward to Bill Falloon, Senior Editor for Finance and Investment at John Wiley & Sons. Third, he took the time to go over the manuscript and offered many helpful suggestions for improvements. Lastly, he was kind enough to write the Foreword. To Bill we owe thanks for guiding us through the publication process—a process that requires patience and a sense of humor.

To Geoffrey Smith (then a graduate student at the Rotman School of Management at the University of Toronto, now with the Canadian Imperial Bank of Commerce) we are grateful for helping us with the library research and interviews with key informants, and for sharing our enthusiasm for the field of enquiry. Jacqui Shoffner offered constructive comments as she read early drafts of the manuscript. In addition, Greg Philpott and Janice Daley provided crucial help in formatting the manuscript and developing the graphics, which were tasks that we could not have done on our own.

Finally, we recognize that our spouses, Sue White and Arthur Labatt, have had to share our preoccupation with this work. In addition to their indispensable support, both have also provided significant help through their knowledge of the worlds of insurance and investment, respectively. For their support, patience, and knowledge we are deeply grateful.

Even with all this help no doubt errors do remain for which the authors alone are responsible.

Every effort has been made to trace and acknowledge ownership of copyright. The authors will be glad to hear from any copyright holders whom it has not been possible to contact.

SONIA LABATT
RODNEY R. WHITE

Toronto, Canada
August 2002

contents

CHAPTER 1

The Emerging World of Environmental Finance

INTRODUCTION

Environmental finance is a recently coined term, one that probably could not have appeared until the closing moments of the twentieth century. It encompasses all market-based instruments designed to deliver environmental quality and to transfer environmental risk. It signals a radical change of direction in the way that modern industrial society has approached environmental challenges in the past.

The modern environmental movement appeared in the second half of the nineteenth century in response to the ugliness and destruction of the industrial revolution. Throughout most of the twentieth century people assumed that there was an implicit trade-off between an attractive environment and economic growth, because this was the lesson they drew from the previous century. People had become wealthier through an industrialization process that blighted the landscape and poisoned the water, the air, and the ground. The lesson seemed obvious. If people in the twentieth century now wanted to restore a healthy and attractive environment they would have to pay for it. There is no logic whatever in this assumption. It is just a simple quid pro quo—if you want something you will have to pay for it. Hence, if you want a decent environment it will cost you something, maybe a lot more than many people want to pay.

Happily, the world is a more complicated and interesting place than this simple assumption implies. The accounting systems that grew up alongside the industrial revolution concentrated on the simplest financial indicators—revenues, costs, and the balance. If a company did not have to pay for its damage to the environment, then it did not show up on its bal-

1

ance sheet. Economists later dignified these omissions as "externalities"—or costs that the firm passed on to society at large.

If we—as citizens, as investors, or as businesses—are now really concerned about these environmental damages, then we should find ways to include them in the balance sheet. Once we make this adjustment the world appears in a more interesting light. If we really *do* value an attractive and healthy environment, then we *will* be prepared to pay for it. The converse of this deduction is even more interesting—the businesses that destroy environmental value should reflect that fact in their balance sheets and be valued accordingly. Can these simple observations be put to good use? We believe they can.

Environmental finance is a field of inquiry and activity that has grown up to address these challenges. If we truly wish to value environmental quality, then we should try to price its worth, in the business context. This is a very different ambition from that of "environmental economics" or even "ecological economics." These approaches have been developed to respond to the values of society at large. Environmental finance, on the other hand, approaches environmental problems from the internal perspective of the firm, acting in its own interest. Its interest will be framed by the personal ambitions, expectations, and values of the managers and owners of the firm, as well as by the regulatory system through which society obliges them to respond to the environmental challenge. Some firms also respond to the expectations of all the stakeholders in the enterprise, including employees and the local community. (See the section titled "Stakeholder Relationships" in the next chapter.)

How might a firm that wishes to achieve certain environmental standards chart its path? First, the firm must have a clear assessment of its situation *in the biosphere now*. (The biosphere is that part of the planet inhabited by living organisms.) Is it causing damage for which it might later have to pay? This is the simple compliance issue, which is driven by legislation. The more complex issue lies over the 20-year horizon. How will the biosphere have changed by then, and how might the firm be responding?

AN EMERGING FIELD

There are many examples of market-based solutions for environmental problems, and in the past 10 years the development of these solutions has begun to play a part in the evolution of the financial services sector. For people who develop and use these products the connections between them may not be obvious. For example, what has "carbon trading"—the trading of carbon dioxide emissions reduction credits—got to do with socially responsible investment? The answer is that both have evolved in response to environmental change. The concept of environmental change embraces all those changes to the physical environment that have happened as a result of the growing impact of humankind on the biosphere, including climate change and local environmental degradation. The development of financial products to respond to environmental challenges has reached a stage such that environmental finance can be recognized as an emerging field of research and practice.

A successful environmental financial product must satisfy two quite distinct criteria. First, it must establish its niche in the marketplace. Second, it must meet the environmental objectives (such as emissions reductions or risk transfer) that it was designed to address. In this book we will not only identify and analyze successful products, we will also do the same for products that might meet one of the criteria but not the other. For example, the establishment of carbon trading will be successful in an environmental sense only if it facilitates the genuine reduction of carbon dioxide emissions. The risk of failure is evaluated in Chapter 7. Regarding the other criterion, the trading of catastrophe options on the Chicago Board of Trade would certainly have been able to transfer risk from insurers to the capital markets had it been possible to establish a sufficiently large and liquid market. Their failure to reach that point is discussed in Chapter 5.

WHY IS IT HAPPENING AT THIS PARTICULAR TIME?

There is no question (optimists notwithstanding) that the biosphere is coming under increasing pressure. The source of pressure is twofold: increasing numbers of people and increasing intake of resources and production of wastes as people grow wealthier. (See Figure 1.1.) Observers have worried about the exhaustion of resources, such as minerals and fossil fuels, for more than a hundred years, but the fear has been dismissed by others who demonstrate that resource shortages raise prices and those higher prices bring in new discoveries and more efficient means of production. Indeed, the nonrenewable resource base does not appear to be a problem today. The resource problem lies with potentially renewable resources that could be managed sustainably, but which are abused. Key problem areas are freshwater, ocean fisheries, agricultural soils, forests, and loss of biodiversity. The other big problem is the wastes we produce, especially greenhouse

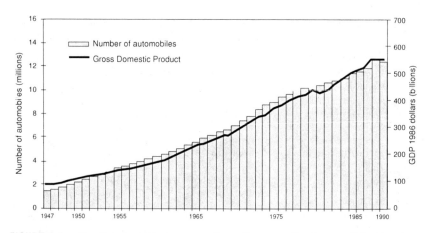

FIGURE 1.1　The Relationship between Gross Domestic Product and the Number of Automobiles in Canada
Source: Statistics Canada 1990a, 1990b.

gases, which are accumulating in the atmosphere and are expected to change the climate. This issue is discussed in detail in Chapter 7.

It is the climate change problem that has pushed environmental concerns to the fore. It is a very large-scale problem that threatens to disrupt the climate on which we all depend for the necessities of life. This is not an aesthetic issue, nor an animal rights issue; it is a survival issue. It has become clear that *something* must be done, even if there is considerable disagreement as to what that something is. It requires governments to make a series of difficult decisions, which is something governments do with reluctance. It requires governments around the world to act in concert for the common good.

Since the climate change and environmental pressure problems were acknowledged at the Earth Summit in Rio de Janeiro in 1992, governments have avoided taking any decisive action. Some have talked courageously about taking up the challenge, but action on the ground has been token at best. Meanwhile, greenhouse gases have continued to accumulate, just as predicted, and the climate has warmed, as expected. (See Figures 1.2, 1.3, and 1.4.)

Even in the heyday of strong central governments in the postwar period, national governments would not have been likely to take decisive action on climate change, because the problem is large and complex, and the benefits we might expect from decisive action lie beyond the political

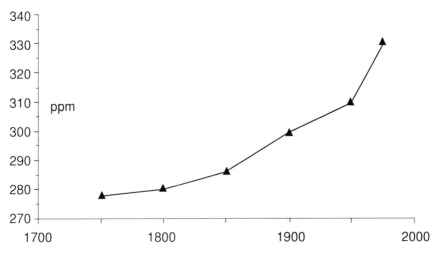

FIGURE 1.2 Carbon Dioxide Concentrations in the Atmosphere, Samples from Ice Cores in the Antarctic
Source: Based on Firor 1990, 51.

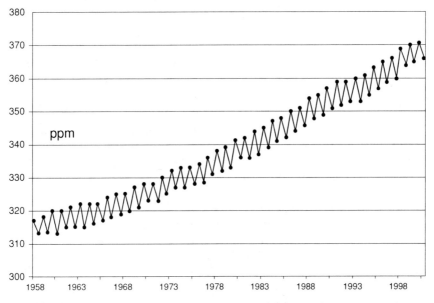

FIGURE 1.3 Carbon Dioxide Concentrations in the Atmosphere, Direct Measurements from Mauna Loa, Hawaii
Note: Data points are taken from May and October, annually, 1958 to 2000.
Source: Based on Keeling and Whorf 2001.

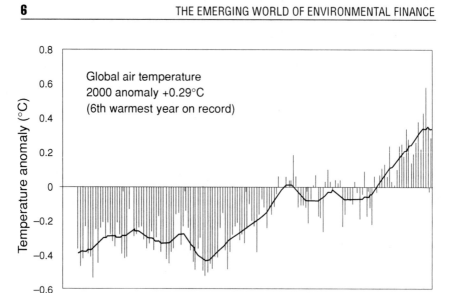

FIGURE 1.4   Global Air Temperature 1850–2000
Source: Climatic Research Unit, University of East Anglia. Available at: www.cru.
uea.ac.uk/cru/info/warming.

time horizon and even beyond the lifetimes of our children. It is even less likely that national decision makers will be decisive today when command-and-control and tax-and-spend styles of government are completely out of fashion.

By default, it falls to the private sector to look ahead and make appropriate plans to protect its own self-interest, although government is still essential to regulate and encourage the development of appropriate policy frameworks. It is interesting that—at this same time—much of the private sector is undergoing a process of globalization, whereby it is acquiring the capacity to make decisions on a global basis, influencing governments and companies around the world. Now the citizens of many countries, in the environmental domain as well as others, can affect shareholders' interests. The tension arising from the interplay between local and global interests is an important part of the backdrop to the themes explored in this book.

Global decision making—meaning decisions that can respond to conditions around the world in real time—has only recently become possible through the revolution in information technology (IT). To the public the IT revolution is mainly visible through the Internet, e-mail, cell phones, and handheld computers. Behind these novelties lies the more powerful world of global positioning systems (GPS), which can abstract terrestrial information from satellites, and of remote sensing and geographical information systems. Together these technologies provide the potential for a global information system that can be accessed in real time. This provides, for the first time, the possibility of a global level of awareness. While this level of support does not provide omniscience, it does provide a heightened sense of global environmental change, which is what we need to meet the challenge.

Nor is this global information capacity restricted to global companies and governments. It is also to some extent available to members of the public, and certainly to international nongovernmental organizations (NGOs), some of which have multimillion-dollar incomes. This global capacity for information exchange at low cost has increased the potential for global pressure to be brought on companies that fail to live up to the public's expectations. This pressure can be exerted through demonstrations, shareholder activism, product boycotts, and legal challenges. The global reach of the international company can be matched by a global capacity of the NGOs to mobilize public opinion. Although the link is difficult to prove, it is certainly no coincidence that many corporations have recently moved beyond "greenwash" (environmental whitewashing) to constructive environmental engagement. Several prominent companies have not only started publishing annual environmental reports on their activities, but they have also had them externally verified (Delphi and Ecologic 1997). This development is analyzed in Chapter 8.

LESSONS LEARNED

Although government regulation and public opinion are essential driving forces, it has been corporate experience with environmental engagement that has accelerated the rate of acceptance of corporate environment responsibility and has recently provided conditions that are favorable to the development of environmental financial products. On the positive side we have the whole range of advice, from the cautious optimism of *Financing Change* (Schmidheiny and Zorraquin 1996), *Sustainable Finance and Banking* (Jeucken 2001), and *Sustainable Banking* (Bouma et al. 2001) to the infectious enthusiasm of *Cool Companies* (Romm 1999), *Factor Four* (von Weizsäcker et al. 1998), and *Natural Capitalism* (Hawken et al. 1999). Books such as these may have helped to reassure the skeptical decision maker that environment and economy are not a zero-sum game but are actually mutually reinforcing.

Even if the skeptic did not gain confidence from such reading, then he or she could not have failed to learn from the hard lessons of environmental neglect. Asbestos was the first environmentally related problem that entailed multibillion-dollar losses and the bankruptcy of several major corporations. It took 30 years to unfold, and the story is still not over. (See Chapter 5.) Concurrent with the asbestos drama was the unveiling of the lethal impact of industrial pollution and inadequate landfills, culminating in the heavy burden of the U.S. Superfund legislation, with which companies are still struggling. (See Chapters 4 and 5.) Some environmental concerns are still gathering momentum, such as lead paint, while others, such as toxic molds and genetically modified organisms (GMOs), have yet to make their impact felt.

There is no doubt that private-sector decision makers had been softened up by these environmental challenges, even before climate change claimed their attention. Timing was critical for this to happen. The Earth Summit met in June 1992, and the Framework Convention on Climate Change was adopted. Then Hurricane Andrew struck in August of the same year, inflicting record damage on the insurance industry. Already there had been speculation that global warming might produce more and bigger hurricanes (still an unresolved issue among scientists). Even the *possibility* that climate change might be responsible for this type of impact, on a more frequent basis, was enough to focus a number of minds on the fact that *scientists did not know exactly what climate change might bring.* Suddenly a very large question mark appeared over balance sheets all around the world. It was possible that the world had embarked on an era of alarming and irreversible change. As Peter Bernstein summarized the issue:

> *If global warming indeed lies ahead, a long string of hot years will not necessarily be followed by a long string of cold years. . . . If humans succeed in destroying the environment, floods may fail to follow droughts. (Bernstein 1996, 182)*

There are risks in inaction, and there are risks associated with mitigation, because both the direct physical impacts of more extreme weather and the economic impacts of mitigative action—specifically, reducing the use of fossil fuels—could be very significant.

Some sectors, like insurance, focused on the first issue and decided that mitigative action was essential and urgent. Others, like the fossil fuel industry, focused on the latter and decided to oppose mitigation vigorously. Opinion in the oil and gas sector has since diverged, with some companies still opposed to action while others are moving swiftly to prepare for life in a carbon-constrained world. (See Chapter 7.)

HOW MIGHT ENVIRONMENTAL FINANCE
PREPARE US FOR THE CHALLENGES AHEAD?

As noted earlier, governments have been extremely cautious about committing themselves (and the taxpayers) to implementing measures to reduce the risks of climate change, just as they have been reluctant to deal forcefully with any environmental issue. Many politicians and bureaucrats are unfamiliar with the underlying science, and they assume, perhaps rightly, that the public is no better informed than they are. The scientists themselves often seem to disagree with one another over the seriousness of many of the issues. You can always find some scientists to disagree on any issue, certainly when it comes down to assigning a level of risk. In the circumstances, caution suggests a noncommittal response, or perhaps no response at all. The very measurements used by the scientists—such as "parts per million" for atmospheric pollutants—seem to indicate that the problem is rather small.

In these circumstances, why should we expect the emerging field of environmental finance to be able to mobilize market forces to tackle the problem?

The expectation is based on the fact that the private sector enjoys several advantages over government when it comes to making decisions under uncertainty. Being private, in itself, confers some advantages. Although companies are being brought more closely under public scrutiny (as noted earlier), they are still not as exposed to the public eye as is a government in a democracy. Private decision makers can change their minds without being publicly accused of inconsistency. They can make incremental decisions and study the effects before taking further steps. In other words, they can experiment. They do not have to pass laws that are binding on all members of society. They face competition and they must remain profitable, but they do have more flexibility. In systems terms, they have a much greater capacity for self-organization. It is this factor that allows ideas to evolve and enables companies to adapt to changing circumstances.

We have seen a willingness to experiment, a searching for solutions to environmental problems, in the way that the field of environmental finance has evolved. In this book we have identified the year 1997 as a turning point in redefining the corporate response to the environmental challenge.

That was the year that the Kyoto Protocol to the Framework Convention on Climate Change was signed. It was also the year that British Petroleum (BP) announced that it was preparing for business "beyond petroleum." (See Box 7.2.) Since then there has been a rapid increase in the development of new financial products. These include: banking products such as green mortgages, weather derivatives to hedge exposure to adverse weather, tradable emission reduction credits for sulphur dioxide and nitrous oxides, catastrophe bonds for earthquake and weather risk, a proliferation of "green funds" as part of the socially responsible investment market, and—potentially most significant of all—the beginning of markets for greenhouse gas reduction credits.

Some companies in the financial services sector have embarked on their own "good green housekeeping" practices to reduce their own environmental impact. Some insurers and bankers now scrutinize their corporate customers' environmental standards to reduce the risk of assuming responsibility for any of their clients' environmental liabilities. Some insurers and bankers even grant more favorable terms if their clients have good environmental records. Environmental reporting has moved from the fringe to mainstream accounting practice. (See Chapter 8.) A number of banks and insurers have signed a statement of commitment with the United Nations Environment Program (UNEP). (See Chapter 3.) Others have contributed to the Intergovernmental Panel on Climate Change, especially in the field of impact assessment.

This is not to say that the environmental challenge has been met so successfully that the problems are under control. Instead these innovations should be seen simply as the first experimental steps along a very long road. Many companies are still looking backward rather than forward. They have yet to commit to serious engagement with the environmental challenges around them. As time passes, the world in which they operate becomes more complex, both in terms of environmental change and the financial instruments that are available for managing their exposure to environmental risk. Ron Dembo and Andrew Freeman observed:

Financial institutions—banks, brokers, and insurers—are nothing more than risk traders who buy one risk and sell another. Their business is based on profit from risk, and they are barraged with opportunities for risk taking. In recent years, as financial markets have become dramatically more complex, these institutions have had to develop innovative ways of controlling their risk exposures. But it is inherently difficult for these banks, investment companies, and insurance compa-

nies to understand the risks they are assuming at any given moment. Their ability to understand risk often lags seriously behind their urgent need to do so. (Dembo and Freeman 1998, 6)

At least decision makers now have a lot more information on what works and what does not work than they had five years ago. This book is offered as an initial assessment of what that information is worth. The assessment runs over a spatial continuum from the local to the global, and a temporal continuum from the recent past (the experience of the past 30 years) to the projected future into the middle of this new century. Although there are some historical references as long ago as the late seventeenth century (the foundation of Lloyd's of London), the beginning of the modern era of environmental risk might be dated to 1969, the year that Clarence Borel filed the first asbestos suit against his employer. (See Chapter 5.) From that date, asbestos and other environmental issues grew relentlessly, eventually affecting all facets of the financial services sector. In the late 1980s, the first billion-dollar weather-related losses appeared, as hurricanes struck the Caribbean, United States, and Japan. From 1992, when Hurricane Andrew struck Florida and Louisiana, severe weather became associated with the impending issue of climate change. The notion of such a momentous change in our living circumstances was widely resisted, initially.

During the course of writing this book the global "landscape of risk" has been completely transformed by two events—the attack on the World Trade Center and the collapse of Enron, an energy trading company that was widely admired for its meteoric rise to prominence in global markets. The phrases "September 11th" and "post-Enron" immediately established themselves in our everyday language; both carry an enormous amount of significance for modern society. September 11th means that no one—even in the tallest tower in the biggest city in the richest country of the world—is safe from terrorist attack. Post-Enron means that no company, however successful and audited by another company with a household name for probity, is necessarily sound. These two events demonstrate conclusively that the unthinkable may happen—and suddenly, without warning. Complacency is out of fashion. As noted in a recent report:

The need for more effective risk management has rarely been so urgent. As CFOs grapple with the implications of events ranging from last September's terrorist attacks to the sudden collapse of Enron, they are reminded of a grim truth: threats to the business can come from any direction. (CFO Publishing Corp. 2002)

Neither of these events is really "environmental" (although both have some environmental implications), yet they have affected the subject matter of the book. The attack on the World Trade Center had a huge impact on insurance availability and insurance rates. Since the attack "the price of corporate insurance has risen 30 percent on average" (CFO Publishing Corp. 2002, 12). Indeed it produced the biggest spike in prices since Hurricane Andrew. Meanwhile the Enron failure has created enormous pressure for companies to show greater transparency in accounting for their exposure to all kinds of risk, not simply terrorism or credit risk.

CONCLUSION

The traditional assumption that there was an unavoidable trade-off between the economy and the environment is now being replaced with a realization that they are mutually reinforcing. This transition to a new paradigm comes at a time when governments continue to withdraw from economic activities that they assumed in the twentieth century, including transportation and public utilities. Their retreat from the days of command and control appears to be accompanied by a reluctance to take a lead in meeting the multiple environmental challenges we face, especially climate change, and especially in the United States.

The private sector finds itself at an interesting crossroads. Some companies believe that they should take a proactive stance in environmental matters, while others do no more than they must to achieve regulatory compliance, and some do not even do that much. Proactive companies include prominent members of the automotive sector, the chemical industry, and oil and gas, even though they have the greatest adjustments to make in a carbon-constrained world. The financial services sector also has its proactive leaders who have developed environmental risk assessment and have started to produce specialized products to help companies meet the environmental challenge. These new products are now significant enough to comprise a new subsector known as environmental finance.

This book has been prepared as an exploration of this emerging situation where financial service companies seek new product niches to support more effective environmental management. The next chapter introduces a toolbox of some basic concepts and financial mechanisms. Chapter 3 provides an overview of recent changes in the financial services sector, especially in response to deregulation and globalization, two powerful drivers for innovation. Those with an environmental background may decide to skim Chapter 2, while those with a broad understanding of the global financial markets may choose to glance briefly at Chapter 3. The next three chapters assess in more detail the worlds of banking, insurance, and investment. Chapter 7 examines the implications of climate change for the financial services sector, indeed the economy as a whole. Chapter 8 analyzes the rise of environmental reporting, which is the key to better management and investment strategy. This is followed by a number of case studies that show how particular companies have responded to a variety of environmental challenges. The concluding chapter, titled "The Way Ahead," draws these experiences together to assess the role of environmental finance in this new, carbon-constrained world.

CHAPTER 2

Concepts and Tools for Developing Environmental Finance

INTRODUCTION

The rate of societal change has been accelerating since the inception of the industrial revolution. We are now increasingly aware that the negative environmental side effects of that revolution are not trivial. Nor are they insuperable or too costly to contemplate. However, until recently many of these side effects were largely ignored. People may have observed some impacts but they were not systematically managed. Some were the responsibility of the public sector (especially nuclear power, water supply and treatment, and solid waste management) and hence rarely a concern of the private sector. Some of the side effects took years to show up (such as long-tailed insurance claims for asbestos liability), and the insurance industry was totally unprepared to manage the risk. Deregulation—often including the activities of formerly public companies—has now brought these concerns to the private sector. In order to reassure the voters, government has brought in a whole array of new regulations ("reregulation") to make the newly privatized operations transparent. Another great force for change has been globalization. Companies have been released from the confines of the regional or national markets and have taken a global stake. The largest companies have been doing this for a hundred years. Now much of the rest of the economy is following. Some newly privatized businesses—like water supply and treatment—find themselves on the global scene for the first time.

Legal redress is becoming globalized also. Ironically, this has been possible for a long time, specifically through the U.S. Alien Tort Claims Act of 1789, which allows foreign nationals to sue American companies in the American courts. This is now being used by diverse groups around the world to sue American companies for damage to their environments (W. Thomas 2001).

Even if companies and their financial service providers had ignored these developments, they could not ignore the very tangible costs of a poor environmental performance. These have been heavy. The costs of asbestos, inadequate landfill management, and oil spills have had major impacts on their balance sheets. Such cases will be identified in the rest of this book. Management failures have led to huge insurance payments and, in some circumstances, eventually to bankruptcy. Environmental problems have pitted old partners—such as manufacturers, insurers, and bankers—against one another.

The September 11 attack on the World Trade Center has intensified this trend toward a more critical assessment of long-standing business relationships in the insurance world.

According to S&P [Standard & Poor's, the ratings agency], reinsurers are reducing their emphasis on long-standing client relationships and adopting a more clinical approach to underwriting as both the insurance and reinsurance markets scrutinise their profitability in the wake of the WTC attacks. The ratings agency predicts that reinsurers will apply even greater financial analysis to the underwriting process, taking a further step back from more traditional, "client-focused" underwriting. . . . Buyers are also taking a more opportunistic stand, helping to drive the shift away from "relationships," according to S&P. (Aon Limited 2001, 14)

At the very least, if an environmental problem is identified for a company—and that problem is not adequately managed—then a company will absorb a reputational risk, which will drive the share price down. Several examples of such cases are presented in the book. The public knows, reminded by nongovernmental organizations (NGOs) and the media, that companies have responsibilities and vulnerabilities. A number of companies now understand this change of paradigm very well and have moved to address it. On the positive side there is increasing evidence that the market rewards proactive environmental management.

ENVIRONMENTAL MANAGEMENT AND SHAREHOLDER VALUE CREATION

Research attempting to link environmental and financial performance (see Chapter 6) reveals a growing sense that sound environmental management can lead to increased shareholder value, which is defined as:

> *Value for shareholders which is created when a business, over time, uses capital at its disposal to earn returns greater than, or equal to, the cost of that capital. (Willis and Desjardins 2000, 9)*

Traditionally, environmental management has been seen as imposing a cost on a company and a "green penalty" on investors, with no corresponding benefit being conferred. The opposing view holds that environmental performance is compatible with, and perhaps central to, competitiveness and superior financial performance (Porter and van der Linde 1995). There is strong evidence that improved environmental behavior has a strong impact on shareholder value (Dowell et al. 2000; Sustain-Ability/UNEP 2001; UBS 2000).

A business case can be made that not only dispels notions that environmental initiatives have an adverse effect on profitability, but holds that they contribute to shareholder value creation. Figure 2.1 demonstrates the linkages between improved corporate environmental performance and the creation of shareholder value.

Areas of strategic decision making within a company's product management, operations, capital assets, and finance departments govern the processes that create value for the corporation, through their impacts on revenues, operating costs, and the cost of capital. Improved environmental management decisions at this level influence these value drivers, which in turn generate shareholder value. The following discussion demonstrates how a focus on environmental issues can lead to increased revenues, decreased operating costs, and a lower cost of capital.

Product Management   A strong environmental focus in the product design can lead to new product development and, in some cases, can redefine markets (U.S. EPA 2000). Considerations of a product's environmental impacts at the design stage can keep a firm in the forefront of market innovation and position it well to reap marketing advantages. From this marketing standpoint, an environmental focus can help improve a company's revenues as its environmentally improved products are differentiated from

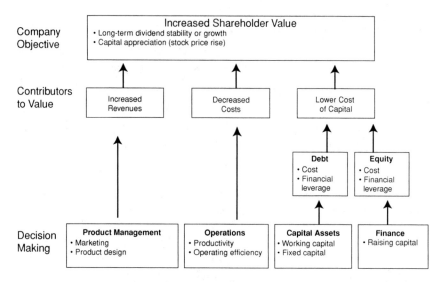

FIGURE 2.1   Shareholder Value Creation Model
Sources: Adapted from Willis and Desjardins 2000; Havemann and Webster 1999.

others, contributing to increased brand recognition and competitive advantage. From a liability perspective, if a company's product has adverse effects on the environment, the company can bear liabilities that strike at the core of its business (Mansley 1994).

Operations   In addition to product management and design, many firms' environmental impacts come from their manufacturing processes. Taking environmental considerations into account in these processes can help firms reduce the energy and raw materials inputs, as well as reduce waste outputs. Process changes that reduce environmental impacts can lead to lower costs and increased operational efficiency.

Insurance specialists have recognized a reduction in risk for firms with strong operational environmental management. Some insurers have created products that translate improved environmental performance into lower premiums. Through the use of environmental criteria in setting policy rates for clients, for example, the insurance specialist Willis Corroon in the United States has offered members of the Synthetic Organic Chemical Manufacturers Association a discount of up to 30 percent on premiums for environmental impairment liability insurance based on their degree of responsible care implementation (Aspen Institute 1998). Thus, a more environmentally sensitive manufacturing philosophy not only reduces operating costs, but can also reduce insurance premiums as well.

Such product and process changes embody the concept of "eco-efficiency" by "creating value for society and for the company, by doing more with less over the entire life cycle" (DeSimone and Popoff 1997, 10).

Capital Assets   A focus on environmental issues when making capital asset investment decisions also helps to lower a company's costs. Not only do investments in environmentally appropriate fixed capital assets lower production costs and make the operating process more efficient, they also help to improve a firm's environmental profile. As a result, a firm that has invested in environmentally favorable assets will be well positioned to comply with new environmental regulations, and to increase its ability to use those assets that benefit the environment over their full operating lives. In addition, the firm will be less prone to environmental incidents, which lead to costly cleanup charges and legal liability.

Lending institutions take into consideration a company's reduction in environmental risk, in considering favorable lending terms. For example, Sumitomo Bank of Japan is highlighted in Chapter 4 for offering "eco loans" to small and medium-sized companies that hope to make fixed asset investments to improve operating efficiencies related to the use of raw materials and energy (Aspen Institute 1998).

Finance   While increasing revenues and decreasing costs help to improve a firm's income, financing decisions are central to the long-term creation of value in the organization. Financing decisions are crucial to the retention of firm value over time, allowing for expansion or acquisitions as well as having an impact on tax and interest expenses.

A firm's two main choices for raising funds are debt or equity financing, although hybrid instruments do also exist. Debt financing refers to the issuance of bonds or borrowing from lenders, while equity financing refers to the issuance of shares. Debt represents a financial obligation, enforceable by law, to pay interest and repay principal. Equity, however, carries no legal obligation, and thus equity holders accept a greater element of risk.

The cost of capital for a firm is defined in terms of the weighted average of its costs of equity and debt, and reflects the company's marginal costs of raising capital (Damodaran 2001). A firm's cost of capital changes if the risk level of its business changes. As risk increases or decreases, so too does the cost of capital. A firm with a lower cost of capital can therefore raise financing at better rates than firms with higher costs of capital.

Firms with poor environmental management, therefore, can be expected to pay higher rates of interest than others, due to the increased risk of environmental liability in the eyes of its investors. This results in a higher cost of debt and larger debt obligations, thus reducing residual earnings that provide a return to equity holders and destroying shareholder value. Return to equity holders consists of dividends paid by the firm as well as the appreciation of the firm's stock price. As with the cost of debt, the perceived level of risk borne by the investor also drives the cost of equity.

The extent and riskiness of a borrower's environmental liability, its capital expenditures and operating costs required for compliance, and its exposure to environmental litigation are all integrated into the credit approval process. Strong environmental management results in a perception of a firm's reduced risk profile. In practical terms, lenders such as NatWest Group offer a reduction of interest rates for credit applicants demonstrating superior environmental performance (Aspen Institute 1998). This lower cost of debt enhances shareholder value. Looking at future financial decisions, Janssen (2000) suggests that investment bankers urge corporate clients to take advantage of the Kyoto mechanisms in order to optimize shareholder value. From another perspective, climate change issues can have a negative effect on the fossil fuel industry; a combination of factors (including carbon taxes and energy efficiency measures) that reduce demand for energy could reduce the upside potential of the carbon fuel industry, thus having an impact on profitability (Mansley 1994).

Lenders may, indeed, view a certain level of risk as too great, and may not be willing to lend to a firm demonstrating poor environmental management. Studies illustrate that the exposure to Superfund liability can decrease the likelihood of loan approval (Garber and Hammitt 1998; Schaltegger and Burritt 2000). Such reticence on the part of lenders can prevent the firm from expanding, and thus stunt the growth of shareholder value.

In project financing, lenders will take into account not only the risk level of the firm, but also the perceived riskiness of the project for which the capital will be used. As a result, aspects of a borrower's environmental profile are used, not only to calculate risk premiums, but also to decide whether a loan for a specific project with a negative environmental impact should be made at all (Blumberg et al. 1997; Koechlin and Muller 1992).

In risk management terms, a firm's beta is a measure of the riskiness of its stock returns compared to the returns of the market as a whole (Damodaran 2001). Research indicates that firms implementing improved environmental management systems and better environmental performance experienced a lowering of their betas (Feldman et al. 1996). With lower betas, these firms would be perceived to add less risk to a diversified portfolio than before, and thus to be awarded a lower cost of equity. As a result, improving environmental performance is a way for firms to reduce their cost of equity, creating greater shareholder value.

Case studies in Chapter 6 offer further evidence of a firm's environmental performance affecting its level of risk profile. Poor environmental performance tends to increase the volatility of the firm's return, as a firm faces environmental operational and compliance costs and potential liabilities. As a result, its stock price, and hence its return, will suffer as these issues come to light. With a higher risk level for its stock price, the firm will be seen as a risky investment compared to the market average, and the firm's cost of capital will rise, thereby reducing shareholder value. Conversely, firms with lower costs of capital will be more likely to earn returns in excess of that cost, other things being equal. If a firm consistently earns more than its cost of capital, its share price will tend to rise, bringing further wealth creation for shareholders. Thus a firm's environmental performance, cost of capital, and share price are tightly linked.

Evidence of Share Price Changes   Research on the impact on a firm's share price of weak or strong environmental management, as signaled by environmental crises or awards, respectively, revealed significant connections. In their examination of the relationship between firms' environmental management initiatives and their market valuation, Klassen and McLaughlin (1996) found that environmental awards tended to bring strong stock price gains ($80.5 million on average) while environmental crises brought strongly negative stock price reactions ($390.5 million on average). Although the stock price changes are asymmetrical, it is clear that the stock market does value environmental events. For the case of a firm that has won an environmental award, this impact can be significant. This lift in stock price may be due to the perceived reduction in risk level that the environmental award signals to the market. In addition to this change in risk level, strong environmental performance may give positive indications about the quality of management in general. Clearly, strong or weak environmental management is creating or destroying shareholder value in the firms under study.

It becomes clear that a consideration of environmental issues in product and process management as well as in financial decision making can benefit both the shareholder and the environment.

ENVIRONMENTAL MANAGEMENT SYSTEMS

An environmental management system (EMS) is designed to control adverse environmental impacts, just as financial management is designed to control a company's economic well-being.

A firm's approach to the development of an environmental management system entails both the formulation of long-term environmental policies and goals as well as the adaptation of current business activities in order to reduce the impacts of the firm's product and process on the environment.

Figure 2.2 outlines the basic components required for the establishment of a comprehensive EMS. The first phase involves the collection and development of evidence of the need for an environmental policy and strategy, followed by top management's commitment and board approval for new environmental management and reporting strategies. Company specifics such as its mission statement and available budget are significant at this stage. Once the commitment has been obtained and the strategy communicated throughout the company, the next phases involve the development of the policy and programs to be implemented and the development of the management system components. Reporting of an environmental policy statement serves to establish the direction the firm is taking as well as to communicate the plan to employees and the broader public. The sixth stage outlined in Figure 2.2 involves the actual implementation of the plan. As the performance of the EMS is measured, it is also evaluated, with feedback then creating the basis for adjusting the programs and perhaps even adapting the environmental policy. Such feedback implies continual improvement within the EMS framework. Finally the company produces both internal and external environmental reports, the development of which is discussed in Chapter 8.

To help the financial services sector meet the requirements of an EMS, a group of British financiers brought out the Forge Report (Forge 2000), which offers practical guidance on the development of an EMS within financial companies. The report pays more attention to the first stage of evidence development and senior management commitment, since financial institutions have historically not seen themselves as a polluting industry. Within this first stage, some institutions may focus on commercial reasons

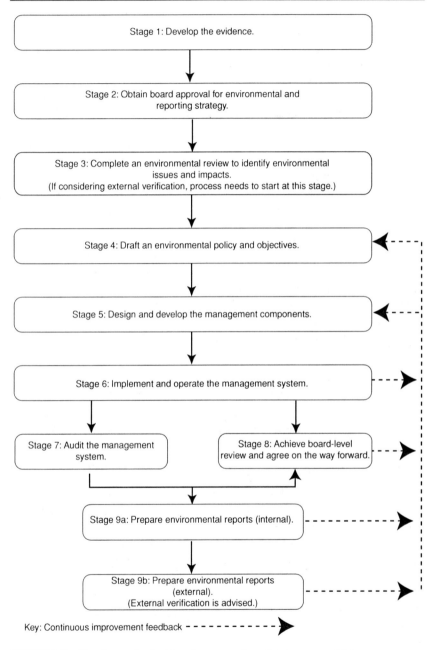

Stage 1: Develop the evidence.

Stage 2: Obtain board approval for environmental and reporting strategy.

Stage 3: Complete an environmental review to identify environmental issues and impacts.
(If considering external verification, process needs to start at this stage.)

Stage 4: Draft an environmental policy and objectives.

Stage 5: Design and develop the management components.

Stage 6: Implement and operate the management system.

Stage 7: Audit the management system.

Stage 8: Achieve board-level review and agree on the way forward.

Stage 9a: Prepare environmental reports (internal).

Stage 9b: Prepare environmental reports (external).
(External verification is advised.)

Key: Continuous improvement feedback

FIGURE 2.2 Key Stages in the Development of an Environmental Management and Reporting System
Source: Forge 2000.

(new products) to examine environmental issues, while others draw on ideological motives.

The implementation of a formal EMS has the benefit of paving the way to international recognition through certification processes such as the European Community Eco-Management and Audit System (EMAS) and ISO 14001. (See Chapter 4, section titled "Internal Environmental Management" and Box 4.4.) Although certification offers advantages in business-to-business dealings in some sectors, in the banking community its greatest importance lies in the sphere of public relations with the communication of a progressive environmental policy to the public at large. Indeed, the Union Bank of Switzerland (UBS) has found that its International Organization for Standardization (ISO) certification has been beneficial in the marketing of its sustainability funds to customers (Jeucken 2001).

The ISO 14000 series, at present, comprises the EMS standard as well as over 20 guidelines that serve as courses of action that companies can take in order to achieve improved environmental performance. Within this series, ISO 14031 offers guidelines on environmental performance evaluation. A group of Swiss and German financial institutions, EPI-Finance 2000, used ISO 14031 to form guidelines for the environmental products and services that banking institutions have developed.

STAKEHOLDER RELATIONSHIPS

The impact of various stakeholder pressures on corporations regarding their environmental performances has a synergistic effect on those companies' environmental and social strategies (Edwards 1998). Historically, shareholders had been considered the only stakeholders of importance with respect to corporate decision making (Friedman 1970). Throughout this volume, readers will become conscious of the influence that other stakeholders have on decision making in industry in general, and within the financial services sector in particular.

Government and other legal aspects are obviously of great importance for companies, and the financial services sector has an obligation to know and understand the effect of these on their clients. Government action, in the form of both strengthened regulations and economic incentives, provides a strong impetus for the financial services sector to develop new products and services that address issues of sustainability. In addition, public law, based on citizens' right to know, mandates the reporting of environmental information and gives rise to programs such as

Toxic Release Inventory (TRI) and National Pollution Release Inventory (NPRI), which provide communities with databases that enable them to hold companies accountable. Further, government regulations pertaining to the private sector, such as liability (strict and several) and contract law (e.g., reporting clean soil) as well as covenants and agreements (e.g., between governments and companies) empower the courts with respect to environmental authority.

The role of media as another external stakeholder, with its coverage of polluting activities and environmental liability issues, also becomes evident in Chapter 6. Media reporting on issues such as ozone depletion and climate change has been instrumental in shaping the globalization of these issues. Further, from a business reporting perspective, increased media understanding of and attention to socially responsible investing and corporate social responsibility have contributed to a growing business awareness of the environmental and social agenda (SustainAbility et al. 2002).

Seen from the internal perspective, banks and insurers are more willing to provide services to environmentally improved companies, while the investment community is demonstrating increasing vigilance with respect to corporate environmental and social behavior. From an employee's perspective, the pursuit of eco-efficiency can motivate a company's workforce to become more innovative, contributing in the long run to a firm's competitive position (Porter and van der Linde 1995). In addition, the attraction and retention of employees becomes easier for a company with a superior environmental and social reputation (Willard 2002). In 1997, the disposal plans for the Brent Spar oil platform and its possible role in human rights abuses in Nigeria caused Royal Dutch/Shell to fall sharply in the estimation of job seekers, while the apparently environmentally friendly British Petroleum (BP) rose in popularity as a place to work (Jeucken 2001). From a positive perspective, ABN Amro has designed an "environmental yardstick" to help employees take ownership of any companywide sustainability initiative (ABN Amro 1998; www.abnamro.com).

Further, Chapter 6 illustrates clearly that consumers are calling for more information with respect to corporate environmental performance (Flur et al. 1997) and investors are making their concerns heard through various manifestations of shareholder activism. In their capacity as investors, banks and insurers join institutional investors in active engagement with companies in order to influence their responses to environmental issues. In Chapter 8, the section titled "Environmental Reporting from the

User's Perspective" emphasizes the diversity of stakeholders with whom companies must communicate, and their varying needs in terms of corporate environmental information. Indeed, a focus on stakeholder governance is emerging in which the one-way system of communications from companies to stakeholders is deemed insufficient and is seen to be shifting to a more deeply engaging process of consultation and collaboration. Furthermore, corporations that have sought feedback from key stakeholders to enhance the value and usefulness of their environmental reporting have also gained valuable insights into the needs and agendas of their stakeholders (UNEP/SustainAbility 1996b).

Corporate dependence on stakeholder trust translates into the hard to quantify yet important quality of corporate reputation. Indeed, a firm's reputation with respect to its stakeholders is described by some as society's authorization of a company's license to operate. Environmental nongovernmental organizations (ENGOs) such as Friends of the Earth and the International River Network (IRN) are increasingly scrutinizing financial institutions for their involvement in large infrastructure investments (roads, railways, dams), new technologies (such as genetically modified organisms), and when dealing with developing countries. NGO activities with respect to financial institutions in these areas of concern include the targeting of Morgan Stanley Dean Witter and the Credit Suisse Group in connection with their participation in the Three Gorges Dam project in China, and similar action against Sumitomo Bank in Japan in connection with its cofinancing of the Sardar Sarovar Dam in India (Jeucken 2001). In addition, IRN publishes its *Bank Check Quarterly* newsletter, which it circulates to other NGOs, allowing them to keep track of financial institutions and to initiate action (www.irn.org).

Figure 2.3 represents a simplified schema of the complex relationship that exists between the financial services sector and its main stakeholders. The influences identified in Figure 2.3, however, are neither unidirectional nor mutually exclusive. Indeed, a two-way exchange often exists between financial principals and their stakeholders.

For example, while banks require a certain level of environmental reporting from a customer in their risk assessment procedures, the same client may also be questioning the environmental performance of its financier (Gray 1998). As banks and insurance companies sign declarations such as the United Nations Environment Program (UNEP) initiatives, stating that they want to foster and play a role in sustainable development, they should be able to withstand critical examination with respect to their own processes and products. In addition, NGOs play a

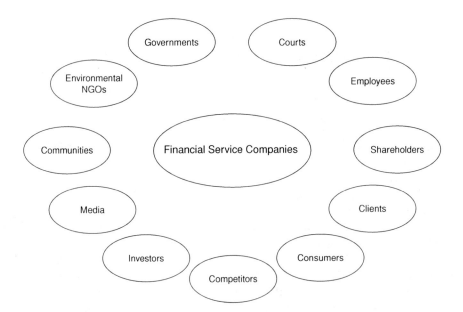

FIGURE 2.3 Financial Service Companies and Their Major Stakeholders

key role in the sustainable development framework in both a confrontational and a supportive role, sharing knowledge and experience and facilitating change in the business world. For example, while some ENGOs have protested against companies' environmental or social performances (see "Shareholder Activism" in Chapter 6), others enter into partnerships with financial institutions to develop environmentally effective financial products. Evidence of this level of influence can be seen in the World Wide Fund for Nature's partnering with insurance giant AMP NPI as well as its involvement with a group of Swiss cantonal banks, Swissca, in designing and publicizing green products (Elkington and Beloe 2000).

Apart from these exchanges of influence between the financial services and their stakeholders, interactions also take place among these stakeholders. Local communities that feel incapable of influencing companies will often enlist the communication skills of the media to help them in their activist role. At the same time, a community often receives its first information from the media concerning environmental issues in its region. The media also interact with the broader public on issues of national and international concern. Moreover, shareholders or ENGOs often operate in tandem with the media in order to effect environmental change within a corporation.

Consumers are mobilized through the media to engage in collective action against certain companies. A prime example of this was the boycott of Shell stations in Europe after the Brent Spar incident and allegations of complicity with state violence in Nigerian oil fields. Interest groups are likely to scrutinize the financiers of these businesses as well, and they may also, then, be affected by consumer backlash.

Thus, the importance of the stakeholder network to corporations, including the financial services sector, becomes clear. Evidence of stakeholder governance is found in the Co-operative Bank's annual report where the bank identifies each of its stakeholders (shareholders, customers, employees and their families, suppliers, and local communities, as well as the broader national and international society). Since the bank's mandate is predicated on the treatment of these stakeholders in an equitable manner, its annual report addresses the values inherent in all components of sustainability (Co-operative Bank 2000).

UBS extends its dependence on client and shareholder trust to the value of its superior reputation that is created through environmental commitment. UBS states that the key factors in determining its good reputation, and thus its success, are its internationally recognized competencies in the area of environmental management as well as its willingness to take its responsibility toward society and the environment seriously (www.ubs.com/umwelt). Its *Environmental Report* (UBS 2000) identifies reputational risk as one of the main value drivers in the asset management, investment banking, and credit business segments of its operations.

LOOKING AHEAD: SCENARIOS AND SIMULATIONS

All business decisions are made under uncertainty, to which there are many contributing factors. Each factor brings its own element of risk. Environmental issues contribute several factors of their own, including more demanding environmental expectations of society, improved detection levels of pollutants, and the impacts from the pollutants themselves. For example, *in the case of greenhouse gas pollutants we have injected a huge amount of uncertainty into the decision-making arena.* In these circumstances there is only one thing that we know for certain, and that is that a linear extrapolation from past experience provides no guidance for the future. This is especially problematic for the insurance industry, because the historical record was the information on which it relied for pricing insurance policies.

There are two broad approaches to looking ahead. One relies on verbal reasoning and exchange of ideas among people with diverse areas of expertise. This type of activity can loosely be classed as scenario building. The other relies on numerical simulation, using the best available data and adding random variables to assess the sensitivity of various physical or financial relationships. In this book we will refer to examples where each approach has been used. For example, there is a discussion of Royal Dutch/Shell's two major scenarios for moving the decision makers' mindset toward a world where fossil fuel would be of diminishing importance. (See Chapter 7.) Numerical simulations are the essence of models of probable maximum loss to the insurance industry from a particular type of event, such as an earthquake in southern California or a hurricane striking Miami. However, even these numerical models are only a best guess because the relationships between many of the physical factors are not well known. What the models do measure is the sensitivity of the result to various estimates of the inputs. For example, estimates can be made of the insurance loss to be expected from earthquakes at various points on the Richter scale of intensity, with epicenters at various distances from the cores of a number of major cities.

The problem of heightened uncertainty due to environmental change varies both between and within sectors of the economy. So far, it is the insurance and reinsurance underwriters who have had to cope most directly with the consequences of this situation, as they have found themselves paying out on huge claims that were never expected when the policies were written. The situation is expanding to embroil bankers and professional investors, too, as climate change is obliging many of their clients to consider how best to adapt to a changing world. The generic problem is the same across the economy: *how to identify new areas of uncertainty and to quantify the risk associated with that uncertainty.* As a partial response to this situation we see the steady rise of environmental reporting among major corporations and trade associations, which is analyzed in Chapter 8. Once the risk can be quantified, the company decision makers should decide which portion they wish to retain and which they wish to transfer.

TOOLS FOR RISK TRANSFER

Traditional Insurance Mechanisms

Insurance will continue to be the principal vehicle for the transfer of business and personal risk. However, there are at least two circumstances in which insurance companies may find themselves unable or unwilling to accept certain risks that they may have covered in the past. First, there is the capacity issue. The magnitude and frequency of major catastrophic losses in the late 1980s and through to the present have challenged the capacity of traditional insurance and reinsurance markets. This was especially true following Hurricane Andrew (in 1992) and becomes an issue again following the destruction of the World Trade Center (in 2001). If the scale and frequency of catastrophes continue to grow, then a wider diffusion of the risk market may become desirable or necessary. This issue is explored in the next subsection.

A more specific issue concerns the types of environmental risk that can be insured. Pollution liability was never intended to be covered by commercial general liability (CGL) policies. Even so, CGL was the door that was opened by the American courts to fund claims for asbestos, lead paint, and Superfund, as well as the accidental spills that it was expected to cover. Attempts to exclude pollution in CGL policies met with mixed success in the American courts. Pollution is now covered by separate environmental policies covering risks associated with asbestos, underground storage tanks, accidental pollution liability, and lead abatement, among others. Special-purpose cover is also provided by specific cleanup cost overruns for remediating polluted building sites. (See Chapter 5.) The old insurance preference for a one-size-fits-all type of policy has been abandoned because of the horrendous losses sustained from the 1970s onward. Insurance companies now hire specialists who understand the challenge of pollution and who can design policies that cover only what is intended to be covered.

Tapping into the Capital Markets

In the wake of Hurricane Andrew there was a widespread and rapid reassessment of just what could be insured by the traditional insurance and reinsurance market. Whereas the major companies were well prepared, others were vulnerable. There was a real danger that government (especially the elected insurance commissioners in each state) would step in to force the solvent companies to fill the breach by obliging them to join involuntary pools to provide backup cover, as had happened so often in the past. That point—examined in Chapter 5—forced some consideration of tapping into the capital markets with their much greater volume of transactions and capital base.

Thus began an exploration of various off-balance-sheet instruments to make this transition. New products were developed to mimic derivative instruments that had been appearing since the mid-1970s to hedge risks in the financial markets, principally volatility in foreign exchange and interest rates (Smithson 1998). Options and swaps are the instruments most widely used. In the 1990s catastrophe options were designed to provide a flexible infusion of capacity through the Chicago Board of Trade, based on the insurance losses due to catastrophes in the United States. Their failure to find a market is described in Chapter 5. Swaps based on exposure to extreme weather events, such as heavy rainfall and both high and low temperatures, have proven more durable. There is now a growing "weather market," driven, so far, by large energy companies hedging their volume exposures in a deregulated world. (This market is introduced in Chapter 5 and examined further in Chapter 9.)

Catastrophe bonds, or "cat bonds," have been developed to bring in additional partners to share the financial risk by going directly to the institutional investors. These bonds have the advantage of being quite simple conceptually, compared with the derivative products described in the previous subsection. The downside is that each bond must be configured for each placement, which takes time and therefore carries a higher transactional cost. The market is growing steadily, so it certainly seems to meet a need. Also, the secondary market in cat bonds is developing quickly, which encourages liquidity in the market and hence further growth. These issues are explored in Chapter 5.

TRADING ATMOSPHERIC EMISSION REDUCTION CREDITS

The issues discussed in the previous two subsections relate to existing risks that can be quantified. These are environmental and weather-related risks that a forward-looking company wants to get off its balance sheet, or wants to hedge, in order to avoid drawing negative assessments from the rating agencies. For strategic planning, the big, overhanging issue is climate change. Although there have been several attempts to assess the costs of climate change and the costs of mitigating (slowing) the rate of change, nobody really knows what it will cost—mitigated or not. This will become clearer only gradually, as climate changes. With this level of uncertainty and so much at stake on the outcome, it would seem prudent to adopt an incremental approach to mitigation (i.e., greenhouse gas emission reduction) that will allow all concerned to develop the most cost-effective approaches to the challenge.

It was for this reason that the notion of trading credits for greenhouse gas emission reduction was included in the Kyoto Protocol to the United Nations Framework Convention on Climate Change in 1997. (The implications of the Protocol are examined in Chapter 7.) The development of a market in these credits requires emission reduction targets to be set for each signatory under an enforceable international agreement. If a country surpasses its reduction targets, then the surplus credits can be sold to countries that failed to meet their target. Such a market is referred to as "carbon trading" or "carbon finance."

It is not yet clear how the world of carbon finance will evolve. Nor is it clear how the roles of companies and countries will be integrated. Some sovereign greenhouse gas trading programs are outlined in Chapter 9. Despite the uncertainty as to the eventual form of this carbon market, some major corporations (like Royal Dutch/Shell and BP) have already started to reduce their emissions by trading within their various operating divisions. (See also the TransAlta case study in Chapter 9.) For further guidance we can also study the operation of existing markets for trading emission reduction credits in pollutants like sulphur dioxide and nitrogen oxides in the United States (Varilek 2000).

CONCLUSION

Environmental finance is developing as a field in response to an acceptance of the idea that sound environmental management is positively correlated with sound economic management. We are no longer tying ourselves to the old assumption that a clean environment is bad for profits. Thus, there is growing confidence that environmental quality is justified by the bottom line. However, because environmental quality cannot be packaged like a physical commodity and sold in a traditional marketplace, innovation has been required to develop new financial instruments that recognize and reward environmental virtue in the private sector. All this is happening at a time when our biggest environmental challenge—climate change—is injecting both uncertainty and urgency into the global situation.

In the remainder of this book we attempt to assess our progress so far. We can admit now that the results have been mixed. This is largely because the development of new financial products can happen only if the regulatory framework is there to make it happen. It requires clear rules that charge the polluters for polluting and reward those who enhance the quality of the environment. This has been demonstrated by the "cap and trade" rules that were put in place for sulphur dioxide and nitrogen oxides in the United States. This approach immediately raises the cost of doing business for those who continue to pollute and it presents opportunities to those companies that have learned to do better. Once the regulatory framework has been constructed, then market forces have the potential to provide a dynamic motor for improved environmental performance. To meet that potential we need a trading infrastructure that provides transparency for price discovery and liquidity to allow traders to enter and leave markets.

The next chapter assesses recent changes in the financial services sector, including globalization, deregulation, and technological innovation, all of which affect the capacity of companies to respond to the environmental challenge.

CHAPTER 3

The Financial Services Sector

INTRODUCTION

In order to characterize the elements of environmental finance that pertain to this book, it is important to establish concepts and structures of both the environmental and commercial setting in which the financial services operate. Much as Chapter 2 has offered background information on the concepts and tools used by financial institutions to develop environmental policies and products, this chapter offers a backdrop to the global marketplace in which they operate. First, the general structure of the global market for financial services and the forces of globalization are discussed. Then the ways the financial services react to these forces are outlined. Once this general background has been established, the core financial services that form the focus of this book are described, along with their areas of environmental exposure. Banking, insurance, and investors' response patterns to environmental concerns are introduced, all of which are expanded upon in subsequent chapters.

STRUCTURE OF THE GLOBAL MARKET FOR FINANCIAL CAPITAL

Today the global capital market is no longer a single, physical marketplace, but a network of individual markets arranged in a hub-and-spoke system. This network is centered on activities of financial intermediaries in the principal hubs in the United States and the United Kingdom, with Japan and Germany providing further cores of financial activity (Barton 2001). Globally, financial intermediation tends to be differentiated on the basis of whether it is primarily driven by market- or bank-based transactions. In the former, the market plays a more important role in attracting savings, allocating new capital, restructuring existing capital, and governing corporations. In the latter case, banks play a much more important role in these functions (Steinherr 1996). Financial intermediation within the bank-based system relies to a greater extent on relationship banking, while the market-based system implies a greater reliance on impersonal markets (White 1998).

European financial systems, such as those found in Germany, Switzerland, and the Netherlands, are characterized by the universal banking system, where both traditional financial activities as well as ownership positions in corporations are carried out by one incorporated entity. Universal banking systems have the capacity to offer a full range of financial services to corporate and personal customers (deposit taking, lending, trading of financial instruments and their derivatives, underwriting new debt and equity issues, brokerage, fund management, and insurance). They also have the capacity to hold equity positions in corporations (Saunders and Walter 1994; Llewellyn 1996). As a means of illustrating one integrated bank's capacity for a full range of services, Box 3.1 indicates the breadth of ING Bank's products and services in the Netherlands, while showing the extent to which environmental issues enter into each segment of its activities.

The structure of financial intermediation in North America is characterized more as market-based systems. Until recently, financial institutions in the United States have epitomized the opposite structure to universal banking, since the Glass-Steagall Act mandated that financial functions be maintained as separate areas of specialization (see "Deregulation" later in the chapter). Similarly in Canada, the Bank Act had, until recent decades, categorized financial institutions according to a "one firm, one function" approach (Kintner 1993).

In recent years, capital markets have displaced bank lending as the major source of capital for large corporations in many countries (Swiss Re 2001). Table 3.1 illustrates how this shift in capital allocation has taken place. In the United States, equitization has had a strong impact on capital allocation, with only 18 percent of corporate funding being provided by banks in the 1990s. In France the issuance of securities has also grown at the expense of the banking industry. In other countries, such as Japan, where depositary institutions have played a greater role, banking institutions continue to predominate in corporate funding.

From an environmental perspective, the dominant financial hubs, as mentioned earlier, are in a position of influencing emerging standards for global financial markets. Investors and issuers within the dominant hubs

BOX 3.1   ING Bank Environmental Banking Products and Services

---

Lending:
  Credit risk analysis.
  Mortgages: green mortgages.
  SME Environmental Plan (services and products for entrepreneurs).
  Environmental loans.
Leasing: Takes advantage of government tax incentive schemes.
Savings: Postbank Groen depositors can save tax-free for investing in
  green projects.
Asset Management: New products and services being considered:
  Sustainable investment counselling.
  Sustainable asset management.
  Sustainability reports of portfolios and investment funds.
Insurance:
  Environmental damage insurance.
  Bank guarantees environmental risks (waste transport, under-
  ground storage).
Consultancy:
  SME Environmental Plan.
  Internal environmental policy.

Source: ING Group 1999.

TABLE 3.1   Relative Share of Bank Loans to
Debt Securities for Financing Corporations,
1983–1995

Country	1980s	1990s
France	44.1%	21.6%
Germany	51.1	56.9
Japan	94.5	90.4
United Kingdom	83.9	72.8
United States	36.4	18.0

Source: Berger et al. 2000, Table 3, p. 79.

must conform to standards of accounting, reporting, and market regulations (see Chapter 8), while intermediaries and investors from the hub have the capacity to spread their standards for transparency, corporate governance, and valuation techniques (Bhatnagar 1999). The position of institutional investors, such as mutual funds, pension funds, and insurance companies, is important in driving the uniform pricing of risk around the world, since institutional investors use similar valuation techniques in markets worldwide. Simultaneously, when leading banks use the same environmental evaluation techniques in all markets, they have the potential to set global standards of pricing as well as risk assessment, including environmental risk. This is important since there are significant differences among countries in accounting and reporting standards, legal protection, and business norms (Barton 2001).

The following section outlines some of the historical and regulatory developments that have contributed to the evolution of financial institutions and their markets.

FORCES RESHAPING FINANCIAL SERVICE INDUSTRIES

The worldwide liberalization of trade and financial markets has contributed to the deregulation of financial institutions, as international corporations and trade patterns demand instantaneous global financial service delivery. In addition, technological developments have contributed to the transformation of financial institutions (Berger et al. 1999; Gros and Lannoo 2000; White 1998).

Historically, institutions within the financial services sector in many countries have been segmented from each other, as a result of regulatory constraints and high transaction costs. As transaction costs fell in the 1980s, due in part to improved technology and globalization, both financial institutions and markets became increasingly integrated (Delphi and Ecologic 1997; Scott-Quinn 1990).

Figure 3.1 illustrates schematically the primary effects that these forces have had on reshaping the financial services marketplace. The following sections discuss the impact of these trends on the structure of financial institutions.

Globalization and Market Forces

Rapid growth in international trade and the spread of transnational corporations have created global markets, which have generated changing pat-

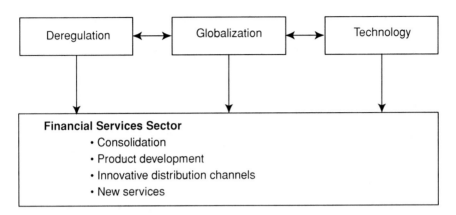

FIGURE 3.1   Forces Contributing to Structural Changes in the Financial Services Sector

terns of demands for products and services offered by financial institutions. The prospect of truly global businesses became even greater with the collapse of communism in Central Europe and the former Soviet Union and the nascent market-oriented transformation of the Chinese economy. At the same time, rivalry for new markets among various financial industries has intensified due to the saturation of some financial services in domestic markets, as well as the increased competition felt as a result of foreign institutions entering domestic markets (Swiss Re 2000b).

The very rapid expansion of domestically oriented businesses into the global marketplace reveals, as well, the environmentally risky side to globalization. Although environmental management has become more commonplace in the developed world, it is virtually nonexistent in many of the emerging economies. There may be regulations in the latter, but often neither the infrastructure nor the culture exists to implement them. As we will see in the following chapters, some progress is being made but change comes slowly. Grossman and Kreuger (1995) suggest that as standards improve in less developed countries, there may be an advantage in adopting a higher environmental standard earlier in countries such as South Korea and Singapore. At the same time, there are increasing occurrences of litigation in which a corporation is sued in its home jurisdiction on the basis of allegations of environmental harm arising from the corporation's activities in foreign jurisdictions. Cases brought against the Papua New Guinea mining company Ok Tedi in the Australian courts serve as a valid example of this type of litigation. Plaintiffs alleged losses due to the effluent of the mine's polluting waters, which adversely affected the adjacent land. Parties in the case reached an out-of-court settlement that included payment to the plaintiffs as well as a compensation package to the region (Cameron and Ramsay 1996).

Technology

In his recent analysis of changes resulting from new international systems and corporate strategies, Friedman (2000, 348) defines globalization as "the product of the democratization of finance, technology and information." As the global economy develops, innovations in information technology are changing the profile of the financial services sector (Berger et al. 1999; Giddy et al. 1996; Street and Monaghan 2001). Within such liberalized markets, increased data-processing capability and increased speed of performing transactions have altered financial firms' internal linkages, as well as their external relationships with clients. Indeed, technological developments are viewed as posing a key threat to relationship banking, which is at the heart of many of the European banking systems, by encouraging competition based on price rather than historical relationships (White 1998).

In the insurance industry, e-business has challenged the role of traditional brokers, causing business strategies of some insurers in a number of countries to shift from a purely sales function toward a service function of providing risk management services, as well as insurance coverage, to clients. In addition, technological developments in Internet access have facilitated the entry of new competitors to the market (Swiss Re 2000c). Within the investment community, the world is also witnessing the linkage of stock exchanges that provide 24-hour trading networks.

Many regulatory systems governing financial institutions that existed until the final decades of the twentieth century were rendered unwieldy, if not out-of-date, by such technological advances. The introduction of electronic delivery channels for retail banking, such as phone centers, online banking, and automated teller machines (ATMs), has created greater economies of scale than traditional branching networks (Flur et al. 1997; Radecki et al. 1997; White 1998). When funds can be transferred instantly, regulated differentiation between financial accounts and institutions becomes onerous and affects competitiveness. Further, advances in information technology provided a means of circumventing regulatory restrictions imposed by chartering authorities. For example, electronic transfer technology that led to the creation of ATMs has enabled banks to overcome many state branching restrictions that existed until recently in the United States (Swiss Re 2000c).

Further trends arising from advances in computing technology and information flow have resulted in significant innovations in product development and risk management tools. Technology has not only created new opportunities for identifying and measuring risk; it has also placed increased demands on investors and investment managers to oversee risk, both from an historical loss perspective (such as in derivative instruments) and in the creation of products in the analysis of risk. Examples can be found in the application of alpha[1] and beta to environmental assessments of investment portfolios in Chapter 6 (Beder 1999).

The following section discusses some structural and operational changes that have taken place within the financial services sector in response to globalization and technological forces.

Deregulation

National governments have, historically, closely governed financial institutions with respect to the products they were permitted to offer as well as the geographic markets in which they could operate. Recent deregulation of these industries has had effects on both of these strategic areas for the financial service industries. First, it has opened geographic markets to these companies that traditionally had been beyond their boundaries. Secondly, changes in government policies have blurred the boundary lines that existed between banking, insurance, and investment services, as previously autonomous core functions of each are integrated across industry lines.

A major reason for this lies in the changing structure of global markets for financial capital as a whole, as outlined earlier in the chapter. With the advent of the international consolidation of markets for goods and services came the demands for currency, loans and other services from international financial institutions. Thus globalization of markets in general has likely contributed to the globalization of financial services firms (Berger et al. 1999). Deregulation of the financial sector is aimed, then, at opening new markets and allowing new products to be developed by newly integrated firms.

The first major change that occurred in the basic function of financial institutions was the dismantling of the Bretton Woods system in 1971, an undertaking that allowed previously fixed currency rates to fluctuate, free of major government intervention (Beder 1999). In 1979, short-term interest rates in the United States were freed from government-mandated levels. This action is viewed as having set off the subsequent wave of deregulation of financial institutions. The following discussion offers an abbreviated view of legislative changes that have affected the financial services sector in different jurisdictions. Table 3.2 summarizes the principal legislative changes in various countries.

United States   In the United States, legislation that influenced financial services with respect to regions and markets in which they can operate were principally the McFadden Act of 1927 and the Glass-Steagall Act of 1933. The former guaranteed the right of state governments to decide issues of branching. The Glass-Steagall Act mandated the separation of investment banking from commercial banking (Benston 1996).

Restrictions on banks' capacity to expand geographically became more lenient in the late 1980s and early 1990s, culminating with the Riegle-Neil Interstate Banking and Branching Efficiency Act of 1994, which permitted U.S. commercial banks to branch nationally (Berger et al. 1999; Economist 1995). In 1999, the Glass-Steagall Act was repealed through the passage of the Gramm-Leach-Biley Act, thus allowing banks to engage in insurance underwriting and investments. The intent of such legislation was to improve U.S. banks' competitive efficiency through improved economies of scale, diversification of risk, and a more efficient price structure (Kim and Singer 1997; Berger et al. 1999).

TABLE 3.2   Legislative Changes Affecting the Financial Services Sector

Country	Date	Changes
United States	1994	• Allowed U.S. commercial banks to branch nationwide
	1999	• Glass–Steagall Act repealed
Canada	1980	• Allowed charters for foreign banks
	1987	• "Four pillars" under one regulatory authority
	1987	• Banks allowed to own securities firms
	1991	• Banks allowed to own trust and insurance companies, and vice versa
European Union	1992	• Single marketplace across EU created
	1993	• Abolition of price and product control and introduction of "home country" control
Japan	1993	• Commercial banks allowed to establish security subsidiaries
	1995	• Foreign pension fund management permitted
	1996	• Big Bang
	1999	• Japanese banks and insurers allowed to sell mutual funds

Canada Historically, Canadian regulations have classified financial services according to a "one firm, one function" approach (Kintner 1993), with commercial banks being regulated under federal legislation, securities investments falling under provincial jurisdictions, and trust and insurance services governed by whichever government granted their charter. Both functional and jurisdictional solutions were sought in an attempt to render these industries competitive in a global market.

In order to address these issues, the Canadian government first amended the national Bank Act in 1980, which made provisions for the chartering of foreign bank operations in Canada. In 1987, all the departments governing banks and insurance services were consolidated to form the Office of the Superintendent of Financial Institutions (OSFI), effectively bringing all federally chartered institutions (banks, insurance companies, trust and loan companies, and pension plans) under a single federal regulatory authority. Also in 1987, parliament passed legislation that empowered banks to own and operate provincially regulated security firms (Freedman 1996; Kintner 1993).

Trends in consolidation of services continued, as the 1992 revisions in the Bank Act allowed banks to own trust and insurance companies at the same time as the latter two were allowed to own banks. With the exception of auto leasing and some insurance products, these revisions allowed banks and trust companies to market financial products that had been, until that time, the sole territory of the other financial pillars (Freedman 1996).

Most recently, legislative changes to the Bank Act (Bill C-8) propose significant changes to the structure of the financial services sector that blur significantly the distinctions between different kinds of financial institutions. Included in these considerations are changes in the ownership structure of financial institutions by allowing the creation of bank holding companies and by instituting a new size-based ownership regime for banks that would replace the current Schedule I and Schedule II classification that categorizes Canadian chartered banks separately from foreign-owned ones.[2] At the same time, Bill C-8 gives foreign banks fuller access to the Canadian markets by allowing certain ones to establish either a full-service or a lending branch of their organizations (Haggart et al. 2001). This change offers banks foreign to Canada the potential to distribute their existing products and services in this expanded Canadian market.

European Union Financial institutions in many countries within the European community, such as Germany, the Netherlands, and Switzerland, are characterized as universal banking systems, where the distinguishing feature is the range of activities allowed within any one corporation. In the

British financial system, by contrast, there has been a clear demarcation between financial institutions, such as the structures found in North America, Australia, and Japan.

With the advent of the European Union (EU), however, financial services within EU countries have also been experiencing forms of deregulation. A series of laws, often referred to as the Single Market Program, have facilitated cross-border operations for financial institutions within the EU. The Single Europe Act, implemented in 1992, created a single uninterrupted marketplace across the EU and eliminated all barriers to cross-border movement of capital. The Second Banking Co-ordination Directive, which came into effect in 1993, created a single banking license valid throughout the European community, and mandated that regulatory control of banking operations be maintained in the bank's home, rather than the host, country (Kintner 1993). This second directive had the important effect of making universal banking structure the norm in the EU.

The insurance industry in Europe has also experienced staged deregulation in European countries. In 1990, insurers were allowed to write policies in other European Union states without actually having registered offices in that state. In 1994, the markets were opened even further, with the abolition of price and product control and the introduction of "home country" control, as with the banking industry. The opening up of national insurance markets and the introduction of the euro have resulted in a consolidation of the insurance market within the EU and brought about the rapid growth of European multinational insurers, with the European community becoming a more significant market for these multinational corporations (MNCs), while purely national insurers are becoming regional providers of coverage and services. As the structures of providers become more unified, so too will the products offered and the terms of business (Swiss Re 2000b).

At the same time, a sequence of directives was introduced that were designed to achieve a single securities market. Within the investment community, the formation of the European Union and the introduction of the euro have also increased the range of investment opportunities. Adoption of the euro in January 2001 was designed to establish monetary union and is anticipated to foster further mergers and acquisitions in this sector (Berger et al. 1999; Gros and Lannoo 2000). In addition, investors are now using European, rather than national, benchmarks to measure performance (Swiss Re 2000b).

Changes that have taken place within some countries in the EU have had the effect of deregulating financial systems (United Kingdom) and, in some cases, of rebalancing the orientation of a country's financial institutions from a bank-oriented system to one with a greater market-oriented focus (France).

Historically, the British banking system has been informally regulated, with supervision relying on self-regulatory principles and the moral suasion of the Bank of England. In contrast to the practice in other countries where banks and the securities industry were separated by law, in Britain the distinction was the product of self-imposed and restrictive practice arrangements of the Stock Exchange. Competitive pressures eroded these historic demarcations in the mid-1980s and spawned the emergence of financial conglomerates.

The movement of banks into securities trading (the Big Bang in 1986) was the result of the competitive pressures in the securities market, at a time when the London Stock Exchange was losing market share, particularly to New York (Beder 1999; Llewellyn 1996). The regulatory catalyst was the government's threat to refer the London Stock Exchange rule book (inhibiting banks from trading securities) to the Restrictive Trade Practices Court. Other competitive pressures also influenced the diversification of major British clearing banks (for example, Barclays, Lloyds, Midland, National Westminster) into insurance. In the mid-1980s, the bank and insurance regulators reached an informal agreement to abandon (nonlegislative) prohibition of cross-ownership links between banking and insurance companies.

Legislative changes in France that were taken in anticipation of the Single Market Act were designed to rebalance the structure of financial intermediation from a bank-based system to one with a greater market focus. Major reform came to this system in 1985 with changes in the French Banking Act, removing old divisions between investment and commercial banking, resulting in the broadening of banks' brokerage and securitization activities. Although banks continued to finance corporations after the revisions to the Bank Act, they tended to do so by investing on the capital market rather than considering corporate loan applications (Melitz 1992). Thus, the liberalization of rules in France meant that its financial profile became similar to North American models, as the French business sector came to depend more on the capital markets than it had previously (Melitz 1990; Berger et al. 2000).

Japan　　The postwar Japanese banking system is characterized as relationship or universal banking, with very close links and consultations between banks and industry, and can be considered an extension of the broader Japanese alliances called the *keiretsu*. In addition to the main bank relationship, *keiretsu* members also have trading relations and cross-shareholdings among its nonfinancial firms.

In contrast to the U.S. system, Japanese banks have been permitted to expand through branch establishments throughout both Japan and the rest of the world. In addition, Japanese banks have been free to function as investment bankers at the same time as carrying out their traditional banking services (Kim and Singer 1997). Experts suggest that the reduced regulatory restrictions that the Japanese banking system has experienced have led Japanese banks to take greater risks in attempting to capture global market share, as well as in their investment selections. Such strategies are viewed as having left Japanese banks in a precarious position in the 1990s, and are leading to the present attempt at regulatory reform in that country (Williams 2001).

Since 1948 in Japan, Section 65 of the Security and Exchange Act (the equivalent of the U.S. Glass-Steagall Act) has prevented Japanese banks from conducting securities business as it established a strict separation between banking and securities business (Hoshi 1996). Deregulation within the Japanese financial sector started in 1993 with the passage of the Financial System Reform Bill, which allowed commercial banks to enter into the securities industry through subsidiaries. By the end of 1994, all major commercial banks in Japan had established securities subsidiaries.

In 1995 Japan deregulated pension fund management, allowing Japanese companies for the first time to hire foreign investment managers. The U.S. company Fidelity Investments was one of the first firms chosen as a foreign pension manager. Fidelity expanded its horizons even further by distributing its yen-based mutual funds through Japanese brokers (Spindle 1998).

In 1996, the Japanese government undertook sweeping moves aimed at overhauling the country's financial system by March 2001. The new system, commonly referred to as the "Big Bang," will allow entry by insurers, banks, and securities firms into one another's businesses. By 1999, authorities were allowing the nation's banks and life insurance companies to sell mutual funds, which until that time had been the sole territory of brokers.

Most recently Japan's economic outlook has been grim, with plunging share prices, rising unemployment figures, and a sharp contraction in gross domestic product. Analysts claim that one of the major problems in this economic system is explained by the massive burden of nonperforming loans in the Japanese banking system. For the first time, Japanese banks have had to account for their large stock holdings at current market value, rather than the original purchase price that had traditionally been used. Plunging share prices, then, will cause further stress to the banks as they absorb any losses to their portfolios, which in turn will erode both the values of the banks' holdings and the share prices of the banks themselves (Williams 2001).

CORE FINANCIAL SERVICES

The three core financial services that provide the focus of this book are commercial banking, insurance underwriting, and the investment community. Their primary and secondary business interests are summarized in Table 3.3. The primary focus for banks is lending and credit extension, while that of insurers is the underwriting of life and non-life insurance, both for corporations and for individuals. The investment community is characterized as counseling clients and unit holders and investing funds on their behalf. Table 3.3 also summarizes the exposure to environmental risk that each industry has experienced.

In most countries, the roles that financial institutions play fall somewhere between the extremes of universal banking and of a specialized function of banking, underwriting, or investing. For the purposes of this book, however, in order to differentiate the impacts of environmental issues on the diverse industries, these core activities are discussed in a somewhat separate manner.

In addition to differences in customer and client needs, the three industries can be differentiated in a number of other ways. The first difference among these industries is found in their interpretation of the fundamental concept of risk. In general, commercial banks are traditionally known for their risk aversion tendencies, with risk management in the banking business being dominated by concerns about the risk profile of clients' assets. For insurers, risk is central to their industry, with their principal source of concern being the behavior of liabilities (White 1998). As such, insurers actively aim to adopt risk and then to minimize or offset it internally. Between these two extremes, investment banks and asset managers are interested in the upside potential of risk, and are active in trading off risk against potential positive financial returns (Delphi and Ecologic 1997; Saunders and Walter 1994).

In a similar vein, the differences in the capacities of the three industries to influence their customers' environmental practices are defined by the contrasts in their customer group types. Although commercial banks are actively involved with large companies, the main source of finance and influence for larger companies is the investment community. Banks' most significant point of influence is among small and medium-sized enterprises, where lenders can both impose environmental conditions on financial transactions and be a major source of environmental counsel for SMEs in pursuit of funds (Delphi and Ecologic 1997).

For the purpose of environmental data collection, underwriters and lenders have contractual means of obtaining information on environmental

TABLE 3.3 Summary of Financial Service Sector's Business Activities and Environmental Exposure

Sector	Primary Activity	Secondary Activity	Environmental Exposure
Commercial banking	Extending credit	Investing for its own account	• Prior to foreclosure: loss of cash flow on real estate collaterized loans • After foreclosure: contamination liability on real estate collateralized loans
Insurance	Underwriting P&C insurance for corporations and individuals	Investing for its own account	• General liability policies (liability for contamination and asbestos) • Environmental impairment liability insurance (poorly defined underwritings) • Global climate change (concerns about exposure to catastrophic risk)
Investment banking	Advising corporate clients on investment and financing options	Investing for its own account	• IPOs, mergers, acquisitions, divestitures, project finance, underwritings
Mutual funds	Investing capital provided by unit holders		• Consumer demands for environmentally screened funds • Shareholder activism • Voting proxies
Pension funds	Investing employee pension fund contributions		• Voting proxies • Change from defined contribution to defined benefit
Venture capital	Providing first-stage capital for new business ventures		• Varies with each investment

Source: Adapted from Ganzi and DeVries 1998.

practices, and in theory have the ability to influence their clients' decision making. Investors, on the other hand, must rely on corporations' environmental reporting or on value-added data provided by vendors of environmental screening tools (see Chapter 4).

Finally, a difference is observed in the outcomes that environmental risk exposure has on the three industries in the financial services sector. Judicial rulings on environmental liability, discussed further in Chapters 3 and 4, have created industrywide crises in insurance underwriting (asbestos and the Comprehensive Environmental Response Compensation and Liability Act [CERCLA]) and lending businesses (Maryland Bank and Trust and Fleet Factors). Investment losses related to poor environmental performance, however, affect the value of securities of specific companies or sectors.

RESPONSE OF THE FINANCIAL SERVICES SECTOR TO DEREGULATION

Consolidation

Following the global changes experienced in other sectors of the economy, industries in the financial services sector have undertaken similar strategies in order to remain competitive. In the face of deregulation, this sector has demonstrated varying strategies of consolidation, designed to provide economies of scale and scope by reducing excess distribution capacity and expanding market presence (Flur et al. 1997). Mergers and acquisitions that have taken place within the financial services sector have "fundamentally altered the competitive landscape for financial intermediaries" (Swiss Re 2001, 21).

From a geographic perspective regarding transactions within the same country, in the U.S. banking industry, for instance, NationsBank set its target on becoming a national bank through the acquisition of banks operating in many states, and then merged with BankAmerica in 1998 (Bryan et al. 1999). That same year a similar national geographic profile was seen in the merger of Union Bank of Switzerland (UBS) with Swiss Bank Corporation in Switzerland, creating the largest bank in Europe (Berger et al. 1999). The phenomenon was also observed in Japan, with the merger of Mitsui Trust and Banking Company and Chuo Trust and Banking in 2000. In Canada quite a different pattern of policy making saw two banking mergers, Royal Bank of Canada with the Bank of Montreal and Canadian

Imperial Bank of Commerce with The Toronto Dominion Bank, disallowed in 1998 (Willis 2001).

Looking at cross-industry mergers within the same country, the legislation in the United States that limited banks, security firms, and insurance companies from entering one another's businesses was repealed only in 1999. This change in legislation spawned such events as the Charles Schwab brokerage firm acquiring the trust and investment services of U.S. Trust Corp. (2000). Also from the service integration perspective, mergers abounded in Canada in the 1990s, with transactions such as the Bank of Nova Scotia acquiring the investment house of McLeod, Young and Weir (1998), while Toronto Dominion Bank acquired Canada Trust (2000).

In the insurance industry, the French underwriter AXA merged operations with UAP in 1996, not only strengthening its business in France, but also substantially expanding its European operations. From a cross-border, cross-industry perspective, AXA's acquisitions of an American investment bank (Donaldson, Lufkin & Jenrette), an asset manager (Alliance), and a life insurance company (Equitable), provide it with a strong foothold in the U.S. financial markets as well (Swiss Re 2000b; Bryan et al. 1999). Other European firms have made sizable acquisitions of U.S. asset management firms, such as ABN Amro with Allegheny Asset Management (2000) and Swiss Re with Conning Corp. (2001) (Swiss Re 2001a). It has been suggested that these transactions have strategic importance for the European firms since the U.S. asset management market is large and well established and such acquisitions bring with them market skills required in the expanding equity culture in Europe (Swiss Re 2001a).

Others insurers have expanded market share through shaping niche markets and developing strategic alliances in their efforts to expand globally. American International Group (AIG), the most global of insurance companies (Swiss Re 2000d), for instance, was the first foreign insurer to enter the potentially promising Chinese market using this strategy (Economist 2001a).

In the investment community, joint ventures between investment specialists such as Scudder from the United States and Investors Group in Canada, or Amvescap's expansion strategies (see Box 3.2), contribute to the creation of a global structure in the delivery of financial services.

The Big Bang financial reform in Japan has created a number of trends in the financial services sector. Due to the effects of the declining importance of savings as bond and equity markets develop, along with increased competitive pressures from new entrants in the field, Japanese banks felt a strong incentive to enter the insurance market in order to establish new opportunities (Swiss Re 2000a). From the insurance underwriters' perspec-

BOX 3.2   How the Amvescap Empire Grew

Incorporated in London but headquartered in Atlanta, Amvescap was formed when the Atlanta-based institutional money management firm Invesco purchased AIM Fund Management of Houston in 1997 (Lappen 1999). As Invesco and AIM continued to operate in their respective fields of core competencies, the newly formed Amvescap purchased Chancellor LGT in 1998, as it pursued its goal of becoming a strong, global player in the investment management arena. It expanded its core regional presence in the United Kingdom (with the acquisition of Perpetual PLC in December 2000) and the United States (with the purchase of National Asset Management and Pell Rudman in 2001), as well as strengthening its hold in other regions with acquisitions in Canada, Australia, and Taiwan.

In the case of the merger with Trimark in Canada (August 2000), the complementary nature of the two organizations fulfilled the desires of each, as Trimark aspired to a global reach, while AIM wanted to strengthen its presence in Canada. Similarly, the acquisition of County Investment Management (January 2001) in Australia created a synergy of local and global branding.

Amvescap's acquisition of Grand Pacific in August 2001 makes it the 11th largest fund manager in Taiwan, and combines Amvescap's growing offshore business with Grand Pacific's strong domestic presence. Amvescap anticipates playing the dual role of both bringing global resources to strong local businesses, and at the same time establishing the company as a significant player in the Asian markets, through its strategy of merging with companies in countries such as Taiwan.

tive, a number of mergers and partnerships have taken place in the insurance industry as part of an overall strategy to fend off competition from other financial services such as banks.

Environmental Implications of Organizational Change

Corporations undertaking restructuring strategies can open themselves to increased environmental scrutiny and exposure. Some companies claim that corporate reorganization through mergers and acquisitions can provide a dynamic opportunity for the implementation of environmental programs. In its 1998 merger with Swiss Bank Corporation, UBS, for instance, found that while its banking processes were being redesigned it was possible to systematically integrate environmental management systems across the corporation more rapidly than would otherwise have been possible (Furrer and Hugenschmidt 2000). Others, however, such as Credit Suisse, claim that restructuring as well as changes in key personnel make environmental control more difficult within their groups of services (Credit Suisse 2000).

Environmental exposure has prompted a different sort of organizational change within the insurance industry. In 1996, CIGNA Corporation, a U.S.-based insurer, split its property and casualty operations into two parts: one unit for ongoing business and a separate inactive unit to handle its more problematic liabilities, such as asbestos. CIGNA sought to set up two reserve funds where only one had existed formerly, to insulate the active funds from the inactive ones. Critics viewed this restructuring with skepticism, raising concern over the protection of policyholders' interests and the capability of the inactive pool to meet its financial obligations without calling on the resources of the active one (Levin et al. 1995; Weber 1996).

Also in 1996, Lloyd's of London created a reinsurance company known as Equitas, to assume responsibility for all the pre-1993 Lloyd's obligations, including asbestos and pollution claims. Under its "Reconstruction and Renewal" plan, Lloyd's also committed to reducing and capping investors' pre-1993 obligations in return for a waiver of all claims by them against the insurer (McClintick 2000). The cumulative impact of environmental and catastrophic losses on Lloyd's capacity is further discussed in Box 5.8.

Delivery of Personal Financial Services

As regulation and geography provide less of a constraint to competitiveness, another new trend is found in the delivery of personal financial services. The financial services sector is now starting to organize its products around consumer needs and economic product delivery. In doing so, many have decoupled the distribution from the manufacture of products (Flur et al. 1997), and are specializing in one or the other. For example, Deutsche Bank announced in December 2001 that it would distribute Invesco's mutual funds throughout its sales network. From another perspective, large financial management companies, such as Fidelity, may focus on their strength in the manufacturing of products and establish a joint venture or partnership with an efficient distributor, such as Schwab. At the same time, many superregional banks may seek to become third-party distributors for best-in-class products (see Chapter 6). Environmental implications of this change in perspective can be witnessed in the investment specialist T. Rowe Price's application of environmental research data from Innovest to its investment expertise, in the construction of its Global Eco Growth Fund being distributed by Daiwa Securities in Japan (Nicholls 2001a). From the regional perspective, Swissca Holdings has designed its Green Invest product in cooperation with World Wide Fund for Nature, which is then distributed through the Swiss cantonal banking network (www.swissca.ch).

FINANCIAL SERVICES' APPROACH TO ENVIRONMENTAL ISSUES

Within the financial services sector, banks and insurance companies, in particular, have been forced to develop an evaluation of environmental risks associated with the financial services they provide to their customers. The first tangible evidence of market response to environmental concerns occurred in the mid-1970s, when the property and casualty insurance industry faced claims relating to the use and manufacture of asbestos (see Table 3.4). Then in 1980 Superfund, which was established under CERCLA, became a significant issue for both bank creditors and insurers. Chapter 4 describes the legal implication of this 1980 law, as it imposed strict legal and retroactive liability for the cleanup of U.S. hazardous waste disposal sites contaminated in the past.

The passage of the Superfund bill, with its definition of potentially responsible parties (PRPs) based on retroactive, strict, joint and several liability, caused banking institutions to develop due diligence procedures aimed at minimizing their risk of incurring costs of environmental remediation. These measures were designed to aid decision making in cases where potentially contaminated real estate was being pledged as collateral in a credit application. More recently, banks have been using a company's environmental record not only for risk assessment, but also to identify possibilities for preferential lending rates as well as growth and profit potential for investing (EPA 2000; Blumberg et al. 1996). These developments are further discussed in Chapter 4.

In the insurance industry, Superfund law also had unforeseen and significant effects, due to the courts' interpretation of general comprehensive liability (GCL) policies. In light of joint and several, and retroactive, liability, adverse court rulings have caused the insurance and reinsurance industries severe capacity shortages, and have precipitated two significant

TABLE 3.4   Summary of the Impact of Environmental Events on the Financial Services Sector

		Industry Activity		
Date	Event	Insurance Underwriting	Extension of Credit	Investing
1969	First asbestos suit filed			
1970s	Asbestos suit filed against Johns Manville (1976)	Environmental impairment liability (EIL) policies created (1977)		
1980	CERCLA (Superfund) establishes joint, several, and retroactive liability			
1982				Johns Manville bankruptcy
1984	Bhopal	EIL pulls back due to losses		
1986	TRI reporting begins	"Absolute pollution exclusion" introduced for GCL policies	World Bank issues guidelines on environmental exposure management	
1988			Maryland Bank and Trust case, first case of lender liability for cleanup	
1989	*Exxon Valdez* runs aground; CERES formed	EIL market reappears	Environmental due diligence in credit becomes more standard practice	Early socially screened funds developed

(Continued)

TABLE 3.4 *(Continued)*

Date	Event	Industry Activity		
		Insurance Underwriting	Extension of Credit	Investing
1990			Fleet Financial found 100% liable for Superfund cleanup	
1992	Hurricane Andrew; Rio Convention	Great P&C losses	UNEP statement on banking signed	Investor Responsibility Research Center (IRRC) offers standard EP data on industrial firms
1994	Cat bonds, weather derivatives		First UNEP global banking conference	Securitization of various categories of environmental risk
1995	Weather derivatives	UNEP statement on insurance signed		
1996	ISO 14000 series released	First UNEP insurance conference		Scudder/ Storebrand Environmental Value Fund launched
1999				Dow Jones Sustainability Group (DJSG) Indexes
2001				FTSE4Good indexes

Source: Adapted from Ganzi and DeVries 1998; Swiss Re 1998.

changes to underwriting policies. The first is a switch in liability coverage from "occurrence" to "claims made" policies. The key feature of the "occurrence" form of GCL coverage is that the occurrence of an event triggers policy coverage, rather than when the claim is filed. Thus individuals suffering today from injuries linked to asbestos exposure in the 1960s, for instance, could file for compensation from insurance policies written on an occurrence basis at that time, even if the policy has lapsed. The "claims made" form of GCL alters this basic relationship insofar as the coverage is triggered by the claim rather than the occurrence of the event. If the claim is not filed within a specified time period, the coverage is not provided (Sutton 1991).

The second involves the development of pollution exclusion clauses in GCL policies, which further limited liability. More recently, several specialty insurers have reintroduced environmental impairment liability (EIL) policies that offer specific and limited environmental coverage (EPA 2000; Ganzi and DeVries 1998; Swiss Re 1998). Chapter 5 examines these outcomes in greater detail.

A further dominant environmental feature of the last decade of the twentieth century was the increase in frequency and severity of natural catastrophes, attributed to climate change. The cumulative losses from claims relating to these events had a severe impact on insurers' and reinsurers' capacity, reminiscent of the capacity shortage experienced previously due to U.S. Superfund liabilities. The insurance industry responded in a number of ways to this new environmental challenge. Among them: the securitization of insurance risk through the issuance of market products, such as weather derivatives and catastrophe (cat) bonds (Swiss Re 1998), and the establishment of Bermuda-based cat reinsurers aimed at bridging the capacity gap. Chapter 7 explores further the significance of these initiatives.

Historically, the equity investment community has not demonstrated as uniform a reaction to environmental issues as have the other two industries in the financial services sector. On the contrary, from the investment analyst's perspective, interpretation and understanding of corporate environmental concerns vary considerably, depending on the industry in question and the purpose of the analysis. Early equity analyses viewed companies' environmental strategies as liabilities (Superfund) or risks (catastrophic accidents). More recently, corporate environmental strategies are viewed as having the potential not only to reduce risks and cost of capital, but also to increase revenues, earnings, and the return on investments. In spite of this change in perception, environmental performance has not generally been integrated into traditional financial performance assessments. The emergence of the use of corporate environmental indicators in the appraisal of socially responsible investment (SRI) suggests a nascent, but growing, change in mainstream equity analysis (see Chapter 6).

CONCLUSION

Globalization and technological advances have contributed to the consolidation and organizational changes within the financial services sector in all countries. These changes have potentially significant implications for environmental issues within the financial services sector. Dominant hubs in the global financial market are in a position to influence the environmental standards of emerging markets. When leading financial intermediaries use uniform environmental evaluation techniques, they also have the potential to set global standards for risk assessment and materiality of environmental issues in investment decision making. (See Chapter 8 section titled "Environmental Reporting from the User's Perspective."). At the industry level, mergers provide opportunities for the establishment of environmental management systems across a broader geographic range and in more groups of services than had previously been experienced. Further, the deregulation of markets, such as in Japan, allows conglomerates to develop and distribute environmental products specifically designed for this previously inaccessible market (see UBS Nihon Kabushiki Eco Fund in Chapter 6). In addition, the opening of geographic markets, such as the European Union, combined with increased levels of competitiveness, stimulates institutions to expand distribution of existing environmental products and services through new channels in new jurisdictions.

It remains to be seen how the changes in the global financial market will affect environmental decision making in the financial services, since policies in different jurisdictions appear to be driven by varying considerations. In North America, consolidation and expansion strategies, cost considerations, and competitiveness are at the heart of policy challenges. Such motivation bodes well for the expansion of markets for environmental products and services. In Europe, the main focus appears to be the establishment of a system in which consolidation and cross-border transactions can take place now that the euro is established as the European Union's single currency. Cross-border consolidation provides fertile ground for the expansion of environmental opportunities into new regions within the European Union. Japan's Big Bang seems to be more of a series of sputters, as governments move slowly toward deregulation of the financial services sector (Kashyap 1999). The opening of the Japanese market, however, does appear to have already created a market for new environmental products.

In the following chapters, we will see that a host of new financial instruments has emerged as a result of increased competitiveness among the different industries in the financial services sector. Many of these new products are in the environmental field, as financial institutions are responding to stakeholder pressures discussed in Chapter 2.

ENDNOTES

1. A company's alpha represents the residual (positive or negative) observed return of its stock, after taking its risk factor into account.
2. Banks chartered in Canada are considered mainly to be Schedule I banks, while foreign-owned banks in that country, which have charters in their home jurisdictions, are classified as Schedule II institutions.

CHAPTER 4

Banking

INTRODUCTION

The effects of environmental issues are felt in three ways in the banking segment of the financial services sector. Regulations and court decisions, as well as internal operations, impose forms of direct risk, while the lending and the extension of credit to clients can cause indirect effects on the banking community. Finally, major environmental reputational risk can accrue to a bank through its involvement in controversial project financing relationships. As well as presenting banks with risks, managing these factors affords financiers opportunities to launch new products and services that integrate environmental and social criteria into their development. The following sections outline the background to some of these environmental concerns and examine the effects of environmental pressures on bankers' decision making and the initiatives that have been undertaken in response to such concerns.

COMMERCIAL BANKING

Environmental issues present significant direct and indirect liabilities for lending institutions, which manifest themselves in a number of ways. Indirectly, there is the credit risk of existing loans. If a borrower is unable to repay such a loan due to the cost of environmental cleanup, the loan default and thus environmental liability fall into the bank's jurisdiction. Secondly, a lending institution becomes linked to a corporate client's land holdings if such property is pledged as collateral in the transaction. In such cases, environmental damage diminishes the land's value and jeopardizes a bank's ability to recover its loan through sale of such assets in the event of a loan default or bankruptcy (Case 1999; Jeucken 2001; Schmidheiny and

Zorraquin 1996). Further, if a bank is forced to repossess a client's property, it encounters the additional direct risk of liability for the full cost of the cleanup of the degraded asset.

The impact of these issues of environmental liability can be severe. Under normal circumstances, a bank has the potential to lose the entire amount of a loan when a borrower defaults. When realizing on a loan secured by land assets, the bank's environmental liability can exceed many times the value of the loan if the site requires remediation (Levy 1992). If, indeed, a bank becomes the owner of contaminated land through bankruptcy proceedings, the bank then inherits a client's polluted property and experiences increased levels of lender liability.

At the same time the impacts that banking services can have on the environment are also twofold. The most direct impact of banking services is that of their internal operations and their business processes. Indirect environmental effects are experienced through the core products and services that banks provide for their clients.

To address such environmental issues banks have integrated environmental criteria into their overall lending and investment strategies. As well, such environmental issues have stimulated the development of a broad range of new products that provide environmentally conscious individuals and businesses with easier access to capital.

DIRECT LIABILITY OF CONTAMINATED LAND

Until the final decades of the twentieth century, fiscal responsibility provided a bank's traditional focus on its management practices as a lender; it focused more on a borrower's ability to repay the loan and interest due than on the client's environmental profile or management practices. In the 1980s, concerns arose within the banking sector regarding contaminated land and environmental liability, since legislation at that time did little to address issues of ownership, control, and fiduciary responsibility with respect to banks' lender liability. What was evident, however, was that if a bank was deemed to have the capacity to influence a borrower's polluting activities, the bank had the potential to be held liable by the courts for the cost of environmental remediation (Levy 1992).

The issue of defining who is in control of polluting activities, then, was central to the clarification of lender liability. The following section outlines trends in environmental regulation that have created such uncertainty for lenders in the United States, Canada, the European Union, Asia, and South America.

United States

North American banks were the first to be affected by legislation and court policies, particularly with respect to credit risks. Although the 1970s Clean Air Act had a great impact on polluting industries in the United States, its regulatory schemes did not appear to affect either an industry's financial transactions or the banks that supported them. In the following years, however, it became clear that remedial laws were needed to address the issue of cleaning up pollution and toxic waste. As a result, legislation was enacted in the United States to address these issues (Box 4.1).

In the Superfund Amendments and Reauthorization Act (SARA) categorization of control groups, lending institutions were exempt from being classed as owners. Several of the U.S. courts, however, have eroded this exemption when lenders were found to be operating, owning, or participating in the management of a contaminated business (Schmidheiny and Zorraquin 1996). Thus, liability under CERCLA has

BOX 4.1   CERCLA and SARA Legislation in the United States

To address environmental issues concerning the remediation of contaminated land in the United States, the Comprehensive Environmental Response Compensation and Liability Act (CERCLA) was enacted in 1976. Along with its 1986 amendment, the Superfund Amendments and Reauthorization Act (SARA), CERCLA gave the Environmental Protection Agency (EPA) the authority to identify sites contaminated by the disposal of hazardous substances and compel the responsible parties to clean them up (Thompson 1993).

Under SARA, the initial cost of cleaning up a contaminated site was borne by the EPA, which in turn was permitted to recover the costs of the remediation from any party involved with the disposal or release of a pollutant.

CERCLA attributes liability for remediation costs to one or more of the following categories of participants: first, the owners or operators of the contaminated facility at the time of cleanup; second, owners or operators on the site at the time of disposal of the contaminants; third, the generators of the hazardous waste; and finally, the transporters of the offending material to the contaminated site (Thompson 1993).

been far-reaching, and the role of financial institutions in the United States has been ambiguous. The following examples serve to illustrate this loss of impunity.

In 1986, the Maryland Bank and Trust (MBT) was held liable for the cleanup of a contaminated site of a waste management company that had defaulted on its loan. In this case, MBT purchased the property at a fore-closure sale to recover equity on a mortgage held by the bank on the property. The court said that MBT was protecting its investment in the site and held MBT liable for the cleanup costs of the hazardous substances. The court argued that CERCLA should not function as an insurance scheme to protect lending institutions from financial losses due to loans secured by contaminated properties. The court observed:

> [Lenders] already have the means to protect themselves, by making prudential loans. Financial institutions are in a position to investigate potential problems in their secured properties. For many lending institutions, such research is routine. (Thompson 1993, 416)

Thus CERCLA would not absolve a financial institution because of its lack of due diligence.

In a 1990 management participation case, the courts ruled that Fleet Factors in Providence, Rhode Island, should be held responsible for the cleanup of environmental degradation of the property of its bankrupt client, Swainsboro Print Works Inc. (SPWI). Fleet Factors had taken the inventory, equipment, and plant as collateral against loan advances. When SPWI filed for bankruptcy, Fleet Factors engaged another company to liquidate the equipment, during which hazardous chemicals were spilled on the site. The courts held that, by acting as operator of SPWI, Fleet Factors was in a position to influence the company's compliance with environmental laws. By holding Fleet Factors responsible for the cost of the site remediation, the court endorsed the finding that CERCLA should not be cast in an insurance role for lenders (Schmidheiny and Zorraquin 1996).

In an effort to clarify both lender and fiduciary liability for the cost of cleaning up environmental hazards, the Asset Conservation, Lender Liability and Deposit Insurance Protection Act amended CERCLA in 1996. The Act narrows significantly fiduciaries' potential liability for the cost of remediation. As it became effective immediately, the Act covered all existing claims that had not been finally settled by the date of the amendment (Fox and Zabel 1997).

Canada

At present, Canada does not have legislation that gives clear guidance with respect to lender liability and ownership of contaminated properties. What does exist is a patchwork of federal, provincial, and municipal environmental legislation that is relevant to lender assessment of environmental risk.

At the federal level, the Canadian Environmental Protection Act (CEPA), which came into effect in 1988, provides a number of sections that are applicable to lender liability. Several sections stipulate that any person who "owns or has charge of" stipulated toxins that are released, or who did "cause or contribute to a release" must attempt to remedy the situation and mitigate any danger to humans and the natural environment (Levy 1992).

Also at the federal level, the Fisheries Act imposes civil liability on those that alter, disrupt, or destroy fish habitat through the deposit of deleterious substances (Levy 1992). Licensed fishers can attempt to recover any income lost due to such deposits from the owner or person who had charge, management, or control of the deleterious substance at the time of deposit. Clearly, receivers or trustees in bankruptcy could be viewed as liable for breaches of the Fisheries Act under these circumstances.

At the provincial level, the principal environmental statute in British Columbia, for example, is the Waste Management Act (WMA). Under WMA a lender, receiver, or trustee in bankruptcy may be penalized if found to be "an owner or occupier, or to be a person in possession, charge or control of a polluting substance" at the time of the discharge of the polluting substance (Thompson 1993, 426). Similarly, under the Ontario Environmental Protection Act the scope of liability has been expanded to include persons who have previously owned or controlled the source of the contamination. In addition, acts such as the Ontario Water Resources Act allow the Ministry of the Environment to issue a cleanup order to any institution that "causes or permits the discharge of a contaminant resulting in damage or risk of damage to human health or the environment" (Levy 1992, 283).

The most notable Canadian decision that addresses the issue of a party's ability to influence a polluter's activities was made by the Supreme Court of Canada in 1978 in the case of *Regina v. The City of Sault Ste. Marie*. In this case, the city had entered into an agreement with a private waste management company for the disposal of the city's garbage. The city's refuse was dumped at a site near a creek and an adjacent river, resulting in the contamination of both these watercourses.

The city, rather than the disposal company, was charged under the Ontario Waste Resources Act with the offense of impairing the city's water (Thompson 1993).

The issue of control was also addressed in the *Regina v. Placer Development Ltd.* case. In 1991 the mining company was charged under the Fisheries Act with depositing diesel fuel into water that served as a fish habitat. The company defended its position by claiming that the responsibility for the contaminating fluid lay in the hands of an independent contractor. This defense was rejected, based on the argument that the position of authority that Placer held over the contractor gave the company the ability to control such offending activities (Thompson 1993).

European Union

European banks were not exposed to the same liabilities as early as their American counterparts, and thus tended to focus more on the development of new products than on risk assessment. Banks' consideration of policy development to address environmental issues started in the mid-1990s (Jeucken and Bouma 1999). This implies that the environmental legacy of vast tracks of contaminated land created during Britain's historic industrial revolution remains for the most part unrecorded and unquantified (Thompson 1995).

Given the U.S. litigious tradition along with court decisions and threats of punitive damage posed by CERCLA, the responsibility for cleaning up contaminants falls to the "voluntary" activities of potentially responsible parties (PRPs). By contrast, the European Union member states accept the main responsibility for primary cleanup. U.K. laws regarding land remediation, however, are more inclined to follow the U.S. model of site specificity. In the U.K. cases, a lender becomes directly liable for land remediation only if it forecloses on a business and becomes the owner of a contaminated site (Thompson 1995).

In 1991 the establishment the Financial Sector Working Group, a subcommittee of the Government's Advisory Committee on Business and the Environment (ACBE), started to address issues of contaminated land in the United Kingdom (ACBE 1993). In 1993, a separate division of the ACBE was established to deal specifically with the larger issues of contaminated land and liability. In 2000, the new Part IIA of the Environmental Protection Act, which addresses issues of contaminated land, was implemented in England and Scotland. Its goal is to provide an improved system of identification and remediation of historically contaminated lands. In this addition to the Environmental Protection Act, activities such as the provision of financial assistance and insurance underwriting have been excluded from liability (Association of British Insurers 2000a; Thompson 1995).

Asia and South America

In Asia and South America, current banking environmental policy changes being seen are attributed more to the influence of standards from multilateral development banks, such as the World Bank, the International Finance Corporation (IFC), and the European Bank for Reconstruction and Development (EBRD), than to local regulatory pressures (Jeucken and Bouma 1999). Evidence of the role that the World Bank has played in encouraging sustainable practices in developing countries and emerging economies is found in the description of the Indonesian Program for Pollution Control, Evaluation, and Rating (PROPER) in Chapter 6, section titled "Sources of Information."

BROWNFIELD REDEVELOPMENT

A further related, yet distinct, area in which lending institutions play an essential role is in financing potential projects of brownfield redevelopment. Traditionally, brownfields are sites located in urban settings that have contaminated soils and are economically remediable. Present and former transportation facilities, such as railway lands, often define the locations of brownfield sites since cities develop around such amenities. Similarly, harbors encourage industrial development on sites that then become contaminated. Facilities such as coal gas plants also have contributed to the brownfield dilemma (Dillon Ltd. et al. 1996).

From a planning and land use perspective, revitalization of brownfields has the potential to create commercially desirable locations in otherwise underutilized urban cores. However, increased awareness of environmental responsibility has created a stigma in some jurisdictions with respect to the redevelopment of these contaminated urban lands. Not only do purchasers avoid buying sites with contaminated soil, but financial institutions also decline to become involved because of issues of lender liability.

In the European Union the use of land for urban expansion is highly controlled in the member states, a condition that severely restricts options available to would-be developers. At the same time, limits to land use alternatives, smaller size and higher density of urban settlements, and the use of greenbelts around major cities in the EU generate a level of land scarcity that is not present in the United States. In combination, these factors have the effect of creating incentives for private sector land reclamation and redevelopment efforts. In addition, EU member states have the capacity to acquire land for any purpose, thus facilitating state action toward brownfield remediation by the private sector. By contrast, U.S. practices constrain such reclamation of privately held contaminated sites, and further oblige state governments to compensate landowners for any restrictions on land use imposed after acquisition by new owners (Meyer et al. 1995).

One indirect incentive identified by the Canadian National Round Table on the Environment and the Economy (NRTEE) to remove barriers to site cleanup and reuse (Dillon Ltd. et al. 1996) is that of reaching standard agreements with respect to lender liabilities in this area of concern. Environmental regulators noted that lenders could be induced to take control of contaminated sites, if certain conditions were negotiated between the two parties. Thus, "lender liability agreements" between regulator and lending institution have evolved. The agreement allows a creditor to commission an environmental audit of a property without triggering liability for its remediation. In a further step, the NRTEE suggested that a bank could take possession of the land, but with a prearranged agreement that limits its liability (Moffet and Saxe 1996).

At present, most jurisdictions include some provision for both standards-based and risk-based remediation in their guidelines. In the first case, a range of guidelines or regulatory standards has been developed to encourage the cleanup of contaminated sites. The site-specific risk-based model is grounded on the concept of flexible cleanup levels, depending on the proposed use of the site. For example, when the intended use of the property is commercial, the necessity of remediating a site to residential standards can be deferred. Also, in response to remediation concerns, purchase/tenant agreements have evolved that can include a purchaser's promise not to sue the former owner at a future date for the cost of cleanup.

Despite the evolution of lender liability protection in North America, revitalized brownfields are still encumbered with a lack of liquidity, following financing. An extremely limited market exists for these kinds of properties, particularly in areas where greenfields are abundant. As a result, a deep discount must be applied to the price of remediated contaminated land, if it is to sell at all (Evans 2002).

RISK MANAGEMENT

In response to these major environmental concerns, commercial banks have integrated environmental criteria into their overall lending strategies and credit assessments. Environmental risk management systems developed by banks help establish the basis of their due diligence, which addresses issues of clients' environmental risk and bankers' lender liability.

Within this environmental scrutiny, potentially high-risk sectors of commercial and industrial lending are classified into three categories according to the magnitude of the environmental issues that are inherent in different industries (Table 4.1). The categories are differentiated according to the level of environmental scrutiny to which the bank will subject the company before providing the required financial support.

Three levels of due diligence exist with respect to risk identification and appraisal, from desktop reviews through internal research to the use of external expertise. Typically, assessments initially look at whether the sector or the site is likely to pose environmental problems. If a dilemma emerges, the application is subjected to further scrutiny at the regional level or head office, and external consultants are called in if the concern persists.

In the first category listed in Table 4.1, external advisers are used selectively to assess environmental concerns. In the second category, consultants may be asked to address risks that are specific to these industries. In the third and most complex category, which includes industries such as petrochemicals and pulp and paper, a qualified consultant is always called upon to undertake investigations. Such scrutiny is commissioned and paid for by the client, thus distancing the bank from any notion of control or management of the business or the property.

At the same time as such assessments are being made, the commercial or industrial client completes specialized questionnaires. These identify the historical use of the property in question, note environmental issues that need managing, and gather information on the company's compliance and licensing records. When real property is being used as collateral security or when a high-risk industry is applying for credit, the risk analyst is charged with determining whether it is possible to eliminate or treat any problem area or to tolerate its existence. Some remediation measures or commitment to capital expenditures for pollution abatement equipment may be required before credit is extended. In addition, the lending officer may also consider spreading part of the risk through the use of insurance on the loan transaction.

TABLE 4.1   Risk Assessment Guidelines for Extension of Credit

Category I	Category II	Category III
• Dry cleaners (depot) • Electric substations • Furniture and fixtures • Laundry and garment services • Leather and leather products • Lumber and wood products • Printing and publishing • Stone, clay, and glass products • Textile industry • Warehousing	• Dry cleaners (facility) • Electrotechnological industries • Fabricated metal products • Farming industries, services and supplies • Galvanizing industries • Garages for repairs (cars/buses/trains) • Ink manufacturing • Metallurgic industries • Mining • Oil and gas exploration • Oil and gas products manufacture • Paint/lacquer manufacture • Petroleum bulk stations/terminals • Pharmaceutical industries • Pipelines (excluding natural gas) • Pipelines (natural gas) • Plating companies • Recycling plants handling solvents, batteries, used oil, or liquid waste • Scrap and waste materials industries • Service stations • Shipyards • Tanneries • Transportation industries	• Chemical and petrochemical industries • Fertilizers • Foundries • Oil and gas production • Pesticide/fungicide/herbicide manufacturers • Petroleum refining • Pulp and paper industries • Resource extractive industries • Steel • Waste management • Wood preservation

Source: Gray 1994.

This environmental risk evaluation process enables a bank to judge whether the client is capable of managing the environmental risk in a way that limits the bank's exposure. The environmental risk is incorporated into the bank's overall borrower risk rating system that defines whether: (1) credit is to be rationed, (2) the term of the loan is to be limited, or (3) the pricing of the loan will be affected. Thus loan agreements are tailored to each situation and include conditions of indemnification and default clauses pertaining to environmental risk management.

A survey conducted by Ganzi and Tanner (1997) suggests that at least half the banks in North America and Europe have some form of assessment of environmental factors built into their credit approval for commercial loans. Deutsche Bank, NatWest (Thompson 1995), Union Bank of Switzerland (UBS), BankAmerica, and Royal Bank of Canada are among the many that publicly report their three-phase due diligence procedures for the systematic assessment of the environmental aspects in their lending operations.

At UBS Warburg, lists of precedent cases are compiled internally to help staffers source information on different sectors and to provide them with checklists of environmental issues to be considered in any investment bank transaction in those known sectors. For industries or deals that are new to Warburg, information is gained from environmental consultants and law firms, in order to determine what issues need be considered (Henshaw 2001).

Risk control and transfer are further components of this bank's risk management procedure. Risk control pertains to both financial and image risk on the part of banks. In their terms, even if transaction-based mechanisms are generally reactive, image risk needs to be dealt with in a proactive manner.

Risk transfer is most often associated with insurance, where quantifiable risk will be borne by the insurer. Issues of risk transfer will be addressed in Chapter 5. While insurance products may be designed to protect banks from monetary losses such as legal costs, no insurance can protect an institution from loss of reputation or image.

ENVIRONMENTAL PRODUCTS AND SERVICES

In addition to risk management tools, banks have developed new products that both encourage improved environmental performance on the part of clients and provide environmental businesses with easier access to capital. Table 4.2 outlines some of the products and services that have

TABLE 4.2   Environmental Products and Services Developed by the Banking Industry

Function	Particulars	Product
Deposits	• Current accounts	• Permanent balance used for loans and investments
	• Savings accounts	• Specific savings products
Lending	• Financing investments in environmentally favorable projects[1]	• Preferential banking package
	• Organizations fulfilling certain ecological criteria	• Environmental rating and due diligence checks
	• Real estate	
	• Environmental mortgages	• Lower interest rates
Credit	• Affinity cards	• Donations to environmental nongovernmental organizations (ENGOs)
Investment banking	• Initial public offering (IPO) due diligence	• Risk management assessment
Advisory service	• Small and medium-sized enterprises (SME)	• Environmentally related counseling
Leasing	• Making government fiscal schemes accessible to entrepreneurs	• Purchase and subsequent lease of environmental products
Venture capital	• Providing capital for new business ventures	• Funds dispensed according to environmental criteria
Insurance	• P&C underwritings	• Lower premiums
	• Investing for own accounts	• Investing in environmentally friendly companies

[1]Environmental technology, energy-efficiency investments, environmental management systems, soil remediation, recycling infrastructure.
Source: Based on Tarna 2001, p. 161.

been developed within the banking industry in response to environmental concerns and stakeholder pressures.

Banks have introduced specific products that meet the needs of their clients through the introduction of payment, savings, and investment products. In addition, in their roles as financial intermediaries, banking institutions have created products such as environmental loans and leases to help in the establishment of new environmental markets (e.g., development of water purification equipment and efficient and sustainable energy products). In addition, financial institutions have become involved in the securitization of projects that are in early stages of development and which are capital intensive with little or no profit; this is most evident in new policies and products that address issues of climate change. Finally, banks have developed advisory products and services that assist companies with their environmental risk management (Jeucken 2001). The following sections give examples of these products and services. Chapter 9 looks at the issue of securitization and climate change in greater detail.

Preferential Banking Packages   Very few products related to environmental care are offered to holders of current accounts. The exceptions to this are found in banks such as the Co-operative Bank in the United Kingdom and Triodos Bank in the Netherlands (www.co-operativebank.co.uk; Triodos Bank 2000). In both these cases, the balance in customers' current accounts is used for loans and investments specifically in the field of sustainable development.

Environmental care products for savings accounts have been, until the present, the purview of niche banks such as the Dutch Algemene Spaarbank voor Nederland NV (ASN) and Triodos Bank. They offer specific savings products from which funds are directed toward sustainability loans and investments. For example, the Triodos North-South Account finances small-scale sustainable economic activities in developing countries (Triodos Bank 2000). ING Bank and Rabobank distinguish themselves among the larger banks with such products. These are tax-driven savings products, stemming from fiscal tax regulations in the Netherlands that are discussed later in this chapter. Rabobank is considering the introduction of "destination accounts" in which individuals can designate where their savings account funds are to be invested (www.rabobank.com/sustainability).

Clients that meet certain environmental criteria are able to take advantage of preferential banking packages that can include lower interest rates on loans, reduced banking charges, or special rates on funds deposited. An interesting example of this positive drive toward sustainability is found in the Co-operative Bank's pledge to sustainability. Companies that are deemed to be acceptable to the Co-operative Bank's criteria are eligible for favorable interest rates, with higher interest rates on savings and lower interest rates on loans. The net savings for a company can be as high as 30 percent when compared to standard interest rates (Green Futures 1998; www.co-operativebank.co.uk/ecology.html).

Green Mortgages   The delivery of "green mortgage" products takes on original formats at different financial institutions. At ING Bank, green mortgages fall within the Dutch government's Green Projects scheme, where buyers of sustainably built homes can negotiate a green mortgage at lower rates. These sustainably built homes must comply with stringent technical requirements in energy and water conservation, use of materials, and internal environment. Buyers profit from an interest rate that is 1.5 to 2.0 percent below market rates (ING Group 1999). Co-operative Bank's green mortgages combine the value of credit with investments that provide environmental benefits. In this scheme, the Co-operative Bank makes payments to Climate Care each year throughout the lifetime of the mortgage. Climate Care is a company that finances carbon-offsetting initiatives such as reforestation, renewable energy, and energy efficiency. The bank's first project was Uganda's Kibale Forest, home of one of the highest concentrations of primates in the world (Co-operative Bank 2000).

Credit Cards   In addition to its sustainability screening of assets and liabilities managed by the institution, the Co-operative Bank has developed a number of tailored ethical and sustainable products, such as its selection of affinity cards with Oxfam, Amnesty International, Greenpeace, and Save the Children Fund. Donations are made to each of the partnered nongovernmental organizations (NGOs) from income generated by the use of the credit cards (www.co-operativebank.co.uk/personal/personal_affinity_cards.html). In addition, Swedbank has developed its World Nature Card in collaboration with the World Wide Fund for Nature (WWF), where 0.5 percent of the total payment transactions made with the card are devoted to the WWF for use in Scandinavia (FöreningsSparbanken 2000). The Royal Bank of Canada has established a similar WWF Visa Affinity Card (www.rbc.com), while in the United States Citigroup offers an Environmental Defense Platinum MasterCard to its clients (www.citigroup.com). These arrangements are made at no cost to either the banks' customers or retailers, since the full cost is borne by the banks involved. These credit card arrangements create a heightened image for the banks, and, as such, are considered a form of cause-related marketing (Jeucken 2001).

Leasing   A number of government initiatives have been designed to stimulate environmental products in lending institutions through the application of contract-leasing models. In Switzerland, Credit Suisse offers an energy contracting model that was developed in response to the Swiss federal government's Energy 2000 investment program. The initiative is based on the concept that a number of companies would purchase energy in the form of heat, refrigeration, light, or steam from an outside supplier that can produce and distribute such energy requirements efficiently (Delphi and Ecologic 1997).

In the Netherlands, close cooperation among the Dutch government, the Dutch environmental technology industry, and financiers has created an interesting and innovative incentive for businesses that are intent on using environmental technology. In this country, the range of environmental funds has increased as the government encouraged investment in new environmentally sound economic activities that are not yet profitable. Wanting to encourage activities such as organic agriculture and sustainable energy, the government introduced financial and fiscal instruments designed to stimulate investments in these areas (Corten et al. 1998; Delphi and Ecologic 1997; Knörzer 2001). Two of these initiatives, the accelerated depreciation scheme and energy investment tax deduction scheme, are outlined in Box 4.2.

Green Certificates   In 1992 the Green Fund System was launched by the government of the Netherlands as a joint venture with the financial services sector. The program represents a number of tax incentives applicable to investments in green projects that meet the criteria for "green certification." Projects financed must show a high environmental return, plus an economic return that indicates the project is self-supporting, although its return is insufficient to attract regular financing. The project should be situated in the Netherlands or another area covered by this regulation, such as the Dutch Antilles, Eastern Europe, and some developing countries (Jeucken 2001; van Bellegem 2001). Private individuals (retail investors) investing in the system are eligible for tax exemptions.

By the end of 2000, every major Dutch bank offered its own brand of fiscal green fund. Most banks in the Netherlands, such as ABN Amro, ASN, and ING, have established a number of green funding sources for sustainable energy projects in order to comply with the Dutch Ministry of the Environment's Green Certificate program (BASE 2001; Jeucken

BOX 4.2 Financial Instruments Designed to Stimulate Investment
in the Environment

The *accelerated depreciation* format for equipment investment offers
entrepreneurs the financial advantages of both increased cash in
hand, as well as more favorable interest rates. A fiscal scheme such
as this is of interest only to taxable companies. However, non-tax-
paying organizations can benefit from the arrangement as well
through the application of operational leases. In this case, the lessor
(a financial company such as ING) invests in the equipment and
claims the fiscal early depreciation. The benefit can then be passed
on to the lessee (entrepreneur) in the form of lower lease installments
(van Bellegem 2001).

The Dutch government's *energy investment tax deduction scheme*
was designed to encourage investment in equipment designed to save
energy or to run on sustainable energy sources. These schemes also
make use of operational leases, making them an attractive option for
entrepreneurs (van Bellegem 2001). Through a "lease construction"
product, ING Bank, for example, makes such fiscal schemes accessible to small business ventures.

Source: ING Group 1999.

2001). For example, deposits made under the auspices of ING's Postbank Groen green certificate program are used to finance certified green
projects, such as district heating, wind power, solar energy, and sustainable construction. Rabobank is the market leader in the field with respect to both the volume of funds and the number of projects financed
(Jeucken 2001).

Through these initiatives, Dutch banks are able to capitalize on a federal tax scheme by offering their private clients an opportunity to save capital gains tax while investing in green projects (www.abnamro.nl;
www.asnbank.nl; www.postbankgroen.nl). The chief beneficiaries of the
tax exemptions have been businesses, as the tax changes are reflected in reduced interest on their credit for projects that qualify for Green Certificates. This has been made even more compelling, as investors seem willing
to accept a lower gross return when the tax advantage is factored into the
overall cost of capital (Jeucken 2001).

Insurance The insurance products of integrated banks also offer environmental benefits to customers and clients. Environmentally friendly companies can enjoy lower premiums, while some banks offer distinct forms of coverage. One such product is recycling insurance offered by Credit Suisse, in which customers pay less for car insurance (up to 20 percent) if recycled parts are used for repairs or replacements. In a similar vein, Tokio Marine as well as Yasuda Fire and Marine offer a 3 percent discount on automobile insurance for low-pollution vehicles. From an investment perspective, insurance companies such as Uni Storebrand in Norway and National Provident Institution (NPI) in the United Kingdom have introduced investment products targeting the growing sustainability market. In addition, some insurers have conditions on certain types of products that allow for donations to environmental causes. In the Netherlands the SNS-Reaal Group donates a fixed amount per policy to causes such as an environmental education project for children in Chad in its Aware Savings Policy program (Jeucken 2001).

Consultancy In addition to the banks' capacity to influence clients through lending programs, there is a good potential for banks to act as a major source of environmental information for small and medium-sized enterprises (SMEs). In this capacity, a number of promising initiatives have taken place. For example, initiatives undertaken by Deutsche Bank, Germany's largest private bank, with respect to its small and medium-sized clients are outlined in Box 4.3.

BOX 4.3 Deutsche Bank's Environmental Assistance for Small and Medium-Sized Companies

In the late 1980s Deutsche Bank's corporate client department drew up an information brochure for pollution control for its medium-sized clients.

More recently, Deutsche Bank has provided information on the Eco-Management and Audit System (EMAS) and consultation on environmental services, products, and technologies for clients other than its largest industrial customers.

In 1996 Deutsche Bank developed an environmental checklist for smaller project financing applications where the cost of environmental impact assessment would be excessive. The checklist, which is completed by a credit officer, focuses mainly on matters of eco-efficiency and eco-audits.

Further, in the Netherlands ING Bank developed its SME Environmental Plan in 1999, which provides a total package of financing, insurance, and consultancy for entrepreneurs. Its SME Environmental Loan component was developed in cooperation with the European Investment Fund (EIF) within the Dutch Growth and Environment Program. In an effort to stimulate SMEs' investments in environmentally friendly projects, EIF issues guarantees for extending credit, while ING Bank issues the actual credits, designed exclusively for environmental investment (ING Group 1999).

In the United Kingdom, National Westminster Bank (NatWest) has launched a series of manuals and computer-based information systems on environmental management, designed to help small and medium-sized businesses (Delphi and Ecologic 1997; Thompson 1995).

In Switzerland, the Swiss Bank Association (SBA) developed a program in 1997 to inform smaller Swiss banks about environmental issues. The association, which is heavily supported by the main large Swiss banks, published a practical environmental guidebook for financial institutions, aimed at helping the smaller Swiss banks get started in environmental management. The handbook acts not only as a tool for internal environmental issues, but also as an environmental primer for credit and investment activities (Delphi and Ecologic 1997).

NICHE MARKETS AND MICROCREDIT

Some would argue that the banks with the greatest potential for embracing sustainability are those whose shareholders hold the same vision and ambitions as the banks. Siddiqui and Newman (2001) illustrate that this is possible with niche players, where the entire focus of an organization is on a niche market, such as that of microcredit. On a larger scale, the Co-operative Bank in the United Kingdom lies somewhere between a mainstream and a niche sustainable banking approach with its comprehensive inclusion of stakeholders in its measurement and reporting.

On a smaller scale, a number of banks have created positions for themselves in the niche market of providing lending for small projects and businesses in the environmental field, where they can have a significant impact. Among these are the Algemene Spaarbank voor Nederland NV (ASN Bank) in the Netherlands, the Grameen Bank in Bangladesh, and Shore-Bank Pacific in the United States.

In the Netherlands, ASN Bank was founded in 1960 with a business approach that included environmental and social principles for society at large, and a commitment to what was good for the local communities as well. With these guidelines in place, ASN considers itself to be a specialized "ethical" bank and a "niche player" (Negenman 2001). ASN Bank applies its clear set of ethical criteria, which are directly related to "green financing," to all projects being considered for its investment portfolio. In addition, savings account funds are invested in accordance with the bank's sustainability investment criteria. The ASN-Trouw Index, based on the same ethical criteria, has been developed with the expectation that the publication of its weekly value will demonstrate that companies included in the index will outperform those in traditional indexes. In short, ASN's ethical niche market approach emphasizes the fact that green financing can take place successfully, with the use of creative products developed at a community level.

While microcredit organizations such as the Grameen Bank often do not have a direct environmental focus, the activities they support frequently will have a positive environmental outcome. The Grameen Bank of Bangladesh is a specialized credit institution for the poor. It focuses on extending lending facilities to landless men and women in Bangladeshi villages, with an eye to breaking the downward spiral of poverty and social and environmental degradation.

Borrowers form into groups of five like-minded people with similar economic and social backgrounds in order to receive a loan. No collateral is required. Loans are repaid in weekly installments at the village meeting. The recovery rate remains stellar, at 98 percent. In attempting to enhance the social welfare of the villagers, the Grameen Bank is seeking to improve family living quarters, drinking water, and sanitation facilities, thus improving the families' general health. In agricultural arrangements, the bank encourages the growth of vegetables and tree plantations to improve both families' consumption patterns as well as their economic condition through the sale of surplus production. Grameen Bank educates its lenders about the adverse effects of using chemical fertilizers and pesticides in the practice of agriculture, and encourages them to establish more environmentally benign agricultural practices. The main portions of loans go toward livestock and fisheries, followed by agriculture, forestry, and manufacturing.

By enhancing human habitation through better housing, the use of better drinking water, better sanitation, and the establishment of environmentally sustainable agriculture, the Grameen Bank serves as a leading example of a microcredit bank addressing aspects of its country's social needs, with its associated environmental results.

The Chicago-based South Shore Bank has created the first conservation development bank in the United States, namely ShoreBank Pacific.

ShoreBank Pacific's aim is to combine community development with ecosystem restoration. A major focus of this new entity is the support of business entrepreneurs' efforts to build green markets for their products. In addition, the bank has introduced "ecodeposits," wherein "ecodepositors" help finance protection of the forests in the U.S. Pacific northwest (Crane 1999).

INTERNAL ENVIRONMENTAL MANAGEMENT

As has been noted, the banking industry can affect the environment through the direct impacts of its internal operations and business processes. Although banks are not normally considered to be part of a severely polluting industry, they have taken steps to reduce their impact on the natural environment. Due to the sheer size of the banking community, any improvement in its environmental performance will be significant. In so doing, banks can also lead by example within the industry, as well as demonstrate superior environmental performance to other sectors. The high-profile energy-efficient buildings that serve as the ING Bank headquarters in Amsterdam (built in the 1980s) and the Commerzbank headquarters in Frankfurt (developed in the 1990s) provide notable examples of this leadership.

Just as in other sectors, the systematic use of environmental management systems is beginning to appear among banking institutions. Some banks are integrating environmental management systems into their policies and operations through the adoption of ISO 14001 (Box 4.4). In this regard, UBS is the first bank to be awarded ISO 14001 certification for its environmental management systems, both for its international banking operations and for its in-house operations in Switzerland.

In Europe the European Commission drew heavily on the pioneering work of the British Standards Institution's BS 7750 (1992) in developing its regulation outlining its Eco-Management and Audit Scheme (EMAS), which became operational in 1995. The concept behind the development of EMAS was to encourage voluntary public reporting on corporate environmental performance.

EMAS introduced European guidelines for the voluntary introduction of environmental management and auditing systems in certain parts of the manufacturing sector. Following an environmental audit, EMAS requires a company to prepare a validated environmental statement or report for each site, and have this statement made available to the public (Pritchard 2000).

BOX 4.4   The International Organization for Standardization Environmental
Management and Performance Evaluation

The International Organization for Standardization published its international set of standards, the 14000 series, of which ISO 14001 describes an environmental management system standard and ISO 14031 addresses environmental performance indicators and evaluation (Pritchard 2000; Skillius and Wennberg 1998).

The ISO 14001 standard for environmental management systems (EMS) requires a validated environmental policy statement that demonstrates a commitment to environmental improvement and also provides overall procedures for its attainment. As well as policy and procedures, ISO 14001's specifications include implementation and review of the EMS, as well as a position on corrective action and continuous improvement (Pritchard 2000). In contrast to EMAS, which is limited to production companies, service companies can take part in the ISO 14001 systems specification and standard operating rules for application.

ISO 14031, the standard set for environmental performance evaluation, identifies two indicators of environmental performance: environmental performance indicators (EPI) within an institution and environmental condition indicators (ECI) outside the institution. The latter group offers a company insight into general environmental conditions and can help a firm determine its influence and impact on the environment.

The EPI are further divided into indicators measuring the management performance (MPI) in the financial services sector, focusing on the drivers of environmental performance, and operational performance indicators (OPI) for the actual financial services, which focus on results.

Source: www.epifinance.com

In Austria, an ordinance allowing for the inclusion of financial institutions to participate in EMAS was passed in 1996. This means that Austria is the first member state of the European Union whose complete banking and insurance industries have been able to participate in the EU's EMAS scheme. In the United Kingdom a group of leading banks, led by National Westminster, is exploring the possibility of extending EMAS to the financial sector.

UNEP FINANCIAL INSTITUTIONS INITIATIVE

The founding of the UNEP Financial Institutions Initiative on the Environment and Sustainable Development (FII) presents further clear evidence that bankers, insurers, and investors, among other institutions, can contribute to environmental protection in a valuable way. The FII represents the continuation of UNEP's 1972 mandate to encourage forms of economic growth that are compatible with the environment, and the 1992 Earth Summit's further emphasis on sustainable development. When UNEP founded its Financial Institutions Initiative, 30 banks originally signed the statement. Now over 170 financial institutions are signatories. The Statement by Financial Institutions was revised in 1997. While not diluting any of the original commitments or aspirations of the original, the revised edition did reflect changes in the makeup of the banking sector that have taken place since 1992 (Kelly and Huhtala 2001).

The UNEP Insurance Industry Initiative on the Environment (III) was launched independently in 1995 to reflect the management styles and concerns of the insurance industry that differ from those of the banking community. To date more than 85 insurers and reinsurers have signed the III Statement. Although the FII and III continue to work independently of each other, the UNEP now combines both initiatives at its Annual Financial Institutions' Round Table (O'Sullivan 2001). To view the statements and the list of signatories for the FII and III, see Appendix A.

The primary objective of the Financial Initiative has been to generate a dialogue among the various industries in the financial services sector, with UNEP initially playing an educational and information-giving role. As banks have became more informed as to their role, UNEP now acts, to a greater extent, as a facilitator of change among informed banks. A secondary objective is to encourage private sector investment in environmental technologies and services. When last surveyed in 1999, over 60 percent of the signatories had introduced specific products or services with environmental, as well as financial, aspects.

In the early years of the twenty-first century, this Financial Initiative represents a voluntary program involving over 275 institutions in the financial services sector. The initiative itself has broadened its horizons to include regional conferences, workshops, and training courses, all aimed at the examination of specific regional issues in areas such as the Philippines and South Africa. In June 2001, the UNEP launched its Global e-Sustainability Initiative (GeSI). GeSI represents a voluntary initiative similar to the UNEP Financial Initiative that tackles the linkage between the information and communication technology sector and sustainable development.

The chair of the interim GeSI steering group states, "At a time in history when our technologies are bringing people closer together, it follows that businesses also work together to contribute to the societies within which they operate." Thus, GeSI will look at contributions that information and communication technologies can make in advancing sustainable development in areas such as climate change, waste reduction, and the digital divide. Participating companies are also looking at how best to pass on their knowledge and expertise in a spirit of outreach, to ensure that businesses around the world can take advantage of new opportunities and expanded markets at the same time as being environmentally and socially responsible (UNEP 2001).

MEASUREMENTS AND REPORTING OF ENVIRONMENTAL MANAGEMENT

As will be seen in Chapter 8, the comparison of the environmental performance between industries and sectors has proven to be difficult. The banking industry proves to be no exception. A number of initiatives have been undertaken to address this weakness within the financial services sector. A summary of these initiatives follows.

VfU

The German Association for Environmental Management in Banks, Savings Banks, and Insurance Companies (Verein fur Umweltmanagment in Banken, Sparkassen und Versicherungen: VfU) was founded in 1994, with a goal of developing industry-specific strategies and tools for environmental management for its members.

In 1997, VfU developed a standardized methodology, specifically for banks, to measure the burden of their internal operations on the environment (Box 4.5). VfU indicators have been adopted by a number of European financial institutions in reporting their efforts to improve their internal environmental performance. Table 4.3 demonstrates the Swiss Sarasin Bank's use of VfU key indicators for its internal environmental reporting.

Other financial institutions, such as the Credit Suisse Group, also provide data on the environmental impacts of their operational activities using the VfU set of indicators. The Credit Suisse Environmental Report (2000) goes further in its analysis of the quality of the data that the bank is able to collect (average to very good), as well as directional trends in the reduction/growth of each indicator.

BOX 4.5   German Association for Environmental Management in Banks, Savings
Banks, and Insurance Companies (VfU)

> VfU methodology draws a distinction between internal and external
> issues, labeling them "operating" and "product" ecology respectively.
> VfU is most applicable to internal operating functions.
>
> VfU-suggested operating indicators include measure of energy,
> heat, water, and paper consumption, as well as business travel and
> CO_2 emissions. Absolute measurements of EPIs (kWh, cubic me-
> ters, tons, and km) are converted to relative terms through the
> use of the company's general information, such as number of em-
> ployees, area of buildings, number of branches, and number of
> workdays.
>
> VfU suggests that companies should use its environmental perfor-
> mance indicators both to compare performance levels on an annual
> basis and to benchmark a company's environmental performance in
> comparison to other institutions.
>
> *Source:* VfU 1996.

TABLE 4.3   VfU Key Figures for Sarasin Bank's Internal Environmental Report

VfU Key Figures	Unit	1996	1997	1998	1999
Electricity	KWh/employee	7,540	7,654	7,123	6,571
Heating energy	KWr/m3 ESA	61	84	70	74
Water	Liter/employee/day	59	80	73	68
Paper	Kg/employee	215	not available	270	238
Recycling		12%		4%	20.6%
Waste	Kg/employee	320	291	276	294
Incineration		60%	72%	70%	46%
Recycling		40%	28%	30%	54%
Business Travel	Km/employee	2,930	3,862	3,372	5,513
Car		13%	10%	17%	8%
Rail		12%	15%	17%	11%
Air		75%	75%	66%	81%
CO_2 emissions	Kg/employee	2,490	3,204	3,047	3,737

Source: www.sarasin.ch/show/content.

Although this schema allows for comparisons across financial institutions, critics say that VfU does not make provisions for company-specific characteristics, such as corporate size or function. In the latter category, it would seem that multinationals would generally exhibit a poorer performance in all categories, but most specifically in business travel (Jeucken and Bouma 1999).

EPI-Finance 2000

In 2000, a group of 11 Swiss and German financial institutions, assisted by E2 Management Consulting, developed a set of environmental performance indicators specifically for the financial services sector. The group's report, known as EPI-Finance 2000, aims to help harmonize reporting practices in financial institutions and to facilitate benchmarking (Box 4.6). EPI-Finance 2000 division of indicators is based on the evaluation methodology outlined in the ISO 14031 standard. Due to the existence of VfU, EPI-Finance 2000 does not include in-house ecology performance; rather, it focuses on the product and management performance of financial institutions.

Table 4.4 illustrates UBS' application of the EPI-Finance 2000 standard to its environmental performance.

The Natural Step

The Natural Step (TNS) is a tool that has been developed to help a variety of organizations assess and reduce the impact of their operations on the environment (Box 4.7).

Two financial institutions that have applied TNS principles to develop programs and assess the environmental impacts of their service channels are the Co-operative Bank in the United Kingdom and ShoreBank Pacific in the United States.

The launch of the Co-operative Bank's Ethical Policy followed by an Ecological Mission Statement contributed to its success in turning around its negative performance figures as well as attracting new customers (Delphi and Ecologic 1997). Taking its environmental commitment even further, the bank adopted a deep ecological approach to educating its staff about environmental risks and opportunities. Using the four "systems conditions" of The Natural Step (see Box 4.7), the bank developed a series of indicators to measure the ecological and social impact of its internal operations and service channels.

The Co-operative Bank's third *Partnership Report* (2000) examines

BOX 4.6 EPI-Finance 2000 Environmental Indicators

EPI-Finance 2000 proposes five environmental indicators for measuring and reporting environmental impacts of financial institutions. They focus on management and operational performance for commercial and investment banking, asset management, and the insurance industry, and are divided into three management (MPI) and two operational (OPI) performance indicators.

Management (MPI) Performance Indicators:

- Know-how (environmentally relevant posts and environmental departments).
- Training (environmental management training).
- Auditing (environmental management audits).

Operational (OPI) Performance Indicators:

- Integration into the core business (environmental risk check/coverage; assets under green management).
- Environmentally oriented services (financing/transactions with/investments in environmentally oriented pioneers; environmentally innovative policies).

Source: EPI-Finance 2000.

the internal indicators of buildings and their maintenance, energy use, waste reduction, and transportation. In addition, the bank has developed some original measures of the social and environmental impact of its delivery of its services to clients. For example, from an environmental perspective, the range of ecological impacts of the manufacture and disposal of credit and debit cards made from polyvinyl chloride (PVC) is assessed. The bank has indicated its intention of developing a PVC-free card made from Biopal, a plastic derived from fermented sugar rather than fossil fuels (Street and Monaghan 2001). The Co-operative Bank views key groups of stakeholders, such as employees and customers, as partners in the bank's activities. Thus, from the social perspective, the bank examines elements of job security and working conditions with

TABLE 4.4 UBS Environmental Performance Indicators, Based on EPI-Finance 2000 Standard

GROUP Employees	Unit	Value 1999	Value 2000
Employees (total)	Jobs (part-time jobs converted to 100%)	49,058	71,076[1]
Employees dealing with environmental aspects in the business process	Jobs (part-time jobs converted to 100%)	n.a.	n.a.
Employees in specialized environmental units	Jobs (part-time jobs converted to 100%)	2.5	3[1]
External Audits			
External environmental audits	Audits carried out	69	9
Number of employees audited	Employees	82	14
Auditing time	Hours (number of audits × average auditing time)	68	15

ASSET MANAGEMENT Employees	Unit	Value 1999	Value 2000
Employees in UBS Asset Management and UBS Switzerland, Private Banking	Jobs (part-time jobs converted to 100%)	9,832	10,545[1]
Employees dealing with environmental aspects in the business process	Jobs (part-time jobs converted to 100%)	n.a.	n.a.
Employees in specialized environment units	Jobs (part-time jobs converted to 100%)	7	7[1,2]
Training			
Training with environmental component	Employees trained	266	926
Training time	Hours (employees trained × average training period)	n.a.	475
Internal Audits			
Environmental audits	Employees audited	11	0[3]
Auditing time	Hours (number of audits × average auditing time)	n.a.	0[3]
Assets under Management			
UBS Group	Billions CHF	1,744	2,469
Assets under green and social management	Millions CHF	627	901

(Continued)

85

TABLE 4.4 *(Continued)*

ASSET MANAGEMENT Employees	Unit	Value 1999	Value 2000
Investment in Innovators			
Unlisted companies with innovative products or services	Number of companies in which invested	1	1
Investment volume	Millions CHF	1.5	2.25
Performance of Environmental Products			
Performance	%	Eco Perf[4] + 47.7% Eco JPN[5] +10%	Eco Perf +1.7[4] Eco JPN[5] −18.6%
Relative performance versus relevant index	%	Eco Perf vs. MSCI: +1.7% Eco JPN vs. TOPIX: −0.1%	Eco Perf vs. MSCI: +15.7% Eco JPN vs. TOPIX: +8.7%

[1]All employment figures represent the state as of December 31, 2000.
[2]Including external partners.
[3]The audits for the business year 2000 will take place in the first quarter of 2001 and will therefore be first released in the Environmental Report 2001.
[4]Eco-performance = UBS (Lux) Equity Fund-Eco Performance.
[5]EcoJPN = UBS (Jpn) Equity Fund-Eco Japan.

INVESTMENT BANKING External Audits	Unit	Value 1999	Value 2000
Employees in investment banking	Jobs (part-time jobs converted to 100%)	14,266	16,955[6]
Employees dealing with environmental aspects in the business process	Jobs (part-time jobs converted to 100%)	n.a.	n.a.
Employees in specialized environmental units	Jobs (part-time jobs converted to 100%)	0.5	0[1]
Training	Number of trained employees		
Training with environmental component	Employees trained	341	39
Training time	Hours (employees trained × average training period)	516	58.5
Internal audits			
Environmental audits	Employees audited	9	0[3]
Auditing time	Hours (number of audits × average auditing time)	6.75	0[3]

Key figures for investment banking products have not yet been established.

(Continued)

TABLE 4.4 *(Continued)*

Employees	Unit	Value 1999	Value 2000
Employees in UBS Switzerland, Private and Corporate Clients (PCC)	Jobs (part-time jobs converted to 100%)	24,098	21,100[1]
Employees dealing with environmental aspects in the business process	Jobs (part-time jobs converted to 100%)	2,900	2,727[1]
Employees in specialized environmental units	Jobs (part-time jobs converted to 100%)	2.5	1.7[1]
Training			
Training with environmental component	Employees trained	939	693
Training time	Hours (employees trained × average auditing time)	700	506
Scope of training	% (proportion of trained employees/employees in target group)	32	25
Internal Audits			
Environmental audits	Employees audited	44	0[3]
Auditing time	Hours (number of audits × average auditing time)	33	0[3]
Scope of auditing	% (Proportion of employees audited, according to activity)	1.5	0[3]
Credit Check			
Total loans of UBS Switzerland, Private and Corporate Clients (PCC)	Billions CHF	172	155
Total loans with environmental relevance to private and corporate clients[8]	Billions CHF	165	150
Proportion of loans to corporate clients with preliminary environmental assessment	%	54	47
Total loans to corporate clients	Billions CHF	98	73

(Continued)

TABLE 4.4   *(Continued)*

CREDIT BUSINESS[7] Employees	Unit	Value 1999	Value 2000
Proportion of loans to corporate clients with preliminary environmental assessment	%	100	100
Number of loans with detailed environmental assessment	Loans	38	35

[6]UBS Warburg employees without PaineWebber employees (21,490 employees).
[7]The key figures in the table concern only Switzerland, they thus do not cover the whole credit business of UBS.
[8]Total loans of UBS Switzerland, Private and Corporate Clients (PCC) without interbank loans.
Source: UBS 2000; 13–14.

BOX 4.7   The Natural Step (TNS)

> The TNS approach is based on the application of four principles or "systems conditions":
>
> 1. Nature cannot withstand a progressive buildup of waste derived from the earth's crust.
> 2. Nature cannot withstand a progressive buildup of society's waste.
> 3. The productive area of nature must not be diminished in quality (diversity) or quantity (volume) but must be enabled to grow.
> 4. Society must utilize energy and resources in a sustainable, equitable, and efficient manner.
>
> *Source:* Nattrass and Altomare 1999.

respect to employees. It also examines issues of convenience and quality of service for clients, as well as "social exclusion" concerns, which arise when some services are more accessible to some groups of customers than to others. Geographic, technological, cost, and competitive factors are all central to the delivery of banking services, and contribute to issues of accessibility within the social economy.

The Co-operative Bank's *Partnership Report 2000* demonstrates other distinguishing features. For example, performance targets are included in the report, with indications as to whether the targets were achieved or whether acceptable progress had been made with respect to the targeted goal.

In the United States, ShoreBank Pacific has also internalized its ecological focus by adopting the four systems conditions of The Natural Step as its basis for the education of staff with respect to environmental risks and opportunities (Crane 1999).

INVESTMENT BANKING

In contrast to the extension of credit by commercial banks, the function of investment banking is to act as an adviser and liaison between corporations or governments that aim to attract investment capital and investors who are aiming to buy securities. Investment banking transactions include initial public offerings (IPOs), mergers and acquisitions, divestitures, liquidations, project finance, underwriting of debt securities and equity issues, and private placements. In addition, investment banks also manage stock and bond transactions, both for individual clients and for their own account. Although their products and services are quite distinct, investment banks are nonetheless affected by many of the same environmental issues as commercial banks.

Environmental considerations form part of most IPO due diligence and disclosure processes, when an investment bank investigates a private company's potential liability before taking it public, a process that can take up to two years. Bond issues made by publicly traded companies or governments raising capital in international markets represent the most common form of IPO. More visible, however, are IPOs of common stocks, since these bring a private company to the public's attention for the first time (Ganzi et al 1998). Considerations in IPO due diligence undertakings can include: compliance with applicable environmental laws; nature and extent of environmental liabilities, such as real estate contamination; and potential future costs associated with anticipated legal and regulatory changes (Henshaw 2001). In the United States, it is in the interest of all concerned, including investment bankers, to observe Securities and Exchange Commission (SEC) standards of disclosure and mitigate environmental issues before filing a new prospectus with that principal regulator.

The depth of environmental due diligence varies, however, depending on the institution, the corporate client, and the type of transaction taking place. It may range from no environmental scrutiny to a nominal focus on present concerns, through to an extensive examination of present and potential future liabilities. In a personal interview, Scott Henshaw (2001) suggested that investment banks tend to be known for their sectoral expertise, rather than any form of environmental knowledge. In his opinion, no investment bank has gained a strong reputation for its environmental know-how. Nonetheless, investment banks such as UBS Warburg are making strides in this direction. UBS Warburg has codified considerations of environmental issues in its Global Environmental Policy. The policy, based on the parent UBS Environmental Policy, is part of Warburg's overall risk policy framework and applies worldwide to all investment banking transactions, such as IPOs, project finance, and underwritings. Asset management performed by Warburg, however, is not covered by the policy.

CLIMATE CHANGE: RISKS AND OPPORTUNITIES FOR THE BANKING SECTOR

The Kyoto Protocol generates a risk that companies that may be regulated by future climate policies will experience a greater cost burden, which will vary by country, by sector, and by a company's ability to reduce its environmental risk of greenhouse gases (GHG) emissions. On the other hand, companies may generate extra returns if they are able to reduce emissions and produce emission permits that can be sold to other companies. Banks that put themselves in a position to provide sound service to these companies will be well positioned to gain from this new market for financial services in the context of the Kyoto Protocol (Janssen 2000).

Risks

Climatic catastrophic events have the capacity to threaten banks with significant physical risks to the projects to which they have already committed loans, since property is often used as collateral. In addition, the prospect of property insurers withdrawing services or a global crash of property-catastrophe insurance reserves would pose dire economic problems for bankers and pension funds, as well as for the insurance industry (Leggett 1995). While the burden of uninsured catastrophic losses could cause loan defaults in the banking industry, whole sectors, such as agriculture and tourism, may also be adversely affected, presenting such industries with problems in arranging financing.

    In 1988, Hurricane Gilbert had just this debilitating impact on Jamaica, which suffered heavy direct losses to housing, agriculture, and public services. Indirect losses to productivity and tourism were estimated to be twice those of the direct damage. At that time, insurance premiums rose and risk management requirements increased, all of which affected enterprises that require insurance coverage as a form of guarantee of loan repayment. At the national level, the local economy was weakened due to the devaluation of the Jamaican currency and increased interest rates. Within commercial banking, the key issue in small island states and coastal zones such as those affected by Hurricane Gilbert is to include the effects of climate change as factors in the risk assessment procedure, since the loss of confidence in a local economy can trigger a "credit famine" and lasting financial damage (Dlugolecki 1996a).

Opportunities

At the same time as presenting these risks, climate change provides great opportunities for the financial services sector to profit from new and adapted products and services that address global warming issues. Banks have an important role to play in addressing issues of climate change, by tailoring financial services and products toward carbon dioxide emissions reduction initiatives. The following discussion highlights the development of new products, such as climate-related investment funds, trading programs for greenhouse gases emissions credits, and weather derivatives, all of which are designed to increase the competitive positions of banks whose corporate clients are active in sectors relevant to these initiatives (Janssen 2000).

SG SG, the investment banking arm of Société Générale, has teamed up with the French insurance company AGF to launch a new fund that will invest in weather derivatives and catastrophe bonds. The $95 million fund Meteo Transformer, launched at the end of 2000, is co-managed by the two firms. While the investment bank is able to offer a new product to its clients that is uncorrelated with equity and bond market movements, the insurance company is able to bolster its alternative risk transfer capability (Nicholls 2001l).

Deutsche Bank Germany's largest bank, Deutsche Bank, has become the first bank to set up a dedicated GHG emissions trading desk, designed to cover the full range of transactions involved in buying and selling carbon credits. The desk will focus on sourcing credits from emissions reducing projects in both the developed and developing worlds, and passing these emissions reductions on to companies that are having difficulty in meeting their emissions reduction targets. Since Deutsche Bank has a substantial presence in the global energy sector as well as a strong role in arranging project finance, it is well positioned to attract both buyers and sellers of emissions permits around the world (Nicholls 2001o).

Goldman Sachs The confluence of increased liquidity in the weather futures market with companies' desire to hedge weather effects on their revenues led the investment banking firm Goldman Sachs to establish a dedicated weather derivatives desk in the fall of 2001, making it the first investment-banking house to enter the weather derivatives market. (See case study in Chapter 9 for an in-depth discussion of this commodity.) The weather desk focuses primarily on temperature-linked contracts in the North American market. Goldman Sachs brings to this venture a history of involvement with alternative risk products, having arranged a number of structured risk transfer deals, including the first and only weather-linked bond, which it arranged for Koch Energy in 1999 (Kirby 2001b).

UBS Warburg In anticipation of fuel cells becoming a key element in future energy supplies, UBS Warburg has developed an investment product identified as "fuel cell baskets," for investors wanting to invest in new and innovative energy technology. The baskets are made up of shares in leading fuel cell companies worldwide. The baskets mature in 2004, and are structured in such a way as to benefit from the first commercial implementation of fuel-cell-powered products. To a certain extent, investment baskets of energy-related products are impinging on the territory of venture capital, perhaps in an effort to remove the "venture" from the financing of incubator and small firms (C. Kennedy 2001).

Fuel cells will play a key role in the automobile industry, as well as in stationary electrical generation facilities (such as the 55 New York schools that have used this technology to date) and as a power source for portable equipment. Table 4.5 summarizes the breadth of investments that are eligible for the fuel cell baskets, from fuel cell producers and users, to suppliers of raw materials and components, to new energy storage technology that can help smooth out power delivery (UBS 2000).

The importance of such investment vehicles is emphasized by the California Air Resources Board (CARB) requirement that 10 percent of all cars sold in California be emission-free, starting in 2003 (see Box 7.4). DaimlerChrysler has made known its intention to offer a class of vehicles with fuel cells at the same price as the gasoline-powered version no later than 2004. Thus fuel cells are viewed as being central to the auto industry's hope for pollution-free motors. At the same time, off-grid distributed

TABLE 4.5 A Selection of Company Stocks That Are Eligible for Inclusion in UBS Warburg Fuel Cell Baskets of Investment

Stock	Product or Service	Country
Ballard Power Systems, Plug Power, Manhattan Scientifics	Produces fuel cells for cars, power stations, medical equipment, home electric supply, portable electronics	Canada, United States
Fuel Cell Energy	Opens access to "molten carbon" technology, which has the potential to provide electricity with multimegawatt plants	United States
SGL Carbon	Produces parts for fuel cells	Germany
Satcon Technology Group	Supplies electrical components for fuel cells	United States
Energy Conversion Devices	Provides storage of hydrogen	United States
Idacorp, Avista, Minnesota Power	Power station operators that have diversified their activities into fuel cell technology	United States
SYMYX Technologies Inc.	Provides fuel cell producers with special raw materials and components	United States

Source: www.bestzertifikate.de/englisch/pdf/fuelcell.

power delivery with so-called "seven nines" reliability is also required within specific industrial sectors. Computer-dependent companies need electricity for 99.99999 percent of the time, rather than the 99.9 percent reliability delivered by traditional electricity grids (Nicholls 2001b; www.bestzertifikate.de/englisch/pdf/fuelcell).

SUSTAINABLE ENERGY FUNDS

Sustainable energy funds represent one more form of venture capital funds that expand a financial service company's product range to address issues of climate change (Knörzer 2001). These funds raise equity capital for unlisted companies at an early stage of development when they are not yet profitable. This becomes an important source of funds for such undertakings when traditional financing is unavailable due to their higher levels of risk. Venture capital funds have a longer time horizon than traditional financing, with investors anticipating profit realization on a horizon of five to seven years, through an exit strategy of either an initial public offering, a merger, or an acquisition. Traditionally a high percentage of venture capital comes from institutional investors such as pension funds and foundations. In sustainable energy funds, however, national governments and energy-related companies also join the group of investors. Investors seek to offset this higher risk of loss with the potential for significant capital gains, often as high as 30 to 40 percent, as the enterprises grow. In the case of sustainable energy funds, returns can be realized in the form of both cash and carbon credits.

Historically, the venture capital industry has had little experience with, or concern for, environmental issues, since environmental factors have not been viewed as significant relative to other risks inherent in such transactions (Ganzi et al. 1998). Recently, however, a number of venture capital funds that specialize in alternative energy and environmental technology have been launched. The publication of an inventory of sustainable energy funds by UNEP (BASE 2001) underscores the importance of this form of environmental financing.

The growth in the international markets for products that address issues of carbon emissions reductions and energy efficiency has given rise to the creation of a number of funds that anticipate that part or all of their returns will be gained from income derived from the reduction of carbon dioxide emissions. The following section outlines a sampling of these types of funds, while Table 4.6 summarizes their characteristics.

Pure Carbon Funds

World Bank Prototype Carbon Fund   The World Bank Prototype Carbon Fund (PCF), capped at $180 million, is aimed at channeling public and private capital into greenhouse gases reduction programs in developing countries and economies in transition. In this case, emissions reduction certificates will be transferred to investors rather than cash.

National governments that have approved participation in PCF are principally Scandinavian, while the private sector participants are mainly Japanese power companies. Their interest stems from the fact that the present high level of efficiency practiced by these Japanese companies makes it expensive to cut their emissions further. Thus it is likely that it will be significantly cheaper for these companies to buy certificates via the PCF than to invest in cutting their own emissions directly.

TABLE 4.6 Characteristics of Carbon Credit Funds

Fund Type	Size	Investors	Emphasis
PURE CARBON FUNDS			
World Bank PCF	$180 million	Governments, strategic investors	Carbon components of CDM/JI projects
ERUPT	$31 million	Dutch government	JI
CERUPT (see Chapter 9)	$6–$15 million		CDM Carbon credits from Central/Eastern Europe
PRIVATE EQUITY WITH CARBON CREDIT-ENHANCED IRR			
REEF	$65 million	IFC, strategic energy, insurance investors	Emerging market countries eligible for IFC financing
Dexia–FondElec EEER	€71 million	EBRD and strategic investors	SME energy efficiency projects in Central/ Eastern Europe
FLACES	$25.5 million	AIDB and strategic investors	Energy efficiency, future carbon credits
FUTURE PRIVATE EQUITY FUNDS			
Black Emerald Group Leasing Fund	€500 million	Financial institutions, energy utilities	Renewables sector, fuel cells in Europe
GOVERNMENT/PRIVATE SECTOR OFFSET PROGRAMS			
GHG Friendly/ GHG Free Fund (see Chapter 9)	$1–$2 million/ year	BP collects funds from fuel sales	Renewables sector, energy efficiency, capture of fugitive emissions in Australia

Source: Adapted from Bürer 2001.

Private Equity Funds with Carbon Credit-Enhanced Internal Rate of Return

World Bank REEF Fund A member of the World Bank Group, the International Finance Corporation (IFC) provides loan and equity financing for private sector projects in the developing world. In 2000 the IFC, along with other founding investors, launched the Renewable Energy Efficiency

Fund (REEF), a carbon equity fund designed to help mitigate the impacts of climate change while generating profitable returns for investors. Projects that are eligible for the fund include on- and off-grid renewable energy and energy efficiency projects in developing countries. Asset managers are anticipating a 20 percent return on the $100 million fund, along with the potential of capturing carbon credits from the projects that would generate further income (Cooper 2000a).

Dexia-FondElec Energy Efficiency and Emission Reduction Fund   Also in 2000, the European Bank for Reconstruction and Development (ERBD) and the Franco-Belgian banking group Dexia launched a new private equity fund aimed at reducing energy consumption and greenhouse gas emissions in Central and Eastern Europe. The $\in$ 150 million ($150 million) Dexia-FondElec Energy Efficiency and Emission Reduction Fund (EEER) has a number of power companies as investors. In addition to cash returns, the chosen projects should also generate carbon credits, which investors will be able to acquire and use directly to meet their own emission limits (Cooper 2000b).

In late 2001, a division of FondElec, the FE Clean Energy Group, launched a Latin America initiative, which carries a similar mandate of promoting energy efficiency on that continent. Investors in its $25.5 million Latin America Clean Air Energy Service fund (FLACES) include the International American Development Bank (AIDB), Sumitomo Mexico, Sumitomo Brazil, and TEPCo of Japan. The primary emphasis of FLACES is on energy efficiency. As this nascent market develops in Latin America, FondElec will examine the potential for the creation of carbon credits from appropriate projects in that region (McGrath 2002).

Future Private Equity Funds

Black Emerald Group   The Black Emerald private merchant banking group specializes in project and corporate financing for environmental technology, renewable energy, and related industries, worldwide. In response to the EU Council's directive to commit to 12 percent electricity production from renewables by 2010, the Black Emerald Group plans to generate significant Green Certificates and carbon credits through lease financing in Western Europe and selected Eastern European countries. Renewable energy projects to be financed include wind, hydro, geothermal, biomass, biogas, fuel cells, and solar technologies. The Black Emerald Leasing Partners fund is expected to raise $\in$ 500 million from private banks, pension funds, insurance companies, and energy utilities that want to participate in the renewable sector in the designated jurisdictions. The group expects to launch its fund later in 2002 (www.blackemerald.com).

By way of contrast to the expectations raised with respect to greenhouse gas reduction and energy efficiency through the implementation of carbon credit funds, it is instructive to observe that UBS was poised in 2001 to launch an Alternative Climate Fund, which would focus on Joint Implementation (JI) and Clean Development Mechanism (CDM) projects as defined in the Kyoto Protocol. In 2002 the Bank abandoned its planned "carbon fund," citing the fact that investors showed little willingness to participate in a product that was tied to such a vague international policy. Another obstacle appeared to be the management fee of 2.5 percent, which was set at the upper acceptable limit to cover the inherent costs of CO_2 procedures such as validation and certification (Stetter and Böswald 2002).

THE PRICE OF CARBON

Despite these proactive initiatives, the market for carbon trades and offsets is fraught with uncertainty. One of the many issues that remain to be resolved is the pricing of carbon, CO_2 and its equivalents (CO_2e). Although there are six main greenhouse gases (CO_2, methane, nitrous oxide, hydrofluorocarbons, perfluorocarbons, and sulfur hexafluoride), since CO_2 is the most common among the six gases, the others are expressed in terms of CO_2 equivalents (CO_2e). Table 4.7 illustrates the carbon equivalents for each greenhouse gas compared to the global warming potential (GWP) of CO_2.

In the absence of any formalized, international trading system, most of the GHG emission trades have taken the form of verified emissions reductions (VERs), which have traded at values between \$0.60 and \$3.50 per metric ton CO_2e. Price differentials can be attributed, in part, to differences in location and vintage (date) of the VERs, since these two attributes help determine whether the reductions will be usable in the event of the ratification of the Kyoto Protocol.

Developing country emissions reductions generated after 2000, as well as those generated in developed countries during the period 2008–2010, are expected to qualify for credit under the Kyoto Protocol. The pricing of CO_2e during these periods is at the higher end of the scale (\$1.65 to \$3.50/metric ton CO_2e), reflecting this expectation of eligibility. The pricing of developed countries' emissions reductions generated between 1990 and 2008 is found at the lower end of the spectrum at \$0.60 to \$1.50/metric ton CO_2e (Rosenzweig et al. 2002).

TABLE 4.7 Global Warming Potentials of
Greenhouse Gases

Greenhouse Gas	Global Warming Potentials
Carbon dioxide (CO_2)	1
Methane (CH_4)	21
Nitrous oxide (N_2O)	310
Hydrofluorocarbons (HFCs)	150–11,700
Perfluorocarbons (PFCs) (especially CF_4 and C_2F_6)	6,500–9,200
Sulfur hexafluoride (SF_6)	23,900

Source: Cozijnsen 2002, Table 1, p. 38.

Despite the fact that these early prices for CO_2 from VERs are considered, generally, to be low, the World Bank has predicted that prices for CDM/JI financing will remain at this level until 2005. However, the prices of some of the emission reduction units (ERUs), bought from Joint Implementation projects under the auspices of the more formalized Dutch ERUPT program, did reach close to $8/metric ton CO_2e. The pricing premium in this case has been attributed to the fact that ERUs from JI projects in Annex B countries will become compliance units if the Kyoto Protocol is ratified (Bürer 2001; Rosenzweig et al. 2002)

REPUTATIONAL RISK

In addition to banks' environmental risk related to loan defaults and lender liability, concerns regarding image risk to their institutions act as drivers in banking decision making (Case 1999). Evan Henry, senior vice president, Bank of America, holds that financial institutions must recognize that environmental risk can include both transactional and image components and must be managed as such (Henry 1999). Within this context, risk evaluation must consider the source and nature of critical opinion, since different constituencies hold varying perceptions of an organization. Indeed, banks, as well as other publicly held companies, are experiencing increased activism from shareholders, as well as nongovernmental organizations (NGOs), the investment community, and the public at large (as noted in Chapter 2). Depending on the vested interest of the stakeholder, image risks can arise due to poor performance records or lack of meeting either self-imposed or externally imposed standards.

Reputational leverage was used by a group of NGOs against a group of financial institutions in 1997 in an attempt to halt funding of the Three Gorges Dam project in China, which is designed to control floods while generating electricity. The NGO group, under the leadership of International Rivers Network and Friends of the Earth, canvassed each of the six investment banking houses involved, and followed up with a media campaign naming the bond underwriters. After a four-year study, the World Bank refused financing for the project, giving the reason that the project carried serious environmental and human rights risks and would likely prove to be economically unviable. The Export-Import Bank of America also refused participation, citing the project's failure to comply with the bank's environmental guidelines. In the final analysis, the companies involved were all exposed to criticism based on their association with this environmentally and socially sensitive project. A number made public commitments to corporate responsibility, with one investment banking firm agreeing to develop social and environmental guidelines for its lending, investment, and underwriting practices (Kearins and O'Malley 1999; Ganzi et al. 1998).

As has been observed, banks do have contractual agreements, such as indemnities, covenants, and warrantees, that can be used to address the indirect risks associated with the loss of value or return on investment. By contrast, image risk is much harder to define and scope, and conventional contractual language does little to placate the situation. Thus, although transaction-based contractual risk control mechanisms can be reactive, those relating to image risk must be proactive in nature.

In order to undertake environmental, reputational risk control measures, banks have attempted to set environmental measurement and reporting standards by which the industry can be measured, as discussed earlier in the chapter. In this vein, a consortium of financial institutions in the United Kingdom, the Forge Group, has produced further guidelines for financial service organizations that are new to environmental management and reporting. Not only are external risks and opportunities defined in traditional financial and legal terms, but also in terms of reputational risks and opportunities for each of the industries within the sector (Table 4.8). The guidelines first define key environmental issues in core financial industries, and then offer guidance for developing management processes, so that "environmental risk can be avoided, governance standards met and business opportunities realized" (Forge 2000, 1).

It has been suggested that banks possess a limited ability to influence larger companies, while smaller companies are more likely to be subject to banking influence (Delphi and Ecologic 1997). The banks are able to

TABLE 4.8　Forge Group's Definition of Risks and Opportunities in the Financial Services Sector

Core Commercial Activity	Risk	Opportunity
Retail banking and personal lending	*Financial:* Reduction in property value used to secure loans Reduced sales value of property *Legal:* Potential lender liability	*Financial:* Market differentiation through offering of environmental products (e-loans) *Reputational:* Enhanced public profile (awareness and education programs) Enhanced reputation because of new products
Commercial banking	*Financial:* Reduced returns on loan repayments or project profitability Reduced value of securities *Legal:* Potential liability with loan default *Reputational:* Damage through association	*Financial:* Increased business from environmental service sector Market opportunities with new loan products Enhanced performance *Reputational:* Enhanced reputation through association with companies with good environmental performance (EP) Improved customer relations Increasing customer awareness
General insurance and reinsurance	*Financial:* Unanticipated financial impact leading to unplanned costs Fall in share price due to reduced business performance Reduced investor confidence *Reputational:* Failing to demonstrate response to emerging market needs	*Financial:* Increased market demand for insurance for emerging environmental risks Improved business planning and risk provision Improved investor confidence *Reputational:* Enhanced reputation Improved business partner relations Competitive advantage

(Continued)

TABLE 4.8 *(Continued)*

Core Commercial Activity	Risk	Opportunity
Fund and asset management	*Financial:* Loss of value Loss of business *Legal:* Meeting the best practice of socially responsible investment Government intervention *Reputational:* Damage through association	*Financial:* Assist market positioning with institutional investors Higher returns *Legal:* Help in meeting legal obligations to deliver maximum returns *Reputational:* Enhanced through selecting companies with good EP

Source: Forge 2000.

influence management of smaller borrowing establishments through lending arrangements and consultancy practices. Bankers, however, are loath to take on the role of environmental police or policy setters. Despite Hector's (1992) claim that banks have become "eco-police," bankers strongly believe that it is not, nor should it be, the responsibility of lenders to police or try to manage their customers' businesses. UNEP banking initiative delegates argue that banks are neither qualified nor resourced to undertake this role, which they believe should rest with regulators and environmental experts. They are comfortable, however, with the role of making sure that the banks' clients can meet the criteria, once standards have been set.

CONCLUSION

The banking sector has been exposed to a combination of direct, indirect, and reputational risks that have had an impact on its approaches to environmental concerns. Certain segments of the banking industry have made progress in their approaches to environmental issues and sustainable development. New products and services with environmental and social central themes have been developed, while environmental criteria have been integrated into overall lending and investment strategies. At the same time, banks have made strides toward incorporating internal operations into their environmental profiles. These changes are being seen not only in large, integrated banking systems, but also in the smaller niche market organizations. It does appear, however, that there are as yet a number of unexploited opportunities to integrate environmental performance into this segment of the financial services sector.

WEB SITES

Citigroup	www.citigroup.com
Co-operative Bank	www.co-operativebank.co.uk
Rabobank	www.rabobank.com/sustainability
Royal Bank of Canada	www.rbc.com

CHAPTER 5

Insurance

INTRODUCTION

The field of environmental finance has evolved in response to the identification of a new class of business risks associated with a broad range of environmental issues. As the concept of insurance was invented in order to redistribute risk, it is not surprising that the insurance industry was the first segment of the financial services sector to become aware of the need to reevaluate its position in relation to the environment. The focus of this chapter is on the property and casualty (P&C) or general insurance business since that is the subsector that has been most affected by environmental issues, principally through damage to property, third-party liability, and business continuity.

This evaluation was not made any easier by the industry's tradition of distinguishing between environmental risk—meaning pollution—and catastrophic risk. Catastrophic risk is generally defined as a large loss resulting from a single event and affecting many insureds and many insurers. In the United States the size of a catastrophic loss was defined as exceeding $5 million until 1997 when the definition was raised to $25 million. The definition would exclude large losses attributable to a single insurer or a single insured, as in the case of a wrecked oil tanker, for example. The classic catastrophic loss arises from an earthquake or an extreme weather event such as a hurricane. For example, Hurricane Andrew resulted in more than 700,000 claims, triggering a payout of more than $16 billion and bankrupting 10 insurance companies. (See Box 5.1.) Although Hurricane Andrew remains the most expensive hurricane in terms of insured losses, it is not an isolated event, as can be seen from the record of losses of the past 50 years (Figure 5.1).

Environmental risk is characterized in the industry as a liability issue,

BOX 5.1 Hurricane Andrew

> *Andrew was a small and ferocious Cape Verde hurricane that wrought unprecedented economic devastation along a path through the northwestern Bahamas, the southern Florida peninsula, and south central Louisiana. Damage in the United States is estimated to be near $25 billion, making Andrew the most expensive natural disaster in U.S. history. . . . In Dade County alone, the forces of Andrew resulted in 15 deaths and up to one quarter million people temporarily homeless. (Rappaport 1993)*
>
> *Following Hurricane Andrew, which made landfall in Florida on the morning of August 24, 1992, property and casualty insurance companies in the state of Florida were faced with over $16 billion in insured losses, a circumstance the companies thought was highly unlikely and were not prepared for. In reaction, an insurance crisis ensued, broadly characterized as a desire of insurance companies to either withdraw from the Florida market or significantly reduce their exposed risk and a desire of the Florida Department of Insurance and legislature to ensure that affordable insurance would be made available to all homeowners and . . . businesses. (Mittler 1997)*

As these quotations indicate, the physical force and economic impact of Hurricane Andrew were unprecedented. Ten insurance companies were bankrupted by the impact. The industry as a whole was left to compare the size of the claims paid with the $11 billion it had collected in premiums in Florida from 1972 to 1992. The Florida legislature could ensure the availability of insurance only by passing emergency legislation that capped premiums, deductibles, and the percentage of nonrenewed policies permitted to each insurance company in the state. Companies were also "mandated to participate" in a "residual market mechanism" created by the state—the Florida Property and Casualty Joint Underwriting Association (Mittler 1997). This temporary solution is still in existence and the association has become the second largest source of homeowners' insurance in the state. This type of solution is known in the insurance industry as an "involuntary pool" (Holtom 1987).

A more fundamental approach to the problem included an investigation by a Dade County grand jury into the effectiveness of

(Continued)

BOX 5.1 *(Continued)*

> the South Florida building code. The jury found the code to be "out of date and inadequate" and concluded that "the effectiveness of the community's building inspection process has been questionable for decades, subject to corruption, at worst, and apathy, at best" (Mittler 1997).
>
> Newspaper coverage of hurricane damage inevitably includes pictures of boats hurled on land and trees that smashed buildings, yet "often the major insured losses aren't a result of direct wind, but from the water damage that follows. As much as 80 percent of the total dollar loss results from the saturation of the buildings' contents. . . . [Thus,] consensus is building for a new approach holding that a majority of property loss—including loss from hurricane wind—is preventable" (Burke 1997).

where a company or individual responsible for a pollution episode is deemed to have damaged the health or property of a third party by contaminating the land, air, or water. The 1980s saw the emergence of environmental liability on a very large scale, especially in the United States where injured parties sought redress through the courts, typically in class action suits. Among the major sources of damage were leachate and other nuisances associated with inadequate landfill practices,[1] sparked by the notorious Love Canal episode in upstate New York (Box 5.2). Leaking underground storage tanks provided another large source of trouble, as did lead paint, especially in housing. Pollution was also associated with industrial accidents and contaminated land.

To these troubles was added the identification of asbestos as a causal agent for asbestosis and mesothelioma, beginning with a suit launched by Clarence Borel, a retired insulation installer, in 1969 in the federal district court in Beaumont, Texas. The asbestos claims have mounted steadily, beginning with miners, manufacturers, and installers, and continuing to people living in buildings with exposed asbestos, to family members, and finally to people who simply lived in the neighborhood of asbestos manufacturers or heavy users of asbestos such as dockyards. (Box 5.3). As asbestos was not considered a pollutant in the traditional sense, this problem area became known in the insurance industry as "asbestos and environmental claims." The problem is so large that it is recorded as a

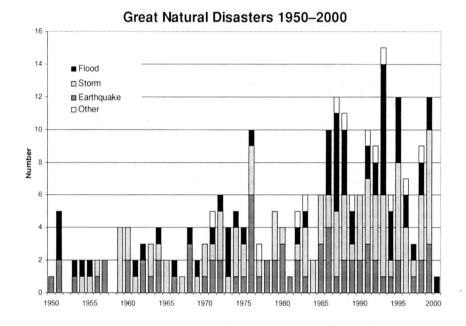

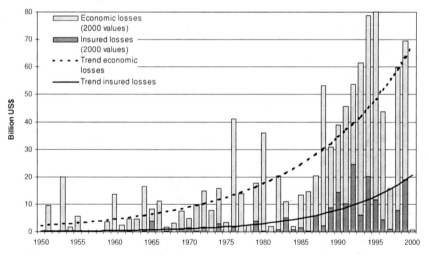

FIGURE 5.1   Trends in Natural Catastrophes
Source: Munich Re 2001b.

BOX 5.2 Love Canal

Love Canal became a municipal and chemical disposal site in 1920. It was the abandoned portion of an incomplete canal that had been planned to connect the upper and lower Niagara River and provide hydroelectric power. Until 1953 it was used by the Army, the city of Niagara, and Hooker Chemical Corporation, a subsidiary of Occidental Petroleum. It was then filled in with dirt and sold to the Board of Education for $1 and a disclaimer that absolved the previous owner—Hooker Chemical Corporation—of any future liability.

The Board built an elementary school in the center of the site; houses and apartments followed soon after. Years of complaints by the residents about odors and substances appearing on the surface produced no effective response until 1978 when the New York State Health Commissioner conceded that a public health hazard existed and recommended that pregnant women and children under the age of two should leave the area. The school was closed. Blood tests conducted by the Environmental Protection Agency in 1980 determined that residents had suffered chromosome damage that carried an increased risk of cancer, reproductive problems, and genetic damage, all of which had been observed in the area over the previous 25 years.

Later that year the federal government provided funding for any of the 900 families who wished to leave. Three years later, residents won a $20 million settlement from Occidental Chemical Corporation, a subsidiary of Occidental Petroleum. Remedial work was done on the site and some homes were offered for sale, but regional banks would not provide mortgages. The Federal Housing Administration agreed to provide mortgages. In 1994 Occidental Petroleum paid $98 million to New York State for cleanup costs, and the following year paid another $129 million to the federal government for its costs. Occidental Chemical assumed responsibility for waste treatment and maintenance on the site.

Love Canal is a landmark case in the history of liability for contamination. Despite disclaimers and years of denial by the polluter, the residents succeeded in attracting the attention of the authorities that finally forced the polluter to pay for cleanup and compensation (Gibbs 2001). Love Canal is identified as the case that gave rise to the Superfund legislation. (See Boxes 4.1 and 5.6.)

BOX 5.3 First Outdoor Asbestos Award Made in the United Kingdom

On October 27, 1995, a High Court justice ordered asbestos manufacturer T & N Plc. to pay £65,000 to Ms. June Hancock, who had
been diagnosed with mesothelioma the previous year and given a
prognosis of two years to live. A second claimant received £50,000
for the death of her husband from the same rare disease, whose only
known cause is asbestos. What made these awards significant was
that the victims did not work in the asbestos factory, nor handle asbestos products, nor wash the clothes of people who did. They simply
lived close to the factory, which was located near Leeds. Ms. Hancock lived there for only five years during her childhood. Her mother
had died of mesothelioma in the 1970s. Another 200 people are
known to have died from the disease in the Leeds area.

Mesothelioma is responsible for about 1,000 deaths annually in
the United Kingdom, but the latency period is between 30 and 50
years, so the rate is expected to rise for another 15 or 25 years, perhaps peaking at 3,000 deaths per year, according to the British Health
and Safety Commission.

Ms. Hancock's legal team argued in court that by the late 1930s
company officials "knew or should have known that asbestos dust
caused lung damage and that by 1943 knew or should have known
that asbestos was probably carcinogenic" (Aldred 1995). The plaintiffs' case received support from Chase Manhattan Bank, which provided their lawyers with thousands of documents proving that T & N
knew of the risks associated with asbestos. The bank was suing T & N
for $185 million for damages from asbestos installed in their New
York headquarters. T & N established a £150 million reserve to cover
asbestos-related claims in the United States and the United Kingdom.

In 1998, T & N was bought by Federal-Mogul, an auto parts
manufacturer. Federal-Mogul became trapped in a dwindling pool of
asbestos defendants and filed for bankruptcy in 2001.

special provision in the annual report of Munich Re, the world's largest
reinsurer (see Table 5.1).

*In the March 1994 report, entitled "Environmental/Asbestos Liability
Exposures: A P/C Industry Black Hole," [A. M.] Best [the rating
agency] developed a range of estimates extending from a "best case"
of $55 billion to a "worst case" of $623 billion for insurer liabilities*

TABLE 5.1 Provisions for Asbestos and Environmental Claims at Munich Re (in € M)

	1998		1999		2000	
	Gross	Net	Gross	Net	Gross	Net
Asbestos	848.9	728.2	1,433.3	1,118.3	1,400.7	1,113.9
Environmental	660.5	585.9	895.5	806.9	888.2	811.2

Source: Munich Re 2001a.

relating to the cleanup of National Priority List sites, litigation costs, natural resource damage costs, non-NPL sites, and asbestos claims." *(Sclafane 1996)*

(See subsection titled "Landfills and Superfund" later in the chapter.)

Why was the industry taken by surprise? How could these huge exposures appear without any warning? The pollution issue will be considered in the next main section, followed by a discussion of the extreme weather contribution to catastrophic risk.

ANGUS ROSS, INVITED AUTHOR'S COMMENT

An Insurer's Perspective of Risk

For many years now, insurers and reinsurers have been affected by environmental impacts. These have ranged from asbestosis to pollution; from oil spills to climate change and a proliferation of extreme events on a worldwide basis. Many risk bearers have shied away from these exposures to the greatest extent possible while others, cognizant of the dangers inherent in them, have nevertheless sought to innovate and create opportunity out of risk.

Climate change is a fairly recent example. As the frequency of extreme atmospheric events has risen over the past two decades, perceptive and forward-thinking risk bearers have made careful studies of the statistics and sought to change their rating structures to meet the higher perceived risks. A far cry from the earlier "pluvius" policies that

(Continued)

An Insurer's Perspective of Risk *(Continued)*

covered rain-outs for specific days' events, new types of covers have now been created to meet new demands: lack of precipitation covers for hydroelectricity generating utilities; lack of snow covers for winter sports resorts; excessive snowfall cover for municipalities who must bear the financial cost of snow removal. Others have gone further in their diversification strategies and instituted investment policies reflecting the growing potential of "green" investments, which will not only benefit the investment portfolio but also help to reduce the impacts of climate change. If the Kyoto agreement is ratified, with an internationally agreed emissions trading scheme, we can expect insurers and reinsurers to offer covers guaranteeing that the credits or trades will actually meet the trading requirements and are valid for trade.

Another area where a few bold underwriters have ventured to tread after so many have stepped in financial quicksand over the years is contaminated site or brownfield cleanup and redevelopment. Contamination of land, particularly in the United States with Superfund legislation, has cost underwriters billions of dollars over the past two decades. Now, however, companies such as AIG, Zurich, ECS, and Kemper (to name a few) are offering new insurance products to facilitate the cleanup of contaminated sites and protect the finances of investors and developers involved in the work. Where until a few years ago underwriters fled from such risks, now policies offer protection against cleanup cost overruns, discovery of new contaminants, changes in legislation post-cleanup, migration of contaminants off-site, and other contingencies.

As underwriters' knowledge and experience grow in these developing areas, they will continue to branch out and offer new protections benefiting not only their own bottom lines but, more importantly for all of us, the environment on which we all depend.

Angus Ross spent more than 35 years in both the brokering and underwriting sides of the reinsurance industry, joining Sorema, a major French-owned reinsurer, as head of its Canadian operations in 1992. Mr. Ross chaired the Insurance Bureau of Canada's National Committee on Environmental Liability. Since 1995 he has been a member of the (Canadian) National Round Table on the Environment and the Economy, where he has chaired the Financial Services Task Force on brownfield redevelopment. He is also a member of the Canadian Climate Programme Board, the co-coordinating mechanism for climate-related activities in Canada.

CONTAMINANTS IN THE ENVIRONMENT

Insurers never expected to pay for pollution, except in cases that were clearly accidental, that is, due to a combination of circumstances that could not have been foreseen by the insured party. A typical case would be a road accident leading to the release of a polluting chemical such as ammonia or gasoline. Insurers use the phrase "sudden and accidental" to define the insured situation. Pollution from a smokestack or a waste pipe running into a river or drain was clearly not sudden or accidental, simply a routine by-product of doing business. The distinction seemed to be quite obvious, so where did the liability arise, and on such a huge scale?

If a date had to be chosen to mark the change in circumstances that resulted in these liabilities, then that date would be 1978—the year that the Love Canal case reached the American courts (Box 5.2). The impact of this incident was further reinforced by the 40-year struggle to gain compensation for victims of methyl mercury poisoning in Minamata Bay in Japan (Box 5.4). In Europe, the Seveso industrial accident is often identified as the critical event that changed public and private attitudes toward the risks that are seemingly inherent in industrial society (Box 5.5).

Love Canal and Minamata confirmed what many people had feared for years, namely that exposure to certain chemicals could lead to a variety of very serious health effects such as impaired mental and physical function, miscarriages, and birth defects. Routine assurances that the public would never be exposed to dangerous levels of contamination from industrial processing or waste disposal were finally abandoned. Although cause and effect in an individual case are difficult to establish, the epidemiological evidence at Love Canal was overwhelming. The concentration of adverse health effects in a small area could not be due to chance.

Landfills and Superfund

As the defendants had long argued that there was nothing unusual about the operation of the Love Canal facility, the acceptance of the epidemiological evidence also implied that many similar landfills might carry similar risks. Eventually a survey by the U.S. Environmental Protection Agency identified 14,000 problem sites, of which approximately 1,500 were placed on the National Priority List. In 1980 this led to the Superfund legislation in the United States, officially known as the Comprehensive Environmental Response Compensation and Liability Act (CERCLA), to provide public funding for the remediation of the most critical sites, although it is estimated that 85 percent of the Fund disbursed to year 1995

BOX 5.4   The Minamata Methyl Mercury Case, Japan, 1956

Minamata disease is a disorder of the central nervous system (affecting vision, balance, and limb control) that is caused by the consumption of fish and shellfish contaminated by methyl mercury. In this case the compound was discharged by chemical plants, one in Minamata Bay, Kumamoto Prefecture, Japan, in 1956, the second along the Agano River, in Niigata Prefecture, in 1965. It was not until 1968 that government researchers agreed that the causal agent for the disease was methyl mercury, biomagnified through the food chain. However, this had first been proposed as the cause as early as 1959. The first response was simply to ban fishing in the area; eventually the plants were closed down.

The first court decision was handed down in favor of the victims as early as 1971. However, the matter remained disputed in the courts until 1996—40 years after the first cases were identified—as the burden of responsibility was tossed backward and forward between the polluting companies and the government. Finally the government agreed to pay the companies to help *them* pay the victims. To date over 3,000 victims have been compensated at a cost of more than $1 billion.

Like Love Canal in the United States, the Minamata case is credited with raising national consciousness of the potentially very serious consequences of the careless handling of industrial wastes. In the 1950s, when these cases came to light, very few people were aware of the chain of cause and effect that we now take for granted.

was spent on legal costs, not cleanup (Patzelt 1995). (See Box 5.6.) Other estimates from the Insurance Information Institute vary from 20 to 70 percent of the Superfund expenditures being spent on legal and administrative fees (Insurance Information Institute 2000).

Although some of the earlier problems of the program have been addressed, others remain. A recent report to Congress stated:

We found it difficult to understand, much less evaluate, the level of Superfund resources going to program management, policy and administrative support functions. EPA spends a large portion of its annual Superfund budget on these activities. . . . A surprisingly large

BOX 5.5   The Seveso Incident and the Seveso Directives

On July 10, 1976, an accidental release of two kilograms of 2,3,7,8-tetrachlorodibenzo-*p*-dioxin (TCDD) from a chemical factory in Seveso, Lombardy, Italy, provoked enough alarm to lay the basis for new European Community law governing the manufacture, storage, and transportation of potentially dangerous chemical products. The 20-minute release of a toxic brew of chemicals formed a cloud that exposed the nearby urban population of 200,000 people, including schools that were immediately downwind of the factory. TCDD's immediate impact produces chloracne, a disfiguring skin eruption that can persist for 30 years, and to which the young are most susceptible. Doctors recorded 200 cases of chloracne in the immediate vicinity after the incident. Previously, chloracne had been recorded only in occupational settings for workers in the chemical industry to a total of 4,000 cases worldwide.

TCDD is a dioxin, an organochloride that is soluble in fat and hence bioaccumulates through the food chain. The long-term health concern lies in the fact that elevated cancer cases are associated with exposure to dioxin. This can affect the function of the liver, the brain, the immune system, and reproduction. Follow-up studies of the 42,000 most exposed people have not yet shown these impacts on the exposed individuals (Bertazzi 1991), although comparisons between the exposed group and a control group led to the following observations:

An excess mortality from cardiovascular and respiratory disease was uncovered, possibly related to the psychosocial consequences of the accident in addition to the chemical contamination. An excess of diabetes cases was also found. Results of cancer incidence and mortality follow-up showed an increased incidence of occurrence of cancer in the gastrointestinal sites and of the lymphatic and hematopoietic tissue. Experimental and epidemiologic data as well as mechanistic knowledge support the hypothesis that the observed cancer excesses are associated with dioxin exposure. Results cannot be viewed as conclusive. (Bertazzi et al. 1998)

(Continued)

BOX 5.5 *(Continued)*

> What this boils down to is that a potentially lethal toxic release from a factory has had relatively small impacts on the local community so far, although with long-term latency serious impacts could still appear. This was a near miss, and it was widely understood that people might not be so lucky next time. The incident was very far from being the worst-case scenario. Such was the impact of the accident—the realization that something similar could happen anywhere, anytime—that the Seveso incident ushered in stringent legislation to govern the handling of potentially dangerous chemicals throughout the European Community. Seveso Directive No. 1 (1982) covered chemical producers, and Seveso Directive No. 2 (1996) extended control to the transportation and storage of potentially dangerous chemicals.

proportion of regional Superfund staff time is not charged to site-specific accounts, for reasons that are not readily apparent. (Probst and Konisky 2001, xxvi–xxvii)

Underground Storage Tanks

Whereas it could be argued that the proponents certainly knew what they were putting into landfill sites and should have been aware of the implications, the same argument could not be used against the owners of underground storage tanks (such as tanks for gas stations and home heating) that subsequently leaked and then contaminated the soil and groundwater. The owners could assert that they had no knowledge of leakage, unless the loss was on a scale that would show up on a gauge. They could also argue that the loss was accidental, even if they could not prove that it was sudden. Questions regarding when the release was triggered became important in policies that required that claims be submitted within a certain deadline after the occurrence.

Asbestos

The reason for the growth of the asbestos tragedy to such momentous proportions was twofold: First, asbestos was widely used, and second, the

BOX 5.6 Superfund and the Insurance Industry

The introduction of the U.S. Superfund legislation (see Box 4.1) was supposed to enable the Environmental Protection Agency (EPA) to identify those hazardous waste sites that posed potential problems for human health; determine which parties had produced, transported, and managed those hazardous wastes; clean up the priority sites; and retrieve the cost of cleanup from the polluters. This sounds simple enough in theory, yet in practice it became a nightmare. Thousands of sites were identified, rather than the hundreds that were anticipated. The net that was used to identify potentially responsible parties (PRPs) was particularly troublesome for the insurance industry because the legislation was retroactive—without any time limit—and treated the parties as having "joint and several" liability.

The retrospective nature of Superfund triggered commercial general liability (CGL) policies that were decades old, dating from an era long before insurers even thought about pollution exclusion clauses. Not only were there no time limits on these policies, there were no loss limits, either! The joint and several nature of the liability was interpreted by the courts as meaning that *any party* to the pollution episode could be held accountable for *any amount* of the cost of the cleanup! Predictably the PRPs went to court, where the insurers found themselves saddled with a "duty to defend" their insureds (Insurance Information Institute 2000).

Successive pieces of legislation provided $15 billion of public funding and the EPA "reached settlements with private parties with an estimated value over $16 billion" (EPA 2001). A tax on chemical feedstocks, crude oil, and imported petroleum products provided further funding, until this tax expired in 1995. Although the problem is far from over, the initial legislative logjam has given way to some positive action. Cleanup technologies have improved, and there is more flexibility on the degree of cleanup required, with variations according to the use to which the remediated site will be put. The emphasis on brownfield redevelopment to reverse urban decay has put the issue in a broader perspective. Some responsibility has devolved from the federal EPA to the states and local authorities. Legislation is now in place that involves much stricter accounting for the handling of potentially hazardous wastes, so there is less confusion about the responsibilities of the various parties. Pollution is now excluded from CGL policies. Time and loss limits are now the norm.

latency period for asbestos-induced diseases to develop was very long, being anything between 30 and 50 years. It is estimated that in the United States alone 27 million people were exposed to asbestos between 1940 and 1979 (Hensler et al. 2001). In the early days, skeptics about the risks of asbestos could say that the observed lung cancer was caused by smoking. Apart from lung cancer, asbestos fibers increase the risk of cancer of the larynx and of the gastrointestinal tract. The fibers also produce asbestosis—a chronic lung infection that causes shortness of breath and permanent lung damage. Mesothelioma (cited in the case in Box 5.3) is a rare cancer of the thin membranes that line the chest and abdomen of which the only known cause is crocidolite, or blue asbestos. Because the disease has only the one cause, it became the signature condition that revealed the seriousness of the whole asbestos problem.

The impact of asbestos claims on the insurance industry outweighed any other single problem until the terrorists' destruction of the World Trade Center in 2001. To date, $22 billion in asbestos claims has been paid out by insurance companies in the United States alone (Hensler et al. 2001). A similar sum has been paid by the insurers in litigation costs. At least 41 asbestos defendant corporations have entered bankruptcy proceedings. The first corporation to become bankrupt was the Johns Manville Corporation in 1988. It had filed for bankruptcy in 1982, but it took the intervening six years to set up a trust fund from the remaining assets of the company to maximize the funds available for asbestos claims. Between February 2000 and July 2001 eight large corporations filed for bankruptcy because of the asbestos liabilities. In October 2001, Federal-Mogul, a major North American auto parts maker, filed for bankruptcy due to asbestos claims. In 1998 it had acquired T & N Plc. (the company featured in Box 5.3) as well as two other asbestos-liable companies. The company's reserves for asbestos liability proved inadequate—perhaps because many of the other asbestos defendants had, by now, declared bankruptcy (Pacelle 2001). Thus there were fewer companies available to provide compensation.

The problem is now global. In July 2000 in the U.K. the House of Lords agreed that:

> *Some 3,000 South African citizens suffering from asbestosis and mesothelioma could continue to bring an action in England against Cape Plc., a UK-based company formerly with South African asbestos mining interests. (W. Thomas 2001)*

Contaminated Land

Another large class of contamination problems for insurers has surfaced through attempts to reuse old industrial sites and transportation corridors. Invariably land that has been under such use for decades will be seriously polluted with hydrocarbons, metals, and synthetics such as polychlorinated biphenyls (PCBs) and furans—the last being highly toxic organochlorines (Lecomte 1999). As discussed in the previous chapter, the reuse of contaminated land has become a widespread problem throughout the old industrial world. Like the banks, the insurance companies do not expect to be held responsible for the cost of cleanup for the reuse of the sites, especially in jurisdictions that would not provide any assurance that once the land was restored there would be no further liability accruing to it. A further problem resides in the possibility that the cost of remediation may be seriously underestimated if conditions prove to be much worse than consultants' assessments indicated. Many sites remain idle waiting for a resolution to the impasse.

The source of the contamination problems for the insurance industry included a change in the public expectations regarding the handling of materials that was supported by gradually improving methods of detection and clearer evidence of cause and effect. The industry was not helped by the ambiguity that surrounded key words such as "pollutant" itself. A simple definition could be that a pollutant is any substance that has been manufactured or manipulated by humans and left in sufficient concentration to cause harm to human health or property. Such a definition does not sound complicated. It has been put even more simply:

> *A clumsy but essentially accurate definition of pollution is "too much of something in the wrong place." (Crathorne and Dobbs 1990)*

Yet on the subject of lead in the paint used to paint houses, a Massachusetts court ruled that lead was *not* a pollutant because a pollutant was something associated with industrial activity, and therefore the insurer's "pollution exclusion" clause was not applicable to the residential property in question. Similarly, in a 1993 California case, *Flintoke Company v. American Mutual Liability Insurance*, the court deemed asbestos not to be a pollutant, and the exclusion of occurrences other than the "sudden and accidental" did not bar claims alleging contamination within a building. Furthermore, across the United States various courts have ruled both for and against arguments that polluters' behavior was not accidental because "they should have known" that their activities would pollute.

Lead Paint

The lead liability issue ran a similar course to asbestos for the insurance industry. The macabre joke in the early 1990s in insurance circles was, "If you liked asbestos, you'll love lead." Like asbestos, lead was very useful, and thus became ubiquitous. Just as asbestos was prized because it was resistant to heat and electrical currents, lead was prized because it was both strong and malleable. It was used to provide secure roofing for important buildings; like asbestos it was ideal for making pipes (especially water pipes); it was used in solder for cans; at the turn of the nineteenth century it was added to paint to provide both durability and luster; in the twentieth century it was put in gasoline as an antiknock additive. Gradually its negative side was understood. If inhaled or ingested it was taken up by the body and stored, and this affected neurological functions. Calculations were made of the negative effect of lead on I.Q. among the young. Throughout the industrial world lead in paint was phased out in the late 1970s, while lead in gasoline was phased out in the 1980s. The remaining problem for the affected population and the insurers was the lead paint in poorly maintained housing. As long as the paint remained securely in place—like asbestos—it did not pose a problem. But once it deteriorated and, in biochemical terms, became "available" and hence could be ingested by humans, it became a *huge* problem.

Typically the humans at risk were very young children, many of them living in public or low-cost housing. As with asbestos, the number of people exposed to this risk was in the millions. Until 1978 houses in the United States, for example, were painted with lead-based paint. The housing stock is typically replenished at only about 2 percent per year. Even allowing that many well-maintained houses would not have a lead paint problem, the number that might be at risk was enormous, potentially twice the number (again in the United States) exposed to asbestos.

> *Today, an estimated three million tons of lead paint still can be found on the walls of some 57 million homes in the United States. As a result, as many as three million pre-school children are believed to have ingested a sufficient amount of lead to have elevated levels in the blood. Children under six years of age are considered to be most vulnerable to lead contamination because their nervous systems are still developing. (Kasouf 1996)*

This situation is far worse—from the impact perspective—because the vulnerable this time were not likely to be cigarette-smoking 50-year-olds. They were very young children facing a lifetime of diminished quality of life and a need for constant care. As the first cases were settled, the average individual cost was more than double that of the asbestos settlements. Single awards of $10 million per individual case were made by juries in the United States, although these types of awards were often knocked down by judges in superior courts or contested by the targeted party.

Suits were entered against the owners of buildings, including public authorities in the low-cost housing sector. Issues emerged that were similar to those in the asbestos claims. Who exactly was responsible for what? What were the insurance policies supposed to cover? In New York (where 6,000 lead paint liability cases were filed between 1993 and 1996) various courts involved in the *Juarez v. Wavecrest* case imposed *absolute* liability on landlords. Absolute in this context means that:

> *Landlords are negligent per se when they fail to continuously inspect pre-1960 multiple-dwelling units in New York City in which children six years of age or under reside, and where a lead paint condition exists and was not abated.* (Kasouf 1996)

This was a dramatic change from the previous supposition:

> *Under common law doctrines defendants would have been negligent only if they had an actual or constructive notice that a defect or hazard existed, and then failed to cure it when reasonably they should have remedied the problem . . .*
>
> *The potential claims exposure to insurers from lead in children is ominous. In New York State alone, one insurance company estimated the potential cost of lead paint claims could reach $100 billion, 60 percent of the total industry capital.* (Kasouf 1996)

As with asbestos claims and the Superfund cases, the legal campaign over lead paint liability has become more complex and wide-ranging as the players have gained experience. The lawyers for the plaintiffs want to bring as many potentially responsible parties into the dock as possible. For lead paint cases the obvious goal for the plaintiffs is to expand from the landlords to the manufacturers of lead paint. Arguments have been made in district courts in New York that *all* manufacturers of lead paint should be held liable to the extent of their *share* of the market, even if the use of their product in a particular building cannot be proved. For example,

Plaintiffs' lawyers are trying to overcome that problem by arguing, in a class action in the U.S. District Court in Manhattan, that nine companies that made lead pigment from 1925 to 1960 should be liable based on their share of the pigment market, or jointly or severally liable on the basis that they all knew the risks and misled customers about them. That suit covers several hundred thousand children under six years old and pregnant women. (Kasouf 1996)

So far the courts have resisted this "market share responsibility" argument.

Two factors became evident over the development of the lead paint issue within the property and casualty insurance industry. First, while the claims people are on the front lines and may be fully aware of the emergence of the potential costs to the company, it can take years for the full scale of the problem to reach the underwriters. For example,

These claims are just emerging, and the impact hasn't been contemplated by insurers and reflected in rates and reserves. At some [insurance] companies only the claims people know what's going on. It hasn't worked its way to underwriting yet. (Kasouf 1996)

Even then a solution to a potentially ruinous financial exposure may not be apparent. For example, in some states, such as New Jersey, lead exclusions on habitational policies are banned. Apart from the legal wrangles, the problem persists because the authorities do not apply the existing laws that govern inspection of properties; insureds likewise do not always fulfill their duties; and insurance companies do not hire the expertise needed for effective loss control.

The problem is most concentrated in the older cities in the northeastern United States such as Philadelphia, New York, and Boston, but cases occur across the country. The problem persists, and the full extent of the exposure remains unknown, because the children who are most likely to be affected belong to low-income families and are the least likely to come forward for screening. Screening is now mandated by both the federal and state governments, but it is difficult to enforce, especially for preschoolers. In a recent case (December 2001) in Manchester, New Hampshire, a three-year-old died from lead poisoning, the first death in 10 years (General Cologne Re 2002).

Public authorities are major property owners and managers in low-income urban areas, and they have been the frequent targets of lawsuits for damages associated with lead paint. Some municipalities have, in turn, sued the manufacturers of lead paint, as happened recently in New Jersey (General Cologne Re 2002).

Common Lessons from Asbestos and Environmental Problems

These problems have a number of features in common. First, they arise from conditions that were widespread and endured for a long period of time. They then came to light through a landmark event and a subsequent legal judgment. The damages awarded in the first few cases are then multiplied by the potential number of claimants. The product of these two numbers is enormous. Understandably, there is resistance and denial among the prospective defendants and their insurers. This attitude can persist for years, greatly adding to the final cost of the problem. In a 1996 report on "Environmental Liability and the Insurance Industry" the rating agency Standard & Poor's concluded:

> *In this area, just as in most lines of business, aggressive and expeditious handling of claims is crucial. Once it has become clear that insurers will likely have an exposure to this issue, those companies who continue in "stonewalling" the issue run the risk of ultimately paying more than those who have been quick to address their exposures and have taken decisive action to resolve that exposure. (Levin 1996)*

While the insurers begin to come to grips with their liabilities, the authorities move to resolve the physical basis for the adverse condition. This can simply be a ban on the use of the materials, such as lead paint and asbestos, which at least limits the scope of the damage. They may also pass legislation, as in the case of the Superfund, which may make the problem worse (see Boxes 4.1 and 5.6). The courts will pass down various judgments, some favorable to one party, some to another. Gradually insurers find ways to manage the problem, such as accepting the cost of endless litigation, excluding the liability from all future underwriting, or hiring specialists to control the loss through tighter inspections of prospective business and through claims management.

In a justice system like that of the United States it seems improbable that these widespread pollution problems will ever be managed without spending many years in adversarial gridlock in the courts. As the relatively poor (blue-collar workers for asbestos, children in public housing for lead paint) are more likely to be among the victims and as the cases will drag on for years, the lawyers will count on contingency fees, paid as a percentage of the awards they win. This gives them a very strong incentive to collect as many plaintiffs in a class action suit as they can muster; they will also wish to maximize the number and wealth (deep pockets) of the defendants; and they will resist accepting a settlement for anything less than the amount they think they might eventually win. Lawyers now advertise on the Internet for people to join class action suits. On the insurers' side there are reasons to ignore the prudent advice of the rating agencies to make adequate reserves for anticipated losses, because such a prudent action could be interpreted as tacit admission of the expectation of an eventual loss in the courts. Thus, the actual amount reserved for the loss might become the target settlement figure for the lawyers.

Meanwhile, companies that went ahead and cleaned up sites before being ordered to do so by the courts were sometimes denied liability coverage on the grounds that the action was voluntary, and that coverage would be triggered only if a court ordered the cleanup or a third party sued for off-site contamination. The courts found in favor of the insureds' claims being paid in landmark cases in the states of Washington, Wyoming, and New Jersey (Wojcik 1996; Niedzielski 1996). Claims have also been upheld for the cost of cleaning up on-site pollution.

As "asbestos and environmental" problems mounted through the 1980s and 1990s, various changes have taken place that should reduce the uncertainty for insurer and insured alike. First, there is much less ignorance about the potential dangers of materials like lead and asbestos, leakages from landfills, discharges from chemical plants (both purposive and accidental), and leakages from underground storage tanks. New landfills are designed to collect liquid and gaseous wastes that are then treated; indeed methane from landfills is now a valued source of power for the electricity grid. New underground tanks are built with double hulls and a monitor that signals if the air pressure between the hulls falls, signifying a breach in one of the hulls. Without this provision insurance cover is not available for new tanks. Asbestos and lead paint are removed from buildings when they are demolished or renovated using specially trained and officially bonded companies to do the work.

The insurance industry has taken steps to clarify the exclusion of pollution liability from homeowners' and commercial policies, indicating that coverage must be obtained separately for environmental impairment liability. The latter is a specialty business that provides coverage only for legitimate accidents. A further innovation has been the offering of "cleanup cost overrun" insurance for those cases where the cost of remediation of polluted land exceeds the consultants' estimate of what the cleanup would cost (Box 5.7).

While the tendency to resist paying environmental claims may still linger in the insurance industry, events of the past 30 years provide two very important lessons. First, the eventual cost of these claims can be huge. Second, environmental problems require a more sophisticated kind of management that understands the physical basis of these problems from an interdisciplinary perspective, integrating the environmental, engineering, and physiological issues. These are not issues that can be handed off to a lawyer who will then find the most favorable expert witnesses to appear in court. The relevant expertise should be developed in-house, so that the insurance company can control the losses.

Almost certainly, the next crop of environmental liability issues will be a lot more complex than lead, leachate, and asbestos. They will evolve from more subtle health effects from such diverse origins as toxic mold, electromagnetic fields, sick-building syndrome, endocrine disruptors, genetically modified organisms, and airborne asbestos emanating from disasters such as the destruction of the World Trade Center.

BOX 5.7   Cleanup Cost Cap Insurance Policies

The uncertainty inherent in remediating contaminated land has been a major factor in discouraging redevelopment even when prime sites in the urban core are available. No sampling procedure—however rigorous—can guarantee that the full scope of the problem has been estimated before remediation begins. In recent years some insurers have offered a solution to the uncertainty problem by offering "cleanup cost cap" policies for owners or buyers of contaminated land. These policies are based on the consultant's estimate of the probable cost of cleanup, and will cover costs in excess of that estimate.

For example, AIG Environmental offers coverage for contamination on the site itself, off-site costs (for pollutants that migrate during remediation), and additional costs incurred through change orders required by the authorities. The coverage is capped at $70 million per loss (AIG Environmental 1997).

CLIMATE CHANGE AND EXTREME WEATHER EVENTS

The lessons learned from losses suffered from "asbestos and environmental" claims have been painful and costly for the victims of the physical impacts, for the insured parties, and for the insurance companies themselves. They were almost terminal for Lloyd's of London, the founders of the modern insurance industry (Box 5.8). However, these costs may prove to be *small* compared with the potential losses to come from extreme weather events and other impacts associated with climate change.

In Chapter 1 we summarized the environmental liability problem as a matter of "paying for the past." With climate change we are looking in the other direction and "preparing for the future."

The unpredictability of the weather creates a lot of business for the insurance industry. As climate change will definitely increase that level of uncertainty perhaps it will create further business opportunities. It will certainly increase the level of risk. Perhaps—like environmental impairment liability—that is a risk that a general insurer would not want to underwrite and would leave for a specialty insurer.

The fundamental problem for the general insurer in an era of climate change is that the underlying probability of various weather events cannot be estimated. By definition, the historical record becomes inadequate as the basis for pricing risk. Even as new events unfold they will not add enough information because the climate will continue to change as long as the atmospheric concentrations of greenhouse gases continue to increase. (These uncertainties are presented in more detail in Chapter 7.) Even when these concentrations are stabilized, the warmer world in which we will then be living may begin to unravel other planetary features that evolved during the colder world of the past. The permafrost in the Arctic regions is already melting and will slowly release important quantities of methane—a powerful greenhouse gas—into the atmosphere. More methane will be released into the overloaded atmosphere as the oceans warm sufficiently to break up methyl hydrates frozen in the Arctic seabed (Leggett 1999). It is also feared that the release of freshwater from the Arctic ice cap may interrupt the northward flow of the Gulf Stream and North Atlantic Drift, which keep northern Europe warm. Thus, even as the rest of the world warms, Britain and her neighbors may move towards a colder climate. This is a level of uncertainty that surely exceeds the appetite of the insurance industry.

What is confidently expected is that a warmer world will intensify the hydrological cycle and thereby increase the frequency of convective storms—thunderstorms, hail, and tornadoes (White and Etkin 1997). It is a matter of

BOX 5.8   Lloyd's: The Cumulative Impact of Asbestos, Environmental, and Catastrophic Losses

Lloyd's of London evolved as a unique entity in the insurance world, beginning as an informal meeting of marine underwriters in the coffeehouse of Edward Lloyd, first referred to in 1688. Until 1994 it was based on the wealth of private individuals, known as Names, who assumed unlimited liability for losses. The "London market," as Lloyd's is sometimes known, includes several syndicates of such individuals who act as primary insurers and also as reinsurers among themselves.* Through the nineteenth century Lloyd's went from strength to strength, a pillar of Britain's global empire. Its loose structure, based on the social cohesion of a few hundred people drawn from a particular slice of society, enabled it to innovate while the broad base of its wealth enabled it to insure risks that might be shunned by companies responsible to shareholders. Its rapid payment of losses incurred in the San Francisco earthquake in 1906 established its reputation for reliability in the United States, from which a growing proportion of its revenue was earned. Within its expanding pool of business in America it wrote liability insurance for a number of asbestos manufacturing companies. As was its custom, Lloyd's reinsured much of this risk within the ranks of its own syndicates.

Even before it was threatened by the rising tide of asbestos and pollution claims in the 1970s, Lloyd's recorded its first ever overall loss in 1965, mainly due to the losses associated with Hurricane Betsy. At that time the number of Names was greatly increased from hundreds to thousands, eventually reaching over 30,000 in the 1980s, while the subscribed capital base went from approximately £1 billion to £10 billion over the same period. Of course, beyond that visible security lay the unlimited liability of the Names themselves.

Then the insurance world was struck by a series of unprecedented events that were to bring Lloyd's to the brink of collapse. Its dominance in the global market and the practice of reinsuring itself became an Achilles' heel as the losses piled up. Major European windstorms (1987); the Piper Alpha oil rig explosion and the

*The London market also includes the Institute of London Underwriters (marine, aviation, and transport business) and the London Insurance and Reinsurance Market Association (reinsurance and nonmarine business).

(Continued)

BOX 5.8   *(Continued)*

> Lockerbie plane crash (both 1988); the oil spill of the *Exxon Valdez*, Hurricane Hugo and another San Francisco earthquake (all in 1989); more European windstorms (1990); typhoon Mireille, a devastating typhoon that struck Japan (1991); and finally Hurricane Andrew in the United States (1992), added to the steady rise of asbestos and pollution claims, brought five years of losses totaling £7.9 billion (Lloyd's 2000). Many of the newer Names simply did not have the wealth to absorb these losses. Some refused or were unable to pay up. Others sued Lloyd's, claiming that they had not been informed of the growing asbestos liability when they were invited to join the exclusive club.
>
> The door was opened to corporate capital in 1994. The obligations of many of the distressed Names were settled out of court. In November 2000, in the London court, Lloyd's was found not guilty of defrauding investors. However, the exclusive association of private individuals insuring major risks around the world is no more.

debate as to whether climate change will mean bigger hurricanes (sometimes called "hypercanes") and/or extend the area over which hurricanes normally occur, perhaps bringing New York and Los Angeles within the normal seasonal swathe. The storms will also produce unprecedented flooding (Munich Re 1997; Partner Re 1997). In the year 2000 serious floods were experienced in places as far afield as Britain (insured losses $700 million, economic losses more than $1,500 million, and 10 deaths) and southern Africa, especially Mozambique (insured losses $50 million, economic losses $660 million, and more than 1,000 deaths) (Munich Re 2001b).

The relevance of these changes for insurers cannot be ignored. Even in a cold country like Canada global warming is threatening. For example, as Angus Ross, until recently chief agent in Canada for Sorema Reinsurance, pointed out:

> *A warming climate carries substantial risks for property and casualty insurers and reinsurers in Canada. Among the events likely to become more frequent are severe precipitation (rainfall, snowfall and attendant flooding/sewer backup) and convective storms (thunderstorms and tornadoes). We could also expect more frequent and possibly prolonged droughts. (Ross 1997)*

There are a number of steps that the insurance industry can take to reduce the impact of climate change. First, it can lobby governments intensively to mitigate climate change by discouraging the use of fossil fuels. European reinsurance companies have been doing this since the first Conference of the Parties to the Framework Convention on Climate Change in Berlin in 1994 (Swiss Re 1994). Over the long run this is the most important priority. As with the pollution problems, such as lead and asbestos, once the source of the danger has been identified the extent of the impact must be limited by banning further use of the materials as soon as possible. For climate change this means greenhouse gases, principally fossil fuels.

Second, in the short term, losses may be reduced by encouraging the insureds to maintain their buildings to reduce susceptibility to heavy wind and rain (roof fastenings, window covers, etc.). Third, they should monitor climate more closely, especially heavy rainfall events, and work with the meteorological authorities to produce data in a more useful form. For example, climate data should be aggregated on a seasonal basis, rather than by a calendar year, with more climate stations in urban locations where most people live, not only at airports that may be 20 miles out of the city. We are living in an era when there never again will be a historical record on which the underwriter can assess probabilities. The next best strategy is to closely monitor the latest trend.

There are also much more sophisticated models for estimating the probable maximum loss (PML) from extreme weather events (and from earthquakes, too). As cheaper computer capacity has become available, it is now possible to develop computer models based on fine-grained geographic information systems (GIS) on either an industry or a firm base (Andrews and Blong 1997). Spatial data will give a much more accurate estimate of firm, and industry, exposure to a particular risk, whether it is windstorm, wildfire (i.e., forest and other fires that encroach on urban areas—a problem for California, Florida, and much of Australia), or hail (Insurance Services Office 1997). Insurance companies will have to decide if they will buy such models off the shelf or develop their own in-house capacity for GIS-based PML modeling.

Much more work is required on event definition, the basis for ceding risk from the primary insurer to the reinsurer (Brun 1997). So long as extreme weather events were not that extreme and were of low probability, this was not a pressing problem. However, Figure 5.1 clearly indicates that we have moved into a different world. As the world becomes more populated and urbanized, and more of its people own valuable goods, "insurance density" increases in the richer countries, including high-risk (earthquake, typhoon) areas such as the Pacific Rim. Inevitably PMLs will also increase. In a warmer world, under a more intense hydrological cycle, various events and impacts will begin to coalesce. For example, hurricanes often generate a swarm of tornadoes in their wake, and the heavy rainfall associated with hurricanes means that rivers will flood. Are these all one event? Such situations will become more common and will generate disputes between insurers and reinsurers that will end up in the courts. Some legal disputes might be avoided if research were carried out on complex events that have already been experienced, such as the "super outbreak" of tornadoes that struck the United States with no less than 148 twisters in 24 hours, April 3–4, 1974 (NOAA 1999). How much would such an outbreak cost the insurance industry today, and how much would fall on the reinsurance industry?

There are several approaches toward developing closer approximations to the risk to which the insurance industry may be exposed by climate change. For the problem of event definition, for example, we can construct tables for hypothetical and historical cases showing how costs will be partitioned between primary insurers and reinsurers, depending on the definition of an event that is used. Using a hypothetical approach, Brun and Etkin (1997) have proposed a "time-space chart" that would allow reinsurance treaty partners to define more clearly the nature of the risk covered by the treaty. A historical approach would take an actual meteorological event and rerun or simulate it for today's population, infrastructure, emergency capacity, and insurance density to determine what impacts it would have today. The Institute for Catastrophic Loss Reduction, a unit of the Insurance Bureau of Canada, has done this for Toronto's Hurricane Hazel (1957) (Cumming Cockburn Ltd. 2000).

Other simulations have been undertaken purely to understand the physical impacts of a historic event. For example, various climate change scenarios were simulated for the Grand River in Ontario, and it was found that:

Modifications to operating procedures and additional reservoir capacity were shown to be moderately successful adjustments to all but the most severe streamflow scenarios tested. (Southam et al. 1999)

An analysis of Canada's capacity to cope with natural hazards uncovered a variety of potential responses that was far more complex than any member of the research team expected, even though the group included insurers, academic researchers, government scientists, and emergency-response officials (Brun et al. 1997). Most tellingly of all, no one in the team included a major urban ice storm among the possible hazards to be considered. The report was published in June 1997. From the 4th to the 10th of January 1998, an unprecedented ice storm struck a region from the Ottawa Valley to northern

New England (Kerry et al. 1998; Lecomte et al. 1998; Higuchi et al. 2000). It paralyzed Montreal for two weeks. It was Canada's first billion-dollar insurance loss, and it resulted in over 800,000 claims, exceeding even the number of claims for Hurricane Andrew in the United States. Yet it was a near miss— that is, not the worst-case scenario. The city of Montreal could not be evacuated, as most of the 17 bridges off the island of Montreal were either blocked or encumbered by ice and stalled traffic. Power failed as the electrical transmission line pylons toppled. As the pylons fell, small fires broke out. Due to the power failure, water could not be pumped. At one point, only four hours of water supply remained in the water treatment plants. If fire had caught hold it would have been very difficult to contain it, due to problems of emergency access and lack of water from the city system. In conclusion,

> *It left 4.7 million people without electricity and heat for a prolonged period in the middle of winter. It caused property damage, insured and uninsured, and economic loss approximating Cdn. $6.4 billion [U.S. $4 billion]. (Lecomte et al. 1998)*

And it was entirely unexpected.

On a quieter note, a more intense hydrological cycle is also likely to produce longer periods of warm, dry weather. This may be bad news for farmers and for water management companies. It has also been expensive for insurers covering properties built on clay soils (Association of British Insurers 2000b). Clay is composed of very fine particles that normally hold a lot of water between them. Under extended warm and dry conditions the water near the surface evaporates and the particles move closer together. The resultant shrinkage of the supporting ground stresses the foundations of buildings, some of which shrink and crack. This has become an expensive problem in Britain since the 1970s when the warming trend first became apparent. The problem has been dealt with in Australia, the United States, France, and South Africa by simply reducing the expectations of the insured—no cover. In Britain, where the idea of a warmer, drier climate is a novel concept, homeowners are still expecting full compensation for the restoration of their damaged property.

In conclusion, climate change implies at least two major challenges for the property and casualty insurance industry. First, the historical record of climate is no longer a reliable guideline for establishing the likelihood of weather-related losses. Droughts, floods, and storms are all likely to increase in frequency and intensity, if they have not clearly done so already. This means that losses will mount, independent of other factors that increase the likelihood of losses such as increasing insurance density as economies grow and urbanization proceeds. Although insurance companies are beginning to use simulation models to understand the PMLs they can expect to manage in a warmer world, the pricing of premiums is still based on the now-unreliable historical record. In a competitive world economy this poses a real difficulty, as noted by Dr. Gerhard Berz, head of the Geoscience Research Group of Munich Re:

> *How long the insurance industry will be able to continue fulfilling its function depends on the speed and agility with which it can adjust to a changing environment. This adjustment can be achieved by applying loss reduction measures, such as introducing adequate deductibles, and, most important, by charging premiums that are truly commensurate with the risk. Unfortunately, this is still today based exclusively on loss experience of the past and, under competitive pressure, corners are often cut. (Berz 1993)*

Second, more complex weather phenomena will make the task of event definition more difficult, which means that the question "one event or two?" is more likely to end up in court.

TRANSFERRING RISK FROM THE INSURANCE INDUSTRY TO THE CAPITAL MARKETS

It has been obvious since Hurricane Andrew rocked the insurance industry in 1992 that events of this magnitude could not be absorbed on a regular basis. Many people rapidly made the calculation that the worldwide capitalization of the P&C insurance industry (then at approximately $250 billion) could not absorb an early repetition of this level of loss. In a competitive market premiums could not be raised dramatically, and in the United States—the most vulnerable country—publicly elected insurance commissioners would not only prevent premium hikes but would also oblige the industry to continue to offer coverage. The usual short-term measures were taken to maintain coverage with the creation of a layered Florida P&C involuntary pool, as has been done many times before after major hurricanes in the United States. (A similar reaction to the Northridge earthquake in California in 1994 had longer-lasting effects through the securitization of the risk, described shortly.)

A more elegant and creative approach to tap into the much greater risk-bearing potential of the American capital markets was offered through the Chicago Board of Trade catastrophe options (White 2001). (See Box 5.9 and Figure 5.2.) Unfortunately, this product failed to gain market support.

BOX 5.9   The Experience of the Chicago Board of Trade with the Offering of Catastrophe Options, 1995–2000

It was widely observed after the shock of Hurricane Andrew that global insurance capacity was unable to absorb such an event on a regular basis. It was also noted that Andrew had only grazed the southern tip of Florida—30 miles further north lay Miami and a probable maximum loss of $50 billion, which would have had a severe impact on a global scale. Finally, it was noted the capital markets are much larger than global insurance capacity and that the daily volatility of the U.S. capital markets far exceeded the total loss from Hurricane Andrew. "However, it was not until insurers had digested the consequences of these losses that they started to believe that a bridge to the capital markets had to be built" (Hague 1996).

The first such bridge was the creation of a market in insurance futures, based on the Insurance Services Office loss data, and offered by the Chicago Board of Trade (CBOT) in 1992. Industry response was lukewarm and the product was soon replaced by a more elegant and flexible concept in the form of catastrophe options contracts, being a call spread based on total catastrophic losses, totaled quarterly and by nine geographic areas, including a national contract (CBOT 1995a, 1995b; Ip 1996; White 2001). Development periods of 6 and 12 months were available. The buyers of the contracts were expected to be the insurance and reinsurance companies exposed to catastrophic risk in the United States. The sellers would be large institutional investors such as pension fund and mutual fund managers. Despite the novel nature of the investment it was expected to be attractive to sellers because the premium would be higher than standard investments and the risk would be completely uncorrelated with market trends, as it would be driven by natural events such as hurricanes, tornadoes, winter storms, and earthquakes. Because of the open and incremental nature of the trading, price discovery would be transparent and the coverage potentially cheaper for the buyer than traditional reinsurance. It would certainly be a great deal more flexible than a reinsurance treaty, as the options could be bought in any quantity and for any spread, 8:30 A.M. to 12:30 P.M., Monday to Friday. The market was launched in September 1995 and interest grew slowly but steadily. (See Figure 5.2.)

(Continued)

BOX 5.9   *(Continued)*

> However, demand was never strong enough to close the bid/ask spread, and trading volume remained low. The development of the Bermuda catastrophe market and the opening of Lloyd's to corporate investors restored capacity to the traditional reinsurance market. Above all, there was no repeat of Hurricane Andrew and certainly not the nightmare scenario of a hurricane landfall in a major urban area. Demand for the CBOT cat options peaked in May 1998, and the product was withdrawn in January 2000 (White 2001).

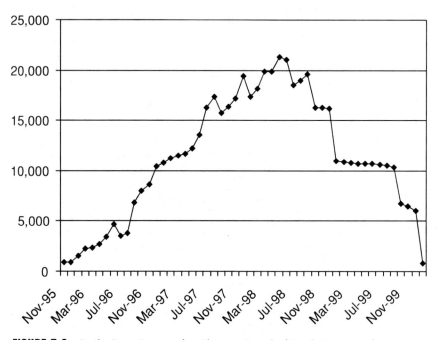

FIGURE 5.2   Daily Open Interest for Chicago Board of Trade Catastrophe Options, 1995–2000
Source: Based on data provided by the Chicago Board of Trade.

If the level of concern in the aftermath of Hurricane Andrew had prevailed, then the story might have been different. The establishment of a new Bermuda-based reinsurance market funded by major investors quickly filled the liquidity gap for reinsurance.

A longer-term response developed from the securitization of various categories of risk, beginning in 1994 with an $85 million bond from Hanover Re to lay off its catastrophe coverage for worldwide property, excluding the United States and Japan (Table 5.2). This has been followed by nearly 50 bonds covering a variety of risks, providing more than $4 billion of additional coverage, mostly tied to extreme weather events and earthquakes. Sellers of these bonds are mostly insurance companies, although corporate sellers are beginning to emerge. The buyers are major investors such as mutual funds and pension funds. The bonds are attractive to buyers because the yield is high and the risk is uncorrelated with other asset classes. Therefore it offers a good return in relation to risk. Indeed, the inclusion of these uncorrelated risks reduces the overall basket of risk assumed by an investor (Hague 1996).

A new market for weather risk is also emerging in various weather derivative and swap deals where companies hedge against moderate weather conditions that are adverse to their business, rather than extreme weather events that affect general insurance companies through damage to property. Simply stated,

> *A weather derivative is a contract between two parties that stipulates how payment will be exchanged between the parties depending on certain meteorological conditions during the contract period. (Zeng 2000)*

The principal players are energy companies that need to hedge their exposure to warm winters (less heating demand) and cool summers (less cooling demand). Their problem is to find a "natural other side" with which to hedge this risk (Hull 2000; Nicholls 2001i). They may find a general investor among the pension funds, mutual funds, and insurance companies, but the price would certainly be lower if they could find counterparties who wish to swap the risk to which they themselves are exposed. (See Box 5.10 and Chapter 9.)

TABLE 5.2 Risk-Linked Securities 1994–2001

Year	Risk Capital ($ Million)	Type of Cedant	Underlying Risks
1994	85	Reinsurer	Worldwide property catastrophe, except U.S. and Japan
1996	6	Insurer	Swiss automobile hail
	10	Insurer	Global
	100	Reinsurer	Global property catastrophe
	45	Reinsurer	U.S., Europe, and other property Lloyd's retro, marine, and aviation
	42	Insurer	Life (variable annuity)
1997	10 (est.)	Insurer	U.S. and other property, marine, aviation, satellite
	158	Insurer	Life (variable annuity)
	90	Insurer	Japanese earthquake
	112	Reinsurer	California earthquake
	35	Reinsurer	East and Gulf Coast hurricane
	400	Insurer	East and Gulf Coast hurricane
	10 (est.)	Insurer	U.S. and other property, marine, aviation, satellite
1998	30	Reinsurer	California earthquake
	80	Insurer	Japanese typhoon
	57 (DM100)	Reinsurer	Multicurrency life
	450	Insurer	East and Gulf coast hurricane
	25 (est.)	Insurer	U.S. and other property, marine rigs, aviation, satellite
	243	Mortgage purchaser	Mortgage default
	431 (£260)	Insurer	Life (unit linked annuities)
	90	Reinsurer	Northeast U.S. hurricane
	30	Insurer	Japanese earthquake
	72	Reinsurer and insurer	Florida hurricane
	54	Reinsurer and insurer	Florida hurricane
	150	Reinsurer and insurer	German wind and hail
	25	Insurer and bank	U.S. Midwest earthquake
	50	Reinsurer	Global property catastrophe
	10	Reinsurer	U.S. property
	100	Reinsurer	U.S. hurricane and earthquake
	566	Corporate	Auto lease residual
	45	Reinsurer	U.S. property

(Continued)

TABLE 5.2   *(Continued)*

Year	Risk Capital ($ Million)	Type of Cedant	Underlying Risks
1999	100	Reinsurer	Japanese earthquake
	49 (€50)	Reinsurer	Multicurrency life
	182	Reinsurer	U.S. hurricane, California, and New Madrid quake
	50	Corporate	Temperature
	50	Reinsurer and insurer	New Madrid earthquake
	80	Reinsurer	U.S. hurricane
	75	Insurer and bank	New Madrid earthquake
	200	Insurer	East and Gulf Coast hurricane
	100	Corporate	Credit following Japanese earthquake
	100	Corporate	Japanese earthquake
	17	Reinsurer	Japanese wind and earthquake, European wind
	100	Reinsurer	New Madrid property
	500	Reinsurer	European commercial trade credit default
	10 (est.)	Insurer	U.S. and other property, marine, aviation, and satellite
	45	Reinsurer	U.S. property
	118	Reinsurer	Multicurrency life
2000	165	Reinsurer	U.S. hurricane
	135	Reinsurer	California earthquake and European windstorm
	129	Insurer	French windstorm and Monaco earthquake
	50	Insurer	Northeast U.S. and Hawaii hurricane
	200	Insurer	East and Gulf Coast hurricane
	90	Insurer	Florida hurricane
	17	Reinsurer	Japanese wind and quake, European wind
	200	Reinsurer	U.S. and Japan quake, European windstorm
	150	Reinsurer	California earthquake
2001	125	Reinsurer	East and Gulf Coast hurricane, and New Madrid earthquake
	100	Reinsurer	California earthquake

Source: Goldman, Sachs & Co., May 2001.

BOX 5.10 Marketing the Weather Risk

Insurance companies have always been closely involved in the impacts of the weather on their clients and hence on their own bottom lines. Traditionally this has mainly been felt through the impact of extreme weather events on property damage (home, automobile, and business) and business continuity. There are also specialty companies that provide crop insurance and protection for the transportation sector.

However, the weather affects businesses in other ways than property damage and disrupted operations. Weather affects profit on a daily basis for several key sectors of the economy, especially energy and agriculture, but also retail sales, the leisure sector, and the construction industry. In the late 1990s the weather risk business emerged as companies examined their own exposure to weather risk and then sought partners with whom they could exchange it or hedge it. The most sensitive sector in terms of the magnitude of the cost of weather variability was the newly deregulated American energy supply industry that was especially vulnerable to warmer winters and cooler summers that reduced demand for heating and air-conditioning, respectively.

The risk could be hedged if accurate data were available and the risk avoided could be priced. In other words, "weather derivative contracts can be straightforwardly priced once the counterparties have agreed on an estimate of the underlying distribution of the weather statistic involved" (Toulson 2000). Unfortunately data, and even language, standardization is some way off and the market has been slow to evolve (Foster 2001). The reinsurers who participated in the first deals, buying the risk ceded by energy suppliers, ran into three warm winters in a row (perhaps predictable in a warming world) and are believed to have lost in the exchange (Nicholls 2001i). However, they have now returned to the market forming alliances with specialist dealers in weather derivatives, who, in turn, are linked up with banks. The latter introduce the weather risk product to their clients for whom they already manage interest and currency risk. One such insurance and dealer alliance includes Aquila Energy—an American weather derivatives dealer—with American Re (subsidiary of Munich Re), Hiscox (a member of Lloyd's), Mitsui Marine and Fire (Japan), and Kemper Insurance (U.S.).

(Continued)

BOX 5.10   *(Continued)*

> The attraction of this market is that a sufficiently diversified port-folio could ensure that one risk would balance another, given the variability of the world's weather, unlike the financial markets that have a tendency to rise and fall together. The challenge for the players in this market is to build a global infrastructure that can take advantage of the diversity of world weather experiences at the time when the market is still in a nascent form. Marketing is expensive and pricing will remain a problem, especially as the climate changes and the underlying weather risk changes with it.

REGIONAL VARIATIONS IN THE RESPONSE OF INSURANCE COMPANIES TO THE ENVIRONMENTAL CHALLENGE

In 1995 several insurance companies worked with the United Nations Environment Program (UNEP) to produce a Statement of Environmental Commitment by the Insurance Industry (UNEP 2000). This committed the signatories:

> *to work together to address key issues such as pollution reduction, the efficient use of resources, and climate change. . . . [and to] reinforce the attention given to environmental risks in our core activities. . . . [including] risk management, loss prevention, product design, claims handling and asset management. . . . [and including a commitment] to manage internal operations and physical assets under our control in a manner that reflects environmental considerations. (UNEP 2000)*

The locations of the signatory companies are revealing. Of the 91 companies signed up as of August 2000, 69 (75 percent) were from Europe (Germany 21, Switzerland 10, United Kingdom 9, Russia 8); 13 from Asia; 3 from Australia and New Zealand; 3 from North America; 2 from Africa; and 1 from South America. (See Appendix A for the Statement of Environmental Commitment and a list of the signatories.)

The regional difference in response to the challenge of environmental issues is most marked with respect to climate change. For European insurers and reinsurers the events of the past 15 years—especially major floods (1995, 1997, 2000) and unprecedented windstorms (1987, 1990, 1999)—appear to indicate conclusively that climate change has begun and will have significant impacts on society as a whole and therefore on the insurance industry. However, in the United States the hurricane and tornado losses since Hurricane Andrew have been absorbed by the insurance industry without any serious financial strain. Even hurricanes that made landfall in the United States, like Floyd (1999) and Georges (1998), have not replicated the alarm that followed Hurricane Andrew (Partner Re 1998). Another reason for different perspectives on either side of the Atlantic is that the catastrophe burden is born disproportionately by the reinsurance industry, as it is designed to be. In Europe, reinsurance is a larger portion of the insurance industry as a whole. Europe is home to the world's two largest reinsurance companies (Munich Re and Swiss Re) and to Lloyd's. The following statement, from Munich Re, is representative of the leadership of the industry in Europe:

> *Changes to the setting in which we operate, e.g., population growth, dwindling natural resources, and the increasing strain on the natural environment, have a major influence on our business and are capable of subjecting it to lasting change. . . . We have even assumed a leading position in the worldwide discussion concerning the effects of climate change and the increase in natural catastrophes. (Munich Re 2001c)*

Thus, despite the growing confidence of the pronouncements of the Intergovernmental Panel on Climate Change (IPCC), to the effect that man-made climate change has begun, we have divergent assumptions on either side of the Atlantic. For Europeans climate change is happening and requires a major response, while in the United States it is still not taken seriously at the national policy level despite the urgings of American scientists, municipalities, corporations, NGOs, and members of the public. Under the Bush administration the United States withdrew from the Kyoto Protocol. President Bush then commissioned a new "American" study on climate change from the National Academy of Sciences, even though the original IPCC studies were overwhelmingly the products of American science. Nearly half of the authors were American, with a quarter from Europe and another quarter from the rest of the world. Indeed, it was thanks to American scientific concern in the 1950s that greenhouse gas accumulation in the atmosphere was first put on the global research agenda (Firor 1990). When the President's new energy policy was unveiled in February 2002, it included some reference to energy conservation, but it relied entirely on voluntary measures to reduce greenhouse gas emissions.

A recent study sponsored by the U.S. Department of Energy and the U.S. Environmental Protection Agency referred to "the remarkable difference between U.S. and non-U.S. insurers on the question of climate change," for which various explanations are offered, including negative views on UNEP in some quarters in the United States and a negative association between anything "environmental" and Superfund (Mills et al. 2001, 106). The authors of the study also identify a fear among American insurers that any explicit admission of the threat of climate change will lead to expectations for them to increase their reserves, which is exactly what happened when the asbestos and Superfund crises deepened. The report also noted "the virtual absence of U.S. insurer perception that climate change mitigation could offer business opportunities and other financial co-benefits for insurers" (Mills et al. 2001, 108–109).

As the climate change trend becomes clearer we should expect divergent views among insurers to coalesce. The likely implications of climate change for the whole of the financial services sector and their clients are the subject of Chapter 7.

CONCLUSION

The insurance industry prides itself on its conservatism, in the sense that it considers itself to be well prepared to absorb the costs of the risks to which it is exposed. To a great extent this self-evaluation is correct. The industry has adjusted quite swiftly to the environmental and catastrophic challenges of the past 20 years. However, there have been some alarming moments. The near sinking of Lloyd's under the asbestos and environmental claims was one such moment. The liquidity crunch in the reinsurance industry following Hurricane Andrew was another.

The next chapter considers the role of investors in meeting the challenge of environmental finance. Chapter 5 simply looked at the role of the insurance industry as an underwriter of risk in property and casualty. However, the insurance industry is also a major investor. To what extent does the industry invest in activities that increase the risks covered by the underwriting side of the business?

ENDNOTE

1. Leachate is "the contaminated liquid draining from a sanitary landfill" (Henry and Heinke 1989). Even "clean" municipal solid waste contains organic material, solids, soluble salts, iron, lead, and zinc; in practice, it could contain anything, depending on how strictly the system is managed.

CHAPTER 6

Investments

INTRODUCTION

In Chapters 4 and 5, we have seen that most mainstream institutions that are involved in the extension of commercial credit and property and casualty (P&C) insurance use contractual information about environmental performance. However, no analogous contractual situation for gathering environmental information on companies exists in equity investments. Within this sector, the understanding of environmental issues varies considerably.

Contradictory evidence exists as to the relationship between a firm's environmental performance and its market valuation. While some hold that an environmental focus of strategic planning suggests a potential fiscal liability to companies, others view progressive environmental management as an opportunity not only to reduce costs, but also to find openings to develop new products and services.

In an attempt to gain insight into the factors supporting this divergence of views, this chapter explores first the evolution of the screening processes that have been used to develop socially and environmentally acceptable investment products. We then review previous studies that have attempted to establish a linkage between environmental and financial performance and the relative performance of professionally managed screened funds relative to the broader investment universe. A preliminary discussion reveals reasons for the existence of conflicting evidence regarding the environment-finance nexus. The chapter further comments on the power that institutional portfolio managers have to move social and environmental prioritization from a fringe activity to the mainstream of investment decision making. Finally, we examine the growth in environmental research and benchmarks that have evolved in response to the needs of the investment community for material information regarding corporate environmental and social performance.

EVOLUTION OF SCREENING FOR SOCIAL
AND ENVIRONMENTAL RESPONSIBILITY

Given the new insights that have evolved from the recognition of concepts such as shareholder value and stakeholder management, the context of "green" and socially acceptable investment products has changed in recent years (Knörzer 2001), with socially responsible investing growing over the past decade. Historically, investors have mainly used financial screens in making investment decisions. More recently, social screens have been developed that allow investors the use of nonfinancial criteria with which to express their social or environmental concerns in their investment decision making.

The first generation of social selection techniques focused on screens that barred investment in companies in particular lines of business, such as the manufacture of alcoholic beverages, tobacco products, nuclear power, and armaments. Included in this process were companies that have attracted adverse attention as a result of environmental pollution.

Within this first stage of screening, a shift occurred in the 1970s that took investors from these single, issue-based screens to an investment strategy of more comprehensive social change. This transformation took place during investors' responses to the Sullivan Principles regarding the apartheid regime in South Africa, when they divested themselves of companies operating in that country (Kinder and Domini 1997).

The next stage of screening brought environmental indicators to the fore. This second generation of activities not only screened out egregious offenders, but started to include a positive element that allowed for investment in smaller pioneering companies in cutting-edge environmental technology (Ganzi and DeVries 1998). Examples of these investments would have been found in firms whose sole purpose was to develop environmentally friendly products and services, as well as those whose products concentrate on pollution reduction, such as waste management companies, the recycling industry, and emission control filters and scrubbers. Although this type of screen tended to introduce typically higher reward/risk investments, it still allowed for the avoidance of complete sectors, such as tobacco and nuclear energy, that were viewed as being problematic in specific areas of environmental activity (Ganzi et al. 1998).

The third stage of investment screening involves strategies that allow for the selection of companies within any sector based on their relatively good performance on environmental issues. Here environmental criteria are applied to the full universe of companies in a "best-of-class" approach. In this case, only the companies with the best environmental records are eligible for investment consideration. Positive screens such as pollution prevention measures, use of renewable energy, and conservation policies apply. Such an investment philosophy allows for greater diversification within a portfolio, with all sectors eligible for consideration. This best-of-class method enables portfolio managers to balance the greater risk perceived in the use of nonfinancial screens with the inclusion of more established stocks found in the major industrial sectors such as natural resources that otherwise may be eliminated on environmental grounds (Elkington and Beloe 2000).

An extension of the best-of-class format is found in the application of the criteria of eco-efficiency that allow investment professionals to recognize the potential for companies to meet environmental challenges at the same time as delivering superior profitability. In this way, investors can include environmental responsibility while meeting their fiduciary responsibility. The use of the concept of eco-efficiency allows for the inclusion of some companies or sectors such as energy companies that might otherwise be excluded from investment considerations. The theory of eco-efficiency implies that companies that meet environmental challenges also deliver superior profitability. Testing for superior eco-efficiency recognizes that it is not only the responsible management of downside risk, but also the strategic and operational ability of that management to identify and take advantage of upside opportunities that contributes to shareholder value and competitiveness (Blank and Carty, forthcoming). Table 6.1 gives examples of negative and positive screens that have been used by investors in attempting to incorporate social and environmental issues into their decision making.

This background to the development of the environmental screening process informs the following sections, which describe studies that attempt to use available environmental information to assess whether good environmental performance adds value to a company's financial performance.

THE RELATIONSHIP BETWEEN ENVIRONMENTAL AND FINANCIAL PERFORMANCE

Publicly available information sources of corporate environmental performance exist in a variety of formats. In some cases companies *voluntarily* disclose environmental data in annual financial reports or in questionnaires from institutional rating services. In these cases, information is conveyed on such matters as pollution control expenditures and progressive environmental practices. In other cases, media reporting represents an *involuntary* form of environmental exposure for individual corporations.

TABLE 6.1 Negative and Positive Criteria Used in Social Investment Decision Making

Criteria for Exclusion (Negative)	Criteria for Inclusion (Positive)
Alcoholic beverages	Disclosure of environmental policies
Nuclear power	Increased energy efficiency
Tobacco products	Increased raw material efficiency
Supply services to gambling operations	Recycling/reusing waste material
Production of military weapons	Reduced emissions, discharges, waste
Pesticides manufacture and marketing	Product's positive environmental
Greenhouse gas production	characteristics
Supply/use of ozone-depleting chemicals	Reduction in toxic releases
Environmental violations	
Intensive farming	
Adverse environmental publicity	
Reputational controversies	

Sources: Elkington and Beloe 2000; Tarna 2001; Willis and Desjardins 2001; Blumberg et al. 1997.

Media reports can be either positive (awards) or negative (disasters). *Collective* sources of information, such as reports mandated by national pollution inventory regulations, have also been used in studies in order to examine corporate environmental-financial linkage collectively, rather than at the individual firm level. The U.S. Toxic Release Inventory (TRI) program and Canada's National Pollutant Release Inventory (NPRI) fall into this category.[1] (See also "Mandated Reporting" in Chapter 8).

Over the past decade there has been controversy as to whether any connection exists between a company's environmental behavior and its financial indicators and market valuation. Table 6.2 illustrates the breadth of financial measures and information sources that have been used in studies attempting to link environmental and financial performance.

Measures of Environmental Management

Many researchers associate positive market reaction with the reporting of progressive environmental management practices. In their analysis of 300 large public companies in the United States, Feldman et al. (1996) concluded that investments in environmental management led to substantial reduction of perceived risk, with its concomitant positive valuation by financial markets. Using institutional rating service data, Hart and Ahuja

TABLE 6.2 Linking Environmental and Financial Performance

Study	Information	Event	Methodology	Impact
Blaccioniere and Patten (1994)	10-K report	• Chemical companies' environmental disclosure before Bhopal	Content analysis; multivariate analyses	• Less negative market reaction
Dasgupta et al. (1997)	Print media	• Rewards, recognition	Event Study	• Increase in market value
		• Spills, complaints		• Loss in market value
Dowell et al. (2000)	IRRC[1]	• Global environmental standards	Bivariate, multivariate analyses	• Higher market value
Edwards (1998)	JERU[2]	• Best in sector green companies	Bivariate analyses	• Positive link; environmental performance (EP) and ROC, ROE
Feldman et al (1996)	Environmental management system (EMS) and firm's risk (beta)	• Reporting of improved EMS/EP	Multivariate analyses	• Improved stock price
Hart and Ahuja (1996)	IRRC[1]	• Emission reductions	Multivariate analyses	• Improved ROA, ROS (operating), ROE (financial) performance
Klassen and McLaughlin (1996)	Print media	• Awards and favorable events	Event study	• Increase in market value
		• Disasters		• Loss in market value
Laplante and Lanoie (1994)	Print media	• Lawsuits	Event study	• No impact on equity value
		• Suit settlement		• Loss in market value
		• Investments		• Loss in market value
Muoghalu et al. (1990)	Print media	• Lawsuits	Event study	• Loss in market value
		• Suit settlement		• No impact

(Continued)

145

TABLE 6.2 *(Continued)*

Study	Information	Event	Methodology	Impact
Patten and Nance (1998)	Media	• *Exxon Valdez*	Event study	• Adverse effect on firm value; product price increase
Piesse (1992)	Print media	• *Exxon Valdez*	Event study	• Lower stock value
Russo and Fouts (1997)	FRDC[3]	• Compliance records; environmental expenditures, waste reduction	Multivariate analyses	• Modest variation in ROA
Stanwick and Stanwick (2000)	Corporate environmental disclosures	• Environmental policy, activities	Content analysis; bivariate analyses	• Higher financial performance (income/total assets)
White (1996)	CEP[4]	• Environmental reputation	Event study	• Positive impact
Collective Information				
Blacconiere and Northcutt (1997)	Enactment of SARA	• Market reaction to SARA	Content analysis	• Negative market reaction
Hamilton (1995)	TRI reporting	• On-site releases	Event study	• Negative impact
Khanna et al. (1998)	TRI reporting	• On-site releases • Off-site transfers • Total toxic waste	Event study	• Reduced • Increased • Negligible effect
Konar and Cohen (1997)	TRI reporting	• Market decline following TRI report	Event study	• Greater emission reductions
Lanoie et al. (1997)	Ministry of the Environment, British Columbia, Canada	• Publication of compliance lists	Event study	• No impact on equity value

[1]IRRC: Investor Responsibility Research Center's Corporate Environmental Profile.
[2]JERU: Jupiter Environmental Research Unit.
[3]FRDC: Franklin Research and Development Corporation Environmental Rating.
[4]CEP: Council of Economic Priorities.

(1996), Edwards (1998), and Dowell et al. (2000) presented similar evidence that investments in environmental management are seen as reducing risk, resulting in improved market valuation.

Others indicate that firms with strong environmental management and reporting practices have better stock price returns after a major environmental disaster such as the *Exxon Valdez* (Patten and Nance 1998; Piesse 1992) or the Bhopal accident (Blaccioniere and Patten 1994; White 1996), and after the passing of SARA legislation (Blaccioniere and Northcutt 1997), than those with poor environmental practices.

Using content analysis to examine the impact of Union Carbide's leak at Bhopal on the valuation of stocks of other firms in the chemical industry, Blaccioniere and Patten (1994) observed a negative market reaction, thereby concluding that the incident reflected poorly on the whole chemical industry. They did, however, find less of a negative stock price reaction to adverse media coverage for companies within the chemical industry that had previously published their environmental records.

While investigating the market reaction of another sector's stock prices in the wake of the *Exxon Valdez* incident, White (1996) found that oil companies with better environmental reputations, as established by the Council of Economic Priorities index, experienced a positive impact from the spill, while the others were negatively affected (Ganzi and DeVries 1998). Stanwick and Stanwick (2000) found further evidence of a relationship between financial performance and environmental disclosure. They concluded that firms' disclosures regarding this environmental commitment have a definite positive effect on their net income/total assets. These findings suggest that investors view such disclosures as a sign that the firms demonstrate the ability to manage present and future exposures to environmental costs.

Measures of Environmental Expenditures

Researchers have made conflicting observations as to the contribution of corporate environmental expenditure information to a firm's valuation. Laplante and Lanoie (1994) found that such investments reduced a firm's equity value, while Dasgupta et al. (1997) recorded a positive market reaction to the announcement of environmental expenditures. Russo and Fouts (1997) are positioned between these opposing views, finding only modest levels of variations.

Discrepancies in findings reflect a lack of consensus that exists regarding the profitability of environmental expenditures. Traditional thinkers have considered the environment as a pure cost center, by which investments in environmental improvements impose a "green penalty" on investors (Gottsman and Kessler 1998). For those, the environment is simply assessed in terms of financial liabilities, with the potential liability measured by the cost of what a company is required to do by legislation compared to estimates of remediation costs (Friends of the Earth 2000; Lanoie et al. 1997). Given the small penalties typically imposed on noncompliant firms, loss of market value is likely to be significantly larger than traditional fines imposed by courts and regulators. In an early study of market reactions to environmental mishaps, Piesse (1992) indicated a loss in market value of £670 million after Shell's oil spill in the Mersey River in 1989. This market loss far exceeded the actual cost of cleanup and the £1 million fine imposed on the company.

Further, Muoghalu et al.'s (1990) results indicate an average decline in stock market value of 1.2 percent due to the public announcement of the filing of environmental lawsuits related to the U.S. Resource Conservation and Recovery Act and Superfund Act. This figure translates into an average loss of $33.3 million in equity value due to environmental enforcement measures (Lanoie et al. 1997), an amount significantly larger than traditional penalties at that time. Similarly, Hamilton (1995) translates a 0.2 percent to 0.3 percent negative market reaction into an average loss of $4.1 million in stock value for firms reporting TRI figures on the day that TRI data was released.

Opponents of this train of thought view progressive environmental management as an opportunity, with pollution efficiency being associated with overall production efficiency and lower compliance costs, resulting in a stronger competitive position and improved financial performance (Lanoie et al. 1997).

An extension of the "green penalty" concept is found in the pollution haven hypothesis of multinational corporations (MNCs) investing in emerging or developing countries. Such arguments suggest that it is cheaper to operate in countries where environmental regulations are either lax or not enforced than it is where strict pollution control regulations are in effect (Eskeland and Harrison 1997). Under this scenario, it would appear that the market value of companies attempting to achieve higher environmental standards when investing in developing countries would be negatively affected. A competing argument would posit that relocation to a pollution haven in order to operate at lower environmental standards would violate firmwide corporate environmental policies, as MNCs pursue global competitive strategies (Dowell et al 2000). A number of studies (Dasgupta et al. 1997; Hettige et al. 1992; World Bank

1999) attempt to address this dilemma. In the examination of the potential impact of environmental regulations on international competitiveness, these studies conclude that pollution-intensive firms generally have not invested or relocated in developing countries in order to benefit from poor environmental regulations or enforcement.

Sources of Information

As seen in the preceding section, measures of corporate environmental performance can emanate from a variety of information sources.

Varied results are seen in studies that use *involuntary* reporting sources, such as media reports of environmental incidents. Muoghalu et al. (1990) and Laplante and Lanoie (1994) offer conflicting results with respect to environmental lawsuits and the resolution of those suits published in the press. In the United States, Muoghalu et al. found a significant loss in market value on the filing of a lawsuit, but no significant abnormal return at the settlement of that suit. In performing a similar analysis in Canada, Laplante and Lanoie found, in contrast, abnormal losses when a company was found guilty and fines were imposed, but no losses when the lawsuit was initiated.

Positive media reports as sources of information, however, demonstrate a greater degree of consensus. Using media reports of environmental award announcements, researchers such as Klassen and McLaughlin (1996) and Dasgupta et al. (1997) demonstrate that positive media coverage has a significant impact on a firm's market valuation.

In the use of *collective* sources of information such as government compliance reports, there is further evidence of a lack of consensus regarding investors' expectations of a company's environmental performance (Cormier and Magnan 1997). Investors' response patterns to Toxic Release Inventory reporting provide an instructive example that investors' expectations are embedded in the prices of corporate stocks. Firms in highly polluting sectors in the United States experienced significant negative market returns after the initial TRI data was reported in the media in 1989—information that was previously unknown (Hamilton 1995; Khanna et al. 1998). Conversely, in a Canadian study of the reporting of noncompliant companies in British Columbia, Lanoie et al.'s (1997) results indicate that the publication of such information had no impact on market values of companies identified by the government as polluters.

Lanoie et al. (1997) suggest the discrepancy between the Canadian results and those from the United States may be explained in two ways. First, they propose that the Canadian list of polluters may not provide new or unexpected information to the investors, since the Canadian report identifies a much smaller market than the U.S. study, in which TRI polluters are likely to be less known and recognizable to investors. Furthermore, Lanoie et al. (1997) advance the argument that the Canadian companies are most likely in the primary sector, where an adverse impact on reputation may affect demand less than the publication of TRI data, which covers a broader set of industries. They also suggest that the U.S. environmental authorities have been more successful in creating a credible threat to polluting firms than have their Canadian provincial counterparts.

In a corollary to these environmental/financial studies, there are implications that public reporting has become the driving force that induces firms to change their environmental behavior. Looking at the market response to the 1989 TRI report, Konar and Cohen (1997) demonstrated that the companies that were most severely affected by negative market reaction were those that showed the greatest reduction in their TRI emissions the following years. In a similar study that examines the effects of negative investor reactions to TRI reporting, Khanna et al. (1998) indicate that, following the release of TRI data, significant stock market losses in the chemical industry were followed by noteworthy reductions in on-site toxic releases accompanied by major increases in off-site waste transfers. They found, however, a negligible impact on the total volume of toxic waste generated.

The Program for Pollution Control, Evaluation, and Rating (PROPER), Indonesia's widely publicized public disclosure pollution control program, provides an insight into the effects of mandated environmental reporting in developing economies. With the help of the World Bank, Indonesian officials have designed a color-coded five-tier scheme by which to rank companies, spanning from beyond compliance (gold) to flagrant violation (black). A World Bank (1999) examination of the initiative concluded that the public disclosure of companies receiving poor environmental ratings under the program caused the companies to improve their compliance records. It could be construed that PROPER spurred change through improving factory managers' information about their own plants' pollution reduction opportunities. Afsah et al. (2000) suggest, however, that the effect of environmental audits worked in tandem with external pressures, and that public disclosure of corporate environmental behavior created an informed society, which in turn pressured companies to improve their pollution abatement records.

In another study related to developing and emerging markets, Dasgupta et al. (1997) concluded that capital markets in Argentina, Chile,

Mexico, and the Philippines appear to react to environmental events involving publicly traded companies, if properly informed by the media. This suggests that the mandated release of firms' environmental performance data in those countries would create a driving force for improved environmental performance, as has been seen with the U.S. TRI data disclosures. Viewed from the perspective of the U.S.-based corporations with global operations, Dowell et al. (2000) indicate that firms adopting stringent global environmental standards have much higher market values than firms that default to less stringent host country environmental standards and enforcement. There are indications, then, that little support exists for the assumption that emerging and developing nations are burdened with a "green penalty" from corporations that operate in their jurisdictions.

PERFORMANCE OF ENVIRONMENTALLY SCREENED FUNDS

The Social Investment Forum trend report (1999) indicates that 79 percent of SRI funds use environmental performance as at least one screen. Thus it is instructive to examine research that has looked at broader socially screened funds, as well as those that specifically address environmental issues.

In early studies of the impact of social screening on fund performance, Hamilton et al. (1993) found no significant difference between the returns of socially screened funds that used a combination of positive and negative criteria and conventional mutual funds. In a similar study using a similar combination of criteria, Guerard (1997) showed that all screens, with one exception, produce portfolios with higher returns. The only social criterion that consistently cost the investor was the military screen. By contrast, in a study of U.S. and German environmental mutual funds, White (1995) concluded that environmentally screened funds underperformed, causing investors to receive lower returns than from conventionally constructed mutual funds. He conceded, however, that the German screened funds came closer to matching the returns of unscreened funds and outperformed their U.S. counterparts. (See Table 6.3.)

Rather than compare performance figures of existing funds, other researchers compare theoretically constructed portfolios to market indexes such as the S&P or Financial Times Stock Exchange indexes. They conclude that the simulated environmental portfolios demonstrate overall performances that are very similar to market indexes that include a larger,

TABLE 6.3 Assessment of Performance of Environmentally Screened Funds

Study	Focus	Comparison	Relationship
Cohen et al. (1995)	Portfolios based on high and low pollution	S&P 500 Index	No penalty for green investing
Gottsman and Kessler (1998)	Theoretical environmental portfolios	S&P 500 Index	Little difference in stock market performance
Guerard (1997)	Socially screened funds	Unscreened funds	No significant association between returns and environmental screens
Hamilton et al. (1993)	Screened mutual funds	Unscreened funds	No difference in returns
Havemann and Webster (1999)	Simulated funds	Financial Times Stock Exchange All-Share Index	Performance similar to market indexes
White (1995)	U.S. and German environmental sector funds	S&P 500 Index, Domini Social Index, Deutsche Aktienindex	Relatively poor returns

general investment universe (Cohen et al. 1995; Gottsman and Kessler 1998; Havemann and Webster 1999).

VARIATION IN RESEARCH RESULTS

Studies involving either individual companies and sectors or mutual fund performance figures illustrate that researchers have used an assortment of indicators, data sets, and techniques in the examination of the environment-finance nexus.

The results of the examination of screened mutual funds consistently suggest that a balanced portfolio of good environmental performers has not harmed investment performance. The authors warn, however, that results should not be interpreted to mean that a "green premium" exists, but rather that there is not a "green penalty" associated with environmentally conscious investing.

By contrast, the comparisons by researchers of the environmental and financial performance of companies or sectors have shown some inconsistent results, ranging from negative through tenuously positive to significant relationships. These discrepancies may be due in part to conceptual differences in the definitions and measurement of environmental performance, as well as to varying methodologies undertaken to operationalize these concepts. Discussions of these variations in definition, data selection, analytical approaches, and financial impacts follow.

Definition and Measurement

Lack of consensus in the definition and measurement of corporate environmental performance across industries adds one level of difficulty for researchers of corporate financial and environmental performance. Interpretation of what it means to be "green" varies as different groups of stakeholders exhibit differing opinions as to what constitutes acceptable environmental behavior.

Measurements of environmental behavior vary as well, from a broad range of inputs such as pollution control expenditure, to internal process and product characteristics, to outputs covering an array of indicators from emissions reductions to stakeholder relations. Analyses are further confounded by the inclusion, in some cases, of qualitative "soft" environmental facts in the measurement of a firm's environmental progress. By their very nature, indicators such as the quality of environmental management or product characteristics often do not lend themselves to quantitative measurement.

Data Selection

In addition, available data used in analyses is a function of existing information sources. Studies using media reports concentrate more on individual firms, while the use of mandated reports lends itself to a broader cross section of companies and industries. Case study methodology, by its very nature, can be applied to only a limited sampling of companies.

The process of compilation of data also engenders certain levels of skepticism. Voluntary corporate environmental disclosure is seen in some cases as primarily an exercise in self-reporting and therefore preconceived as being partial.

Reputational indexes, such as the Fortune 500, which are also informed through corporate self-reporting plus interviews with company executives, are viewed by some as being purely perceptual and by others as simply a measure of overall management, rather than specifically environmental management. Mandated reporting such as TRI, although a publicly available data source, is also viewed as being a self-reported measure and, as such, lends itself to accusations of corporate bias (Griffin and Mahon 1997).

Finally, others suggest that data gleaned from survey instruments, such as content analysis, reputational indexes, or pollution control investments, are used as surrogate measures of corporate environmental performance and, used in isolation, capture only part of the complete environmental portrait of a firm (Waddock and Graves 1997).

Analytical Approaches

Further, we observe a variety of analytical approaches used in these studies. In some cases, event studies are used to ascertain whether new information about a company's environmental behavior has a financial impact on the firm. Others attempt to establish a link between environmental and financial performance through the use of content analysis, as well as correlation and regression analysis. Methodologies using content and multivariate analysis of corporate environmental disclosures, however, depend very much on the purposes for which the relevant sources of information were originally created (Waddock and Graves 1997). Finally, performance indicators are used to construct theoretical portfolios, which are then compared to a benchmark over some specified period of time (Repetto and Austin 2000).

Measuring corporate social and financial performance across industries is seen as adding another level of difficulty to these analyses. Indeed, different industries inherently experience differing issues and pressures due to diverse political cultures and configurations of stakeholders (Griffin and Mahon 1997; Pritchard 2000; Elkington and Beloe 2000; EPA 2000). Thus not all measures are applicable to every industry. For example, in the chemical industry resource use and toxic releases would be given more importance. By contrast, in financial services companies the quality of environmental management and their product characteristics take on a greater importance (Joly 2001).

Financial Measures

Finally, different indicators reflecting environmental impacts on companies' financial performance have been used. In some cases historical accounting measures such as return on assets (ROA) and return on earnings

(ROE) are used. In others, financial impact is measured by excess market valuation and abnormal returns in response to environmental disclosures (alpha). Still others examine risk instruments, such as beta (e.g., Feldman et al. 1996).

SOCIALLY RESPONSIBLE INVESTMENT
PORTFOLIO PERFORMANCE RATINGS

In 2000, Morningstar, the leading mutual fund analyst in the United States, noted that only 13 percent of socially responsible investment (SRI) funds received its five-star performance rating in 2000, compared to 21 percent the year before. This drastic downturn was tied, in no small way, to an overexposure to technology stocks, which have taken a beating over the past two years. In addition, many SRI funds avoided investments in energy and oil stocks, which had a good year due to rising fuel prices (Bayon 2001a). This was the explanation given for the Domini 400 Social Index's poor performance relative to its S&P benchmark in December 2000, with its overexposure to the computer hardware industry and underexposure to the energy sector (Environmental Finance 2001a).

Conversely, smaller, more specialized groups benefited from their large holdings in alternative energy companies. Funds such as New Alternatives and Green Century outperformed the market by 52 percent and 13 percent respectively. The Green Century fund, for instance, is solely concerned with companies that are environmentally sensitive and proactive. As a result, it gravitated toward companies in fuel cell production as well as wind and solar energy industries, all of which performed well in 1999 compared to traditional technology companies (Bayon 2001a).

Investment baskets of environmental technology stocks have shown impressive returns compared to typical information technology funds. Environmental technology companies have been in existence since the 1970s, but their performance was often tied to macroeconomic conditions. When times were prosperous, the environment was in vogue and environmental cleanup was affordable. During economic downturns, their performance was less robust. Now, however, increased stakeholder pressures and deregulation of the basic services (energy, water supply and treatment, and waste collection and treatment) have created opportunities for environmental technologies (Simm and Jenkyn-Jones 2000). In order to reduce the risk of investing in individual companies or subsectors of environmental technology, many companies are developing baskets of investments that include related components across these markets. (See UBS Warburg fuel cell baskets in Chapter 4.)

Havemann and Webster (1999) have shown that the use of ethical criteria in the selection of portfolios can have a variety of effects upon investment performance. They demonstrate that screening designed to develop an Environmental Management Index led to an overweighting in resource, consumer goods, and utility stocks, with an underweighting in financials and services, compared to the FTSE All-Share Index. Conversely, their development of an Environmental Damage Avoidance Index tends to overweight services and financials, while it underweights industrials, utilities, and resources in general. In fact, there are no companies in the resource sector left in this index.

Kurtz (1995) adds that SRI screening can also result in an underweighting of large-cap companies, since technology firms tend to be smaller or medium-sized. In addition, there are not enough stocks that pass the screening process that can substitute for excluded large caps such as General Electric or Philip Morris.

A further factor affecting SRI indexes and portfolios is found in issues of currency exchange rates. In 2000, the Dow Jones Sustainability Index (DJSI) exhibited a very poor performance, falling 18 percent in dollar terms, compared to 14 percent for its benchmark, the Dow Jones Global Index. The reason for this becomes apparent in reviewing the index's portfolio. The DJSI is heavily weighted toward euro-zone stocks, which fell as the euro plunged 8 percent against the dollar, dragging the DJSI with it (Cooper 2001).

Variations in levels of performance are also found between actively managed funds and passively managed index funds. Since index funds are 100 percent invested all the time, they typically outperform actively managed stock funds in rising markets, since the latter are not fully invested to the same extent that index funds are. By contrast, actively managed stock funds do better in volatile and declining markets, in part because a portion of the portfolio is retained in cash, which is less vulnerable in uncertain markets (Barnes 2001).

INSTITUTIONAL PORTFOLIO MANAGERS

By virtue of the size of their investment portfolios, managers of institutional portfolios such as pension funds and mutual funds have the power to move environmental prioritization from a niche market to the mainstream of investment decision making through the use of environmental screens, active engagement, and divestment strategies.

According to the Social Investment Forum (1999), the United States has the most advanced SRI market, with approximately 12 percent of professionally managed assets in socially responsible portfolios. SRI represents about 3.2 percent in Canada (SIO 2000), while comparable figures for Australia stand at 0.7 percent of managed equity funds (Allen Consulting Group 2000). Recent trends do indicate, however, that SRI awareness is rising in Australia and Asia (Box 6.1).

Among institutionally managed portfolios, pension funds alone account for over one-third of corporate equity in the United States and United Kingdom, making them substantial shareholders. As such, they hold a potentially high degree of influence over corporate policy (Neale 2001).

Until recently, traditional fiduciary responsibility of pension fund administrators has implied purely financial benefits for pension fund beneficiaries. Indeed, one of the most common arguments against inclusion of nonfinancial investment criteria in the Employment Retirement Income Security Act (ERISA) in the United States is that inclusion would violate ERISA's definition of fiduciary responsibility (Aspen Institute 1998). Thus, pension fund managers have viewed their role almost exclusively as promoting shareholder value.

BOX 6.1   Indications of Increased SRI Awareness in Australia and Asia

In Australia, Rothschild Australia Asset Management launched two socially responsible funds in 2001, following a survey that indicated growing demand for such products (Environmental Finance 2001c). In Japan, nine new SRI funds were launched since the beginning of 2000 (Marshall 2001).

As well, in 2001, the Association of Sustainable and Responsible Investment in Asia (AsrIA) launched a new web site, www.asria.org, aimed at raising awareness and promoting the development of SRI across the region. In its intent to promote global best practice in Asia from the outset by pursuing SRI as a market mechanism within the investment community, AsrIA has the distinction of having an industry association established before industry arrives in the area (Marshall 2001).

Historically, pension fund managers have maintained an arms-length relationship with companies in which they invest, never feeling that it was their prerogative to apply any form of screening process. Nor did these managers have much involvement with pension fund beneficiaries in determining investment policies (Neale 2001). Indeed, in the mid-1980s, the legal limits of social activity in pension funds were defined in a U.K. high court ruling against the National Union of Mineworkers' attempt to end oil industry investment by the coal industry's pension fund. At that time, the judge argued that the sole purpose of a pension fund was to promote benefits, and that the trustees therefore should do nothing to damage financial performance, including social screens or constraints (Neale 2001).

Recently, with changes in fund manager policies and new regulations governing pension fund reporting, there appears to be a significant change in how fiduciary responsibility is being interpreted. One change that started in the United States has been in the definition of the fiduciary guarantee, and therefore the responsibility, of some private and occupational pension fund administrators. It has been changed from defined benefit, where the company guarantees an employee's pension, to defined contribution, where the individual has the opportunity to manage his/her own money. Under these circumstances, retirement plans have the potential to allow beneficiaries to express their environmental and social preferences through their pension plans. Since these schemes are intended to act in the interest of their members, those same beneficiaries can now apply pressure for a socially responsible approach to their retirement funds (Aspen Institute 1998; Friedman 2000; Neale 2001).

In July 2000 in the United Kingdom, changes in the Pension Disclosure Regulation obliged trustees of pension funds to state the extent to which social, environmental, and ethical considerations are taken into account in the selection, retention, and realization of the fund's investments. This shift in disclosure requirements may signal a potential change in the characterization of fiduciary responsibility. The success of the U.K. regulation is making other countries consider similar rulings. For example, in January 2001 the Green Members of Parliament in Germany succeeded in inserting disclosure regulations for private pensions into legislation that is being proposed to reform that country's pension system (Kahlenborn 2001).

The Dutch pension fund giant ABP provides further evidence of the inclusion of SRI criteria in pension investment strategies. In July 2001, ABP created two new SRI portfolios with the help of Innovest's rating methodology (see Innovest case study later in chapter). Using this technique, ABP will invest in the same companies and sectors as its fund's mainstream benchmarks, the Morgan Stanley Capital International (MSCI) Europe index and the S&P 500, but will change the weightings according to social and environmental criteria.

Recent pension legislation in Hong Kong provides another opportunity for the institutionalization of SRI in this part of Asia. In 2000, the Hong Kong government legislated the development of private pension schemes for all employees. Although this compulsory program provides members with choices in the mix of equity and fixed income, there is not as yet any option for socially responsible investing. "This is likely to change," says Euan Marshall (2001), the business director at AsrIA, "since a number of Hong Kong pressure groups are already demanding such product choices."

These changes in definition of fiduciary responsibility and disclosure requirements may signal that not paying attention to environmental and social issues in the future could be interpreted as a dereliction of responsibility.

Shareholder Activism

The complete picture of socially responsible investing is painted by the Social Investment Forum (1999) as comprising three strategies: positive and negative screening practices, shareholder activism, and community-based investment programs.

Individual groups of environmental investors are now responding to poor corporate environmental management through active shareholding practices such as shareholder resolutions and divestment strategies, in order to pressure targeted companies to improve environmental or social performance (Bayon 2001b; Elkington and Beloe 2000). Shareholder resolutions such as those filed at the Shell 1997 annual general meeting illustrate the public's increasing expectations with respect to multinational corporations' behavior patterns (Marinetto 1998). If such tactics fail to trigger the required response, these stakeholders may register their disapproval by selling the stocks of the company concerned. While dissatisfied customers can undertake product boycotts, which affect a firm's cash flow and profitability, the exit of dissatisfied investors can lead to a decrease in corporate market value along with a concomitant increase in the cost of capital (Angel and Rivoli 1997; Kinder and Domini 1997).

Pension and mutual fund managers have a sliding scale of responses that they can use to encourage companies to heed their environmental advice. These fund managers can make their voices heard through policies of active positive engagement with companies under scrutiny. They can meet regularly with top corporate managers to encourage and persuade them to improve environmental performance. An exit strategy of selling the company's shares is not always practical for pension and mutual fund managers, since the divesture of a large holding would, of its own accord, depress the selling price. But if active discussions fall short of their intended goal, fund managers can ultimately still vote against reports and accounts at annual general meetings of the companies in question (Beloe 2000).

Shareholder activism by institutional investors appears to have had some effect on changing corporate governance strategies of targeted companies (Smith 1996). Strategies of active engagement, shareholder voting, and divestment have all been used in the institutional investment field, and are noted in the following subsections. With few exceptions, however, hardly any institutional investment manager attempts to measure his engagement success. Although debate continues as to how to measure the success of institutional investors' SRI strategies, the United Kingdom's Friends Provident has kept a detailed record of all engagement contacts and reports since the inception of its Responsible Engagement overlay in May 2000 (Nicholls 2001c).

Pension Funds

The Teachers Insurance and Annuity Association–College Retirement Equities Fund (TIAA-CREF) has the potential to influence social investing through its scrutiny of firms' governance issues in its Social Choice Equity Fund portfolio (Carleton et al. 1998). In addition, the New York and California state pension funds have become leaders in developing their roles as active shareholders. The California Public Employees' Retirement System (CalPERS), well known for its shareholder activist strategies, recorded significant stock price reactions in targeted companies held by CalPERS as it successfully engaged in an active dialogue to change the companies' governance structures.

Under the leadership of its president and chief executive officer, Claude Lamoureux, the Ontario Teachers Pension Plan demonstrated similar action in 2001, by voting against proposals to upgrade stock options and other incentive plans put forward by companies such as retailer Hudson's Bay Company, printing multimedia company Quebecor Inc., fertilizer producer Potash Corporation of Saskatchewan, and real estate giant TrizecHahn Corporation (Silcoff 2001).

Mutual Funds

In the United Kingdom, two leading fund managers, Henderson Global Investors and Morley Fund Management, have incorporated SRI principles into their investment criteria, with guidelines indicating a threat to vote against reports and accounts of any of the FTSE 100 companies that fall short of expected levels of social behavior (Nicholls 2001a). Indeed, Morley, the fund management arm of the United Kingdom's largest insurance group, CGNU, has stated that it will vote against the reports and accounts of any of the 100 largest U.K. companies that do not publish a stand-alone environmental report (Tindale 2001).

Similarly, in partnering with the Calvert Group in the United States, the Vanguard Group of funds (Box 6.2) not only applies the Calvert Social Index to its screening process, but also adopts Calvert's pledge of social and environmental activism and, as such, actively votes the shares held in its SRI funds to encourage better environmental and social performance.

Going one step further, Walden Asset Management in the United States chose a divestment strategy, and sold its holdings in Safety-Kleen, created in a 1994 merger of four environmental service companies, because of continued hazardous waste violations both in the United States and abroad (Elkington and Beloe 2000).

BOX 6.2   Vanguard Calvert Social Index Fund

> Vanguard Calvert Social Index Fund uses the social index designed by the Calvert Group's broadly diversified SRI index to screen companies' environmental performance and their approach to labor relations, product safety, and policies on animal welfare, military weapons, community relations, and human rights, including the rights of indigenous people. In addition to screening, Vanguard has declared it will vote its shares held in SRI funds in line with its environmental and social expectations. A further impact that Vanguard will have is on SRI fees and expenses, since it charges less than 0.3 percent (30 basis points), compared, for example, to Calvert's own Social Index fund, which tracks the same index and charges almost triple that amount.
>
> *Source:* Bayon 2001b.

In contrast to the SRI managerial activism by U.S. funds, their United Kingdom counterparts seem to be taking a less aggressive approach, preferring behind-the-scenes dialogue to exercising shareholders' rights (Nicholls 2001b). At its 2001 annual general meeting in the United Kingdom, British Petroleum (BP) was presented with two resolutions by environmental and human rights groups. One, organized by Greenpeace, would have BP withdraw its 2 percent ($580 million) investment in PetroChina on human rights grounds. The other directed BP to set out its plans for reducing and eventually phasing out its production and sale of fossil fuels, in line with its recent adoption of the slogan "beyond petroleum" (Bahree 2001). The activists were supported by only 7.4 percent of the votes cast on the environmental issue, and even less for the human rights concerns, with none of the U.K. SRI fund managers backing the environmental resolution. Fund spokespersons indicated a greater desire for active engagement and an equally strong desire not to upset BP's management if the company has given a commitment to the issue at hand (Nicholls 2001b).

Corporate Perspectives on Shareholder Activism

Shareholder activism and market pressures can also be viewed from the company's perspective. The widely publicized attack on Canada's largest independent oil producer, Talisman Energy Inc., in 2001 and its participation in a Sudanese oil consortium serves as a classic example of the ultimate effect of shareholder activism and market pressures. In the face of rising pressure by dozens of advocacy, religious, and ideologically affiliated groups to divest themselves of their oil operations in war-torn Sudan, Talisman's stance has been that it is doing more good than harm by providing Sudanese with jobs and development, as well as by trying to pressure the Sudanese government to observe human rights conventions. Nor did the divestment of Talisman stock from the portfolios of a number of pension funds have any visible effect on the company. But when the New York Stock Exchange threatened to remove Talisman from its roster, executives of the firm considered selling its controversial stake in Sudan's oil fields rather than lose access to U.S. capital markets. This concern was further heightened after the terrorist attacks on the World Trade Center in New York City, when Talisman feared a ban on investments in any countries suspected of harboring terrorist activities (Nguyen 2001).

ENVIRONMENTAL PRODUCTS IN FUND MANAGEMENT

The socially responsible investing sector is, according to some estimates, worth over $2 trillion in the United States and over £25 billion in the United Kingdom (Elkington and Beloe 2000). The management of funds, therefore, becomes a focus of consideration, as fund managers not only take into account financial considerations, but also give priority to social and environmental issues. The following subsections look at techniques of SRI analysis as well as the selection criteria of a number of mutual fund managers. Later in the chapter the section titled "Investable Indexes" will examine further the potential for investing in passively managed funds that are based on the development of a number of social indexes.

Sarasin Bank's Oekosar Sustainable Development Fund   Bank Sarasin & Cie. launched one of the earliest eco-efficiency funds in 1994. The Oekosar Sustainable Development Fund uses the seven-step analysis, based on the Basel Concept of Eco-Controlling, that is outlined in Table 6.4.

The deciding factors for the investor are: how management is using environmental protection as a strategic opportunity rather than merely risk control, how the strategy is implemented, and how the combination of environmental and economic success contributes to shareholder value (www.sarasin.ch/sarasin).

UBS (Lux) Equity Fund—Eco Performance   In addition to monitoring the dynamics of the markets, interest rates, currencies, and traditional financial analyses, UBS Asset Management looks at companies' environmental and social performance from a best-of-class perspective. Their analyses are then validated by a plausibility test, carried out by the Basel-based rating agency ecos.ch ag, which examines companies' environmental and social claims. The use of its industry-specific criteria allows for a standardized comparison between companies.

UBS (Lux) Equity Fund—Eco Performance (1997) pursues a twin-track strategy in selecting individual companies by investing in both eco-leaders and eco-innovators. With this investment strategy, the portfolio managers address some performance issues introduced earlier in the chapter. They are able to combine industry eco-leaders, which are usually large, often blue-chip, companies such as Sony and Unilever, with eco-innovators, which tend to be small and medium-sized companies. This latter group of companies offer products and services that promote innovative approaches for saving resources, such as renewable energy sources. Thus

TABLE 6.4 Seven-Step Analysis of Sarasin's Oekosar Sustainable Development Fund

Step 1—**Financial analysis:** Verification of eco-efficiency with ratios such as percent change in production or cash flow/percent energy consumption, waste generation, or CO_2 emissions, which indicate whether the selected environmental strategy has influenced the market position positively or whether some pollutant reduction has simply been reached by discontinuing certain activities. Some environmental values, such as water consumption and energy use, directly affect the profit-and-loss statement, while others, such as the company's impact from CO_2 emissions, bear a more tenuous interpretation.

Step 2—**Negative screens:** Companies with important activities in sensitive industries such as defense, auto, nuclear power, and agrochemicals are excluded as investment possibilities. Social problems such as employment of minors and tobacco consumption are taken into account as well.

Step 3—**Benchmarking:** All enterprises are measured according to previously defined minimum standards that take into account the environmental impacts and advantages attributable to different activities and sectors. Measurements are registered on a gradation of three possible levels of environmental behavior.

Step 4—**Questionnaire:** Along with the financial data compiled under Step 1, the questionnaire provides a subset of data management within the eco-controlling cycle. In this step, the management is evaluated on its position concerning four dimensions of sustainable development:

Environmental policy/strategy—helps with assessment of corporate image.

Production processes—resource use and waste emissions, also includes supplier linkages.

Products—including materials used, packaging, final disposal, and research and development (R&D) for continual improvement.

Environmental management systems—according to which standard the company works (EMAS, ISO 14001, BS7750).

Step 5—**Evaluation/weighting:** The four sustainable development dimensions mentioned in Step 4 are subjected to different valuations according to the specific conditions of the industry or sector under scrutiny. This step helps clarify the ecological leverage of products and services with respect to economic consequences.

Step 6—**Published material:** Outside material included in the evaluation includes studies by industry associations and environmental protection agencies, publicly available databases, and press releases.

Step 7—**Environmental contribution:** This step represents the ultimate evaluation of the enterprise and positions the company within its sector. The combination of environmental and economic criteria gives a simplified aggregate, which is then used to evaluate eco-efficiency.

Source: Schaltegger and Sturm 1998.

the investment strategy combines the strengths and success of large companies with the innovative potential of smaller ones. The fund's asset mix is approximately 80 percent in eco-leaders and 20 percent in eco-innovators. Such a distribution allows for diversification across all important industries (www.ubs.com/funds).

UBS Nihon Kabushiki Eco Fund   This fund, called Eco Hakase (Doctor Eco) for short, was launched in Japan in 1999. Eco Hakase is designed exclusively for the Japanese market and contains only securities in Japanese companies. The predominant investors in this product are women. The environmental analysis of Japanese companies is carried out by the Japan Research Institute in Tokyo. Criteria applied are, for all intents and purposes, the same as those used by the ecos research specialists used by UBS in Zurich (www.ubs.com/funds).

CASE STUDY: Storebrand Investments

Storebrand Investments is a subsidiary of Storebrand Group of Norway. The parent company, Storebrand Livsforsikring, a charter member of the UNEP Insurance Initiative, has a strong policy on corporate social responsibility. Its focus on environmental issues has provided it with new business opportunities and has improved its reputation among customers, as revealed in a public survey (Joly 2001). In addition to its standard investment management activities, Storebrand also offers both managed environmental funds and discretionary investment management services that use socially responsible criteria.

Storebrand Principle Group of Funds

Storebrand Scudder's Environmental Value Fund (EVF), launched in 1996 in a joint venture with Scudder, Stevens and Clark Ltd, was converted in 2000 to the Storebrand Principle Global Fund (PGF). PGF represents Storebrand's SRI flagship, and has been broadened to include three new, related SRI funds: Storebrand Principle U.K. Fund, Storebrand Principle Europe Fund, and Storebrand Principle European Bond Fund.

These funds are actively managed using eco-efficiency criteria to derive data that is generated internally. For Storebrand, eco-efficiency is defined as the degree to which a firm is able to generate more goods and services while producing less pollution or causing less degradation of natural resources than its competitors (Storebrand Scudder 1996).

Originally, the Environmental Value Fund (EVF) screening process involved nine environmental indicators, including an indication of the firm's environmental liabilities. Table 6.5 indicates the metrics used in the quantification of these eco-efficiency indicators. Using the EVF methodology, analysts for the PGF also apply certain negative screens related to issues of the production and sale of land mines, tobacco, chemicals, or pesticides on UNEP's list of banned persistent organic pollutants (POPs), as well as genetically modified crops that produce sterile seeds.[2]

TABLE 6.5   Indicators Used in Storebrand Analysis for Socially Responsible Investing

Indicator	Unit
Global warming	Tons of CO_2 per unit of sales
Ozone depletion	Tons of chlorofluorocarbon (CFC) equivalent per unit of sales
Material intensity	Tons of waste per unit of sales
Toxic releases	Tons of toxic release per unit of sales
Energy intensity	Terra joules per unit of sales
Intensity of water use	Million cubic meters per unit of sales
Environmental liabilities	Percent of shareholder equity
Quality of environmental management	Points
Product characteristics	Points

A point worthy of note is that Storebrand's Principle Group of Funds has removed the environmental liability indicator from its original list of environmental criteria, due to a lack of available data to evaluate this criterion. The issue of the reporting of future liabilities will be raised again as an important component in the discussion of environmental reporting and verification as outlined in Chapter 8.

The remaining eight criteria are selectively weighted according to how appropriate an indicator would be for a specific sector. In the chemical sector, for example, all criteria are relevant, but a greater weighting is put on material intensity and toxic releases. By contrast, many of the criteria are not applicable in the financial sector. Consequently, quality of environmental management and product characteristics alone determine their ratings.

Storebrand marks this group of funds solely in Norway, but the company has partnered with other organizations to extend its SRI reach beyond that country's borders. Storebrand and the Sancroft Group have undertaken a joint venture to service the U.K. institutional savings and pensions market, while in France, Cortal (a subsidiary of BNP-Paribas) distributes the Principle Funds mainly to individuals, and Apogé-Acacia distributes the same funds mainly to associations, foundations, and corporations. Tower Asset Management distributes a variant of the Principle funds in New Zealand and Australia.

STOREBRAND'S TRIPLE RETURN REPORTING

Storebrand's Principle Group of Funds has initiated a creative format of sustainable development in its triple bottom line reporting (Box 6.3), which enables investors to appreciate the environmental and social rewards of SRI in terms of the criteria used by Storebrand in stock screening.

In order to reveal further insights into the decision-making process, Storebrand makes some of its sector analyses publicly available. In addition, it publishes policy position papers that attempt to reflect societal values as well as fiduciary requirements. Summaries of two sector analyses and two position papers are provided in Box 6.4.

BOX 6.3   Storebrand's Triple Return Reporting

Storebrand's Triple Return comprises financial return in excess of the benchmark MSCI World index, an Environmental Return reflecting the investment's eco-efficiency record, and a Social Return recording the company's strong social performance.

The Environmental Return for a given fund is measured by the difference between the average eco-efficiency of the companies held in the portfolio and the market average. This figure will always be positive for firms selected for inclusion in the Principle Group of Funds. Indeed, given the stringent stock selection process, the market average refers to only those companies selected to be in Storebrand's database, and as such the true market average is likely to be much lower. The Environmental Return represents a measurable benefit to the environment created by the companies in which the fund has invested.

Source: Joly 2001.

BOX 6.4   Storebrand's Industry Analyses and Position Papers

HEALTH AND PERSONAL CARE

Two of Storebrand's eight environmental indicators were used to rate firms in this industry. The indicators chosen were: quality of environmental management (given an 80% weight) and product characteristics (20% weight). These two indicators were chosen because data for the other indicators were unavailable. Out of 14 firms analyzed in this sector, four were admitted into the investment universe. Storebrand also provided a company report for L'Oreal. This report showed L'Oreal's scores on both indicators, as well as its overall rating. The report was thorough, discussing specific strengths and weaknesses in the company's environmental approach and providing guidance for areas that need improvement.

CHEMICAL INDUSTRY

Seven of the eight available indicators were used to assess firms in this industry. The indicators chosen were weighted as follows: global warming (15% weight), material intensity (15%), toxic releases (15%), energy intensity (10%), water intensity (10%), product characteristics (10%), and quality of environmental management (25%). The

(Continued)

BOX 6.4   *(Continued)*

---

ozone depletion indicator was not used because most firms in this industry have virtually eliminated all use of such substances, rendering this indicator largely irrelevant. Storebrand provided a company rating for Bayer. Bayer was rated above average on six of the indicators, and slightly below average on the material intensity indicator. Its combined environmental index score was enough to qualify Bayer for inclusion in the investment universe. As in the L'Oreal example, the report discussed specific strengths and weaknesses of Bayer's approach and listed areas for improvement.

GENETIC ENGINEERING POSITION PAPER

To be included in the investment universe, companies involved with producing or selling genetically modified organisms (GMOs) must document the products' benefits and manage GMO-related risks, in addition to performing extensive testing of the products. Companies using gene protection technologies that result in sterile seeds are excluded from the investment universe altogether.

TOBACCO INDUSTRY POSITION PAPER

Given the legal liabilities and negative public opinion associated with this industry, Storebrand excludes tobacco manufacturers and distributors from its investment universe. Companies deriving more than 10 percent of their sales or revenues from the tobacco industry (both suppliers and retailers) are also excluded from the investment universe.

Source: www.storebrand.com/storebrand/com/Publications.nsf.

ENVIRONMENTAL RESEARCH AND RATING ORGANIZATIONS

The response of the investment community has spawned not only a rise in environmental mutual funds, but also the growth of a new industry in environmental research. As seen in earlier chapters, the banking and insurance industries have developed their own specific environmental risk rating methods that look at a combination of regulatory, technological, operational, and event risk. Now companies that undertake environmental rating and ranking have developed with a view to providing investors, fund managers, and financial analysts with material information regarding corporate environmental performance.

Some rating strategies evolved as a result of financial repercussions due to environmental catastrophes, such as the *Exxon Valdez* and Bhopal incidents. These systems take into account historical compliance records as well as the risk of regulatory intervention and third-party damage claims. Other rating and ranking systems assess the current environmental management of a company through an analysis of emissions and litigation reports as a means of linking present activities to future compliance. Still others have developed analytical tools designed to uncover potential corporate value from strategic environmental management. In general these tools attempt to balance a company's environmental risk with its capacity to both control that risk and capitalize on environmentally driven opportunities. And finally, some have expanded their horizons to add ethical performance to their environmental base (Aspen Institute 1998; Skillius and Wennberg 1998).

This environmental, social, and ethical research has been undertaken by organizations as diverse as trade associations, NGOs, charitable groups, and fee-for-service enterprises. Targeted markets for these ranking services include institutional investors, brokers, high-net-worth individuals, foundations and endowments, hedge funds, boards of directors, public authorities, communication and marketing consultants, as well as insurance companies and law firms.

The following section describes a sample of such systems, including examples of different categories of research as well as different types of organizations that have evolved with the goal of filling clients' needs in assessing corporate social and environmental behavior.

Liability Systems

Loss Prevention Council   The Loss Prevention Council in the United Kingdom, supported by the insurance industry's Association of British Insurers and Lloyd's, has designed a framework for pollution risk assessment for "suitability for liability cover." The system demonstrates many elements that are similar to the bankers' risk assessment tool outlined in the "Risk Management" section in Chapter 4. It focuses on the risk of on-site pollution occurring, as well as the off-site consequences of an incident. The procedure is divided into four levels:

1. A proposal form that records basic information on industry type, location of sites, and management systems.
2. A detailed questionnaire that identifies not only on-site management processes, but also consequences of off-site initiatives.

3. Insurance survey or site survey.
4. Site investigation by an environmental consultant if earlier assessment levels indicate a high risk of a pollution incident.

The assessment results can be used in a risk assessment matrix to compare the degree of hazard (low, medium, high) to an estimate of the competence of the company's managers to control the hazard (poor, average, excellent) (Loss Prevention Council 1997).

Safety and Environmental Risk Management Rating Agency   Safety and Environmental Risk Management Rating Agency (SERM) is a U.K. environmental rating agency whose rating approach involves evaluations on a 27-point scale analogous to Moody's and S&P's bond credit ratings. SERM ratings focus to a greater extent on downside risk, deriving a residual risk figure from direct and indirect costs of potential environmental and safety incidents, as well as the likely effectiveness of a company's risk management procedures to avoid or mitigate such risks. This figure is then measured against the scrutinized company's market capitalization to come up with a residual risk to capitalization percentage that is classified on a 27-point scale. This comparison between residual risk and market capitalization provides one method of quantification of a company's risk, and produces a profile that is useful from fund managers' and insurers' perspectives. It does not, however, attempt to quantify other critical aspects such as overall environmental performance, nor does it identify environmentally related opportunities.

As a research and rating organization, SERM provides three levels of reporting. The first is a publicly available outline derived from questionnaires. The second is a verified outline that includes further research and meetings with the company. The final type of report is a full rating, usually undertaken at the request of a client company (Nicholls 1999/2000; Pritchard 2000).

Compliance Systems

Investor Responsibility Research Center   The independent, nonprofit U.S.-based Investor Responsibility Research Center (IRRC) mainly examines the environmental performance of S&P 500 companies through the use of emissions, compliance, and environmental litigation information compiled from government records and company reports. The quantitative data is normalized by considering the environmental risk per unit of revenue, thus allowing for comparisons of companies of different sizes. IRRC's research information is supplied to investment analysts, who then in turn develop their own ratings (Skillius and Wennberg 1998).

Environmental and Social Strategic Systems

Whereas the rating agencies discussed to this point take into account past environmental liabilities, historical compliance records, and present environmental management in their rankings, the following organizations go one step further by linking strategic decision making to potential corporate value. In these cases, researchers identify not only the company's capacity to manage environmental risk, but also its capacity to capitalize on opportunities those environmental challenges present.

Öekom Research The German Öekom Research system mainly rates the environmental and social performance of European companies. Its environmental assessment takes place in three areas: environmental management; product and service development in the environmental field; and environmental data. Each field carries a specific weighting: 25 percent for the first and last categories and 50 percent for product and service development. Each section is assessed on a 12-point scale from A+ to D–, with A+ denoting a particularly progressive approach to environmental challenges. The grades for the three areas are combined, according to their weightings, to form a final rank that is applied to the company for use in comparison within its specific industry (www.oekom.de/ag/english/index_unternehmensliste.htm).

Kinder, Lydenberg, Domini Kinder, Lydenberg, Domini & Co. (KLD) is a "social choice" investment advisory firm, with ratings that cover nine areas of environmental and social performance through the application of 60 criteria. The firm is best known for its Domini 400 Social Index (DSI 400), launched in 1990 to serve as a benchmark for socially screened equity portfolios. Screens are applied to S&P 500 companies, with 400 of these being selected for the DSI 400 on the basis of their superior social performance. KLD offer investors the possibility of socially responsible investing through KLD's proprietary funds, as well as by investing in passively managed funds based on its DSI 400 index.

Companies are assessed using exclusion criteria similar to those suggested in Table 6.1. A company's positive environmental and social records are included through the application of qualitative positive screens, such as diversity, employee relations, product safety, and environmental record. KLD company profiles flag areas of strength and concern with respect to any of the nine areas analyzed (Elkington and Beloe 2000; Skillius and Wennberg 1998).

KLD also offers a Corporate Social Rating Monitor service, known as SOCRATES, which makes continually updated CDs available to subscribers for use in the screening of personal or institutional portfolios for negative and positive social and environmental performance (www. domini.com).

Michael Jantzi Research Associates Michael Jantzi Research Associates (MJRA) is the Canadian equivalent of KLD, and, as such, monitors and reports on the environmental, labor, and social performance of more than 300 publicly traded Canadian companies, producing the Jantzi Social Index (JSI). Company profiles are available to social investors as well as more detailed, customized reports (www.mjra-jsi.com). MJRA has undertaken a number of strategic partnerships that validate the value and construction of its database. JSI is calculated in real time through a partnership with Dow Jones. Any individual or client can access this valuation on the Chicago Board of Trade. In addition, State Street examines the construction of the JSI on a continuing basis, looking at, among other factors, asset allocation, the influence of beta and price/earnings (P/E) ratios, the criteria used, and the weighting used per company/sector. JSI is the first definitive index with real-time pricing that examines the effects of social screening on financial performance in Canada. In 2001 JSI was licensed to the Meritas Mutual Fund Company as the core investment tool for its Meritas Jantzi Social Index Fund (www.meritas.ca). Meritas is Canada's newest socially responsible mutual fund company, established as a joint venture of the Mennonite Savings and Credit Union (Ontario) Limited, the Mennonite Foundation of Canada, and the Mennonite Mutual Aid.

Sustainability Asset Management Headquartered in Zurich, Sustainability Asset Management (SAM) Sustainability Research Group seeks to identify proactive sustainability-driven companies among both large (leaders) and small to medium-sized (pioneer) firms through its Corporate Sustainability Assessment program. By looking at industry-specific environmental and social trends as well as the driving forces behind these trends, SAM focuses less on past performance and is assessing to a greater extent future sustainability potential both of sectors and of individual companies. Corporate activities are continuously reviewed and monitored through SAM's Corporate Sustainability Monitoring system. In this way, the researchers can observe a company's ongoing involvement in critical environmental and social issues, as well as its management of these issues. Companies that score poorly in Corporate Sustainability Monitoring are excluded from the annual Corporate Sustainability Assessment process. Companies that successfully pass both these stages qualify for the Dow Jones Sustainability Indexes (DJSI) (see "Investable Indexes" section later in the chapter).

SAM differs from the majority of rating companies in that it not only assesses and monitors companies in its rating research division, but also offers its own brand of funds by applying its research to investment products, such as its Sustainable Water Fund (www.sam-group.com). Most recently, SAM has raised $60 million for its new Private Equity Energy Fund, which will invest in expansion-phase firms in Europe and North America that are involved in emerging energy generation and conversion, energy management systems, energy storage, and power quality. The majority of the investors are global energy companies, such as Norsk-Hydro Technology Ventures (NVT), the Norwegian power firm's venture capital fund. NVT was itself set up in early 2001 to invest in companies developing technologies of relevance to Norsk-Hydro's operations (Environmental Finance 2001d).

CASE STUDY: Innovest Strategic Value Advisors

Innovest Strategic Value Advisors is an internationally recognized investment advisory firm specializing in environmental finance and investment opportunities. It has developed an environmental rating system called EcoValue'21. The ratings are industry-relative, with a company being rated, within its sector, from best to worst (6 to 0 or AAA to CCC) using a list of over 60 data points and performance metrics within a proprietary algorithm. The procedure examines factors that hold the greatest financial significance in the areas of environmental risk, environmental management, and environmental opportunity. Components of the EcoValue'21 rating model are summarized in Box 6.5. The risk component includes all quantitative data such as toxic emissions, resource use efficiency, and a number of industry-specific criteria. The management classification addresses issues of energy and resource efficiency as well as the incorporation of the environment into business strategy. Opportunities include the degree to which a firm engages in environmentally friendly products and services and innovative approaches to new environmental product and service development (www.innovestgroup.com). The company profile of STMicroelectronics provides an example of the application of EcoValue'21 in the semiconductor industry (Figure B.2 in Appendix B).

In addition, Innovest has created a supplemental analytical platform, Sustainability[Plus], that provides a social overlay to its environmental EcoValue'21 model. While these additional drivers cannot yet be linked as rigorously to stock price performance as the core EcoValue'21 model itself, Innovest's analysis of these factors does add valuable investment insights into sustainability that are becoming more critical in analyses of sustainable development. The Sustainability[Plus] overlay includes over 50 indicators that lie within subcategories of the six principal value drivers: human capital development, supply chain, community/stakeholder engagement, products and services, strategy and management,

BOX 6.5 Innovest's EcoValue'21 Rating Model

Historical Contingent Liabilities:
  Superfund/contaminated land.
  Resource Conservation and Recovery Fund (RCRA) and equivalents.
  Toxic torts.
Operating Risk Exposure:
  Toxic emissions.
  Product risk liabilities.
  Hazardous waste disposal.
  Waste discharge.
  Supply chain management risk.
Sustainability Risk:
  Energy intensity and efficiency.
  Resource use efficiency and intensity.
  Product life-cycle durability and recyclability.
  Exposure to shifts in consumer values.
  Social community license to operate.
Financial Risk Management Capacity:
  Balance sheet strength.
  Insurance coverage adequacy.
Strategic Management Capacity:
  Strategic corporate governance capability.
  Environmental management systems strength.
  Environmental auditing/accounting capacity.
  Social issues performance.
  Supply chain management.
  Stakeholder relations.
Sustainable Profit Opportunities:
  Ability to profit from environmental and socially driven industry and market trends.

Source: Innovest SVA 2001.

---

and international considerations. General Motors' company profile provides an example of Sustainability[Plus] in the automotive industry (Figure B.1 in Appendix B).

Within the context of the EcoValue'21 and Sustainability[Plus] databases, Innovest has the capacity to investigate in detail issues of particular relevance to different sectors. For example, its reports within the steel sector provide a detailed carbon profile of companies, and categorize each company in the sector on a carbon sustainability rating scale, as well as classifying (none to extreme) the sector's overall risk from climate issues. An example can be seen in the company profile for Usinor (Figure 6.1). In the integrated oil and gas sector,

Usinor

USI

Carbon Profile

Industrial Sector:	Steel	Carbon Sustainability Rating:	**40** out of 100	3-Oct-2000
1999 Sales ($ millions):	13,745	Main region:	EU	1999 Production: 22,200,000 tons steel

Financial Carbon Related Risk Exposure

Equivalent tons CO$_2$ Generated in 1000s

Base Year:	1990
Target Year:	2012
Market capitalization ($M):	2.714
Discount rate:	6%
WACCR*:	8%
Expected yearly industry growth %:	2%

Product/Service Embedded

Indirect (e.g. power purchased)

Direct (in-house)

0.0E+00 5.0E+06 1.0E+07 1.5E+07 2.0E+07 2.5E+07 3.0E+07 3.5E+07 4.0E+07 4.5E+07

	Exp. case	Min case	Max case
Carbon Cost ($/ton CO2):	85	40	120
NPV costs to meet Kyoto target year ($1000):	572,230	38,151	1,373,421
Exposure (% of current market value):	21.1%	11.7%	28.4%

Total Direct CO$_2$ Emissions (tons): **38,742,366**

Normalized CO$_2$ equivalents (tons/$ M sales):	2.819
Regional benchmark (CO$_2$ tons/$ M GDP):	527
Ratio: company-to-benchmark:	5.3 High exposure to CO2 related market risks.
Normalized CO$_2$ equivalents (kg/ton steel):	1,745
Sector benchmark (kg/ton steel):	2,300
Ratio: company-to-benchmark:	0.8 Above average carbon efficiency performance.
Carbon improvement vector:	2% reduction since 1990.
Kyoto Commitment of main operational region:	8% reduction by 2008-2012 compared to 1990.

Overall sector risk for climate issues:	None	Low	Moderate	High	⚠ Extreme

Climate Change Policy and Strategy

Rating Scores

Usinor has a skeptical attitude regarding the climate change potency of man-made emissions of CO2. However, it has adopted a precautionary measure to control its CO2 emissions and energy use more strictly. Usinor non-regret strategy hinges around extending the use of scrap steel into integrated plants and making more efficient use of gas by-products from blast furnaces and steelworks.

1 = poor; 10 = superior

Mitigation and Innovative Measures

In the aftermath of the two oil shocks, Usinor has dedicated resources to reduce its energy use by 20% by 1990 since 1970 levels. Since then, energy use per ton of steel has only been reduced by 2%. The company claims it has reached its optimum energy efficiency inherent to integrated steelmaking infrastructures. Usinor is working on increasing its use of scrap metal beyond current 20% which should reduce associated CO2 emissions. Unlike some of its competitors, no CO2 reduction targets have been set. The company does not plan to use pulverized coal injection technology as a way to reduce CO2 emissions from coking operations.

5.0

Carbon Management

Direct Carbon Risk (from in-house operations and emissions)

As a major integrated steelmaker, Usinor has a high carbon risk. The company emits annually 44 million tons of CO2, i.e. 3,200 tons / $ million sales, in comparison to the OECD average of 780 tons of CO2 / million GDP. If the EU were to enforce a carbon tax to achieve a 5% reduction by 2008-2012 from 1990 level, Usinor will have to cut its CO2 emissions by a further 3% on absolute terms, which would be equivalent to a total of US$ 26.4 million at a likely $20 per ton for carbon emission permits.

3.5

Carbon Market Risk Embedded in Offered Products and Services

Steel products do not carry embedded CO2, and the company has no CO2 product liabilities.

Carbon Risk

Carbon Related Profit Opportunities

Whereas some steelmakers diversify their production facilities by acquiring minimill capacity, thus allowing for a higher rate of scrap metal consumption, Usinor pursues a more traditional approach by focusing on integrated steelmaking only. Usinor does not disclose any innovative technology to curb the coke making, structural CO2 emissions.

3.8

Emissions Trading

Usinor is taking part in a CO2 permits trading simulation system.

Carbon Profit Opportunities

*Weighted Average Country Carbon Reduction (by 2008-2012 from 1990 level)

I N N O V E S T
Strategic Value Advisors

New York: 1-212-421-2000 Toronto: 1-905-707-0876 London: 011-44-1225-312-051 www.innovestgroup.com

FIGURE 6.1 Innovest Carbon Profile of Usinor
Source: Innovest SVA. Reprinted with permission.

Innovest provides a detailed examination of key downside risks such as global climate change, as well as key opportunities such as investments in fuel cells and renewables and participation in emissions trading. Innovest company profiles, then, outline not only risk factors, but also strategic profit opportunities for each company.

EcoValue'21 also allows for a web-type mapping of a company's ecological footprint. The example of such a mapping is found in the GM company profile in Appendix B, where measures of resource and waste efficiency, as well as global warming, ozone depletion, eutrophication, photochemical ozone, and acidification potentials/$ revenue are recorded. The measures of each indicator are joined, creating a spider web-like illustration of the company's impact on the environment.

Innovest has demonstrated that its eco-efficiency rankings provide not only environmental differentiation, but also return differentiation (Innovest SVA 2001a). That is to say, the stocks of higher-ranked companies on an environmental basis purportedly will deliver higher investment returns compared to the lower-ranked counterparts in the industry. Innovest analysts argue that careful examination and quantification of a company's environmental behavior produces a ranking that captures information not normally utilized or available to investors as they attempt to determine prices at which a stock should trade. In these terms, superior eco-efficiency rankings suggest superior management quality, which in turn generates financial outperformance and increased shareholder value (Kiernan 2001).

Due to the depth of research and flexibility of its algorithms and databases, Innovest is able to provide an extensive cluster of products and services, including:

- Customized portfolio analysis for individual portfolios, in order to uncover hidden risks and value opportunities not accounted for in traditional equities analyses.
- An alpha overlay index product that assists clients in constructing enhanced index and enhanced sector index portfolios.
- Portfolio management that helps clients construct actively managed portfolios in best-of-class sector funds.
- Strategic industry sector reports that provide in-depth research on hidden outperformance opportunities in high-risk sectors, such as oil and gas, chemicals, and power generation.

Council of Economic Priorities   The Council of Economic Priorities (CEP), a not-for-profit advocacy group in the United States, researches companies' environmental and ethical factors in nine issue areas of social performance. The environmental component involves environmental risks as well as accomplishments and efforts of companies to improve their environmental performance. The ethical component includes minority advancement, charitable giving, community outreach, family benefits, and workplace issues. Corporate documents and/or a questionnaire provide the information used by CEP. Ratings of A to F (outstanding to poor performance) are developed, based on a weighted average of 13 measures of corporate environmental performance: releases, policy, packaging, recycling, raw materials/

waste, toxic reduction, community impact, energy conservation, natural resources, accidents, Superfund sites, compliance, and environmental technology, as well as on size/type of industry (Elkington and Beloe 2000; Skillius and Wennberg 1998).

Ethical Investment Research Service (EIRIS Services Ltd.)   EIRIS Services Ltd. is a subsidiary of the U.K.-based registered charity Ethical Investment Research Service that was established in 1983 with the help of churches and charities that needed a research organization to help them apply their ethical principles to their investments. EIRIS is the oldest and largest specialist research company in the United Kingdom, assessing corporate activity in 30 principal areas. These cover both negative and positive criteria, outlined in Table 6.6.

The application of EIRIS data can be used to provide services for all types of clients, from checking a portfolio to creating and implementing an ethical investment policy. EIRIS also provides data required by certain analysts and managers, such as Friends Provident Stewardship Trusts and Fund, allowing investment analysts and fund managers to draw their own conclusions as to rankings. In addition, EIRIS information services can be obtained and sold by independent financial advisers, such as Global and Ethical Investment Advice (GAEIA) (Skillius and Wennberg 1998).

WEIGHTINGS

The different ranking systems just discussed illustrate that companies are scored using proprietary algorithms that calculate a company's score across a range of different criteria. In most cases, companies are given relative weightings before an intra- or intersectoral comparison is carried out. However, within different algorithms, different weightings may be used to ascribe extra value to certain parameters. Four types of weighting systems are described next.

Financial   Innovest Strategic Value Advisors looks mainly at the environmental and social issues that have a material effect on a company's value. It therefore uses the correlations between stock market price and these criteria to develop a weighting system that is financially based. The system takes into consideration three broad clusters of issues that revolve around this relationship: a company's risk profile on social and environmental issues, its management's capacity to deal with that risk, and how well the company is positioned to take advantage of trends in these areas.

TABLE 6.6   Criteria Used by EIRIS in Assessing Corporate Environmental and Ethical Activity

Negative Criteria	Positive Criteria
• Production/sale of alcohol • Animal testing • Gambling • Greenhouse gas emissions • Health and safety breaches • Activities in countries with poor human rights records • Involvement in intensive farming and meat production • Contracts with the Ministry of Defense • Production/sale of goods for military purposes • Involvement in nuclear power • Contribution to ozone depletion • Marketing of pesticide products • Involvement in pornography/adult films • Involvement in road-building activities • Exploitation of the third world • Tobacco production/sales • Extraction/sale/use of tropical hardwood • Involvement in water pollution incidents	• Provision of positive products or services (pollution control, health care, utilities, education industries) • Community involvement • Disclosure of information • Grading of companies' environmental policies, reports, and management systems • Good record on equal opportunities (policies, training) • Grading on retailers' and food manufacturers' policies on foods containing genetically modified organisms

Source: www.eiris.u-net.com (Elkington and Beloe 2000).

Social Responsibility   Socially responsible weighting criteria used by analysts such as the Calvert Group (see Box 6.2 earlier in the chapter) recognize the fact that some sectors are deemed to be problematic in specific areas of environmental and social activity. Companies in such sectors are weighted accordingly in their overall scores before stock selection is made for investment funds (Elkington and Beloe 2000).

Confidence   Confidence weighting recognizes the fact that some data sets are more reliable and robust than others. Confidence weighting is used by organizations such as CEP that ascribe a positive weighting to particular information sources when the data has been, or can be, verified.

Sectoral   In some instances, weightings are applied to particular sets of data according to their applicability to different industrial groups or sectors. As seen in the case study earlier in the chapter, weightings used by the Storebrand Group emphasize those issues that are most important within a specific sectoral cluster (Storebrand Scudder 1996).

INVESTABLE INDEXES

The primary role of any constructed investable index is to reflect the behavior of some subset of the market. Thus the inclusion of a company or sector in a particular index and the weighting it is given reflect the characteristics that the index is trying to emphasize. Indexes are made available for general investment purposes through licensing agreements between the initiator of the index and an investment management institution (Whittacker 2001). For example, the investment company T. Rowe Price has based its Global Eco Growth Fund on the S&P 500 index, which is then weighted for environmental performance using Innovest's EcoValue'21. The DSI 400 and JSI, described earlier, provide other examples of investable socially responsible indexes as they are applied to KLD and Meritas groups of funds, respectively.

Other traditional indexes, such as the S&P 500 and the FTSE 100, have been accessible to investors through products offered by a number of investment houses. These indexes have been modeled on different investment universes and apply different sets of criteria in the stock selection process. More recently, new versions of these two financial indexes have been developed in order to provide social and environmental products for passive investment proposes.

Dow Jones Sustainability Indexes

In September 1999, Dow Jones and its partner SAM launched one new global sustainability index; three new regional indexes (Europe, North America, and Asia-Pacific); and one country index covering the United States, with the intention of ranking companies within different economic sectors according to their principles of sustainability (www.sustainability-indexes.com). The aim of the Dow Jones Sustainability Indexes (DJSI) is to provide a bridge between companies that implement principles of sustainability and investors wishing to profit from favorable risk-return profiles and shareholder value created by companies committed to prioritizing environmental and social concerns. This allows for a geographically diversified, yet specialized set of indexes.

The DJSI yardstick of sustainability ranks a company's management of sustainable opportunities and risk deriving from economic, social, and environmental developments. These opportunities and risks are directly related to a company's strategic commitment at the board level, as well as concrete management initiatives and instruments, use of new technology, and a host of industry-specific measures (Flatz et al. 2001).

The Dow Jones Sustainability Indexes have been licensed to a number of leading banks and insurers, such as Rabobank, Baloise Insurance, and State Street. In the case of Invesco (mentioned in Box 3.2), the DJSI is licensed to this asset management firm to benchmark one client's managed account specifically at that client's request (Environmental Finance 2001d; Harrison 2002).

FTSE4Good

In mid-2001, FTSE International launched a similar family of equity indexes of socially responsible investment for the United Kingdom, Europe, the United States, and the world. A tradable index and a separate benchmark index have been developed for each region covered. The FTSE4Good family of indexes bases its definition of socially responsible investment on three basic principles: the promotion of practices that mitigate damage to the environment, the encouragement of relations with stakeholders, and support of and respect for the protection of international human rights. Of the more than 1,600 companies that were assessed for their compliance with social, environmental, and humanitarian measures, the top 50 were selected for the British and European tradable indexes, with a total of 100 companies appearing on the U.S. and world equity indexes.

While the indexes have been the subject of some skepticism, they do recognize the possibility of a positive relationship between good environmental management and superior stock market performance. It is anticipated that these new sets of equity indexes will increase the competition between companies and lead to improved corporate social and environmental performance (Dupont 2001).

CONCLUSION

This chapter illustrates that great efforts have been made in an attempt to link environmental and financial performance. We have seen, however, that there is little consensus as to the definition and measurement of environmental performance. Part of this discrepancy lies in the range of options and metrics used to communicate environmental management activities and performance to capital markets. Under these conditions, it becomes difficult to relate environmental and financial performance, and even harder to convince analysts and investors of the creation of value from strategic environmental management decision making.

In response to some of the issues of data collection and imperfect communication of information, a number of benchmarking efforts have been made to gather and disseminate information on corporate social and environmental performance. Financial institutions and portfolio analysts have developed dedicated research departments or use the services of specialist research companies to either screen or select superior environmental opportunities. In addition, investable indexes such as DJSI and FTSE4Good have been developed to act as passive investment vehicles, much as the FTSE 100 and S&P 500 have been used in the past.

Implications of some of the measurement issues revealed in this chapter will be explored in Chapter 8, where the need for improved environmental reporting structures is discussed.

ENDNOTES

1. The Toxic Release Inventory (TRI) was mandated under the Superfund Amendments and Reauthorization Act (SARA) of 1986. Firms subject to the Act were originally required to report, by location, their annual on-site releases and off-site transfers of approximately 320 specified toxic chemicals. Later a further 286 chemicals were added to the list. The first public disclosure of TRI data on toxic emissions appeared in June 1989. Modeled on the U.S. TRI, the Canadian National Pollutant Release Inventory (NPRI) was mandated under the Canadian Environmental Protection Act (CEPA) in 1993 (www.ec.gc.ca/pdb/npri/). NPRI is designed to collect annual, comprehensive, national data on releases to air, water, and land, as well as transfers for disposal and recycling, of 176 specified substances.

2. The aim of genetically modified (GM) plants and animals is twofold: first, to solve the problems of population growth with its concomitant conditions of malnutrition and hunger; and second, to achieve an environmentally compatible intensification of plant production with the use of proportionately less pesticides, herbicides, and fertilizer. The four main GM crop plants are soybean, maize, cotton, and oilseed rape. Increased volume of GM plants depends on consumer attitudes, and thus demand, as well as on farmers' decisions as to what they will plant and produce. Consumer acceptance of genetic modification is declining globally, and farmers have found that higher yields have failed to materialize while the prices for GM products are coming under pressure due to the increased demand for conventional goods from the food and fodder industries outside the United States. In addition, marginalized farmers are incensed at the costs involved due to the planned use of "terminator genes" in GM seeds, resulting in sterilized crop plants that prevent replanting (Munich Re 2001c).

WEB SITES

Association of Sustainable and Responsible Investment in Asia	www.asria.org
Calvert Group	www.calvertgroup.com
Domini Social Index	www.domini.com
Dow Jones Sustainability Indexes	www.sustainability-indexes.com
EIRIS	www.eiris.u-net.com
Innovest	www.innovestgroup.com
IRRC	www.irrc.org
Öekom Research	www.oekom.de/ag/english/index_uternehmensliste.htm
Meritas Mutual Fund Company	www.meritas.ca
Michael Jantzi Research Associates, Jantzi Social Index	www.mjra-jsi.com
Sarasin Bank	www.sarasin.ch/sarasin
Storebrand	www.storebrand.com
UBS	www.ubs.com/funds

CHAPTER 7

Climate Change and Financial Vulnerability

INTRODUCTION

Climate change is the largest element of environmental change, as it covers the globe and extends to time horizons beyond the lifetimes of people alive today. It is essentially irreversible. Despite the seriousness of the probable impacts of climate change, it has been very difficult to bring to the public forum for debate because many established interests feel threatened by the adaptive and mitigative actions that appear to be required. The financial services sector is already in the process of adapting to the expected impact of climate change, but even here—where the impacts are already visible—it has been difficult to develop consensus on the best way forward.

ACCEPTING CLIMATE CHANGE AS A REAL PHENOMENON

There is a growing understanding that climate change is a real phenomenon that has potentially serious consequences for human society. This consensus has emerged very slowly. The possibility of greenhouse gases such as carbon dioxide and methane accumulating in the atmosphere and thus warming the climate was raised at the beginning of the nineteenth century. However, it was not until the middle of the twentieth century that scientists became sufficiently concerned to begin to take direct measurements in the atmosphere. Very quickly the accumulation became evident (see Figure 1.1). The measurements were sensitive enough to show seasonal variation reflecting the carbon absorption capacity of tree growth. Verification of the long-term accumulation of greenhouse gases since the beginning of the industrial revolution was obtained from bubbles of air trapped in ice cores extracted from the Arctic and Antarctic ice fields (see Figure 1.2). In addition to carbon dioxide and methane, the currently targeted gases are nitrous oxide (N_2O), hydrofluorocarbons (HFCs), perfluorocarbons (PFCs), and sulfur hexafluoride (SF_6).

It was to be another 30 years before the temperature signal became unequivocal (Figure 1.3). The graph shows a transition period of fluctuating temperatures between 1945 and 1975, followed by a steadily warming trend. The 1980s and the 1990s are the warmest decades on record. In 1988 an international conference in Toronto issued a report entitled *The Changing Atmosphere*, asserting that climate change was underway and could have dire consequences (Environment Canada 1988). What differentiated this environmental problem from its predecessors was that some of the greenhouse gases—including carbon dioxide, the principal contributor to warming—are very long-lived in the atmosphere, exceeding 100 years. This has two serious consequences for managing the problem. First, the gases have enough time to become well-mixed in the atmosphere; hence the problem becomes global, rather than regional or local like many other pollutants. Second, even if all the contributing sources around the globe could be shut off tomorrow, we would still have to live with the impacts for at least that duration. In other words, all the nations of the world have to agree to a very long-term strategy of abatement. Given the potentially negative short-term economic consequences of eliminating greenhouse gas emissions, it is obvious that consensus will be difficult to develop. For large sections of society the problem is just too long-term to contemplate. It is crowded out by other serious problems that are seemingly much more urgent and can perhaps be resolved without unanimity and over a relatively short time frame.

Despite the serious potential for discord, indifference, and hostility, certain sectors of society have resolved to address climate change for fear of the consequences of simply pretending it is not happening. For example, at the International Council for Local Environmental Initiatives:

> *ICLEI's Cities for Climate Protection Campaign (CCP), begun in 1993, is a global campaign to reduce the emissions that cause global warming and air pollution. By 1999, the campaign had engaged in this effort more than 350 local governments, who jointly accounted for approximately 7 percent of global greenhouse gas emissions.*

Further information is available from: www.iclei.org/co2/index.htm.

Within the financial services sector, the major reinsurance companies were the first to go public with their concerns, producing television programs and publications aimed at the public and their clients, the primary insurance companies. The reality of climate change and the hazard it represents were difficult messages to communicate, partly because the phrase "global warming" had already become current and sounded fairly harmless to the public. At the same time, those sounding the alarm could easily be interpreted as simply promoting their own business rather than public well-being. Swiss Re took a typically low-key approach in its 1994 document *Global Warming: Element of Risk*:

> *Occurrences such as Hurricane Andrew in 1992 and the Mississippi–Missouri flood of 1993 cannot be directly attributed beyond any shadow of doubt to such climatic change. . . . Andrew need not necessarily be a result of climatic change. But climatic change could lead to an accumulation of such events in future or to their occurrence in hitherto unknown regions. . . . More extreme weather patterns could cause damage which not only poses a threat to individual citizens, families and enterprises but could also jeopardize whole cities and branches of the economy and—on a global scale—entire states and social systems. (Swiss Re 1994)*

At the same time there was a hardening of the opposition to taking any immediate action to respond to climate change. Certain corporate and national interests estimated the potential costs of mitigation as being extremely high and subsequently dismissed the risks of inaction as the exaggerated fears of a handful of environmental extremists. The Organization of Petroleum Exporting Countries (OPEC) as well as fossil fuel, chemical, cement, and transportation companies could all see how their businesses could no longer be run as usual if greenhouse gases were targeted for reduction. Early in the 1990s a group of companies strongly opposed to mandatory action on climate change formed the Global Climate Coalition (GCC) to lobby against national reduction targets (Leggett 1999). (See Box 7.1 for the impact of this coalition and its subsequent transformation.)

However, even among the major oil companies there were leaders who could see that change was inevitable and the best policy was to prepare for a time when the reduction of greenhouse gas emissions became an important goal for every type of business, including those currently selling fossil fuels and their products. In May 1997, John Browne, chief executive officer of British Petroleum (BP) (a former member of the

BOX 7.1   The Role of the Global Climate Coalition

The name Global Climate Coalition sounds as if this is a worldwide organization dedicated to the protection of the climate. In fact it is an organization dedicated to persuading the American government that it should take no action to enforce the reduction of greenhouse gas emissions; specifically, it should not participate in the UN Framework Convention on Climate Change, nor join the Kyoto Protocol that emerged from the convention. The coalition—sometimes referred to as the "Carbon Club"—consisted of major energy, automotive, and chemical corporations such as BP, General Motors, and DuPont. Representatives of the coalition lobbied at the Conference of the Parties to the Convention (see Box 7.3), ran advertising campaigns in the United States, and supported members of Congress who shared their views. They believed that American action on climate change should be left to the voluntary initiatives of American corporations. They built their campaign on the concern that government action would significantly raise energy prices and endanger American jobs.

There is little doubt that their views were widely shared in the United States. The public was largely apathetic or had so little understanding of the science of climate change that they could not believe that the situation required urgent mitigative action that carried the potential for economic disruption. Yet opinion changed through the 1990s as an appreciation of the seriousness of the threat spread from the scientific community to politicians, the public, and some corporations. *If* the scientific predictions were plausible *then* we had a problem to face, sooner or later. The lessons from asbestos and tobacco showed that stonewalling on an issue of this size could become extremely costly. Large corporations make many major decisions on a 20-year horizon or even further in the future. Some of those corporations looked ahead and changed their views on the best course of action.

DuPont was one of the first to leave the Carbon Club. BP left shortly after John Browne's 1997 Stanford speech indicating that BP was planning for a life "beyond petroleum" (see Box 7.2). The next to go, in 1998, was Royal Dutch/Shell. Ford followed in 1999, with its chairman (the great-grandson of Henry Ford) announcing, "I expect to preside over the demise of the internal combustion engine," and "Membership in the Global Climate Coalition has become something of an impediment for Ford Motor Company to achieving

(Continued)

BOX 7.1   *(Continued)*

its environmental objectives." The following year saw the departure of DaimlerChrysler, Texaco, and General Motors.

Some ex-members of the coalition, such as BP, Shell, and DuPont, joined the newly established Business Environmental Leadership Council, supported by the Pew Center on Global Climate Change. The Council represents over 20 corporations, including IBM, Sunoco, Toyota, and Boeing.

The Global Climate Coalition restructured itself to accept only trade associations as members, making the loss of major corporations less visible. On its web site it states that "GCC members collectively represent more than 6 million businesses." Perhaps it can claim some success in the withdrawal of the Bush administration from the Conference of the Parties (COP) process. But it could also be said that opinion in many of the corporations that will be most affected by climate change has moved ahead of that of the administration. Confident that the government's position was consistent with its own, the Coalition announced in 2002 that it had been "deactivated."

Sources: Global Climate Coalition, www.globalclimate.org; Pew Center on Global Climate Change, Business Environmental Leadership Council, www.pewClimate.org/belc; Worldwatch Institute, www.worldwatch.org/chairman/issue/000725.html; Leggett 1999.

Global Climate Coalition), made a major policy speech at Stanford University in which he said:

The time to consider the policy dimensions of climate change is not when the link between greenhouse gases and climate change is conclusively proven, but when the possibility cannot be discounted and is taken seriously by the society of which we are part. We in BP have reached that point. . . . It will be a long journey because the responsibilities faced by governments are complex, and the interests of their economies and their peoples are diverse, and sometimes contradictory. . . . The private sector has also embarked upon the journey, but now that involvement needs to be accelerated. (Browne 1997; our emphasis)

Subsequently BP made a major investment in solar photovoltaic technology, set up an in-house carbon dioxide emission reduction trading scheme, and redefined its acronym to mean "beyond petroleum" (see Box 7.2). Historians in the future will probably identify 1997—the year of Browne's Stanford speech—as a watershed year, marking growing acceptance of the potentially serious consequences of climate change. In December of that same year 160 nations signed the Kyoto Protocol to the UN Framework Convention on Climate Change. A commitment was made by the signatories to begin the process of reducing greenhouse gas emissions to 5.2 percent of 1990 emissions by 2008–2012 for Annex 1 countries, although there was no agreement at that time on how the process was to be managed (see www.unfccc.int). Five years later there is still a serious lack of clarity.

BOX 7.2   "Beyond Petroleum"—The Challenge for BP

In 2000 BP began an advertising campaign in which the company acronym stood for "beyond petroleum." Within its health, safety, and environment policy it has a "simply stated goal—to do no damage to the environment."
Regarding climate change, the policy states:

The prospect of global climate change is a matter of genuine public concern. We share this concern.

The amount of carbon dioxide (CO_2) in the atmosphere is increasing and the temperature of the earth's surface is rising. Although there is a lot of uncertainty about the magnitude and consequences of these developments, the balance of informed opinion is that mankind is having a discernible effect on the climate and scientists believe there is a link between the amount of CO_2 in the atmosphere and increased temperature.

Faced with this uncertainty, BP believes that adopting a precautionary approach to climate change is the only sensible way forward in these circumstances. What BP proposes to do is sustainable, real and measurable. That is why BP has set itself a goal to reduce its emissions of greenhouse gases by 10%, from a 1990 baseline, by the year 2010. (In fact, this goal was achieved in 2002.)

(Continued)

BOX 7.2 *(Continued)*

Overall, BP is pursuing a goal of "lower carbon energy"; thus:

Gas is the fastest growing source of hydrocarbon energy. Switching from coal to gas as the primary fuel for generating electricity can result in a 50% reduction in CO_2 emissions per unit of electricity generated.

Recent technological advances have made renewable energy more economically accessible. The annual growth rate for wind and solar photovoltaic generated electricity is around 20–30%. Other sources of renewable energy are being actively pursued throughout the world and will contribute to broaden the energy mix.

BP has established BP Solar, one of the largest producers of solar technology, with solar products in more than 160 countries around the world.

BP carried out a greenhouse gas emissions audit in all its operating units as a prelude to the launch in 2000 of an intracompany carbon trading regime, which will enable it to meet its emissions reduction target. It had its inventory verified by independent auditors, Ernst & Young. The reporting guidelines issued within the company are posted in full on the company web site.

Sources: BP health, safety and environment performance, www.bp.com/corp_reporting/hse_perform/index.asp; BP environmental performance—group reporting guidelines, www.bp.com/downloads/273/Environmentalguidelines2000.doc; BP today, www.bp.com/our_company/bp_today.asp.

Despite the unsteady platform provided by the Kyoto Protocol, many cities, various corporations, and some European countries moved ahead to develop a capacity to operate in what came to be known as a carbon-constrained world. These players expected that carbon dioxide emissions would be regarded as a liability in that world, and hence the ability to reduce emissions would become an important asset. The trading of credits for emissions reductions was one of the "flexible mechanisms" identified by the Kyoto Protocol to encourage reductions at the lowest possible cost. (See later in the chapter for details on this and other flexible mechanisms.)

The extent to which trading of emission reduction credits could be used to meet national reduction targets was left for future Conferences of the Parties to the Protocol. (See Box 7.3.)

The degree of certainty/uncertainty that surrounds the issue is illustrated by a quotation from a representative of Royal Dutch/Shell at the Sixth Conference of the Parties at the Hague in November 2000: "The cost

BOX 7.3   The Conference of the Parties to the Framework Convention on Climate Change

The titles are cumbersome and the acronyms are numerous, but the main elements of the international negotiations on climate change are fairly simple. Based on the scientific reports of the Intergovernmental Panel on Climate Change, the United Nations General Assembly, in December 1990, established an Intergovernmental Negotiating Committee. This committee, in turn, drew up the United Nations Framework Convention on Climate Change (UNFCCC) that came into force in 1994 with the requisite 50 signatures. Almost all members of the United Nations have now signed this Framework Convention.

At the UN, a convention is like a "problem statement." Eventually the means to address the problem should be agreed to in a treaty. The steps from convention to treaty may take many years, and indeed some UN treaties remain unratified after decades of negotiations. The bridge from a convention to a treaty is a protocol, which might be thought of as a draft treaty without the dotting of the i's and the crossing of the t's. The negotiations along this process are called Conferences of the Parties (to the Framework Convention on Climate Change), known as COPs. The first COP took place in Berlin in 1994. In addition to the national delegations there were many other interested parties including the Global Climate Coalition (Box 7.1), representatives of the insurance industry, and numerous nongovernmental organizations (NGOs).

The third COP, in 1997, produced the Kyoto Protocol. Many parties signed the Protocol, and some have even had their agreement ratified by the national governments. However, the parties were divided into two distinct groups—the richer countries that signed Annex 1, and the poorer countries, which did not. Only Annex 1 committed governments to emissions reductions. The Kyoto Protocol was a very tentative agreement that produced a deadlock between

(Continued)

BOX 7.3 *(Continued)*

Annex 1 parties at COP 6 at the Hague in 2000. In March 2001 the United States withdrew from the negotiations. In July of that year the remaining Annex 1 parties rebuilt an agreement in Bonn (officially known as COP 6 Part II), but still with many crucial issues undecided. COP 7 at Marrakech developed some of the operating rules but postponed difficult issues such as the legally binding nature of the agreement and the inclusion of developing countries in the treaty. (Annex 1 countries are listed in Appendix C of this book). Generally, COP 7 is viewed as a qualified success that will keep the process moving toward ratification, even without the participation of the United States (Nicholls 2002).

The UNFCCC story is far from over. As David Victor predicted in the fall of 2000, "The story about Kyoto is not how hard the negotiators worked, but how easy it was. Progress was rapid, and the speedy creation of an emission trading system seemed too good to be true. It was."

Sources: COP 7 meeting at Marrakech, www.unfccc.int/cop7/index.html; UNFCCC home page, www.unfccc.int; Grubb et al. 1999; Victor 2001.

of a ton of carbon might be $5, $50, or $100—we don't know. But not zero" (Innovest SVA 2001b). This type of public statement by a major oil company signifies a historic reversal of the trends in the relative prices of materials (including energy) and labor. Innovation throughout the twentieth century was dominated by the search for higher labor productivity to counteract its rising price as standards of living and expectations rose. In the same period the price of materials and energy was falling. The attribution of a price—as yet conjectural—to carbon dioxide emissions promises to change all of this. Understanding the implications of this shift is emerging slowly, and the market has yet to respond. For example:

> *At present, virtually none of the substantial differentials in companies' carbon risk exposure are currently being captured by traditional securities analysis. Yet under plausible scenarios, the discounted present value of potential future carbon liabilities within a single energy-intensive manufacturing firm could represent as much as 40% of its entire market capitalization. (Innovest SVA 2001b, 1)*

The potential enormity of the shift in focus implied by this development has placed attention on the cost of adaptation and the extent to which the trading of emissions reduction credits can bring the cost down.

The expectations raised by such "flexible mechanisms" fueled a growing interest in encouraging market-based mechanisms for emissions reduction, discussed later in the chapter. The journal *Environmental Finance* began publication in October 1999 to cover the impact of environmental issues on the financial sector and its corporate clients, including emissions trading as well as the risks and opportunities provided by the Kyoto Protocol. It also organized conferences specifically on the topic of "carbon finance." However, we are still some time away from the day when carbon becomes an important tradable commodity. Emissions reductions can become valuable only when governments commit to making them mandatory. So far this has not happened. The failure to reach agreement at the Hague was a great disappointment to the traders-in-waiting. The U.S. government's withdrawal of its Kyoto commitment in March 2001 was another step backward.

The Bonn meeting in July 2001, COP 6 Part II, revived the Protocol but still without quantifying the extent to which the buying of emissions credits can be used to meet a national commitment to reductions. The agreement evaded the point by stating, "Domestic emissions reductions must be a significant element of the effort made by each party [i.e., country]" (Nicholls 2001n). In the meantime, some countries, such as Britain, are launching national trading schemes (Rosewell 2001). (See Chapter 9 for further details on national carbon dioxide reduction initiatives.) In October 2001 the European Union outlined its own trading scheme, which is scheduled to begin in 2005. The will to persevere despite the political complexity is driven by a strengthening consensus on just what the physical consequences of climate change will be.

PHYSICAL IMPACTS OF CLIMATE CHANGE

Even before government policy makers and corporate leaders became more publicly concerned about the likelihood and implications of climate change, scientists had been producing detailed reports on the subject, beginning with the First Assessment of the Intergovernmental Panel on Climate Change (IPCC) in 1990. The report included the key conclusion "that rising concentrations of carbon dioxide and other greenhouse gases in the atmosphere were caused by human activities and would cause global temperatures to rise, with accompanying climatic changes" (Grubb et al.

1999). In 2001 the panel produced its Third Assessment (IPCC 2001a, 2001b, 2001c), which is available on the Web at www.ipcc.ch.

Each assessment exercise involves thousands of scientists from around the world, and each line of the draft reports is scrutinized in detail before it is approved. At first—sometimes for overtly political reasons—there was some reluctance to make any unequivocal statements about the fact that the climate was changing due to manmade emissions of greenhouse gases. The implications of such a simple admission were very widespread and deeply disturbing. However, in the recently released Third Assessment the language is very clear:

> *Available observational evidence indicates that regional changes in climate, particularly increases in temperature,* have already affected *a diverse set of physical and biological systems in many parts of the world. Examples of observed changes include shrinkage of glaciers, thawing of permafrost, later freezing and earlier break-up of ice on rivers and lakes, lengthening of mid- to high-latitude growing seasons, poleward and altitudinal shifts of plant and animal ranges, declines of some plant and animal populations, and earlier flowering of trees, emergence of insects and egg-laying of birds.* (IPCC 2001b, 3; our emphasis)*

There are some potentially positive implications of projected climate change, such as:

- Increased crop yields in some midlatitude regions for small temperature increases.
- Potential increase in timber supply from appropriately managed forests.
- Increased water availability in some water-scarce regions.
- Reduced winter mortality in mid and high latitudes.
- Reduced energy demand for space heating.

However, the impacts are mostly negative, including:

- General reduction in crop yields in tropical and subtropical regions.
- Reduced crop yields in midlatitudes for anything other than small temperature increases.
- Decreased water availability in many water-scarce regions, especially in the subtropics.
- Widespread increased risk of flooding from heavier precipitation events and sea-level rise.
- Increased energy demand for space cooling.

The lists may appear confusing, and the actual implications for the financial services sector and the rest of the global economy may be unclear. It is, however, possible to summarize the present state of knowledge quite briefly as follows. Because we are releasing greenhouse gases to the atmosphere faster than those gases can be absorbed from the atmosphere by the ocean, they accumulate in the atmosphere. There they enhance the greenhouse effect, which keeps the surface of the earth and the lower atmosphere warmer than they would otherwise be. This is the primary impact. The enhanced warming effect will have three main secondary effects: sea level will rise (due to thermal expansion of the oceans and melting glaciers and ice caps), the hydrological cycle will become more intense (producing more frequent and heavier rainfall events), and the rate of evaporation of moisture from the earth's surface will increase. These physical changes will in turn affect our ecosystems and society in a number of ways, as summarized in Table 7.1.

There are still very large areas of uncertainty. In general, scientists know the direction in which the changes will go, but not the rate of change

TABLE 7.1   Secondary and Tertiary Effects of Global Warming

Secondary Effect	Tertiary Effect
Sea-level rise	• Coastal and estuarine flooding • Impeded drainage off the land • Increased impact of storm surges
Intensified hydrological cycle	• More intense rainfall events, overland flooding • More frequent and violent convective storms • More powerful windstorms • More frequent and/or prolonged droughts
Increased rate of evaporation of moisture from the earth's surface	• Reduced moisture available for plants, with negative impacts for crops, trees, and livestock; hence greater demand for irrigation water • Increased cost to supply water to human settlements, industry, conventional energy producers • Impedance of transportation by inland waterways, such as the Great Lakes • Desiccation and subsidence in some soils, especially clays

or its ultimate magnitude. For example, the IPCC's Third Assessment predicts sea level rise from 1990 to 2100 of between 0.09 and 0.88 meters, and a globally averaged surface temperature increase in the same time period of between 1.4°C and 5.8°C (IPCC 2001a, 23). Some major elements of the climate system may, or may not, change. It is not known whether hurricanes will increase in distribution, frequency, or intensity. It is not known how quickly the Arctic and Antarctic ice caps are melting. If the Arctic ice goes quickly, then the resultant reduction in salinity of the ocean could reduce the flow of the North Atlantic Drift, which currently warms northwestern Europe. It is not known whether the Asian monsoon system will strengthen under warmer conditions. Finally, it is not known how the predicted tertiary effects will interact to produce more complex interactions, such as the permafrost melting and thereby releasing methane to the atmosphere, or the impact of warmer weather on forest fires, perhaps turning the forest into a source of carbon dioxide for the atmosphere instead of acting as a sink that takes up carbon dioxide. An adverse combination of these interactions could significantly speed up the rate of global warming, producing the so-called runaway greenhouse effect. The consequences of such a development are largely unpredictable but are hardly likely to be beneficial to human society.

IPCC Working Group II, on Impacts, Adaptation, and Vulnerability, produced a table of extreme climate-related phenomena and their effects on the insurance industry, which is summarized as Table 7.2. The expected changes will have implications for health, life, property, business interruption, crop, vehicle, flood, marine, and aviation insurance.

VULNERABILITY BY ECONOMIC SECTOR

If we assume that the world economy will become carbon-constrained and that international trading of emissions reduction credits (carbon trading) will become a reality, then the implications for the world economy will vary sharply between sectors and by companies within sectors. This can already be seen to be happening in Britain where a combination of the Climate Change Levy (a tax on the business use of energy) and the Non-fossil Fuel Obligation (green energy mandated for 10 percent of supply by 2010 for energy producers) simultaneously discouraged carbon-based fuel and encouraged renewables. The policy has since been replaced by a new "Renewables Obligation" (U.K. Department of Trade and Industry 2002). As the cost of using carbon-based fuel is increased by the tax, there will be more pressure to achieve energy efficiency, and hence demand will soften

TABLE 7.2 Extreme Climate-Related Events and Their Effects on the Insurance Industry

Changes in Extreme Climate Phenomena	Likelihood	Type of Event Relevant to Insurance Sector	Sensitive Sectors/Activities	Sensitive Insurance Branches
Temperature Extremes				
Higher daily maximums, heat waves	Very likely	Heat wave	Electricity reliability, human settlements	Health, life, property, business interruption
		Heat wave, drought	Forest, agriculture, water resources, electricity demand and reliability, industry, health, tourism	Health, crop, business interruption
Higher daily minimums, fewer cold waves	Very likely	Frost, frost heave	Agriculture, energy demand, health, transport, human settlements	Health, crop, business interruption, vehicle
Rainfall/ Precipitation Extremes				
More intense precipitation events	Very likely over many areas	Flood	Human settlements	Property, flood, vehicle, crop, business interruption, life, health, marine
Increased summer drying and associated risk of drought	Likely in most mid-latitude continental interiors	Summer drought, land subsidence, wildfire	Forest, agriculture, water resources, (hydro)electricity, human settlements	Crop, property, health
Increased intensity of midlatitude storms	Little agreement	Snowstorm, ice storm, avalanche	Forest, agriculture, energy distribution and reliability, mortality, tourism	Property, crop, vehicle, aviation, life, business interruption
		Hailstorm	Agriculture, property	Property, crop, vehicle, aviation

(Continued)

TABLE 7.2 *(Continued)*

Changes in Extreme Climate Phenomena	Likelihood	Type of Event Relevant to Insurance Sector	Sensitive Sectors/Activities	Sensitive Insurance Branches
Intensified droughts and floods associated with El Niño events	Likely	Drought and flood	Forest, agriculture, water resources, (hydro)electricity, human settlements	Property, flood, vehicle, crop, marine, life, health, business interruption
Wind Extremes				
Increased intensity of midlatitude storms	Little agreement	Midlatitude windstorm	Forest, electricity distribution and reliability, human settlements	Property, crop, vehicle, aviation, life, business interruption
Increase in tropical cyclone peak wind intensities, mean and peak precipitation intensities	Likely over some areas	Tropical storm, including cyclone, hurricane, typhoon	Forest, electricity distribution and reliability, human settlements, agriculture	Property, crop, vehicle, aviation, life, business interruption

Source: Adapted from IPCC 2001c.

for that type of fuel. If these measures were supported by the elimination of subsidies of fossil fuels, then the trend toward "decarbonizing" energy would be further accelerated (Mansley 1994).

Although attention is usually focused on the cost of economic response to climate change, there will also undoubtedly be companies that will prosper. The most obvious gains will be in the energy sector for firms that provide renewable energy, fuel cells, and any form of power generation that has a low environmental impact. They will be able to enjoy a "pro-climate change" premium (Innovest SVA 2001b). Similarly, providers of information technology that contribute toward lower carbon budgets (e.g., video-conferencing versus face-to-face meetings) also stand to benefit.

The list of vulnerable sectors is much longer, yet within each sector there will be some companies that do relatively well and, as long as there is continuing demand for the services that they provide, then they will prosper. For every company there will be opportunities to use energy more efficiently and to switch to less carbon-intensive sources. Nowhere is the positioning for such advantage more evident than in the automobile industry, which has already been subjected to air quality regulation for several decades. California began this revolution in 1990 with legislation that requires every major producer selling automobiles in the state to make zero-emission vehicles account for 10 percent of annual sales by the year 2003. (See Box 7.4.) Environmental success in the automobile industry means much more than financial benefit for individual companies, because it would also reduce public pressure to ignore climate change for fear of significant lifestyle changes, specifically being pressured to exchange private automobiles for public transport. This fear of public resentment is one of the major forces for inertia in governmental climate change policy, the other being fear of losing international competitiveness.

Major impacts will be absorbed by the fossil fuel industry itself, from coal, oil, and gas producers to electricity generators. Other highly energy-

BOX 7.4   "Power to Change the World"—The Story of Ballard Power

"We are faced with accelerated global warming and mounting evidence of the threat that global warming and air pollution pose to our quality of life." (Firoz Rasul, Chairman and CEO of Ballard Power Systems, Inc.)

The development of the fuel cell began long before some of the big oil and gas and automotive companies agreed that climate change was a real threat and that action was required. It was developed as a response to the urban air quality problems that were being exacerbated by the proliferation of vehicles powered by the internal combustion engine. The first fuel cell patent was granted in 1880, but there was no demand for it then, and none appeared in the twentieth century as long as the public was content with end-of-pipe solutions to air pollution. But there is no end-of-pipe solution for carbon dioxide emissions from motor vehicles.

Ballard's fuel cell is based on a proton exchange membrane (PEM) that converts hydrogen into electricity in the presence of a platinum catalyst. The hydrogen can be obtained from natural gas, methanol, petroleum, or renewable sources. Its exhaust consists of unused air and water vapor. It has enough power density to run an automobile and a bus. It produces energy at more than twice the efficiency

(Continued)

BOX 7.4 *(Continued)*

of an internal combustion engine and at the same level as a battery without the time-consuming process of recharging the battery. (Batteries depend on electricity, which is mostly derived from fossil fuels.) Thus the fuel cell is both efficient and pollution-free. Prototypes have been on the road since 1994. Why is it taking so long to be brought to the market?

The answer is that it requires a great deal of money to fund the research and development (R&D) required to replace a major, mature industry. As long as there was no demand there was no need to make this investment. Like the emergence of the renewable energy industry, it required regulations that state that the old system is no longer acceptable. In the case of the application of fuel cell technology to automobiles, the key legislation was passed by the state of California in 1990, requiring the six leading automakers to ensure that 10 percent of the cars sold in 2003 would be zero-emission vehicles (ZEVs). Other states, mainly in the northeast (including New York and Massachusetts), adopted the California requirement. A biennial review process has seen some scaling down of this target over the years, balanced by an enlargement of the requirement for "near zero-emission vehicles." In January 2001 the current requirement was confirmed and no further reviews were planned. Reaction from the industry was mixed: Ford said it could make the target, while General Motors remained opposed to the legislation.

For Ballard Power, it was extremely important that California remained on track. To sustain itself through the long period of R&D it formed a partnership with DaimlerChrysler and Ford, both of which hold significant shares in Ballard (43 percent combined). It formed other partnerships in California, Europe, and Japan. And it targeted three separate markets—automotive (both automobiles and buses), stationary power generation, and portable generators. It has conducted field trials for several years, and it opened its first production facility next to the corporate headquarters in Burnaby, British Columbia, in 2000.

Sources: Ballard Power Systems, 2000 Annual Report, available at www.ballard.com/pdf/annual/Ballard-AR2000-full.pdf; DaimlerChrysler Environmental Report 2001, available at www.daimlerchrysler.de/index_e.htm; Ford Motor Company, see "Environmental Initiatives" and "Environmental Vehicles" at www.ford.com/servlet/ecmcs/ford/index.jsp; Kennedy 2001; Plungis 2001.

intensive industries, such as chemicals, iron and steel, and metallurgy, will also come under intense pressure to reduce emissions. The cement industry has its own particular problems, as it creates large amounts of carbon dioxide directly from the production process.

The water supply and treatment business—now increasingly private and organized on a global basis—will come under a variety of pressures, some from climate change and some from the reduced availability of the basic resource. However, for the companies that understand the issues and are preparing themselves for a more complex operating environment there are major opportunities. For example, despite the growing shortage of available water at traditional (low) prices, many large cities in industrial countries still have *no* treatment of wastewater. The European Commissioner for the Environment identified (2001) more than 30 such European Community cities with a population over 150,000, and a similar number with inadequate treatment measures. Ironically, the most famous city with inadequate treatment was Brussels, the commissioner's seat of office (European Commission DG XI 2001). The water industry will have to deal with a more irregular supply, higher evaporation losses, a rise in sea level, and a more intensive hydrological cycle.

The vulnerability of multinational companies to climate change will vary greatly from region to region. Although the greatest temperature increases are projected for the higher latitudes, it is the poorer, tropical countries that are most vulnerable to the impacts of climate change because they have less resilience in their socioeconomic systems to enable damaged areas to be restored. For example, whereas hurricanes may leave areas of the United States without power or water for a number of days, the same impact in a poorer country could linger for weeks and months. Even among the richer countries, resilience may be less than we assume. Canada is vulnerable to even small increases in temperature, as this will produce predictable increases in the risk of forest fires:

> *Under a warming climate, large increases in the areal extent of extreme fire danger and a lengthening of the fire season were found. Moreover, the impacts will include more frequent and severe fires, shorter growth periods between fires, proportionally younger stands, and a decrease in the carbon storage of northern Canadian forests. (Natural Resources Canada 2000; http://sts.gsc.nrcan.gc.ca/adaptation/ sensitivities/map3.htm)*

Likewise, although Britain historically enjoys an equable climate with year-round rainfall, climate change is already producing altered conditions, with wetter winters and drier summers, especially in the water-stressed southeast (Wade et al. 1999). As the West Yorkshire drought of 1995 proved, even the wetter parts of the country can be taken by surprise and subjected to unusual conditions (Bakker 2000).

ANTICIPATING HUMAN RESPONSE TO CLIMATE CHANGE

The present concentrations of greenhouse gases in the atmosphere are such that we are already committed to a changed climate. We can adapt to these new conditions as far as we understand them. Mitigative action to reduce emissions will serve only to reduce the speed at which climate changes and determine the ultimate conditions in place when concentrations peak and fall. Although this situation is becoming more widely understood, the speed with which society makes a significant response to curb emissions is very difficult to predict, as were the outcomes from two key Conferences of the Parties (the Hague, November 2000, and Bonn, July 2001). Even so, while politicians may prevaricate and try to assess the public mood, companies must plan ahead while making certain assumptions.

If we stay with the basic premises of this chapter—that the world will become carbon-constrained and that international trading of carbon credits will evolve—then some business options become more attractive than others. The big lesson that should have been learned from the asbestos problem was that *delay does not pay*. Companies that could have taken positive action on asbestos liabilities in the 1970s and 1980s and did not do so became bankrupt in the 1990s. As climate change is now widely accepted as a real condition that is not going to fade away, then almost every enterprise needs to factor this into its strategic plan. The two most salient planning assumptions are that both energy and water—essential for every activity—will become more expensive relative to other inputs. Capital will also become more expensive or difficult to attract for a company that fails to develop an environmentally sound strategy.

Under this much uncertainty, projections are of little use. Instead, the planning process must be built around scenarios, imagined conditions that would constitute a feasible response to the current challenges. For example, in 1995 Royal Dutch/Shell developed two long-term scenarios for energy use. One required a transformation to "cool power," based on renewables and advanced natural gas technology. Under this scenario it was assumed that the economy would continue to grow and energy use would rise proportionally. The second scenario was based on "dematerialization" and improved energy efficiency, founded on innovation in information technology, telecommunications, materials, and biotechnology (Romm 1999). These two scenarios are not exclusive; the path we take could (and is likely to) contain elements of both. What are the factors that will influence the path we take? Will the innovative companies suffer for the risks that they assume, or will they seize the first mover advantage?

CRITICAL FACTORS IN HUMAN RESPONSE TO CLIMATE CHANGE

The Future of the Kyoto Convention

The Bonn Conference of the Parties in July 2001 rescued the Kyoto Protocol from the Hague impasse and the subsequent unilateral withdrawal from the negotiations by the United States delegation. Ironically, at Bonn the European delegates accepted many of the U.S.-led proposals that they had rejected at the Hague (Nicholls 2001n). However, much of what was agreed to at Bonn is still unclear, and it does not provide an adequate basis for companies to develop plans to manage their carbon risk.

Beyond those very important details (such as the role of emissions trading), the biggest factor that determines the immediate future of the Kyoto Protocol is the likelihood of the participation of the United States government. In the early 1990s, as a negotiating mechanism for the Convention on Climate Change was being developed, the most vocal opposition came from the Global Climate Coalition (Box 7.1). This coalition was made up of global companies, most of them headquartered in the United States and dominated by big oil. For them the UNFCCC represented an unacceptable alliance of two of their favorite targets—the United Nations and the environmentalists. Much of the rest of the American political landscape was less antagonistic. For example, the central administration of the Clinton-Gore White House supported the conferences on climate change. Toward the end of his second term of office President Bill Clinton starkly outlined the need for the rich countries to move first on climate change in order to demonstrate their sincerity and resolve to developing countries:

> *There's no way in the world we'll be able to convince our friends in India or China, which over the next 30 years will become bigger emitters of greenhouse gases than we are, that they can take a different path to development, and that we're not trying to keep them poor, unless we*

can demonstrate that we have . . . evidence that a different way will work. Every member of Congress here will tell you that a huge portion of decision makers in our country and throughout the world—and most troubling, in some of the biggest developing nations—still believe that you cannot have economic growth unless you pour more green-house gases into the atmosphere. There is nothing so dangerous as for a people to be in the grip of a big idea that is no longer true. It was once true that you had to put more greenhouse gases into the atmos-phere to grow the economy, to build a middle class, make a country rich. It is not true anymore. (U.S. President Bill Clinton to the Democ-ratic Leadership Council, May 28, 2000)

American science, much of U.S. business, and sections of the public sup-ported an active engagement in response to climate change.

The election of President George W. Bush reversed this trend, at least at the top of the federal government. The new president presented an en-ergy strategy that appeared to address popular alarm at the California en-ergy deregulation debacle, including blackouts and spiraling prices for natural gas. More power supply was the answer, relying on fiscal encour-agement for fossil fuel producers, a reference to energy efficiency, and re-newed support for nuclear power as a clean environmental alternative. It was like a reversion to the position in the early part of the decade, with the difference that much of the rest of opinion had moved on. When a climate change policy was eventually presented in February 2002 it was limited to voluntary measures to improve energy efficiency, with no commitment to absolute reductions (Biello 2002c).

It is not yet clear when and how these differing U.S. perspectives on climate change will be resolved. Fear pulls in two quite opposite directions. The anti-Kyoto view is that compliance by the rich countries will put them at a competitive disadvantage with developing countries who have yet to make a commitment to reductions. The pro-Kyoto (or perhaps something like Kyoto) view is that failure to become engaged in the problem of cli-mate change *now* will put the United States at a competitive disadvantage vis-à-vis Europe and Japan *later*, when the impact and danger of climate change can no longer be ignored.

In addition—even without the withdrawal of the United States from the negotiations—several fundamental problems make the future of the Kyoto Protocol very difficult to predict. No matter how the negotiations are con-ducted, the basic problem is extremely complex. Verification of compliance and punishment of noncompliance have barely been touched upon in the negotiations. Also, no official proposal has been made to fully enlist the support of developing countries in the global need to reduce greenhouse gas emissions. These issues will be briefly outlined later in this chapter.

Taxes on Energy and Carbon Emissions

There is a general understanding that greenhouse gas emissions cannot be reduced by a classic "command and control" approach, relying on laws passed by national governments and enforced by teams of government inspectors. Every one of us is responsible for carbon dioxide emissions. The climate change process is far too diffuse to be reversed by command and control. The next possibility along the spectrum from control to laissez-faire to anarchy is to use taxes to increase prices, in order to meet the policy objective of reducing demand for energy. If the price is increased artificially by a tax, then demand must go down—a nice blend of command and control and the market, perhaps. This is the logic behind "sin taxes" on alcohol, cigarettes, and such. It may produce revenue for the taxing authority, but there is little evidence that it can significantly reduce demand when that demand is entrenched in personal expectations such as automobile-based mobility.

A gasoline tax does little to reduce the number of miles driven. However, it does have other desirable environmental effects. It encourages the development of energy-efficient technologies. A more discrete approach is to tax the carbon content of fuels, rather than simply taxing the use of all fossil fuels. This will certainly shift consumption from the most carbon-intensive fuels to the less intensive. In other words, it will move consumption for electricity generation along the coal to oil to natural gas transition, and finally it will move consumption from fossil fuels to renewables. Britain has applied a Climate Change Levy on energy users while reducing employers' contributions to unemployment insurance in an attempt to make the measure revenue-neutral. This has the advantage of making it more expensive to use energy while making it cheaper to employ people.

It is possible that some national governments will ratify the Kyoto Protocol and then use a carbon tax to achieve their national reduction targets. The concern is that this approach will impose costs on producers and consumers throughout the countries that sign and ratify the Kyoto Protocol with unpredictable—and possibly very negative—effects on their economies. There are concerns that national governments (who are the negotiators at the Conference of the Parties) will never take this kind of political risk. Even the greenest countries will hesitate in case they disadvantage their economies while the free riders continue to do nothing about climate change. We could commit ourselves to a global game of chicken and all go over the cliff together. The dangers inherent in this carbon taxing approach make the untried complexities of carbon trading quite attractive by comparison.

Trading Credits for Carbon Dioxide Emissions Reduction

One reason that important elements of the private sector, including some energy producers, have become supporters of policies to reduce emissions is that the trading of reduction credits could become a huge and lucrative business. The logic is simple and powerful. If climate change is recognized as a potentially serious problem, then something must be done about it. The something could be a binding international agreement among national governments that then enforce reductions through command and control measures. This solution is quite unlikely because the command and control approach is out of fashion, and governments are finding it extremely difficult to develop an agreement, anyway. It is widely feared that this approach would be both highly expensive and ultimately ineffectual. From the early deliberations on an international climate change agreement, various mechanisms were proposed to give the implementation process some flexibility. Of these flexible mechanisms, carbon trading was the most popular.

An alternative approach to command and control is to encourage the development of markets to trade reduction credits. It would still require an international agreement to cap emissions at successively lower levels in order to reduce the speed at which climate changes. But the driving dynamic would be provided by the profit motive, not simply regulation and enforcement. Likewise, a market approach would still need agreement on measuring and continually verifying compliance. In terms of motivation, the essential difference is that under the command and control approach everyone will pay throughout their lifetimes for a benefit that may not be enjoyed until several generations later. Under the market approach some people—the successful emissions reduction experts, the carbon traders, and the providers of their trading infrastructure, such as lawyers and consultants—will begin to benefit immediately. Some companies have already invested heavily under the assumption that emissions reduction will soon become a major driving force for the global economy. (See Box 7.5.)

Even while the Kyoto process is still struggling for definition and ratification, carbon trading has already begun. There was a useful model to analyze in the successful trading of NO_x and SO_2 reduction in the United States. Live simulations were run to see how a trading system could be made to work. Companies like BP, Shell, and TransAlta set their own reduction targets and established in-house trading systems between different

BOX 7.5   Renewable Energy—What Is Driving the Market?

"Imagine a world where energy is so clean it causes zero pollution and so simple you hardly know it's there. No sound, no smoke, no CO_2—just pure power. That world is here now. That world is solar." So opens the web site for BP Solar, advertising solar power as "the natural source for electricity." This is quite a change of direction for the seventh largest company in the world, the third largest oil and gas producer, and a founding member of the Global Climate Coalition. (Size is measured in terms of revenue in 2000 [Economist 2001b]). What forces are making the renewables market attractive to the likes of BP?

The main driver is the growing realization that climate change is a real phenomenon that requires attention now. The response will include a change in the energy mix that powers the modern world. The minute portion of that mix that comes from renewable sources is growing rapidly, estimated at a rate of 30 percent per year. It is becoming a large enough niche to attract the traditional energy producers like BP, Shell, and Texaco. Renewables are being taken from the domain of the eccentric and becoming real business. In the words of Admiral Richard Truly, director of the U.S. National Renewable Energy Laboratory, "Our engineering choices are limited—either we significantly reduce or eliminate these [greenhouse gas] emissions or sequester CO_2 to offset potential global climate changes. Or we wait and see, and hope for the best."

The U.K. Renewable Energy Advisory Group defined renewable energy as "the term used to cover those energy flows that occur naturally and repeatedly in the environment and can be harnessed for human benefit. The ultimate sources of most of this energy are the sun, gravity and the earth's rotation" (quoted in Boyle 1996). Renewables include solar energy (passive and photovoltaic), wind, waves, running water, biomass, tidal, geothermal, and energy from waste.

In addition to concerns over climate change, the renewables market is being driven by a desire for security of power supply. Businesses dependent on information technology require a highly dependable energy supply—one that provides energy despite extreme weather events (like the Montreal ice storm in 1998 and hurricanes), despite the uncertainties arising from deregulation (outages in California in 2000), and despite the threat of terrorism. As renewable energy cannot be depleted—by definition—the price should be less volatile than

(Continued)

BOX 7.5   *(Continued)*

prices of oil and gas, subject as they are to interruptions of supply. In fact, the price should fall steadily as the market grows and the technology improves.

The growth of renewable energy is being hastened by regulation throughout the industrial world from the United Kingdom to Texas. "Texas, the quintessential oil and gas state, is expected to install around 1,000 MW of renewable energy power plants this year—more than has been built in the state during the previous 100 years" (Sloan 2001). Most (90 percent) of this new renewable energy will come from wind power, and the rest from landfill gas and renovations to existing hydroelectric power. It is enough to provide power for 250,000 "average Texas homes." It is being driven by regulations requiring that a percentage of an electricity retailer's output must be renewable and is being facilitated by trading renewable energy credits.

Sources: BP Solar, www.bpsolar.com; National Renewable Energy Laboratory, www.nrel.gov; Boyle 1996; Sloan 2001.

business units. The United Kingdom, Denmark, Norway, and Switzerland have established—or are in the process of establishing—the rules for national trading schemes. In the United States a regional scheme is under development at the Chicago Climate Exchange. (See Box 7.6.) The European Union scheme is scheduled to begin in 2005. Although these are very early days it is not impossible to imagine that carbon trading might evolve like other commodity markets. At first trading may be local, perhaps even confined to national boundaries, but eventually these regional schemes will link up to become a global system with international standards for payment and quality.

Other Flexible Mechanisms

From the beginning, the climate change deliberations were haunted by the specter of world poverty that is reflected in the disparate levels of emissions per capita from rich and poor countries. Typically, a member of a rich country is responsible for about 12 tons of carbon dioxide per year while the average poor country inhabitant emits about one-eighth of that amount. (See Table 7.3.) Most of the excess carbon dioxide in the atmosphere was put

BOX 7.6 Carbon Trading at the Chicago Climate Exchange

Despite the reluctance of many national governments to become engaged in the business of reducing greenhouse gas emissions, some representatives of the business community have already begun to build the infrastructure to support the trading of emissions reduction credits. Companies like CO2e.com have been set up specifically to develop the business. In the United Kingdom the government has established a national Emissions Trading Scheme with support from the business community. In the United States a private-sector initiative has set up the Chicago Climate Exchange "to design and implement a voluntary private pilot market first based in 7 U.S. Midwestern states (Illinois, Indiana, Iowa, Michigan, Minnesota, Ohio, and Wisconsin), and later to be expanded to include national and international sources" (Environmental Financial Products 2001).

Environmental Financial Products, using a grant from the Joyce Foundation to the Kellogg Graduate School of Management at Northwestern University, is administering the pilot scheme. The 7 states chosen for the exercise have a population of 52 million people and a diverse economy representative of the United States. The approximately 40 participating companies include energy (such as BP), chemicals (including DuPont), automotive (such as Ford), insurance (Swiss Re), timber products, renewable energy, and agriculture. The mix includes both major carbon dioxide emitters and sectors that could provide emission offsets—agriculture, timber, and renewables.

Chicago and Mexico City are the first municipalities to join this trading scheme. The Chicago Climate Exchange began development in 2001. "Trading will begin for the entire United States starting in January 2003. Expansion to Canada and Mexico is to follow soon thereafter. The companies participating in the design phase have CO_2 emissions of approximately 800 million tons, which is roughly equal to those of Germany" (Walsh 2002).

Environmental Financial Products has identified 12 steps that need to be taken to establish the market:

Market Establishment: 12 Steps
1. Clearly define the commodity.
2. Establish market oversight.
3. Define baselines.

(Continued)

BOX 7.6 *(Continued)*

> 4. Set emission targets, allocate permits, and monitor emissions.
> 5. Establish uniform allowances, and define eligible credits.
> 6. Develop an allowance clearinghouse.
> 7. Employ existing exchanges and trading systems.
> 8. Develop auctions.
> 9. Refine and develop trade documentation practices.
> 10. Foster harmonization with other research and markets.
> 11. Develop appropriate accounting principles.
> 12. International linkages.
> (© 2001 Environmental Financial Products LLC. Reproduced with express written permission.)
>
>
> *Sources:* CO2e.com—The Global Hub for Carbon Commerce, www. CO2e.com; Emissions Marketing Association, www.emissions.org/; Environmental Financial Products, Chicago Climate Exchange, www.chicago climatex.com; Rosewell 2001; Sandor 2001, 2002.

there by rich countries in the course of their development. It is not realistic to assume that the rich countries could expect the poor to reduce, or cap, their emissions if this means they will remain mired in poverty. Nor is there any means available to enforce such a proposition, even if some would like to support it. That is the political situation.

However, the global nature of the atmospheric situation requires action of some kind to avoid seeing any emissions reduction on the part of the rich countries being wiped out by the growing emissions of the poor.

Two of the flexible mechanisms are Joint Implementation and the Clean Development Mechanism, which may provide a partial solution to this conundrum. Joint Implementation refers to joint projects between Annex 1 parties. The Clean Development Mechanism is an attempt to curb emissions (actual and projected) in poor countries without actually requiring them to pay for doing so. The rich countries would finance these projects and in return receive emissions reduction credits against their own Kyoto commitments. This apparently neat solution to the conundrum could, of course, be interpreted as a means to allow rich countries to continue their own upward trend in emissions while making the

TABLE 7.3 Carbon Dioxide Emissions by Countries Grouped by Income, and the Six Largest Emitters in 1996

	Total in Billion Tons		Tons per Capita	
Countries	1980	1996	1980	1996
Grouped				
Low income	2.1	5.1	0.9	1.5
Middle income	2.8	6.9	3.3	4.8
High income	8.7	10.7	12.3	12.3
World total	13.6	22.6	3.4	4.0
Six Largest				
United States	4.6	5.3	20.1	20.0
China	1.5	3.4	1.5	2.8
Russian Federation	—	1.6	—	10.7
Japan	0.9	1.2	7.9	9.3
India	0.3	1.0	0.5	1.1
Germany	—	0.9	—	10.5

Source: World Bank 2000, Table 10: Energy Use and Emissions, pages 248–249.

poor reduce theirs, thereby not contributing to a genuine solution to the climate change problem.

Commitment from Developing Countries

Developing, or poorer, countries are not Annex 1 signatories to the Kyoto Protocol and therefore have been placed under no obligation to reduce their emissions. Their sole obligation, at this time, is to measure those emissions. This lack of commitment has been criticized by the government of the United States and offered as a reason for its withdrawal from the negotiations. For the obvious reasons stated earlier, at some point there must be a commitment from every country, poor as well as rich. The question revolves around the timing and the distribution of responsibilities for reducing emissions.

One such proposal is known as "contraction and convergence" (Global Commons Institute 1999; Meyer and Cooper 2000). It is based on the principle of equal per capita rights to use the atmosphere as a sink for greenhouse gas emissions. As with all the other approaches, there would be a need for a capping of emissions and the steady reduction of this cap, hence "contraction." Eventually everyone will be accorded the same right either to use or to sell, hence "convergence."

No one can say at this point how the economy will evolve in a carbon-constrained world. Even so, everyone has an interest is seeing that all countries, companies, and people discover a means to bring greenhouse gas emissions down to a level that will stabilize the climate.

CONCLUSION

There is a growing acceptance in the business community that climate change is a real phenomenon. Even the Global Climate Coalition, which vehemently opposed the process that led to the Kyoto Protocol, accepts this now, although it disagrees on the nature of an appropriate response. But it does conclude that "a new approach to climate policy is needed."

The approach adopted by businesses has been quite varied, both by sector and by region. The insurance industry, especially reinsurance and property and casualty, has been voicing concern and taking action for nearly a decade. Insurers believed that the cost of delay could be extremely high, as was their experience with asbestos and environmental liability. Extreme weather events associated with climate change could transform the industry overnight. Banks have been less responsive despite islands of concern, reflected in the signing of the UNEP declaration. In general, the banks have waited for their major clients to raise the issue rather than take the lead on climate change.

Eventually even those sectors that will have to make the most radical changes to respond to climate change—oil and gas, and the automotive industry—have begun to do so. Even now, though, there are wide differences in the degree of acceptance of the need for an active response. BP and Royal Dutch/Shell, for example, are swiftly repositioning themselves as energy providers, and both have set up intracompany trading schemes to reduce greenhouse gas emissions (Kirby 2001c). Since 1997 the competitiveness issue has been reversed. Companies that are not preparing for climate change are the ones that may lose their competitive edge. There is now a growing belief that although adaptation to climate change and acceptance of the necessity to reduce greenhouse gas emissions will entail costs, these costs are likely to be more bearable than the potential costs of procrastination.

As we can see no obvious low-cost solution to the problem, flexibility is essential. Trading credits for emission reductions is a key element of that flexibility in a carbon-constrained world. We are now living with a new business metric in which carbon becomes a liability and the ability to reduce carbon dioxide emissions becomes an asset. Carbon trading is emerging as a new business activity in its own right, whether intracompany, regional, national, or—eventually—international. Once the goal of emissions reduction has been widely accepted, trading credits becomes part of the way forward, rather than a means of evading the climate change issue.

WEB SITES

Ballard Power Systems, (2001) Annual Report 2000	www.ballard.com/pdf/annual/Ballard-AR2000-full.pdf
BP Solar	www.bpsolar.com
Chicago Climate Exchange	www.chicagoclimatex.com.
Climatic Research Unit, University of East Anglia	www.cru.uea.ac.uk/cru/info/warming
CO2e.com—The Global Hub for Carbon Commerce	www.CO2e.com
COP 7 meeting at Marrakech	www.unfccc.int/cop7/index.html
DaimlerChrysler Environmental Report 2001	www.daimlerchrysler.de/index_e.htm
Emissions Marketing Association	www.emissions.org
Environmental Financial Products, Chicago Climate Exchange	www.chicagoclimatex.com
Ford Motor Company, see "Environmental Initiatives" and "Environmental vehicles"	www.ford.com/servlet/ecmcs/ford/index.jsp
Global Climate Coalition	www.globalclimate.org
Global Commons Institute	www.gci.org.uk
International Council for Local Environmental Initiatives	www.iclei.org/co2/index.htm
National Renewable Energy Laboratory	www.nrel.gov
Pew Center on Global Climate Change, Business Environmental Leadership Council	www.pewclimate.org/belc
U.K. Climate Impacts Programme	www.ukcip.org.uk
UNFCCC	www.unfccc.int
Worldwatch Institute	www.worldwatch.org/chairman/issue/000725.html

CHAPTER 8

Environmental Reporting and Verification

INTRODUCTION

Environmental reporting has taken on a greater level of significance for capital markets as lenders, insurers, financial analysts, and investors as well as other stakeholders demand increased levels of information from companies regarding their environmental performances. This chapter explores the evolution of corporate environmental reporting systems as well as trends in the use of environmental reports on a geographic basis. Issues that arise from both the report user's and preparer's perspectives are reviewed, followed by a discussion of progress that is being made in the growing field of environmental reporting and verification.

TRENDS IN ENVIRONMENTAL REPORTING

In 1993, two of the earliest surveys were undertaken that explored the practice of environmental reporting among leading global institutions. KPMG's *International Survey of Environmental Reporting* (1994) was designed to explore the environmental reporting practices of leading international companies in 10 different countries. The findings showed that environmental reporting was starting to be an acceptable form of communicating environmental information to a number of stakeholders. The authors further commented on the nature of these reports, noting that some companies mentioned environmental issues in their annual reports, while others were beginning to produce separate annual environmental reports.

Another environmental survey in 1993, *Coming Clean*, developed a taxonomy of environmental reporting, recognizing five different stages of development of the format of reporting (DTTI et al. 1993). The classification developed in this study identifies a number of stages, from the first type of short "green glossies" through to environmental management reports identified in KPMG's early study. *Coming Clean* goes further, however, and predicts the advent of sustainable development reporting as the fifth and highest level of its taxonomy, which at that time was "unoccupied territory" (UNEP/SustainAbility 1994, 19). The report's authors viewed environmental reporting very much as an iterative process in which companies moved from one stage to the next over a period of time.

A joint UNEP/SustainAbility (1994) project focusing on environmental reporting trends further elaborated on this five-stage reporting model, while also identifying the contrast between Anglo-Saxon and Rhine reporting models. The former focused on policy and management systems and was favored by most North American and U.K. companies. The Rhine model is based more on the input-output life cycle across a company's operations and is favored by European firms.

A further survey was carried out in 1998 by the UNEP Financial Institutions Initiative, to assess the environmental practices of the signatories to its Statement on the Environment and Sustainable Development (UNEP FI 1999). In signing the statement (see Appendix A) institutions made a public commitment to sustainable development. The main objective of the survey was to review the progress made by the signatories in their considerations of environmental issues within their companies and their business activities. The *Financial Institutions Initiative 1998 Survey* found that, in corporate lending and project finance, over 40 percent of respondents would either decline a transaction or include specific conditions in the loan agreement in order to control environmental risk. Reasons for declining loan approvals included the presence of contaminated land, noncompliance with environmental standards, and projects that were not environmentally sound. However, several banks cited examples where preferential financing conditions were made available to support environmentally friendly projects, such as solar energy stations and modernization of power plants. For investment banking and insurance, there were no common methods used to control environmental risk.

Results indicated that a significant number of the respondents had specifically documented policies covering their core financial products such as corporate credit (74 percent) and project finance (63 percent). Fewer had policies covering investment banking (53 percent) or insurance (38 percent). Only 20 percent had formally integrated environmental risk into overall investment portfolio management. The most popular means of communicating and receiving feedback on the environmental performance of the financial sector were through conferences (66 percent) and articles in journals and magazines (62 percent). Less than 50 percent of the organizations produced any form of external environmental report.

Comments offered in the survey suggested that the most significant obstacles to integrating environmental issues into credit and investment analysis were the translation of environmental impacts into financial terms, the availability of comparable data between companies, and the perceived lack of materiality of environmental issues to bottom-line performance (UNEP FI 1999).

KPMG conducted two further surveys on environmental reporting, in 1996 and 1999. The three KPMG reports indicate a steadily increasing trend in environmental reporting, with 13 percent of companies surveyed in 1993 publishing reports, 17 percent in 1996, and 23 percent in 1999. The 1999 KPMG survey included analyses of reports from sectoral, content, and country perspectives.

From the *sectoral* point of view, the KPMG report indicated that chemicals and synthetics industries led the way in environmental reporting, followed by forestry, pulp and paper, utilities, and oil and gas sectors. These results suggest that the industries that are subject to greater public scrutiny are the most likely to report their environmental performance. Looking at the sector that forms the focus of this book, it is interesting that less than 15 percent of companies in the financial services sector produced environmental reports in 1999. These sectoral findings are further supported by a recent Canadian study, in which the majority of the companies that published detailed sustainability reports were in the resource sector, reflecting high government and stakeholder interests in these areas (Stratos Inc. et al. 2001).

In the *contextual* assessment, the 1999 KPMG survey took note of the rising trend of companies choosing to have part or all of their environmental reports externally verified. The main reasons given for verification include "credibility, stakeholder and financial pressures and the benchmarking of environmental reports" (p. x). Companies in the chemicals and synthetics, oil and gas, and utilities sectors led the way in the practice of verification.

From a *country* perspective, the rate of publishing external environmental, health, and safety reports increased over the past several years in all countries except the United States. Considering the total population surveyed in 1999, and compared to 1996 results, Germany published the greatest number (36 percent of the top 100 companies compared to 28 percent in 1996), followed by Sweden (34 percent and 26 percent respectively), the

United Kingdom (32 percent and 27 percent), and Denmark (29 percent, up from 8 percent in 1996). By contrast, the rate of publishing in the United States dropped from 44 percent of companies surveyed in 1996 to 30 percent in 1999.

The results of later analyses provide further support for KPMG's findings. Figure 8.1 indicates that European countries, excluding Scandinavia, account for 59 percent of global environmental reporting, with the U.K. and German corporate environmental reports being the most prevalent. Scott (2000) notes that if Eco-Management and Audit Scheme (EMAS) and International Organization for Standardization (ISO) reporting were included, Germany would be the most productive in terms of environmental reporting, since it accounts for nearly 80 percent of all EMAS reports. North America, including the United States and Canada, accounts for 17 percent of global environmental reporting, while the Asia-Pacific region accounts for 9 percent. Figure 8.1 also demonstrates that Scandinavian countries account for 15 percent of all global environmental reporting, with countries such as Norway and Sweden responding to recent legislation dictating public environmental reporting for corporations (www.corporate-register.com; Scott 2000).

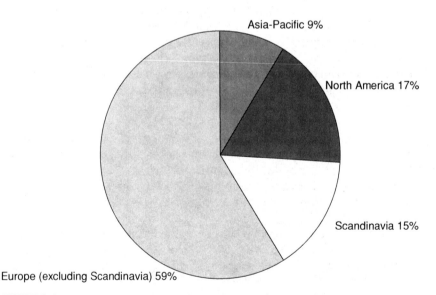

FIGURE 8.1   Environmental Reporting by Region, 1990–2000
Source: Scott 2000.

Stepping Forward, the 2001 report on the status of corporate sustainability reporting in Canada, further supports the KPMG findings, and adds that 26 percent of the top 100 Canadian companies prepare environmental or sustainability reports (Stratos Inc. et al. 2001). This level of participation is approximately the same level as for Denmark and the Netherlands, but well below the leading reporting countries.

A number of forces may account for the difference in reporting rates among countries. Clearly, the results from Denmark can be attributed to the effect of the "green account" requirement legislated in 1996 for companies with significant environmental impacts (Schaltegger 1997).

Scott (2000) explains the observed differences in levels of reporting in terms of the contrasting political regimes that exist in North America and Europe. In the United States, government-industry relations regarding environmental policy have been characterized as adversarial in nature. Due to the litigious nature of the American culture, U.S. companies are reluctant to publish any environmental information that is neither mandated nor already in the public domain. Progressive companies are discouraged from publishing anything broader, fearing that costly lawsuits will be launched by plaintiffs who may argue that expanded environmental reporting demonstrates a company's prior knowledge of environmental concerns (Scott 2000; Skinner 1994).

Further differences are seen due to the choice of policy instruments. In the United Kingdom, the Netherlands, and a number of other European countries, voluntary agreements are more prominent as government-industry relationships have tended to focus more on consultation and cooperation, whereas in the United States, government regulation is the primary policy tool (Goodin 1986; Labatt and Maclaren 1998). Seen from a policy perspective of the U.S. Securities and Exchange Commission (SEC), however, directives such as SEC Rule 10b-5 may provide an incentive for managers to preempt bad quarterly earnings due to environmental liability by issuing some form of environmental report, since stockholders' lawsuits are typically based on the obligation of managers to disclose material information in a timely manner (Skinner 1994). Interestingly, companies such as the Co-operative Bank in the United Kingdom report both positive and negative results in their attempts to reach social and environmental targets; the Co-operative Bank refers to its own sustainability *Partnership Report 2000* as a "warts and all report" (Co-operative Bank 2000, 12).

A further study revealed that companies based in Asia still have a long way to go to meet even average Western standards of reporting, let alone any form of Internet disclosure. *The Internet Reporting Report* suggests that Chinese and Taiwanese companies shy away from providing even financial data, let alone environmental information (UNEP/SustainAbility 1999). Although environmental reporting has had a slow start in Asia, the number of reports emanating from Japanese companies has grown recently. Most notable among these are reports from Omron, Toyota, and Honda. Japan also leads the world in ISO registration and reporting, with well over 2,000 companies reporting, compared to Germany's 1,500 and the United Kingdom's 1,000 (KPMG 1999).

MAIN TYPES OF ENVIRONMENTAL REPORTING

The practice and format of environmental reporting are developing in response to the needs of producers and users of environmental information as well as to the various pressures that are compelling industries to report their environmental performance. In this section, a classification of reports is described, in order to clarify the many influences that affect environmental reporting.

Involuntary Reporting

We have seen in Chapter 6 that independent media exposés and court investigations represent different forms of involuntary reporting. In addition, nongovernmental organization (NGO) publications, such as Friends of the Earth's 2000 report of *Capital Punishment: UK Insurance Companies and the Global Environment*, add other dimensions to public disclosure of corporate environmental behavior.

Self-Regulation and Voluntary Reporting

Autonomous Self-Regulation   The European Community Eco-Management and Audit Scheme (EMAS) and ISO 14001 schemes, discussed in Chapter 4, provide illustrations of environmental reporting where industry is given total autonomy as to whether, and how widely, it reports its environmental performance. Such schemes encourage industries to adopt environmental policies, integrate environmental management systems within their strategic operations, and evaluate and report on their outcomes. Registration in either system is voluntary, but stakeholder pressure is seen to be a competitive factor in providing an incentive for adoption of these programs.

Industry Self-Regulation   The development of industry-specific programs through trade associations has proven to be an effective way of informally regulating an association's constituency regarding environmental factors. The Responsible Care program launched in 1985 by the Canadian Chemical Producers Association (CCPA) provides one of the earliest examples of this form of self-regulation. The initiative comprises a set of guiding principles as well as six codes of management practice, compliance with which is a condition of membership. CCPA issues annual reports that outline the progress members are making in reducing emissions and addressing other environmental issues. Since 1985, chemical producers in 39 countries worldwide have adopted the Responsible Care program. In addition, other sectors such as the petroleum, forestry, and mining industries have adopted similar voluntary programs for their members. Effective sanctions within these organizations can have the effect of public regulations that these operations are striving to avoid.

Self-Regulation within a Legislative Framework Governments will often establish frameworks of rules and then challenge companies to report information, which governments deem the general public has a right to know, but for which they are reluctant to set up full-scale codes and regulations. In these cases, the framework provides a detailed structure within which companies can report environmental performance, but the obligation to do so is imposed by peer group pressure (Ross and Rowan-Robinson 1997). Good examples of this type of self-regulation can be found in many countries. In the United Kingdom, the Environmental Protection Act, Section 34, imposes a duty of care on all companies involved in the production, management, treatment, transport, and disposal of waste (Ross and Rowan-Robinson 1997). Elsewhere in Europe, other programs, such as Germany's Blue Angel eco-labeling program, can be considered as examples of product environmental performance reporting.

In the United States, the Environmental Protection Agency's 33/50 program called for voluntary reductions of the releases of 17 toxic chemicals by industry by 33 percent (relative to 1998 levels) by the end of 1992 and by 50 percent by the end of 1995. The 50 percent reduction level was achieved ahead of schedule in 1994 (EPA 1996). In Canada, the Accelerated Reduction/Elimination of Toxics (ARET) invited industry to voluntarily reduce and eliminate the use of a similar list of toxics by the end of 2000. Environment Canada reports annually on the results of this program by facility and organization, as well as by sector (www.ec.gc.ca/aret/Default.htm). Another voluntary challenge developed as a result of the commitment Canada made to reduce its greenhouse gases levels at the Climate Change Convention. The Voluntary Challenge and Registry (VCR) program invites companies and organizations to develop action plans to limit their greenhouse gas emissions. Annual progress reports that are available to the public reveal the commitments and achievements of all participants (www.vcr-mvr.ca).

Confidential Disclosure Commercial relationships such as those between buyers and suppliers, contractors and subcontractors, lenders and borrowers, and insurers and insured provide a different, yet related, form of environmental disclosure that develops within the framework of common law and public regulation. In these cases, environmental information is disclosed confidentially in contractual negotiations in order to avoid the risk of civil or criminal environmental liability. The motivation to produce and use environmental information in this context has arisen from increased scrutiny on the part of financial institutions with respect to environmental issues, such as contaminated land discussed in Chapter 4. The demand by larger firms for environmental awareness from their suppliers presents an interesting form of motivation, wherein confidential environmental disclosure on the part of suppliers and subcontractors becomes a condition of doing business (Corten et al. 1998).

Nonconfidential Environmental Disclosure A related yet distinct form of voluntary disclosure is that of nonconfidential environmental reporting on the part of industry. This category is differentiated from both confidential and involuntary reporting, since a company itself wishes to publicize its environmental performance, and therefore instigates press conferences, newsletters, and press releases, as well as all forms of individual corporate environmental reports.

Mandated Reporting

Compliance with environmental legislation is perhaps the greatest driving force behind industry's response to environmental concerns. In this context, industries are obliged by legislation to produce certain types of environmental information. In some situations, companies are required to produce environmental information when applying for a license or permit to operate. In others, environmental protection agencies are mandating the registration of activities that reflect a corporation's environmental behavior on a regular basis. The U.S. Toxic Release Inventory (TRI) and Canada's National Pollution Release Inventory (NPRI) are examples of pollution registers that have been mandated in those countries.

In the United Kingdom, the Pension Disclosure Regulation, described in Chapter 6, represents another form of regulation; it obliges trustees of pension funds to state the extent to which social, environmental, and ethical considerations are taken into account in the selection, retention, and realization of the fund's investments. In January 2001, Green MPs in Germany added social disclosure regulations to legislation reforming pension fund disclosure systems. Although the legislation has yet to be passed, the prospects for new pension fund disclosure rules look promising (Kahlenborn 2001).

POLLUTION RELEASE AND TRANSFER REGISTERS

This section outlines the most prominent regulations that have been imposed on companies to account for, and report on, specifics of the release and transfer of pollutants.

North America

United States   The Toxic Release Inventory was authorized under Title III of the Emergency Planning and Community Right to Know Act of 1986 in the Superfund Amendments and Reauthorization Act (SARA) of 1986. Firms subject to the Act (manufacturing facilities under the SIC codes 20–39) were originally required to report, by location, their annual on-site releases and off-site transfers of approximately 320 specified toxic chemicals. Later a further 286 chemicals were added to the list. Firms with fewer than 10 employees or firms with releases below a designated level are exempt from reporting. Also exempt are federal facilities, as well as companies that can justify nondisclosure on grounds of proprietary information (Bowen et al. 1995; Khanna et al. 1998; Konar and Cohen 1997). The first public disclosure of TRI data on toxic emissions appeared in June 1989.

Although the TRI data is the most comprehensive source of information on toxic releases and transfers in the United States, critics claim that it is inadequate on a number of fronts. First, there is no accommodation made for levels of toxicity of the pollutants. Further, not all toxic chemicals are covered, nor are all polluting sources required to report. Nor is there any requirement to report the quantities of toxic chemicals actually used in production or the amounts that are embodied in a company's product. Without this level of reporting, the public has no way of knowing whether the TRI data reported is reliable. Since there is little or no reporting enforcement, there is no way of challenging the accuracy of facility reporting (Schaltegger and Burritt 2000).

Canada Modeled on the U.S. TRI, the Canadian National Pollutant Release Inventory (NPRI) was mandated under the Canadian Environmental Protection Act (CEPA) in 1993 (www.ec.gc.ca/pdb/npri). This is a federal initiative designed to collect annual, comprehensive, national data on releases to air, water, and land, as well as transfers for disposal and recycling of 176 specified substances. NPRI is exposed to much of the same criticism and valuation-relevance discussions as the TRI.

Europe

Scandinavia and the Netherlands Denmark was the first Scandinavian country to legislate public environmental reporting (Rikhardsson 1999). In 1996, companies with significant environmental impacts were required to publish "green accounts." The Netherlands passed legislation mandating environmental reporting, starting in fiscal year 1999 (KPMG 1999). In Norway and Sweden, new Accounting Acts require that all companies include the impacts of their activities and proposed remedial actions in their annual financial reports from 1999 onward. In addition, the offshore industry in Norway has concluded a covenant with the Environmental Department on emission reductions, as well as an agreement on a standard for environmental reporting (KPMG 1999).

United Kingdom In 1991, the U.K. reporting system drew NGO criticism when Friends of the Earth called for improvements to its Chemical Release Inventory (CRI) (Taylor 1995). In response to this and other pressures, the first compilation of emissions data was mandated in 1994, with the registry being renamed the Pollution Inventory (PI) in 1999. The PI covers the emissions of over 150 chemicals of the 2,000 largest industrial processes in England and Wales. Emissions are reported by type, industrial sector, and local authority.

European Union In the European Union, member states are required to register and report emissions data to the European Commission under the mandate of the Integrated Pollution Prevention and Control (IPPC) Directive. This implies that national governments have had to enact new regulations with respect to national emissions registration and reporting systems that comply with the IPPC Directive (KPMG 1999). The EU Pollution Emissions Registry (PER) is based on the U.K. PI and the U.S. TRI, and as such, is intended to improve transparency and availability of information for citizens. The first PER was published in 2001 on the basis of emissions data collected the previous year (Schaltegger and Burritt 2000).

Asia-Pacific

In Australia, companies are expected to give information on performance with respect to environmental regulations that apply to them under that country's amended Corporate Law. In addition, the new National Pollution Inventory, based on the U.S. TRI, requires industrial companies to report emissions and inventories for a specified group of chemicals (KPMG 1999).

ACCOUNTING PROFESSION AND SECURITY REGULATORS

Further forms of mandated reporting come from the securities regulators' and accounting profession's disclosure requirements for risk and environmentally related matters. Since the costs of complying with CERCLA and the Superfund, for example, can have a material effect on a company's financial condition, the Securities and Exchange Commission (SEC) and the practice of accounting with its generally accepted accounting principles (GAAP) have enunciated rules within their professions that address disclosure requirements for potential material corporate environmental liabilities.

Accounting Disclosure Requirements

Inclusion of environmental information in companies' annual reports or financial statements are required in the United States, Canada, Norway, and Sweden (Skillius and Wennberg 1998). In the United States, Financial Accounting Standards Board (FASB)'s Statement 5 (Statement of Financial Accounting Standards SFAS 5) provides authoritative guidance regarding accounting for contingent liabilities. This statement requires companies to accrue contingent liabilities if the loss is "probable" and the amount of the loss can be "reasonably estimated" (FASB 1975). As such, it carries with it important implications in the field of environmental liability, for example, in its application to the future remediation costs of contaminated land. The standards, however, allow for a good deal of managerial discretion in their application, as seen in the variations in Superfund liability estimations (Campbell et al. 1998). FASB's Interpretation No. 14 (SFAS 14), as expressed in *Accounting for Environmental Liabilities* (FASB 1993), specifically addresses the environmental component of contingent liability. In it, further guidance is offered for the estimation of loss despite uncertainties, with the proviso that new information can be added at a later date (Barth and McNichols 1995; Repetto and Austin 2000; Kass and McCarroll 1997; Campbell et al. 1998).

Recognizing the potential for financial repercussions due to future site remediation costs, the Canadian Institute of Chartered Accountants (CICA) incorporated provisions for these possibilities into its CICA handbook in 1990. The section "Capital Assets" requires that corporations accrue liabilities for future removal and site restoration costs when the likelihood of their being incurred is established by law or company policy, and if these costs can be reasonably determined (Li and McConomy 1999). In the natural resources sector, for example, companies are required, by law, to return land and water resources to their original productive state after extractive activities have been terminated. In the case of the mining industry, no uncertainty exists with respect to cost allocations for site remediation since it is a required step after extractive operations (Campbell et al. 1998). For this sector, it can be assumed that reclamation costs are not uncertain and can be reasonably determined, since companies are obliged to provide site closure plans and financial security for such plans to provincial governments. Li and McConomy (1999) maintain that such disclosures provide valuation-relevant information as investors attempt to assess the impact of these future liabilities on capital markets.

In the European Union, the Accounting Advisory Forum (AAF) published its *Environmental Issues in Financial Reporting* (1995), stating that the need to disclose environmental issues related to financial reporting depended on the extent to which they are material to the financial performance or financial position of an undertaking (Skillius and Wennberg 1998).

Securities and Exchange Commission

In the United States, the Securities and Exchange Commission (SEC) requires disclosure in Form 10-K on legislative compliance, judicial proceedings, and liabilities related to the environment (Campbell et al. 1998; KPMG 1999; SEC 1993). The SEC calls for risk and environmentally related matters to be disclosed to the extent that they materially affect present operations and future outlook, so that investors will not be misled by financial statements. Failure to comply with SEC rules can result in prosecution, although most cases in the past have led to an agreement by the charged company to develop a comprehensive environmental audit program, and then to report its findings to the SEC (Kass and McCarroll 1997). Foreign companies wanting to finance their operations through the U.S. securities market as well as U.S. issuers with foreign operations are also subject to SEC Regulation S-K. Disclosure requirements are also set forth by the SEC in its *Management Discussion and Analysis* requiring the reporting of:

> *material events and uncertainties known to management that would cause reported financial information not to be necessarily indicative of future operating results or future financial condition. (Repetto and Austin 2000)*

Together, then, these requirements oblige corporate managers to disclose financially material environmental costs, liabilities, and future risks.

Clearly, uncertainties arising from environmental issues such as future contaminated land remediation and climate change effects on industry come under such disclosure requirements and are potentially material to investors. However, the environment is not specifically referenced in the SEC's guidelines as to what constitutes materiality. Critics argue, therefore, that the SEC rules do little to encourage firms to disclose information about their environmental performance (EPA 2000). Another study claims that the SEC is not enforcing its disclosure rules (Repetto and Austin 2000). Thus, in certain sectors, companies are failing to disclose material environmental risk, in breach of the SEC rules. The study further argues that, of the more than 5,000 administrative proceedings brought by the SEC in the past 25 years, only 3 were based on inadequate environmental disclosure (Nicholls 2000b).

Chapter 6 has indicated that variations in analytical results exist due to the use of differing definitions of environmental performance, data sources, measurements of financial and environmental performance, and analytical approaches. The surveys described in this chapter reveal further evidence of weaknesses in environmental reporting for users of this information. The following sections examine more closely some of the issues brought forward in these surveys, both for corporations preparing environmental reports and for users of such information.

ENVIRONMENTAL REPORTING FROM THE PREPARER'S PERSPECTIVE

Data Collection At present there are no consistent or established ways of measuring either environmental performance or levels of improvement achieved. Nor is there a consistent foundation for choosing indicators, as we have seen in Chapter 4. In addition, although investors and analysts are demanding more specific environmental information, reporting institutions have little idea as to what that information should include (Corten et al. 1998; Flur et al. 1997).

Currently, there are two broad types of indicators that are used to measure environmental performance:

1. Measures of environmental management, which include compliance, environmental management system, and environmental integration into strategic decision making.
2. Operational indicators designed to quantify environmental performance of a company.

Indicators include energy consumption, materials use, emissions, waste, and environmental incidents. These measurements can range from absolute basic data (total CO_2 emitted in a specific time frame), relative data (consumption per unit of output), or a combination of the two (total CO_2 output per unit of production per year) (Skillius and Wennberg 1998; SustainAbility/UNEP 1999).

Targeted Groups of Stakeholders   Since environmental reporting is viewed as a form of communication to a company's stakeholders, it is clear that the potential audience for such a report can be extremely diverse, including government agencies, shareholders, consumers, investors, and nongovernmental organizations (NGOs). Different stakeholder groups do have different content requirements that can affect both the format and content of corporate environmental reports (CERs). While regulatory authorities require information on compliance, shareholders and investors are interested in financial impacts of noncompliance and liability issues. Employees, local communities, and customers may be more interested in qualitative social aspects, while environmental NGOs want answers to their ecological concerns (Azzone et al. 1997; Döbelli 2001; FEE 1999; Schaltegger 1997; Tarna 2001).

In addition, there is a mismatch between how companies think that stakeholders use corporate environmental reports and how they are actually used. Companies think that stakeholders use CERs primarily as sources of reassurance and as a means of identifying examples of best practices. However, the UNEP/SustainAbility survey (1996b) suggests that stakeholders place more emphasis on measuring, monitoring, screening, comparing, and benchmarking companies and industries. Indeed, while "companies are treating CERs primarily as a public relations vehicle, stakeholders are increasingly using CERs to differentiate between companies on the basis of environmental performance data" (UNEP/SustainAbility 1996b, x).

In recognition of the importance of stakeholder commitment, there has been a major shift by proactive corporations seeking feedback from key stakeholders in order to enhance the value and usefulness of CERs. In so doing, corporations gain valuable insights into the needs and agendas of their stakeholders (UNEP/SustainAbility 1996b).

Reporting Demands   In addition to issues of data collection and stakeholder content requirements, preparers of CERs face the daunting problem of fulfilling the number of reporting demands faced by corporations. Table 8.1 demonstrates the plethora of reporting requirements that exist at varying levels of governance and different levels of corporate decision making. Efforts are being made through initiatives such as the Global Reporting Initiative (discussed later in the chapter) to "synchromesh" existing reporting requirements in order to make corporate environmental reports more meaningful and easier to produce.

The following section outlines issues that have emerged with respect to corporate environmental reporting and the potential users of such information.

ENVIRONMENTAL REPORTING FROM THE USER'S PERSPECTIVE

Although public environmental reporting has satisfied the requirements of some audiences, it has appeared in diverse formats with limited utility for the investment community. It is difficult to apply environmental criteria and measurements rigorously if the information is not presented in a precise manner for investment analysts. Moreover, if indicators cannot be measured with a degree of accuracy and consensus, it is difficult to create a business case to demonstrate materiality to investment analysts. These issues that relate to the use of CERs are discussed next.

Format   Variations in the quality and format of environmental data collection and reporting contribute to investors' and analysts' confusion regarding a company's environmental performance. This diversity of format and data confounds the investor who is concerned about a company's environmental performance and the magnitude of costs and liabilities associated with poor environmental records (Beets and Souther 1999; FEE

TABLE 8.1 Summary of Financial Factors that Generate Demand for Environmental Information

Company Level	Governance Level				
	Local	Subnational	National	Continental	Global
Product	• Product standards	• California automobile emissions standards • Green procurement policies		• EU eco-labeling • EU chemical labeling • OECD green procurement • OECD chemicals program	• Forest Stewardship Council (FSC) • ISO 14040 life cycle inventory
Project	• Local environmental action plans • CDM • JI		• EIA requirements	• EIA requirements by regional banks • ECE conventions	• CDM • JI • World Bank guidelines
Facility	• Zoning PRTR in Nakaru, Kenya	• State DEPs • Environmental inspectorates • Permit applications	• Canada NPRI • U.S. TRI • U.K. CRI • Australia NPI • Indonesia, Philippines rating system • Japan PRTR	• EPER • OECD/PRTR manual • EMAS (EEC)	• ISO 14001 • ISO 14031
Corporation			• SEC • U.S. charters • Denmark green accounts • Sweden • Netherlands • Columbia	• CEFIC	• GRI • WBCSD eco-efficiency • WRI-WBCSD • Greenhouse gas protocol

(Continued)

228

TABLE 8.1 *(Continued)*

Company Level	Governance Level				
	Local	Subnational	National	Continental	Global
Sector			• Kyoto targets	• CEFIC	• Montreal Protocol • UNEP finance initiative

CDM—Clean Development Mechanism
CEFIC—(European) Chemical Industry Council
CRI—Chemical Release Inventory
DEP—Department of Environmental Protection
ECE—Economic Commission for Europe
EEC—European Economic Community
EIA—Environmental Impact Assessment
EMAS—Eco-Management and Audit Scheme (1995) based on EEC Regulation EEC No. 1836/93
EPER—European Pollution Emissions Register
FSC—Forest Stewardship Council
GRI—Global Reporting Initiative
NPI—National Pollutant Inventory
OECD—Organization for Economic Cooperation and Development
PRTR—Pollution Release and Transfer Register
WRI-WBCSD—World Resources Institute—World Business Council for Sustainable Development
Sources: Irwin & Ranganathan 2000; White 2000.

1999). Further, it hinders investors' decision making with respect to divestment of equities in environmentally lagging companies and industries (Schaltegger 1997).

Materiality Investment analysts historically have viewed environmental concerns as nonfinancial issues and as such have given them a low priority. In fact, investment analysts generally view a company's reputation after spills and accidents as poor management rather than a cost (Descano and Gentry 1998). From a positive perspective, good corporate environmental performance and good management are viewed as "one and the same thing" with no specific financial benefit being attributed to superior environmental behavior (Waddock and Graves 1997). As a consequence, the environment has had a limited impact an analysts' valuations of companies, compared to traditional financial valuation factors.

Until recently the prevailing view within the mainstream investment community was that the environment represents, at best, a liability. The perception of financial environmental risks has been limited to compliance and land remediation costs, with environmental practices such as pollution prevention and resource efficiency receiving limited attention in any valuation process (Descano and Gentry 1998; Stillius and Wennberg 1998).

At present the mainstream equity investment community remains unconvinced that a linkage exists between environmental and financial performance (Pritchard 2000). Analysts receive little of the business rationale for corporate environmental practices, with corporations having done little to explain that environmental strategies do, indeed, increase shareholder value (see Chapter 2). If core business environmental strategies create market and savings opportunities, analysts and their clients must be shown how environmental performance has a material and positive effect on financial performance. Otherwise, equity investors will fail to incorporate environmental information into financial analyses, thereby undervaluing companies' strategic environmental decision making (Beder 1999; Pritchard 2000; EPA 2000).

The application of the concept of materiality is a complex one, since its application may depend on the nature and circumstance as well as the scale of the event being considered. For example, the capacity for a medium (air, water, or land) to absorb a pollutant will affect the consideration of whether a release or discharge of pollutants into such media is material. Further, when considering different stakeholders, what may be considered material by one user group may be immaterial to another (FEE 2000). Thus the needs of users as well as their application of this information are important factors in determining relevance and materiality.

A number of forums have been established to demonstrate the materiality of environmental behavior to investment professionals. As has been described in Chapter 4, the United Nations Financial Institutions Initiative on the Environment meets each year to examine financial, market, and economic implications of environmental matters on business performance and economic development. Other organizations, such as the New York Society of Security Analysts and the Aspen Institute, bring together leaders from all disciplines (industry, government, the market, and advocacy groups) to develop an expanded model of shareholder value that can include positive environmental issues, thereby demonstrating the important role that proactive environmental undertakings play in future performance, profitability, and growth (Descano and Gentry 1998).

Terminology   There is a basic lack of common language used in describing environmental performance, with financial analysts, environmental managers, and environmental advocates using different terminology to describe common concerns (Beloe 2000). Analyses reported in Chapter 6 reveal that a general lack of uniformity exists in corporate environmental reporting, where a variety of criteria and metrics have been used by different companies. At present, analysts lack the means to translate environmental issues into financial terms in order to integrate them into existing security valuation methodologies. Environmental metrics must be communicated, then, in ways that are useful to the financial community, with terms such as tons of emissions and waste being translated into financially relevant terms that allow for comparisons within, as well as across, industries (Aspen Institute 1998; Skillius and Wennberg 1998; EPA 2000).

Data Collection   While data received from firms varies in quality and completeness, it never was developed to meet the needs of financial analysts. The majority of the information required by socially responsible investment (SRI) analysts either is not publicly available or is available but not in an easily comparable format. Analysts are often obliged to seek information from a variety of sources, in both financial and environmental terms, before they can gauge whether the company under scrutiny should be approved for investment. In addition, for financial analysts there is a dearth of information on the environmental attributes of products, as well as inadequate coverage of companies' activities outside their home countries (www.irrc.org).

One useful single source of information is the company itself. However, much of the reporting by companies depends on what information they are willing to divulge. This impediment is exacerbated by the varying impact of specific environmental concerns to different industries, and thus to their financial performance (EPA 2000). If all reliable and comprehensive information is not found in a company's reports, analysts can turn to publicly available proxy information gathered under mandated disclosure legislation. As seen in Chapter 6, data on environmental performance pertaining to toxic chemical releases, hazardous waste management, or contaminated land liabilities has been used in the United States to assess companies' environmental behavior patterns. Despite the fact that overall regulatory data is limited in Europe, the U.K. Environmental Agency's "pollution log" serves as one useful source of information on amounts of substances released into air, water, and land by companies (Mason 1999).

Further information can be obtained from specialist companies whose core business is researching and communicating information on corporate social and environmental performance (see Chapter 6). Groups such as the Investor Responsibility Research Center (IRRC), Öekom Research, and Innovest SVA can provide SRI data to researchers analyzing specific issues (SustainAbility 2000).

Further hindrances to the quality of available information arise from the high cost of research (Beder 1999; Schaltegger 1997) and the time lag (Beets and Souther 1999) between data collection and its inclusion in screens. Regarding the cost of reporting, however, Schaltegger (1997) claims that, while mandated reporting has brought down the cost of data received by stakeholders, it has also diminished its quality.

Comparability The situation is further confounded by the fact that, even if environmental data is forthcoming from a corporation, it is compromised by the fact that often it is not comparable across or between sectors (Pritchard 1999; SustainAbility 2000). There is no reason to believe that environmental performance is an equal driver of value across all sectors and industries. Indeed, environmental assessments can vary according to an industry's exposure to risk. For the paper industry, for example, the age of equipment, with its corresponding emissions levels, is an important variable, while in the power generation sector the choice of energy sources is of prime importance. Nonfinancial environmental measures, then, are often peculiar to a single industry or even a specific company, making both intra- and intersectoral comparisons difficult (Economist 2001c; Reed 1998; Skillius and Wennberg 1998).

PROGRESS IN ENVIRONMENTAL REPORTING

Recognizing that new demands are becoming increasingly important to corporate environmental reporting, a number of organizations have developed frameworks for an improved focus on environmental benchmarking, verification, performance indicators, and "full cost accounting and sustainability." The following sections provide examples of the wide range of efforts currently being made in these areas.

Environmental Measurements and Benchmarking

World Resources Institute In 1995, Hammond et al. developed a systematic approach to assess environmental policy performance around the pressure/state/response framework, within the context of sustainable development. This framework is mirrored by ISO's subsequent distinction of three types of environmental performance indicators, namely operational, management, and state-of-the-environment indicators.

In this World Resource Institute (WRI) model, the state component indicates the stress or pressures from human activities that are causing environmental change. The pressure indicators are designed to measure the effectiveness of policies through the tracking of environmental agreements, commitments, and compliance issues. Response gauges the efforts taken by an organization to improve its environmental behavior. Examples of this framework are given in Table 8.2.

In 1997, Ditz and Ranganathan expanded WRI's research on environmental policy to develop a framework specifically to track corporate environmental performance. Their framework, outlined in *Measuring Up*, emphasizes resource efficiency, pollution prevention, and product stewardship, and calls for the measurement of four categories of environmental performance: materials use, energy consumption, nonproduct output, and pollutant releases. The WRI study argues that the full potential of such corporate indicators is realized only when decision makers use them both internally to drive improvements in resource efficiency and profitability and externally to report to stakeholders such as lenders and insurers an improved environmental profile.

National Round Table on the Environment and the Economy In 1997 Canada's National Round Table on the Environment and the Economy (NRTEE) examined the feasibility of designing and implementing meaningful and robust indicators for three elements of environmental measures of eco-efficiency: energy intensity, materials intensity, and pollutant dispersion.

For energy intensity, the indicator tested was energy consumed from all sources (in joules) per unit of output (physical, operational, financial). The level of testing for these indicators, whether site, product, business unit, or total company, varied from one company to another (www.nrtee-trnee.ca/eco-efficiency).

Two indicators for materials intensity were used. The first was the total weight of material used directly in a product compared to the total output of product, again measured in physical, operational, or financial terms. The second material indicator includes total direct and indirect materials used in production, the latter being materials used but not part of the final product, such as packaging.

NRTEE gained a number of insights throughout the study. Material intensity indicators were found to be more relevant for primary and secondary manufacturing industries and less so for the extractive industries (mining) or the service industries (e.g., telecommunications). Second, it

TABLE 8.2 World Resources Institute's Matrix of Environmental Indicators

Issue	Pressure	State	Response
Climate change	Greenhouse gas emissions	Concentrations	Energy intensity; environmental measures
Ozone depletion	Halocarbon emissions; production	Chlorine concentrations; O_3 column	Protocol signing; investments/costs
Eutrophication	N, P water, soil emissions	N, P, BOD concentrations	Treatment connection; investments/costs
Acidification	SO_x, NO_x, NH_3 emissions	Deposition; concentrations	Investments; signing agreements
Toxic contamination	POC, heavy metal emissions	POC, heavy metal concentrations	Recovery of hazardous waste; investments/costs
Urban environmental quality	VOC, NO_x, SO_x emissions	VOC, NO_x, SO_x concentrations	Expenditures; transportation policy
Biodiversity	Land conversion; land fragmentation	Species abundance compared to virgin area	Protected areas
Waste	Waste generation— municipal, industrial, agricultural	Soil/groundwater quality	Collection rate; recycling; investments/costs
Water resources	Demand/use intensity— residential/industrial/ agricultural	Demand/supply ratio; quality	Expenditures; water pricing; savings policy
Forest resources	Use intensity	Area degradation; forest use/ sustainable growth ratio	Protected area forest; sustainable logging
Fish resources	Fish catches	Sustainable stocks	Quotas
Soil degradation	Land use changes	Top soil loss	Rehabilitation/ protection
Oceans/coastal zones	Emissions; oil spills; deposits	Water quality	Coastal zone management; ocean protection
Environmental index	Pressure index	State index	Response index

BOD—biological oxygen demand
N—nitrogen
NO_x—nitric oxide & nitrogen dioxide
P—phosphorus
POC—products of complete combustion
SO_x—sulfur dioxide
VOC—volatile organic compound
Source: Hammond et al. 1995.

found that changes in product mix could result in a change in material intensity that does not necessarily reflect improvements in material intensity at a plant or company. NRTEE felt, however, that the energy intensity indicator is an eco-efficiency indicator that has broad applicability, since energy, unlike materials, is a common currency unit in all businesses and countries.

In conjunction with the completion of the program, in 2002 NRTEE published *Calculating Eco-Efficiency Indicators: A Workbook for Industry* to help companies with their calculations and reporting of environmental information (www.nrtee-trnee.ca/eco-efficiency).

United Nations/SustainAbility Project   In an attempt to develop a benchmarking tool for measuring environmental performance, the survey *Engaging Stakeholders* (UNEP/SustainAbility 1996a), referred to earlier in the Chapter, establishes 50 elements of environmental performance, divided into five clusters, that can be used in benchmarking environmental performance (Table 8.3).

From these indicators, a revised five-stage ranking model is used to assess a corporation's environmental record of improvement (Figure 8.2). Since most companies have passed through the two basic stages of reporting, Figure 8.2 indicates Stages 3 to 5, with specific detail being given to the revisions undertaken in Stage 4.

The rapid expansion of environmental rating agencies and the ever-increasing comparison of companies' environmental performance are driving the need for, and design of, benchmarking initiatives. At the same time, many of the analysts that use this rating information play a key role in determining the company's valuation. This link between environmental performance and shareholder value was discussed in Chapter 3.

Verification of Environmental Performance and Reporting

In the light of uncertainty created and varying formats of corporate environmental reporting, a number of authors make the case for the need to develop not only uniform reporting standards, but also guidelines for standardized third-party verification (Beets and Souther 1999; Schaltegger 1997).

A variety of terms are used to describe the practice of verification of environmental reports by a third party. The International Organization for Standardization (ISO) refers to "auditing" of environmental management systems under the ISO 14001 standard. The Fédération des Experts

TABLE 8.3 UNEP Clusters of Reporting Measurements

The Five Reporting Clusters	The 50 Reporting Ingredients	
I. Management Policies and Systems	CEO statement	Legal compliance
	Environmental policy	Research and development
	Environmental management system	Programs and initiatives
		Awards
	Management responsibility	Verification
	Environmental auditing	Reporting policy
	Goals and targets	Corporate context
II. Input/Output Inventory	*Inputs*	*Outputs*
	Material use	Wastes
	Energy consumption	Air emissions
	Water consumption	Water effluents
		Noise and odors
	Process Management	Transportation
	Health and safety	
	Environmental impact assessments and risk management	*Products*
		Life cycle design
	Accidents emergency response	Packaging
		Product impacts
	Land contamination, remediation	Product stewardship
	Habitats	
III. Finance	Environmental spending	Environmental cost accounting
	Liabilities	
	Economic instruments	Benefits and opportunities
		Charitable contributions
IV. Stakeholder Relations	Employees	Consumers
	Legislators and regulators	Industry associations
	Local communities	Environment groups
	Investors	Science and education
	Suppliers	Media
V. Sustainable Development	Global environment	Technology cooperation
	Global development	Global standards

Source: UNEP/SustainAbility 1996a.

FIGURE 8.2 Stages of Environmental Reporting

	Stage 4 State-of-the-Art Company Environmental Reporting			Stage 5 Sustainability Reporting		
Stage 3 Late 1990s Entry Level Descriptive Reporting	4.1 Quantity	4.2 Quality	4.3 Comparability	Company Triple Bottom Line Responsibility	Government Triple Bottom Line Accountability	Market Triple Bottom Line Sustainability
Annual reporting, linked to environmental management system, but more text than figures.	Provision of full (e.g., TRI) performance data on annual basis. Clear targets linked to policy and auditing process. Corporate and site reports. Information on capital and operating costs and savings.	Clear reporting of significant effects and performance against targets. Linking company activities to key environmental issues and global priorities. Third party verification. Financial provisions. Provision of information online or on diskette.	External verification. Reporting against recognized (global) standards. Detailed financial information. First use of discussion of sectoral indicators and benchmarking. Printed and online time series available.	Full standardized, state-of-the-art environmental, financial, and social reporting. True and fair view of global and local impacts. Reporting in all world regions against global operating standards. Responsible lobbying. Internal and external evaluation of social and environmental performance.	Minimum mandatory reporting frameworks. Common environmental and social accounting methodologies and indicators. Enforceable Environmental Quality Standards (EQS). Punitive measures for corporate nonperformers. Environmental and social tax reform. Sustainability-screened public procurement and investment.	Pressure for greater corporate disclosure across the triple bottom line. Information needs made explicit. Use of disclosed information in all investment and consumption decisions. Rewarding good performers and penalizing laggards. Striking a balance between rights and needs as shareholder, consumer, and citizen.
One-way communication with stakeholders.	"Two-way" (passive) communication with stakeholders (e.g., feedback slips and market surveys).	"Multi-way" (active) dialogue with some stakeholders (e.g., roundtables and discussion panels).	"Multi-way" (active) stakeholder dialogue in all countries.	Institutionalized "multi-way" stakeholder engagement.		

Source: UNEP/SustainAbility 1996a.

237

Comptables Européens (FEE), the representative organization for the accountancy professions in a number of European countries, refers to such an undertaking by the term "assurance," while the German Institut der Wirtschaftsprüfer in Deutschland (IDW) refers to the activity as its "attestation." Further, the International Auditing Practices Committee (IAPC) of the International Federation of Accountants (IFAC) draws a line of distinction between different levels of commitment to verify as "audit" for high levels of assurance and "review" for moderate levels. Although some differences do apply in the use of these terms, for present purposes they will be treated as interchangeable.

A number of advocates do exist for the development of a standard environmental reporting verification or assurance service. The following section examines the extent to which accounting associations, particularly in Europe, are addressing this issue. In 1995, the IDW issued an auditing standard regarding the provision of independent environmental report assurance. In 1999, IAPC published its draft assurance standard, which distinguishes between different kinds of verification engagements, as well as making provisions for the assurance document on environmental reports. In a further development, FEE prepared a discussion paper on such engagements in order to further provision of assurance with respect to corporate environmental reports (FEE 1999).

Recognizing that a number of environmental reporting guidelines have already been developed, FEE (2000) has examined a number of assumptions arising from the accounting profession, as underpinnings to environmental reporting. One is that of materiality, which has been discussed earlier. Other assumptions addressed by FEE include: the application of the accrual basis of accounting, and the "going concern" assumption (Adams et al. 1999).

Accrual Basis of Accounting   In financial accounting, the practical application of the accrual basis allows for the reporting of future financial impacts of sales, profits, and revenues in the financial statements of the period to which they relate (Adams et al. 1999; IASC 1994). The purpose of the accrual convention is to inform users of financial statements of a company's future obligations and resources. An example could be that of the recognition of revenues or profits on a percentage completion basis in the case of a long-term contract (FEE 2000). In the case of environmental reporting, the application of the accrual basis would imply that the liability for the ultimate environmental disturbance be reported, at current values, at the point and time of the event. The disposal of future radioactive waste, for example, would have to be provided for in full at current values at the time that the environmental damage is caused, before discounting, and not recorded in separate parts in every period when radioactivity occurs (Adams et al. 1999; Schaltegger 1997).

Going Concern Assumption   The second accounting assumption examined by FEE in environmental reporting is that of the going concern. This implies that the company has neither the intention nor the need to liquidate or curtail the scale of its operations (IASC 1994, 41). In most cases, it is considered that enterprises will continue operations for the foreseeable future, unless otherwise indicated. Since long-term environmental impacts and changing environmental legislation can have a significant impact on the financial well-being of a corporation, FEE recommends that any new environmental reporting standard should require an indication of whether a corporation is capable of funding remediation or cleanup procedures in the future. A related consideration may be to require companies operating in environmentally sensitive areas to set aside financial provisions for known long-term liabilities. FEE suggests that provision of such resources could be made through conventional insurance products or some form of environmental bond. Indeed, Merkl and Robinson (1997) recommend the use of insurance in the management of future environmental liabilities, both to address uncertainties of future cost as well as to provide a tool for structuring risk transfers that can move environmental liabilities off a company's balance sheet.

For producers, users, and verifiers of environmental reports, both accrual and going concern assumptions are important, with their implications that future environmental impacts will be considered in the present.

Emergence of Internet-Based Environmental Reporting

The Internet is a new but very important vehicle for communication of corporate environmental information. Since Internet information is available instantly, continuously, and in a broad choice of languages, it is transforming stakeholder expectations with respect to corporate environmental disclosure. With this in mind, historical case studies of environmental performance hold less interest for stakeholders than a major company's present thinking and strategic plans for the future with respect to environmental concerns.

The majority of companies that do use the Internet for reporting offer print-style reports as Portable Document Format (pdf) files (Jones and Walton 1999; SustainAbility/UNEP 1999). In many cases, principal corporate web sites provide direct links to their environmental reports, as well as offering expanded details of environmental programs or products through linkages on their web sites. For example, UBS offers more detailed information on products, such as its fuel cell certificates, than are described in its Annual Environmental Report. (See www.ubs.bestzertifikate.de/englisch/pdf/fuelcell, which is found at www.ubs.com.)

Not only are corporations reporting their environmental performance on the Internet, but investment companies are also using the Internet to report performances of their environmental or sustainable development funds. For instance, the financial performance of Swissca's Green Invest product, designed in cooperation with World Wide Fund for Nature, is posted on its web site (www.swissca.ch).

In addition, the public can obtain results of mandated reporting schemes through the use of the Internet. Examples include: results of the Indonesian PROPER environmental reporting initiative (www.bapedal.go.id/info/proper/merah97/html) (Afsah and Ratunanda 1999), environmental information reported under Denmark's statutory reporting scheme (www.publi-com.dk/GroenneRegnkaber/hside.htm) (Rikhardsson 1999), and Canadian NPRI and ARET data described earlier in the chapter.

Further, in early 1998, U.S. EPA mandated additional Internet disclosures of companies in five of the largest industries: oil, steel, metals, automobiles, and paper. EPA designed an Internet reporting format that designated companies must use, which includes facility-level information on inspections, compliance records, pollution releases, and racial and income profiles of those living in the neighboring communities (Beets and Souther 1999).

Despite the fact that Internet reporting is less costly, is rapidly accessible, and is easy to update, critics claim that it will create an information divide between those that have access to the Internet and those without. In addition, Jones and Walton (1999) argue that the reduced costs due to fewer printing and distribution costs of traditional reports could be nullified by the increased costs of investing in management time and improved technology in order to exploit the medium to its fullest advantage.

Some users have found that sections of texts or important tables and figures that exist in hard-copy environmental reports are missing from on-line versions. Or, in some cases, only summaries or excerpts from the full report are offered online. To address this concern, many companies are reproducing their hard-copy environmental reports as pdf files, which requires specialized software, such as Adobe Acrobat Reader, to view them. This allows the report to retain the same design and formatting features as the hard-copy version, while making it easily available to the public (Jones and Walton 1999).

The Global Reporting Initiative

Throughout this book, reference has been made to a number of initiatives that were undertaken to address issues pertaining to environmental and social measurement and reporting. Table 8.4 summarizes some characteristics of these undertakings, noting whether they recommend both measurement and reporting of environmental effects, and whether indicators reflect only environmental issues or take into consideration the full complement of sustainability measurements, including social and economic along with environmental components. The most recent concern of third-party verification is also noted.

At present, the most powerful initiative aimed at standardizing corporate environmental reporting is the Global Reporting Initiative (GRI), which was launched in 1997 by the Coalition of Environmentally Responsive Economies (CERES—a U.S.-based nonprofit organization), UNEP, and several other partners.

The GRI is a long-term, multi-stakeholder, international undertaking whose mission is to develop and disseminate globally applicable

TABLE 8.4   A Summary of Characteristics of Voluntary Environmental Measurement and Reporting Initiatives

Initiative	Measure	Report	En	S	Ec	V	Country of Origin	Constitutency
VfU	X	X	X				Germany	Business
EPI-Finance 2000	X		X				Germany/Switzerland	Business
Forge	X	X	X			X	United Kingdom	Business
The Natural Step	X		X	X			Sweden	NGO
EMAS	X	X	X			X	European Union	Intergovernmental
ISO 14031	X		X				Switzerland	Multistakeholder
WRI	X		X				United States	NGO
NRTEE	X		X				Canada	Multistakeholder
SustainAbility/ UNEP		X	X	X			International	Business/ intergovernmental
FEE			X				European Union	
GRI	X	X	X	X	X		International	Multistakeholder

En—Environmental.
S—Social.
Ec—Economic.
V—Verification recommended.
Sources: Based on Ranganathan and Willis 1999; FEE 2000.

sustainability reporting guidelines for voluntary use by organizations reporting on the economic, environmental and social dimensions of their activities, products and services. (GRI 2000, 1)

The core mission of the group is to establish the foundation for uniform, global corporate sustainability "triple bottom line" reporting (environmental and social issues, as well as economic measures), through a multistakeholder consultation process. Specific objectives for the initiative are: to elevate sustainability reporting practices to the level of financial reporting, to design and promote a globally applicable standardized reporting format, and to "ensure a permanent and effective institutional host to support such reporting practices" (Ranganathan and Willis 1999, 1).

In 1999, the GRI issued a draft set of *Sustainability Reporting Guidelines* for comment and pilot testing. Although they do not offer support for actual data collection, the guidelines do demand that each GRI report include certain elements, such as:

- A CEO statement.
- An overview of the company, in terms of size, market, and type of products.
- A summary of key indicators.
- A vision and strategy.
- The company's policy, governance structure and management systems.
- Presentation of qualitative and quantitative aspects of performance.

The *Guidelines* have been revised and reissued for general use and feedback both in 2000 and 2002. This ambitious undertaking is aimed at developing a model that will address both site-specific detailed information, such as EMAS, as well as broader issues such as environmental policies and strategies throughout a company (www.globalreporting. org). The first level of GRI guidelines is applicable to all organizations, while a second tier of industry-specific guidelines has been designed for the chemical, mining, and financial sectors. The main goal of this program is to address many of the issues raised in the environmental reporting sections earlier in the chapter, and in the final analysis reach a consensus among reporters and report users, clarify corporate environmental and social behavior patterns, and facilitate comparisons between companies over time.

In April 2002, GRI became an independent institution with headquarters in Amsterdam (Bayon 2002). As of March 2002, more than 110 companies had already used the guidelines in preparing sustainability reports.

A sign of the initiative's success to date is the fact that the guidelines are being used in widely divergent sectors in all parts of the world (air and transport in the United Kingdom, appliances in Sweden, chemicals in India, auto manufacturers in the United States, and mining in Canada). Interestingly, the GRI methodology has also been used by researchers such as Stratos et al. in their assessment of the status of corporate sustainability reporting (2001).

The GRI approach comprises 10 assessment categories, which include not only leadership, stakeholder relations, and the triple bottom line indicators, but also measures of a company's willingness to extend a leadership role in sustainability upstream and downstream to suppliers and customers. It also takes into consideration the extent to which a corporation recognizes the interactions among the economic, environmental, and social measures.

ALAN WILLIS, INVITED AUTHOR'S COMMENT

The Global Reporting Initiative—An Accountant's Commentary

It is common knowledge that the financial statements used by the world's investment community and capital markets are all prepared in accordance with widely accepted accounting and disclosure standards often referred to as generally accepted accounting principles. The result is financial information that should be relevant to users' decisions: reliable, meaningful, verifiable, and, in particular, comparable between companies and over time.

But we find that even today accounting standards are still growing and changing to keep pace with new types of businesses and ever more complex transactions. What's more, there is not yet a single set of accounting standards followed by all companies in all countries around the world. Instead, in spite of recent efforts to accelerate international harmonization, each country has its own set of accounting and disclosure standards used by businesses in its own jurisdiction, even by multinationals. An earnings number calculated in one country can look confusingly, if not alarmingly, different when calculated under the accounting rules of another country.

And, needless to say, it is being increasingly recognized that finan-

(Continued)

**The Global Reporting Initiative—
An Accountant's Commentary** *(Continued)*

cial statements are intrinsically unable to measure and communicate effectively the underlying value of corporate commitment to sustainability principles and key indicators of environmental performance that various stakeholders want to track. To remedy this limitation, companies began some while ago to experiment with ways to report externally their environmental performance, but there was no widely accepted way to measure and report such information. Indeed, there was not even global consensus as to what should be measured and reported.

Enter the Global Reporting Initiative in 1997. A small Boston-based group of organizational pioneers and visionaries, led by CERES, decided to devise a worldwide environmental reporting framework that all companies could use to produce comparable, relevant, reliable, and verifiable information—valuable to, and trusted by, all stakeholders. Four years later, remarkable progress has been made down this ambitious road, but much still remains to be done. The scope of the challenge was soon expanded to include social and economic performance, beyond just the environmental aspect. Another challenge among the many external stakeholder groups is that there is wide diversity in what most concerns them—some, for example, are more interested in social equity than in ecological integrity, and many still wrestle with holistic interpretations of sustainability. There is also the risk that a sustainability report may provide an excess of data and indicators that together become overwhelming and meaningless.

In spite of such formidable challenges, it seems reasonable to pursue the cause if only because there are now clear signs of a shift away from relying on just financial statements for a clear and complete understanding of a company's performance and prospects. The need is emerging for a broader, comprehensive business reporting model, in which financial statements are just one element. Capital market users are now beginning to look for new but credible types of information. This broader model, exemplified, for example, by Kaplan and Norton's *Balanced Scorecard* (1992) will attempt to uncover, measure, and communicate aspects of business performance and value creation that financial accounting was never designed to deal with. Even a good management's discussion and analysis report may not be able to provide all the information expected by all stakeholders, but at least

(Continued)

The Global Reporting Initiative—
An Accountant's Commentary *(Continued)*

it can provide a more complete business context for understanding past financial performance and future prospects. Environmental and social factors can be part of this context.

Sufficient research has been done to establish a clear relationship between superior environmental and social performance and a company's long-term value creation—perhaps it's to do with reputation and trust building, perhaps with superior risk management, efficiency, or innovation. Whatever the case, it is only a matter of time before the investor community will seek robust, reliable, and relevant information about these other dimensions of performance. Innovest's analytical methodologies, the Dow Jones Sustainability Group Index, and leading-edge ethical and social investment funds are drivers of this growing demand. Already, of course, companies themselves that see the business value of strong stakeholder relationships are turning to better, more meaningful, and more trustworthy ways of reporting performance to such stakeholders.

The bottom line of all this, then, is simply that the Global Reporting Initiative is becoming widely recognized worldwide as being by far the most promising solution to the quest for an internationally accepted framework for companies to use in reporting their "triple bottom line" performance to investors and other stakeholders. This is not the whole answer to the broader, comprehensive business reporting model, but it is certainly a substantial part, and one that accountants alone could not possibly develop. As the GRI reinvents itself in 2002 to become an independent institution dedicated to this particular reporting mission, its success will be reflected in the uptake, use, and continuing development of the GRI *Guidelines* by the wide group of organizations, disciplines, and constituencies that have had the vision and commitment to bring it so far in four short years. I hope accountants will increasingly participate in, and contribute to, this journey.

Alan Willis is the Canadian Institute of Chartered Accountants (CICA)'s representative on the GRI Steering Committee (1997–2002) and chair of GRI's Verification Working Group (1999–2002). He also participated in the (Canadian) National Round Table on the Environment and Economy's work on eco-efficiency from 1997 to its 2001 *Workbook.* Mr. Willis has written a number of publications, including coauthoring CICA's (2001) publication *Environmental Performance: Measuring and Managing What Matters.*

CONCLUSION

Much progress has been made in the field of environmental measurement and reporting. Those companies that obviously interact strongly and visibly with the environment, such as resource companies, tend to produce environmental reports. Other companies in sectors like chain retailing, transportation, information technology, and leisure industries are developing sustainability reports as it is becoming evident that their environmental impacts can be quite significant.

In order to move forward, however, there are a number of issues that need to be resolved. Environmental reporting still remains a somewhat random activity. Environmental measures that are meaningful must be developed in order to fulfill the broad range of corporate environmental information that is required by diverse stockholder groups. Included in these would be measures that are meaningful to analysts that specifically inform the equity valuation process. To make the case for the materiality of environmental performance, investment professionals must have access to current, comparable, complete, and pertinent industry-specific information, which they will then be able to use to demonstrate to investors the contribution of environmental performance to value creation for the firm. Finally, there is a need for a greater integration between reporting and strategic business decision making, and a shift from one-way communications emanating from companies to a more deeply engaging process of consultation and collaboration with stakeholder groups.

WEB SITES

Accelerated Reduction/ Elimination of Toxics (ARET)	www.ec.gc.ca/aret/Default.htm
Corporate Register	www.corporate-register.com
Stratos Inc.	www.stratos-sts.com.

CHAPTER 9

Strategies for Managing Environmental Change

INTRODUCTION

So far this book has covered the major subsectors of the financial services sector separately and also jointly as they face a common challenge (climate change) and attempt to develop a common methodology (environmental reporting). In this chapter we will integrate the lessons drawn from the previous work within the framework of developing corporate strategies for managing environmental change. We will use examples from the financial institutions and from their clients. We expect that financial service providers and their clients will begin to work more closely together on environmental issues as their common problems become more evident.

Corporate strategy will be shaped in this context by those aspects of environmental change that are most salient to the particular corporation. For some, the diminishing availability of cheap, clean water will be of prime concern; for others it may be the remediation of contaminated urban land to prepare it for reuse. For many it will be the uncertainties of climate change that will dominate the process of evaluation. Whatever the driving environmental concern, most companies—certainly any large corporation—should consider the potential benefits of "green housekeeping." Reduction in the use of energy and water and in the production of wastes—solid, liquid and gaseous—is in the interest of every company because it will save recurrent expenditures, improve the company's image, and probably improve the health and productivity of its employees. An evaluation of its own internal operations will probably identify the need for training in environmental management. It may also point the way to a new hiring policy, to bring in new people with specific expertise in environmental management. For example, companies in the weather derivatives business found that it was simpler to hire meteorologists and show them how to trade than it was to turn a trader into a knowledgeable meteorologist. There may also be opportunities for setting up internal trading systems to reduce problematic emissions such as carbon dioxide and methane.

Once a company's internal operations are better understood (and baseline conditions identified), that company is capable of taking the next step by producing regular environmental reports on its improvements. This enables it to report to its board and shareholders. It also makes its activities visible to environmental rating agencies that provide comparative assessments to the socially responsible investment (SRI) community. For the environmentally successful companies this should lower the cost of capital, lower the cost of insurance, and enhance shareholder value.

The first two components of an environmental management strategy are focused on examining how the company affects the physical environment in which it operates. The companies that look ahead will also want to monitor the ways in which the physical world is changing around them. What is the latest estimate of the rate at which the world is warming, for example? Has the reduction in sulfur dioxide emissions (to reduce environmental damage on the ground through acidification) accelerated atmospheric warming, as expected? What are the latest estimates of the population level at which the world will level off, and what is the expected date for this to happen? What is the state of the climate change negotiations, and how will this affect the potential for global carbon trading?

Which new financial products are being developed to address environmental problems? How is the world of environmental finance, itself, evolving? To what extent can a firm's environmental strategy be developed from products that are available off the shelf, and to what extent will it have to be prepared to invest in developing in-house solutions? Can these solutions then be marketed to other companies facing the same problem? For example, BP has already benefited from its experience in emissions reduction and are marketing this expertise to other oil and gas companies (see www.bpenergy.co.uk/products/consulting/index.html). Similarly, some of the energy companies that developed the weather derivatives market to hedge their own exposure to changeable weather turned their weather desks into derivatives brokerages to market trades for other companies.

These are the small-scale components that would go into an environmental management strategy. They may point the way to larger-scale decisions such as strategic partnerships with companies that have complementary skills, or—going further—a merger with, or an acquisition of, the same. It is probably no coincidence that very soon after BP announced its commitment to a lower-carbon future it acquired Amoco, whose energy mix included a very high percentage of natural gas, compared with oil, which has a higher carbon content per output of energy. In many cases companies have concluded that the fundamental nature of their business needs to change if they are to remain profitable. Thus many forward-looking companies have redesigned themselves not as producers of physical products, but as producers of services. Some have gone further, and reformulated their business as the provider of knowledge.

GREENHOUSE GAS EMISSION TARGETS: RATIONALE, TYPES, AND METHODS

The Pew Center on Global Climate Change (Margolick and Russel 2001) has recently issued *Corporate Greenhouse Gas Reduction Targets*, a report on its study of the motivations behind GHG reduction targets made by a number of prominent international companies. The report explores the companies' reasons for adopting targets, their choice of targets, their methods for reaching these targets, and their progress toward these goals. Based on these case studies, the report also provides guidance to other companies that are considering establishing similar climate-related targets. The following subsections summarize this important and timely study.

Reasons for Adopting Climate-Related Targets   A number of factors play important roles in why companies have decided to adopt climate-related targets as part of their overall environmental management strategies. One of the strongest driving forces is the anticipation that future regulations will be imposed that will create serious financial constraints on operations, particularly for the energy industry. Companies are therefore motivated to take voluntary action with respect to greenhouse gas reductions, to demonstrate to government policy makers the value and effectiveness of flexible approaches to climate change. Thus climate-related targets become part of a larger effort to manage regulatory risk and "stay ahead of the regulatory curve." Other driving forces are related to economic benefits, with energy conservation and efficiency leading to decreased energy costs and an improved competitive position.

Classification of Targets   In deciding to adopt climate-related targets, a company must first decide on the type and level of target to adopt. In order to do this a company must answer three questions: Where in the product life cycle should the target be applied? Should the target focus on greenhouse gas reduction or on energy efficiency? And will the target be expressed in absolute or relative terms? Table 9.1 outlines the publicly

TABLE 9.1 Targets Announced by a Selection of Major Corporations

Company	Sector	Target Description	Baseline Year	Placement[1]			Focus of Target		Type of Target	
				In-plant	Purchased Electricity	Product Use	GHG	Energy	Absolute	Relative
ABB	Electricity generation and transmission equipment	• Plant-specific energy efficiency targets • Reduce GHG by 1%/year (1998-2005) • Develop environmental product declarations for every product	Annual	*	*	*	*	*	*	*
Alcoa	Aluminum	• Reduce direct GHG emissions by 25% by 2010	1990	*			*		*	
BP	Petroleum	• Reduce GHG emissions by 10% by 2010	1990	*	*		*		*	
Deutsche Telekom	Telecommunications	• Reduce energy use by 15% by 2000	1995	*				*	*	
Dow	Chemicals	• Reduce energy use/lb production by 2005	2000	*				*		*
DuPont	Chemicals	• Reduce GHG emissions by 65% by 2010 • Hold energy use constant • Source 10% from renewables	1990	*	*		*	*	*	*
Entergy	Electricity generation and natural gas distribution	• Stabilize CO_2 emissions through 2005	2000	*			*		*	

Company	Sector	Commitments	Baseline year						
Ford	Auto manu-facturing	• Improve fuel efficiency of SUVs 25% by 2005	2001		☆			☆	☆
		• Reduce GHG emissions of European fleet by 25% by 2005		☆	☆	☆	☆		☆
IBM	Computers and semi-conductors	• Improve energy efficiency by 4% annually	Annual	☆			☆	☆	☆
		• Reduce CO_2 emissions by 4%/year	Annual	☆		☆	☆		☆
		• 90% of models Energy Star compliant/year[2]	Annual		☆				
		• Reduce PFC emissions 10% by 2010	1995	☆	☆	☆	☆		☆
Ontario Power Genera-tion	Electricity generation	• Stabilize CO_2 emissions through 2000 and beyond	1990	☆	☆	☆	☆	☆	
Shell	Petroleum	• Reduce GHG emissions by 10% by 2002	1990	☆	☆			☆	☆
		• Meet energy targets/ton of product for global business units	Annual	☆		☆	☆		
Trans Alta	Electricity generation and marketing	• Return GHG emissions to 1990 levels by 2000	1990	☆		☆	☆	☆	

(Continued)

251

TABLE 9.1 *(Continued)*

Company	Sector	Target Description	Baseline Year	Placement[1]			Focus of Target		Type of Target	
				In-plant	Purchased Electricity	Product Use	GHG	Energy	Absolute	Relative
TransAlta (cont.)		• Achieve zero net GHG emissions from Canadian operations by 2024	1990	*			*		*	
Chicago Climate Exchange participants	Mix of GHG emitters and potential sequesterers (e.g., agriculture, forestry)	• Reduce GHG emissions to 2% below 1999 levels by 2002 • Achieve further 1% reduction/year after 2002	1999	*	*		*		*	

[1]Placement of target in the production cycle.
[2]Energy Star is a joint program of the U.S. EPA and the U.S. Department of Energy.
Source: Margolick and Russel 2001.

announced targets that a selection of major corporations have adopted with respect to these questions.

The scale of a company's emissions reduction target is related to both where the target is placed in the product life cycle as well as the baseline that is established based on a business-as-usual scenario. For example, most of the energy consumed during the life cycle of electrical equipment is during the use of the product, rather than during its manufacture. This has influenced AAB and IBM, for example, to set targets related to the use of their products, in addition to targets on in-plant emissions. By contrast, emissions from electricity production emanate from combustion of fossil fuels and not from product use. Therefore the electricity generator and gas distributor, Entergy, set its target of stabilizing CO_2 emissions from its in-house operations.

The choice between energy efficiency and greenhouse gas (GHG) emissions as a target derives from cost-effective considerations. For Entergy, for example, the most cost-effective way to reduce emissions is by shifting its fuel mix. Thus a GHG emissions target is its the best choice. By contrast, manufacturing companies use relatively little fuel directly. Thus it seems reasonable that they target energy efficiency rather than GHG emissions, since they have little control over the carbon content of their electricity. In addition, they can realize cost savings along with their efficiency target.

Methods and Progress   Different companies have shown varying strategies for implementing their emissions reductions action plans. The energy company ABB, for example, relies on pledges by more than 500 sustainability officers around the world, through its environmental management system framework for the implementation of targets at the facility level. Targets at IBM, by contrast, are governed by a central directive that covers the company's worldwide operations, even though energy management is implemented on a decentralized basis. Entergy Corporation has established a $5 million internal corporate CO_2 emissions reduction fund to finance emissions reduction projects. Proposals for funding are evaluated not only on their potential to improve future emissions reduction efforts, but also on the basis of their potential to further other corporate objectives, such as regional employment and poverty alleviation.

Most large companies already manage GHG emissions and energy use within their larger sustainable development framework, but the adoption of actual targets may bring in the need for other ways of reaching their goals. Thus a number of companies are turning to programs such as internal trading programs and/or carbon offsets to reach their targeted goals. Internal carbon trading programs spread carbon reduction activities across operating units of a company so as to minimize the total cost of reaching the company's target. One example is found in the case study of TransAlta in the following section. Another worthy of note is the Shell Tradable Emissions Permits System (STEPS)—a voluntary cap-and-trade system for GHG emissions launched in 2000. In this case, permits equivalent to 98 percent of GHG emissions in 1998 were allocated to certain business units operating in the developed world that are responsible for 30 percent of the company's total emissions. The program allows for trading of these permits since emissions reduction costs vary widely among Shell's largely autonomous core businesses as well as across units operating in different countries. It also improves the company's understanding of the costs and actions needed to reach its targets and allows the different units to gain experience in permit trading for the future. Shell's action plan also includes "shadow pricing'" as a fundamental investment strategy for analyses of potential capital expenditure projects over a certain size, with prices of $5 and $20 per ton of CO_2 equivalent being used in estimations of project acceptability.

Energy intensive industries, where fuel choice and energy efficiency have already been optimized, may opt for investments in emissions reductions from outside the company, in the form of offsets. Ontario Power Generation (OPG), for instance, has chosen to meet its GHG stabilization target by investing in external emissions reduction offsets. In 2000, OPG met 80 percent of its targets by purchasing carbon offsets from sources both in North America and internationally. The other 20 percent reductions were generated through internal energy efficiency projects.

The Pew Center's findings with respect to communication of these emissions reduction initiatives to the public are of particular interest in light of the discussion of corporate environmental reporting in Chapter 8. The Pew study suggests that annual reports are being augmented by environmental reports on a regular basis by many large companies. In addition, a number of companies in the study embrace the concept of the triple bottom line (environmental, economic, social) and report on activities that they have taken not only to improve environmental and economic results, but also to make improvements to the society in which they operate. To incorporate GHG emissions in the social context, Shell has established a Climate Change Advisory Panel, which includes representatives from local communities, to assist in the GHG management and planning with respect to its partial ownership of the Canadian Athabasca Oil Sands Project. At BP, internal communication has been flagged as an important means of informing and engaging its employees with respect to emissions reductions. BP has launched a best practices web site to publicize successful initiatives and facilitate their reproduction throughout the company.

GREEN HOUSEKEEPING

It might have started out as a public relations exercise, but green house-keeping has rapidly become a serious part of business. In some cases it has become a major part of the motivation to make a long-term assessment of the environmental future of society, and not just the company itself. The following case study of TransAlta, originally simply a power supply company in Alberta, Canada, illustrates just how far the transformation can go.

CASE STUDY: TransAlta Corporation

TransAlta Corporation is a Canadian electric utility company that owns and operates thermal and hydroelectric power plants as well as electric transmission and distribution systems. TransAlta is the largest investor-owned electrical utility in Canada. Its three coal-fired plants account for 95 percent of TransAlta's Alberta electrical generation, supported by 13 hydroelectric plants. The company has moved from being a traditional provincial power company in Alberta to an international operator in Ontario, New Zealand, Australia, and the United States.

TransAlta Utilities services close to two million people directly and indirectly, and counts its domestic and industrial rates as being among the lowest internationally. At the same time, TransAlta is the second largest point source of greenhouse gas emissions in Canada. The risks associated with such an emissions profile have stimulated TransAlta toward proactively integrating a strategy of CO_2 reductions through programs such as an internal emissions trading system and an internal carbon tax. Much of TransAlta's initial efforts to reduce CO_2 emissions focused on internal projects such as switching fuel from coal to natural gas and renewable energy sources in its generation facilities, an undertaking that has a payback period of less than five years.

In Canada, the Voluntary Challenge and Registry (VCR) program, encouraging organizations to limit their greenhouse gas emissions voluntarily, was initiated in 1995. Well before that time, however, TransAlta had undertaken its own activities designed to meet the challenges of climate change. As early as 1992, TransAlta established its own baseline of CO_2 emissions by setting a goal to return GHG emissions to 1990 levels by the year 2000 for its generating business unit. This clearly measurable goal paralleled targets agreed to in the Rio conference and was instrumental in putting into operation TransAlta's commitment to sustainable development. More recently, the company has proposed a net GHG emissions level of *zero* in 2024 (www.transalta.com).

In 1993, TransAlta introduced an internal trading system among three of its power plants. The motivating factors behind these endeavors were twofold: first, to create a higher level of awareness of environmental costs involved with emissions; and second, to create an understanding of how such programs might work if enacted externally. To implement the program, each plant was charged $2 per ton for its CO_2 emissions. In order to reduce this cost, plant employees were encouraged to identify both internal inefficiencies and offset projects in other parts of the company, such as in transmission and distribution units.

In addition to the trading program, TransAlta also introduced an internal carbon tax in 1993. As with the trading program, the goal of the carbon tax was to raise awareness within the generation unit of the environmental costs for emissions. The original tax was set at approximately $20 per ton CO_2, but was adjusted over the years to settle at $2 per ton CO_2, which reflects the prices TransAlta felt it could pay for offset projects. Although the carbon tax has never been tied to real money, it is used for argument's sake in the capital expenditure approval process. Thus the carbon tax allows for ranking of projects with equal rates of return, and allows for the comparison and ranking of all projects in the generation business unit that are competing within a budgetary constraint (Thompson 1998).

Although it had been implementing its own efforts to reduce GHG emissions, TransAlta was an early driver in the Canadian government's 1995 establishment of its Voluntary Challenge and Registry (VCR) program, designed to encourage voluntary GHG emissions reductions. The Pembina Institute for Appropriate Development recognized TransAlta's action plan submitted to VCR as being one of the best action plans in Canada (Pembina 1998).

There are several key issues that will play major roles in influencing TransAlta's emissions reduction strategies in the future. The first is that the deregulation of electric utilities in Canada has played a major role in TransAlta's purchase of renewable energy. In addition, deregulation may provide utilities with increased flexibility to apply resources where they believe the most cost-effective reductions can occur. At the same time, however, deregulation introduces a heightened state of competitiveness among the utilities, putting market pressure on capital investments, resulting in more stringent requirements for rates of return on viable projects.

As cost-justifiable projects became scarce, TransAlta included other types of projects, such as renewable energy purchases, cogeneration facilities, and offset projects, in its emissions reductions portfolio. Deregulation in other provinces in Canada allows TransAlta to operate in those regions. In Ontario, for instance, TransAlta operates three cogeneration plants that run more efficiently and emit less CO_2 than traditional coal-fired plants. These independent power plants provide site heat requirements along with 250 megawatts of electricity.

In 1997, TransAlta reported that 23 percent of its CO_2 emissions reductions were due to internal efficiency improvements. Of these, 90 percent were due to thermal plant energy conversion and improvements in the transmission and distribution units, and 10 percent were due to its purchase of renewable energy. Under the Small Power Research and Development Act (Alberta, Canada), TransAlta contracted to purchase wind, biomass, and small hydro sources of energy at legislated prices.

TransAlta's projected growth puts pressure on the firm's ability to reduce its emissions levels, causing the firm to place greater emphasis on the identification and financing of domestic and international offset projects. The net emissions reductions allowed by such projects reduce the financial burden that could otherwise restrict its business strategy in the changing electric utility market. Because many of the possible cost-effective internal projects, such as heater basket improvements, had been completed, TransAlta has investigated and invested in a number of domestic and international offset projects. The diverse projects in which TransAlta participates include:

- The Saskatchewan Soil Enhancement Project that encourages farmers to adopt low-disturbance seeding practices, which reduce tillage, lower summer fallow, restore organic matter, and thus lead to increased carbon content in the soil. (This is estimated to have reduced net CO_2 emissions by 1.2 million metric tons.)

- The Edmonton Composting Centre's design to process the city of Edmonton's municipal waste and sludge into usable compost (CO_2 equivalent reduction of 240,000 metric tons).
- The sale of ash from TransAlta's coal-fired treatment plants for use in the manufacture of concrete, thereby substituting the use of concrete for cement and displacing some of the energy required for the production of cement. The sale of 115 thousand metric tons of ash reduced CO_2 emissions by more than 21,000 metric tons (emissions from energy use in manufacture of concrete).
- The India Development project, located in Gujarat, India, which enhances milk production from cattle while reducing the amount of methane produced during their digestive process. TransAlta estimates that it will receive rights to greenhouse gas reductions from this project for 30 million metric tons of CO_2 equivalent reductions over the next three decades.
- In June 2000, TransAlta announced its first transatlantic trade of carbon dioxide emissions reductions with the German electric company Hamburgische Electricitäts-Werke AG. The 24,000 tons trade, brokered by Natsource of New York, represents the annual emissions of approximately 3,000 cars (www.transalta.com).

TransAlta anticipates a greater dependence on offset programs as internal programs become more costly. Indeed, the company has issued a request for proposals in order to increase the number of potential projects from which it can choose (www.transalta.com). Questions of additionality[1] and supplementarity[2] still exist, however, as do the definition and admissibility of "credible" projects. The choice of such a diverse mixture of offsets reduces its risk should restrictions be set on certain types of offsets (Thompson 1998).

ENVIRONMENTAL REPORTING

Just as a simple commitment to green housekeeping can change the course of a company's development, so can the equally simple commitment to environmental reporting. This is not to say that either of these activities is easy to implement, only that the decision to commit the company to undertake them is easy to comprehend. The reporting exercise usually uncovers unexpected information and may provide unsuspected opportunities, thus confirming the old management adage that "what is not measured is not managed." Admittedly, the ambition of the U.K. utility Wessex Water to become a "truly sustainable water company" went far beyond the norm (Howes 2001). In this case, it meant that it had to "identify where the company is in terms of its environmental impacts, to determine appropriate 'sustainability' targets or standards to aim for, and to work out the most cost-effective way for the company to close that 'sustainability gap' " (Howes 2001).

CASE STUDY: Wessex Water Services

Wessex Water, one of Britain's recently privatized regional water and sewage utilities, views itself as steadily becoming a more energy-intensive company as it strives to deliver the same services in the future as it does today. This growth in energy needs is attributed mainly to the range of new activities that are required to comply with ever-increasing regulatory standards. Despite this growth in energy requirements, the company hopes, nonetheless, to shift away from a heavy dependence on energy derived from fossil fuels to an increased use of energy from renewable resources.

In order to meet present goals and future targets to reduce its dependency on fossil fuels, Wessex looks for alternative fuels from processes such as the thermal drying of treated sewage or biosolids. It already derives some energy from renewable sources such as biogas and hydroelectricity. The company has also started to use short-rotation crops such as coppiced willow and elephant grass as "carbon-neutral" fuel sources for smaller combined heat and power (CHP) plants.

Recognizing that methane is judged to be a more potent greenhouse gas than CO_2, Wessex already uses a great deal of biosolids collected throughout the wastewater treatment system to produce electricity. However, high levels of investment will be required to ensure the maximum amount of methane is collected for this purpose. To ensure that its environmental program is understood and applied at all levels of decision making, Wessex has developed a "green guide" with associated software for its engineers, who are required to evaluate emissions and other environmental costs at the earliest possible stages of planning and decision making (Scott 2000).

Along with other decisions that address sustainability concerns, Wessex Water has undertaken two separate forms of reporting to communicate environmental information to its stakeholders. The first, *Striking a Balance* (Wessex Water 2000), is presented in a format developed for the sustainability management system pilot project "Sigma." This project, launched by a group of stakeholders including Forum for the Future, seeks to produce a process that combines the rigor of existing management systems with the fundamental principles that underlie the concept of sustainability. In attempting to do this, Forum for the Future defines all aspects of a business in terms of five corporate "blocks of capital": the environment, customers, employees, infrastructure, and finance. *Striking a Balance* looks at all the assets of the company from this viewpoint, and reports the progress made and challenges ahead within each category. Knowing that its energy consumption will rise in the future, for instance, Wessex Water indicates its goal of cutting the use of fossil fuels by targeting 20 percent of all energy to come from renewable resources by 2005, and 50 percent by 2020. Similar performance projections are made in its transportation activities.

Striking a Balance goes further in its environmental reporting by calculating carbon dioxide emissions or their equivalents that are attributable to Wessex's water service operations. To do this, emission data from its production activities and the transportation of raw materials, as well as the intermediate goods used by the company are calculated. Finally, the report lives up to its title of striking a balance by examining whether the benefits from corporate expenditures are balanced between the company and its external stakeholders (Wessex Water 2000).

In an attempt to "green" its accounting practices, Wessex Water published a set of environmental external accounts alongside its conventional financial statements in its Annual Review of Accounts, *Tapping into Your Water Source* (Wessex Water 2001). (See Table 9.2.) In this context, monetary figures are generated in order to relate environmental information to improved corporate environmental and economic performance.

TABLE 9.2 Wessex Water Services Environmental Accounts
(for the Year to March 31, 2001)

Environmental Impacts	Emission (Metric Tons)	Reduction Target (Metric Tons)	Unit Cost £/Metric Ton (Where Relevant)	£000s
IMPACTS ON AIR				
Direct Energy				
Electricity consumption				
195.1 million kWh				
CO_2	86,235	51,741		
NO_x (NO and NO_2)	234	140		
SO_2	488	293		
Total (avoidance costs)				1,950
Natural gas consumption				
11.07 million kWh				
CO_2	2,103	1,262	6	8
Diesel oil				
18.91 million kWh				
CO_2 only	4,728	2,837	6	17
Methane Emissions				
Estimated at 4,340				
metric tons				
expressed as CO_2e				
(GWP of 21)	91,140	54,684	6	328
Road Transport				
Company cars				
(petrol and diesel)				
2.3 million kms				
CO_2	403	241	6	2
NO_x, HCs, and PM	1	<1	14,000	8
Commercial vehicles				
(petrol and diesel)				
13.2 million kms				
CO_2	3,918	2,381	6	14
NO_x, HCs, and PM	30.5	17	2,400–14,000	323
Private vehicles				
business kms				
2.2 million kms				
CO_2	438	263	6	2
NO_x, HCs, and PM	4	<1	7,200–14,000	26

(Continued)

TABLE 9.2 *(Continued))*

Environmental Impacts	Emission (Tons)	Reduction Target (Metric Tons)	Unit Cost £Ton (Where Relevent)	£000s
Commuting				
6.1 million kms				
CO_2	1,856	1,114	6	7
NO_x, HCs, and PM	12	7	7,200–14,000	73
Contractors				
11.41 million kms				
CO_2	2,500	1,500	6	9
NO_x, HCs, and PM	37	17	7,200–14,000	282
IMPACTS ON WATER				
Abstraction: Provision for alternative supplies at priority sites				5,170
IMPACTS ON LAND				
Contaminated land				120
Rounding				2
Total sustainability cost				8,341
Profit after taxation per the financial accounts				72,000
ENVIRONMENTALLY SUSTAINABLE PROFIT				**63,659**

NO_x—nitric oxide and nitrogen dioxide.
HCs—hydrocarbons.
PM—particulate matter.
Source: Modified from Wessex Water Services 2001; Howes 2001.

Following the United Nations recommended valuation procedure for environmental cost adjustments, Wessex Water valued its environmental impacts on the basis of avoidance and restoration costs. The most significant component of the cost estimate is the development of alternative supplies of water to those currently being abstracted from vulnerable sites. Another major cost is that associated with the avoidance of each ton of GHG emissions related to energy consumption.

This methodology estimates what Wessex Water would need to spend in order to avoid the impacts in the first place, or, if actions are deemed unavoidable, the cost of restoring the damage caused to the environment by these activities. The cost of reducing 60 percent of emissions associated with electricity derived from fossil fuels, then, is the cost of developing on-site renewable energy supplies purchasing such energy from a third party. Costs associated with the purchase and installation of technology for sequestering hydrocarbons and particulates from transportation carbon dioxide emissions are used to value these reductions in road transport. On the positive side, Wessex Water includes offsetting grants and savings, mainly arising from an exemption from the Climate Change Levy and tax rebates for vehicles retro-fitted with carbon reduction technology (Howes 2001).

In making the link between environmental and financial measures of performance more visible, Wessex Water helps decision makers reduce costs and business risks, while adding shareholder value. This comes at a time when financial analysts and other stakeholders are demanding greater disclosure and reporting on financially related environmental data to help them distinguish between good and bad performers.

GLOBAL MONITORING

One important side effect of globalization is that a greater proportion of the economy is now affected by issues around the world, including demographic, political, and economic change, as well as environmental change. For some companies this is not a new situation. Indeed, for the reinsurance sector, globalization is a very important contributor to the essential diversification of their business. Of course, if catastrophes become more frequent and more widespread then this strategy could become counterproductive. It is this danger that makes global monitoring an indispensable part of the reinsurance business. Many of the major reinsurers support an impressive range of up-to-date publications to keep their clients and the public informed on the nature of catastrophes, especially natural hazards, regardless of whether there is a significant insurance loss. No company has done more to make such information available than Munich Re.

CASE STUDY: Munich Re

Founded in 1880, Munich Re is the largest reinsurance company in the world, closely followed by Swiss Re. Both are considerably larger than their nearest competitors[3]. The Munich Re Group (including primary insurance business) wrote more than 30 billion euros of premiums in 2000 (Munich Re 2001a). It reinsures 5,000 primary insurers in 150 countries. Assets under management exceed 143 billion euros.

Since 1973 it has supported the Geoscience Research Group, which comprises geographers, geophysicists, geologists, meteorologists, and hydrologists who monitor natural disasters around the world and, since 1994, has published an annual review of catastrophes (Munich Re 2001b). In 1999 the company published a special millennium version of this review, which provided "documentation of major natural catastrophes in the last one hundred and, wherever possible, the last one thousand years, in order to present a complete picture of the entire range of extreme natural events in the various regions of the world and their damaging effects" (Munich Re 1999, 5).

The trends of these effects are quite clear. The good news is that the loss of life associated with natural catastrophes in the richer, industrialized countries is going down. The bad news is that the economic and insurance losses have been going sharply upward. (See Figure 5.1 and Table 9.3.) The question is: why? A significant clue is given by the fact that 19 of the 21 events that resulted in losses of a billion dollars or more were due to extreme weather events, which "is almost certainly attributable, at least in part, to the combustion of fossil fuels," according to Gerhard Berz, the director of the Geoscience Research Group (Munich Re 2001c, 16). The Group is careful to point out that the increase in economic and insured losses is not due solely to an increase in the frequency of extreme weather events. Other important contributory factors are the increase in population; the growing concentration of people in cities; greater wealth, which increases the insurance density in many parts of the world; and the growing propensity of people to live in vulnerable places like flood plains and coastal locations in storm-prone regions.

Dr. Ernst von Weizsäcker[4] wrote an article in Munich Re's publication *Perspectives: Today's Ideas for Tomorrow's World* (Munich Re 2001), entitled "Financial Services and the Environment" in which he stated:

> If we want to prevent climate change from accelerating and stabilize today's CO_2 concentrations, we will have to reduce annual global emissions by at least half. . . . Furthermore, the use of other raw materials like water and soil must be reduced dramatically if we want to give back to nature the space it needs and thus stop the horrendous loss of plant and animal species, currently to the tune of about fifty a day.

He noted that the company conducted an environmental audit of its own operations and has gone on to develop a program to reduce that impact. He also advised the company to use its investment weight to support companies that are environmentally sound and to avoid companies that "rely to a large degree on exhaustible resources" (Munich Re 2001c, 10–11). The company appears to be following von Weizsäcker's advice. In its Annual Report for 2000 it promises to make sure that environmental standards guide its relationship with clients and influences the investments it makes:

> The main emphasis of our work will continue to be on striving to ensure, in close dialogue with our clients, that expertise accumulated at Munich Re finds its way into appropriate measures for loss prevention, to the benefit of the environment. . . .

TABLE 9.3   Comparison of Losses over Decades in U.S. $ billions (2000 values)

	1950–1959	1960–1969	1970–1979	1980–1989	1990–1999	1991–2000
Number of losses	20	27	47	63	89	84
Economic losses	$40.7	$73.1	$131.5	$204.2	$629.2	$591.0
Insured losses	Unknown	$7.0	$12.0	$25.5	$118.8	$104.4

Source: Munich Re 2001b, 15.

> *Criteria related to environmental protection and sustainable development will play an additional role in our investment decisions, along with the classic principles of security, profitability, and liquidity. We will intensify research in this area in our asset management. (Munich Re 2001a, 78)*

CLIMATE CHANGE PROGRAMS

In addition to the deregulation of the financial services sector, national and regional governments have undertaken a number of climate change initiatives that have the potential to affect the fiscal capacity of the financial sector's clients, most specifically power producers and energy-intensive businesses. The Kyoto Protocol has provided the basis for carbon trading programs that are appearing in different jurisdictions. The following section provides a brief outline of CO_2 trading initiatives, both on regulated exchanges and within the private sector, that have emerged since the Protocol was conceived.

National Carbon Reduction Initiatives

Denmark   In January 2001, Denmark introduced the world's first binding greenhouse gas emissions trading scheme for its power sector, under its CO_2 Quota Act. The program covers nine generators that account for 90 percent of electricity production in that country. It is a straight cap-and-trade system, with the cap declining from 23 million metric tons CO_2 in 2000 to 20 million metric tons CO_2 in 2003. There are financial penalties of 40 Danish kroner per ton (about $5–$6 U.S.) for noncompliance but no allowances for subsidies. The rationale for a program focusing solely on power producers is twofold: First is the fact that this sector is the only major GHG-emitting sector in Denmark that is not covered by carbon taxes or energy efficiency measures; secondly, the Danish power sector has experienced rapidly increasing exports of fossil fuel generated electricity to other Scandinavian countries (Helme 2001; Rosenzweig et al. 2002; E. Thomas 2001).

United Kingdom   In April 2001, the United Kingdom introduced its Climate Change Levy (CCL), which represents a tax on the business use of energy. In April 2002, the United Kingdom launched its national emissions trading scheme (ETS), which is ambitious in both size and complexity, to help the country meet its planned GHG emissions reductions target. In contrast to the Danish GHG market, which targets nine companies in the power sector, the U.K. ETS system covers end users, with the exception of transportation and home heating, rather than generators (thereby protecting the coal industry). Companies can join the U.K. emissions trading system by:

- Agreeing to absolute emissions targets (CO_2 equivalents/year) in which companies must take absolute emissions targets for 2002–2006 that are below a 1998–2002 average.
- Agreeing to relative targets related to levels of output (based on energy efficiency).
- Entering climate change agreements (CCAs) with government.
- Developing specific, voluntary U.K.-based emission reduction projects that can sell credits created to both absolute and relative sectors. (www.defra.gov.uk/environment/climatechange/trading/index.htm; Biello 2002a)

By participating in climate change agreements with the government, many companies have negotiated an 80 percent reduction to their Climate Change Levy (CCL) in exchange for accepting energy-use targets. Under such circumstances, these companies have automatically joined the ETS (Nicholls 2002b). Noncompliance renders agreement participants ineligible for CCL reductions for that year.

Thirty-four companies that were not able to have all their GHG emissions covered by the CCL agreement were encouraged to make reductions with financial incentives worth £215 million of auctioned funds. Noncompliance at this level results in ineligibility for annual financial incentive payments (Rosenzweig et al. 2002; Rosewell 2001). The use of multiple tracks and incentives is seen to contribute both strength and baffling complexity to the U.K. system, which is to run until 2006, according to current plans (Helme 2001).

European Union   With the intent of ensuring a compatible trading program for its member states under the proposed Kyoto Protocol, in 2001 the European Commission (EC) issued a directive proposing a European Union (EU)-wide emissions trading system. It suggests a two-phase program. The first stage, from 2005 to 2007, would allow member states to gain experience with the trading system; the second phase would coincide with the first compliance period of the Kyoto Protocol. Initially the initiative would cover only CO_2 emissions, and would include all sectors (power, iron and steel, refining, cement, pulp and paper). The penalty for noncompliance during the first period would be the greater of either €50/excess ton or twice the average price of CO_2e for a previously agreed-upon period of time. For the 2008–2012 compliance period, the financial penalty would rise to the greater of €100/excess ton or twice the average market price of CO_2e (http://europa.eu.int/comm./environment/climate/home_en.htm; Rosenzweig et al. 2002).

While Denmark, the United Kingdom, and the European Union itself are the most advanced with national plans for emissions trading, other countries have signaled their intention to develop similar national initiatives. Non-EU member Switzerland has released a directive to implement a carbon dioxide law, which would see a domestic emissions trading system introduced possibly by 2004 (Janssen and Springer 2001). For its part, the Netherlands had introduced a national climate change strategy, planned as a cap-and-trade system for 2004–2005, but decided to wait, instead, until the EU trading scheme takes effect in 2005 (Mathias 2002b).

Compatibility of Existing Systems Complications arise as these national systems are developed in the absence of a clear international trading framework, as each country has the potential to introduce features that are incompatible with another country's scheme. Table 9.4 compares some of the characteristics that define the Danish, U.K. and EU emissions trading systems.

The U.K. and Danish systems, for instance, cover different gases and economic sectors, as well as using different mixes of allowance and credit-based approaches. It would appear that these differences would pose a barrier to trade between firms in these countries. However, one swap of emissions allowances has taken place in 2002 between Shell (U.K.) and the Danish electrical company Elsam. Although the counterparties did not disclose the terms of the trade, Shell did express its need for Danish allowances for its generating capacity in Denmark, and Elsam explained that the swap allowed the company to build a longer-term portfolio than the Danish program allowed, that is to say, until 2006 rather than 2003 (Nicholls 2002d; Rosenzweig et al. 2002).

At the moment, however, it appears that neither of these national programs is completely compatible with the EU-wide trading scheme. A number of key differences exist already between the U.K. system and the EC proposal that have sparked controversy as to the compatibility of the U.K. scheme with the EU rules. The first is that the U.K. program is voluntary while the EU-wide system would be mandatory. In addition, the EU would not allow subsidies, such as the incentives being offered by the British government to potential ETS participants. Another difference is the fact that

TABLE 9.4 Comparisons of the Danish, U.K., and EU Emission Trading Programs

Characteristic	Denmark	United Kingdom	European Union
Voluntary/ mandatory	Mandatory	Voluntary	Mandatory
Compliance periods	2001–2003	2002–2006 for direct participants 2002–2010 for agreements	2005–2007 2008–2012
Gases covered	CO_2	CO_2 only or all 6 GHG (company chooses coverage)	CO_2 initially
Sectors	Electricity generators only	Industrial sectors, electricity sectors excluded	Industrial and energy sectors; chemical sector excluded
Targets	Absolute	Absolute and relative	Absolute
Financial incentives	None	Auctioned funds for direct participants CCL discount for agreements	Not anticipated
Financial penalty	40 Danish kroner per ton ($5–$6 U.S.)	Loss of incentive payments and CCL discount	(2002–2007) ∈ 50/ton or 2× average allowance price (2008–2012) ∈ 100/ton or 2× average allowance price

Source: Adapted from Rosenzweig et al. 2002, Table 3, p. 34.

the U.K. program explicitly excludes electricity and heat generators, covering instead electricity consumers, whereas the EU proposals include them. And finally, the U.K. compliance regime has no mandatory financial penalties as foreseen in the EU scheme, other than cancellation of incentive payments and CCL discounts. The lack of compatibility that exists among these initiatives is seen by some as a significant barrier to accessing the economic benefits and cost-saving opportunities that arise from an international trading scheme (Helme 2001; Rosenzweig et al. 2002).

A further dilemma arises regarding the Danish government's concern with the EU's proposed "burden-sharing" agreement, designed to divide the EU's 8 percent overall cut among its members. Denmark argues that it cannot meet its designated target if the base year is set at 1990 levels, a year in which its emissions were unusually low (Goodfellow 2002).

Canada Countries in other jurisdictions have also developed initiatives at the national and regional levels, as well as within the private sector. In Canada the Voluntary Challenge and Registry (VCR) program represents an existing government/industry initiative to reduce greenhouse gases, while the National Round Table on the Economy and Environment (NRTEE) is studying the possibilities of a national trading scheme. In addition, the Greenhouse Gas Emissions Reduction Trading Pilot (GERT) provides a baseline protection scheme in western Canada, while trading is happening among private sector companies through programs such as the Pilot Emissions Reduction Program (PERT) in Ontario.

United States Despite the unwillingness of the United States to ratify the Kyoto Protocol, two northeastern states, New Hampshire and Massachusetts, have proposed caps on CO_2 emissions. Massachusetts has set CO_2 emissions limitations on six existing fossil-fired power plants operating in its jurisdiction. In April 2001, two sets of restrictions were established: First the six plants will be required to make an absolute CO_2 emissions reduction of 10 percent from a 1997–1999 average baseline by October 1, 2002; they then must achieve a relative emissions rate of 1,800 lbs. CO_2/megawatt hour by October 1, 2006. The requirements can be met through internal actions such as fuel switching (coal to natural gas) or through the purchase of offsets from emissions reduction projects, although specific rules governing the latter have not yet been developed (Chartier and Powers 2002; Rosenzweig et al. 2002).

In New Hampshire, a cap on CO_2 emissions, which applies to three power plants operating in the state, has been established under the state's Clean Power Act. The Act allows for emissions trading to help the companies meet the targeted cuts of CO_2 emissions to 7 percent below 1990 levels, a goal that must be reached by December 2006 (Biello 2002b).

Government/Private Sector Climate Change Initiatives

ERUPT and CERUPT The Dutch government's Emission Reduction Unit Procurement Tender (ERUPT) program is designed to help the Netherlands achieve its national emissions reduction obligation through the purchase of emission reduction units (ERUs) generated by flexible mechanisms, that are based on the rules for Joint Implementation projects, but found in Annex B countries. The government has developed a second program, Certified Emission Reduction Unit Procurement Tender (CERUPT), with a similar purpose, with the intention of purchasing reductions generated, in this case, from Clean Development Mechanism (CDM)-like projects (Rosenzweig et al. 2002).

Thus ERUPT operates in a carbon procurement strategy similar to the World Bank Prototype Carbon Fund (described in Chapter 4), in which carbon credits are bought directly on behalf of investors, rather than investing in energy efficiency and renewable energy projects that generate the credits. In the ERUPT initiative, independent banks that are associated with the program provide the project financing. As with the World Bank Prototype Carbon Fund (PCF), a division of labor exists in these undertakings, where the fund managers originate and structure the commercially viable projects, while the leading institutions such as the Dutch government or the World Bank verify and certify emissions reductions in exchange for some or all of the tradable carbon credits (Bürer 2001).

GHG Friendly/GHG Free Fund   In 2000, the Australian federal government launched a GHG Friendly/GHG Free offset program designed to endorse carbon-neutral products whose GHG emissions are offset by renewable energy and energy efficiency programs as well as projects that use landfill methane for electricity. BP was the first company to commit to this initiative through its clean fuel strategy, which offsets emissions arising from the use of its premium fuel, Ultimate 98. An Australian energy company and an international transport firm with operations in Australia are expected to announce their participation as well in the near future (Bürer 2001; Nicholls 2000d).

Private Sector Initiatives

Chicago Climate Exchange (CCX)   Although there has been little progress made in GHG trading at the federal level in the United States, a private sector initiative, the Chicago Climate Exchange (CCX), does exist. (See Box 7.6.) The project is led by Chicago-based Environmental Financial Products and financed by the private sector with grants from the Joyce Foundation, via the Kellogg Graduate School of Management at Northwestern University. The initiative represents a voluntary GHG reduction pilot program that targets emission sources and offset projects in the American Midwest. More than 40 entities, including DuPont, Ford, International Paper, and Wisconsin Energy, will participate in the trading scheme. Its goal is to design and implement a voluntary pilot market, first in seven Midwestern states, and later to include national and international sources (www.chicagoclimatex.com).

GHG Emissions Management Consortium (GEMCo)   In Canada, GEMCo, which represents a consortium of power producers, is a private sector initiative that identifies and develops carbon offset projects for emission reduction credit trading and GHG management solutions. GEMCo assists its members in identifying and securing reductions and offsets for their own use, as well as establishing a formal commercial mechanism for emission reduction credit recognition (www.gemco.org).

NEW WEATHER-RELATED PRODUCTS

Much of this book is about developing new products to meet environmental goals. Examples run from cost cap overrun insurance policies, designed to facilitate the cleanup of contaminated land, to carbon trading. Barriers to innovation abound, including lack of familiarity and information to bring potential buyer to potential seller, lack of government regulation to make what is environmentally desirable into a marketable product, lack of suitable data, and the time and costs involved. These are the common problems associated with the development of new products in environmental finance. In this chapter on the development of strategies for managing environmental change we will take as examples three classes of new products that address climate change: risk transfers with respect to catastrophic events and adverse weather conditions, and trading pollution reduction credits.

The securitization of risk has the potential to mobilize the power of the capital markets by expanding reinsurance capacity and providing hedging tools in the event of major natural catastrophes and mild or extreme weather. To do this, risks pertaining to natural catastrophes and weather are packaged into some form of a standardized financial product that can then be bought or sold in capital markets. This section outlines the characteristics of instruments developed to meet capacity needs in the face of natural catastrophes and weather-related issues. Figure 9.1 identifies the manner in which securitized transfer of risk links investors, insurers, and corporations through hedging instruments.

Within the conventional insurance industry, insurers and reinsurers raise capital from investors. Insurers, for their part, offer coverage to clients, and hedge excessive potential losses through the purchase of reinsurance. Although capacity can be increased by increasing flows of capital through this structure, an alternate means of spreading risk and increasing capacity exists where investors bear some of the risk by purchasing catastrophe or weather instruments (bonds, options, and swaps) offered through the capital markets. Such instruments can provide hedges for insurers or directly for firms such as energy companies. The following subsections discuss the functions of catastrophe and weather hedges currently available to investors.

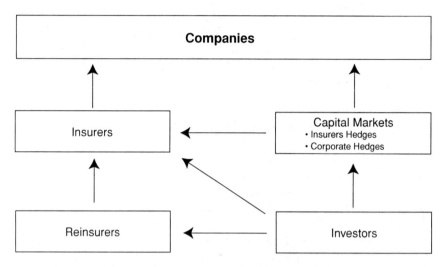

FIGURE 9.1   Linkages of Derivatives to the Markets
Source: Based on Doherty 1997.

Catastrophe Bonds and Swaps

Primary insurers that are very exposed to catastrophic risks such as hurricanes on the U.S. east coast and earthquakes in California actively seek reinsurance for these regional risks. However, reinsurers who already have concentrated exposure to both are not likely to want to assume further risk in either the region or the peril. This need on the part of insurers presents an opportunity for capital markets to provide a form of "synthetic" reinsurance through new forms of financial instruments, such as catastrophe (cat) bonds and swaps. Returns on these instruments that convert reinsurance contracts into securities are uncorrelated with the returns from traditional assets held in investors' portfolios (Canter and Cole 1997; Canter et al. 1996). In addition, since returns are determined solely by the loss pattern relating to a natural catastrophic event, securitized products offer a diversification effect to any portfolio.

Cat Bonds   A typical cat bond provides insurance coverage in the event of a natural catastrophe, such as a hurricane. This transaction involves three parties: the cedant insurer, the investor, and a special purpose shell company that issues the bonds to the investor. Figure 9.2 depicts schematically how these parties interact.

The issuer enters into a reinsurance contract with the cedant, and si-

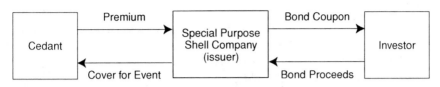

FIGURE 9.2 Catastrophe Bond Payment Structure
Source: Based on Swiss Re 1999, p. 5.

multaneously issues cat bonds to the investor. The shell company is structured as an independently owned trust that is licensed as a reinsurer in an offshore location, such as the Cayman Islands or Bermuda. Its sole purpose is to transform reinsurance risk into an investment security.

The funds provided by the investor are deposited in a trust account that earns the London Interbank Offered Rate (LIBOR). The bond coupon paid comprises investment earnings on the deposit, as well as the premium that the cedant pays for the insurance coverage (Swiss Re 1999b, 2001b). Cat bonds traditionally yield higher returns, since investors demand a premium to compensate for the investment's lack of liquidity. From the perspective of the capital invested, some of these bonds are "principal protected" where an investor can lose only the interest. Others are "principal at risk" where the return of the principal is linked to a specific catastrophic event, in which case a percentage of the capital, related to the severity of the event, can be lost as well as the interest (Mathias 2002a).

If there is no qualifying event during the time period specified, the principal amount is returned to the investor along with the final bond coupon. If, however, a catastrophe takes place, causing losses that surpass a specified amount (trigger) in the geographic region and time period delineated in the bond, the issuer of the cat bond pays the cedant's claim with the funds from the bondholder's funds, which can include the investor's interest, a portion of the entire principal, or both (Canter and Cole 1997; Swiss Re 1999b, 2001b).

Two issues of cat bonds serve as illustrations of the different class of bonds that can be offered to investors with different risk profiles. The first example is that of the two classes of bonds issued in 1997 by USAA, a Texas-based insurer, both of which were tied to LIBOR. USAA's $164 million A-1 bonds were offered at LIBOR plus a 282 basis point premium. In the case of these bonds, the coupon was at risk, with principal being guaranteed. USAA's $300 million A-2 bonds, by contrast, were offered at LIBOR plus 575 basis points. With these higher-paying bonds, the principal is completely at risk. A default of either of these notes would be triggered if there were a hurricane on the east coast of the United States between June 15 and December 31, 1997, that resulted in more than a billion dollars of claims against USAA.

The second example is that of the three classes of cat bonds covering earthquakes, which were brought to market in 1997 by Swiss Re. These issues differed from the USAA bonds in that the triggers for the Swiss Re bonds were indexed to an industry-wide exposure computation that is published by the Property Claims Services (PCS). Each of the three classes of bonds issued was triggered by a different indexed amount (Jones 1999).

Cat Swaps   An alternative way to securitize catastrophic risk is through a swap transaction. In this case, a series of fixed predefined payments from the cedant is exchanged for a series of floating payments from the counterparty (see Figure 9.3). The value of the floating payments depends on the specifications related to the occurrence of the designated catastrophic event that is being insured. The cedant can enter into the swap directly with the counterparty or can use the services of a financial intermediary. Swaps are simpler in structure and less costly to implement than cat bonds. Unlike bonds, they do not tie up capital in a special purpose vehicle. They do, however, entail an extensive credit risk assessment (Swiss Re 1999b, 2001b).

Weather Derivatives

Whereas the evolution of the cat bond market arose from the need for greater capacity within the (re)insurance industry, the weather derivatives market has evolved directly out of the oil and gas options/futures markets, since climatic variability is a major contributor to volatility in demand for energy. Deregulation of the energy sector also played an important part in the development of weather trading, as price and volume volatility that once was absorbed by the taxpayer became the responsibility of energy producers and users (Ertel 2001).

A derivative is defined as "a financial contract whose value derives

FIGURE 9.3   Cat Swap Payment Structure
Source: Based on Swiss Re 1999, 6.

from the value of some underlying asset, such as a stock, bond, currency or commodity" (Swiss Re 2001, 8). Weather options and swaps are derivative products traded daily on world markets as commodities on the energy desks of both financial firms and energy companies around the world. In contrast to the cat bonds market, weather markets are continuous, dynamic, and volatile. Table 9.5 summarizes some of the different characteristics of catastrophe bonds and weather derivatives.

Weather Instruments Typically, the weather conditions that affect energy companies are warm winters and cool summers, when there is less power demand for heating/cooling. To address these conditions, weather contracts are undertaken to hedge losses due to such unseasonable weather, in the form of financial agreements between two entities that allow one company to transfer its weather risk to another. Parties involved in weather derivatives come to an agreement on the threshold temperature (the "strike") as well as the amount of payment to be made (the "tick") per unit of weather index, depending on the contract period and the index used. Temperature, precipitation, wind, snow, and stream flow appear among the weather conditions that form the backdrop for these derivatives. For temperature-based contracts, most weather data used to date is from the United States. More recently, precipitation, snow, and stream flow based weather derivatives products have gained some currency with hydroelectric power producers, to help manage their price and volume risks. Table 9.6 describes a number of indexes that have been used to capture these different forms of weather exposure. A degree day is a measure of the variation of one day's temperature (t_{av}) against a standard reference temperature (t_{normal}), which is typically set at 65°F. If the average temperature on a given day is 55°F, then 10 heating degree days (HDD) are reported for that day ($t_{normal} - t_{av}$). On the other hand, 10 cooling degree days (CDD) would be recorded if the average daily temperature is 75°F ($t_{av} - t_{normal}$). Due to the definition of these indexes, HDD and CDD are always positive values (McIntyre 2000).

TABLE 9.5 Different Characteristics of Castrophe Bonds and Weather Derivatives

Characteristic	Cat Bonds	Weather Derivatives
Trigger	Catastrophic event	Temperature, precipitation
Transactions	Static	Dynamic
Financial instrument	Security	Commodity
Temporal	One event	Period of time
Source of trade	Insurance	Financial and energy firms

TABLE 9.6 Daily Indexes Used to Hedge

Daily Index	Description
T_{min}, t_{max}, t_{av}	Minimum, maximum, and average temperature
HDD	Heating degree days = $t_{normal} - t_{av}$
CDD	Cooling degree days = $t_{av} - t_{normal}$
EDD	Energy degree days = HDD + CDD
GDD	Growing degree days = DD between 50°F and 86°F
VDD	Variable degree days = same as HDD or CDD except t_{normal} replaced by a value other than 65°F
Precipitation	Inches of rainfall
Snowpack	Inches of snow
User defined	A customized index using a combination of the above

Source: Ellisthorpe and Putnam 2000.

The trade described in Box 9.1 between Sacramento Municipal Utility Department (SMUD) and Kansas City–based trading firm Aquila in 2000 represents a classic example of a precipitation-based swap.

The three most commonly traded instruments that are available in weather markets are weather-based call options, put options, and swaps. Each contract involves a buyer and seller who reach an agreement on the contract period, the weather index (W) that will serve as the basis for the contract, the threshold for that weather index (strike S), and the price per unit of weather index (tick k). At the outset, the firm seeking weather protection pays for a contract with an up-front premium to the seller. At the

BOX 9.1 A Precipitation-Based Swap

In an attempt to protect itself against the effects of low levels of precipitation on electricity production, the Sacramento Municipal Utility Department (SMUD) entered into a weather contract. The trading firm Aquila agreed to pay SMUD up to $20 million annually when less water flowed through the utility's hydro plants, while SMUD would pay Aquila the same amount during wet years. Although precipitation deals represent a very small proportion of the overall weather market, growth in this area is anticipated to come as much from agriculture firms as power producers, as farmers attempting to protect their crop incomes from drought (Saunderson 2001a).

end of a call option contract, the seller pays the buyer an amount equal to the difference between the realized index value W and the predetermined strike level S, times the tick of the contract k, or $P = k(W - S)$. In a call option, there is no payoff below the strike level. A put option is the same as a call except that the seller pays the buyer when the weather index W is less than the strike level (W < S). In the case of a put option, the payment is represented by $P = k(S - W)$ and there is no payoff above the strike level.

A weather swap, by contrast, is a combination of a call sold by one company and a put sold by another. Weather swaps require no up-front premium, and the strike is selected so that the call and the put command the same premium. At the end of the contract, a payment is made by one company to the other depending on the realized temperature (Ellisthorpe and Putnam 2000; Zeng 2000).

A number of companies have also designed products that use both cat bonds and weather derivatives, the latter being described in the following section. These companies, such as Société Générale Insurance Derivatives (France) and Willis Corroon Catastrophe Management (Bermuda), have developed fledgling funds that comprise catastrophe bonds and weather hedges. Their principal investors would be insurers and pension fund managers who lack the resources and expertise to examine and compare these two complementary, yet distinct, climate-related products.

Weather Markets Considering electricity as a crucial commodity, it possesses some characteristics that are unusual among commodity products as a whole. First, electricity must be produced on a continuous basis in order to meet consumption levels. At the same time, the energy trading industry is vulnerable to even momentary imbalances in its production and consumption, with excess supply creating power overload and excess demand causing brownouts or blackouts. Unpredictable weather patterns can have a devastating effect on this delicate balance of anticipated supply and demand.

In addition, variations in generation technology further complicate energy management. Generating plants with high fixed and lower operating costs are better utilized in providing the "baseload" amounts of electricity on a continuous basis, while other plants with lower capital costs-to-operations ratios are better suited to adjust supply incrementally or come on line quickly in order to meet peak period demand (Brennan 2001).

Energy generators and utility firms, which demonstrate differing sensitivities to weather exposure, and experience these uncertainties, use weather put and call options or swaps to hedge unpredictable supply and demand patterns. In order to assess and price weather exposure risk, these companies must identify the points in the following list (Ellisthorpe and Putnam 2000; Zeng 2000).

■ The business index (revenues, profits, sales) they assume will be affected by weather conditions.
■ The weather index that best matches the business risk (temperature, precipitation, snow, stream flow).
■ The nature of that weather exposure.
■ The contract type required (call, put, or swap).
■ The contract period.
■ The threshold (strike).
■ The amount of payment per unit of weather index (the tick).
■ The premium to be paid.

Weather instruments are sought after in the energy trading industry as a vehicle for gaining a grasp on future volume requirements. Power plants, for example, are characterized as capital-intensive assets and, as such, are temperature and capacity dependent. As average temperatures rise above 65°F, an increase in air conditioning is predicted for cooling purposes, while temperatures below 65°F see an increase in demand due to heating requirements. If either scenario surpasses the utility's capacity, the power plant will have to purchase power on the spot market to meet its peak demand. In this case, payout options for weather can be used to finance purchases of spot power. Similarly, a power company can hedge against economic loss due to the opposite situation of a cool summer in which there is less demand for power, volume demand is low, and prices are unlikely to spike. In this case, operational costs can be hedged with the purchase of a maximum temperature put option at the beginning of the season that pays a fixed sum if the maximum temperature never exceeds the strike level ($t_{max} < t_{strike}$).

Certain power plants and natural gas distributors may want to hedge against lower than expected revenues due to reduced volumes of sales reflected in a warm winter. The company could hedge its sales volumes through the use of HDD derivatives, by buying a put option based on the total heating degree days for the period in question (cumHDD) or selling a cumHDD swap. Table 9.7 offers a simplified example of weather hedging using these two instruments, if a company's normal revenue ($100 million) is assumed to change by $60,000 per HDD (tick price) because of a warm winter.

When the seasonal daily temperatures are aggregated (cumHDD), the put option protects the company during a mild winter while the company retains its advantage of increased volumes and revenues in the event of a cold winter. If, however, the company chooses a swap, it is liable for the payout to its counterparty in the event of a cold winter. With a swap, therefore, the financial exposure is leveled out, irrespective of weather (Ellisthorpe and Putnam 2000; Millette 2001).

TABLE 9.7 Weather Hedges Using cumHDD Put Options and Swaps (in $ millions)

Type of Winter	cumHDD (W)	(S – W)	Payout (P) in $M[3]	Unhedged Revenue $M	Hedged Revenue $M
cumHDD Put Option					
Mild	3,800	200	12	88	100
Normal	4,000[2]	0	0	100[1]	100
Severe	4,200	–200	0	112	112
cumHDD Swap					
Mild	3,800	200	12	88	100
Normal	4,000[2]	0	0	10[1]	100
Severe	4,200	–200	–12	112	100

[1]Normal revenue.
[2]Strike.
[3]Payout = (S – W) × tick price of $60,000/HDD.
Source: Adapted from Ellisthorpe and Putnam 2000.

The swap undertaken by two Japanese companies that face opposite weather risks serves as a good illustration of this derivative product. Tokyo Electricity Power (Tepco), which experiences increased demand for electricity during an unusually warm summer, swapped a portion of this weather risk with Tokyo Gas (Togas), which experiences a decreased demand for gas-fired water and central heating under the same extreme weather conditions. In 2001, the two firms entered into a swap for a time period of August 1 to September 30. An agreement was reached whereby Tepco would pay Togas if the average temperature in Tokyo was above 26.5°C, and the reverse if the temperature fell below 25°C, up to a limit of 700 million yen. When the average temperature was found to be 24.5°C, Tepco was paid 320 million yen on the swap (Nicholls 2002).

Several other transactions illustrate the use of different indexes that serve as the basis for varying weather contracts. Axia Energy Europe, a subsidiary that emerged from the merger of the power company Entergy and the oil and gas group Koch, has provided precipitation protection to a consortium of corn farmers against the possibility of a drought (Saunderson 2001b). Fear of a mild winter, on the other hand, has prompted the Canadian snowmobile manufacturer Bombardier Inc. to base swap contracts on availability of snow (Millette 2001). In Japan, organizations as diverse as ferry operators, ski resorts, and theme parks have bought protection through the derivatives market against declining revenues due to adverse weather conditions. Indeed, Hiroshima Bank created a humidity derivative for a company that makes throat lozenges, as a protection against weak sales during humid spells (Economist 2002; Nicholls 2002c).

CASE STUDY: Goldman Sachs

One of the interesting developments in the use of capital markets for financing risk has been the entry of investment banks into the field of reinsurance. The investment-banking firm Goldman Sachs, which has a history of involvement in alternative risk products, launched Arrow Re in 1999, and more recently, in partnership with AIG and Chubb Insurance, established Allied World Assurance Holdings. Both of these companies are Bermuda-based insurance and reinsurance organizations, but have been set up for different purposes. Goldman Sachs views its involvement in Allied World as a minority, passive investment, which can be included in clients' portfolios either as a direct investment or as part of a composite such as in GS Capital Partners 2000 (GSCP 2000) investment funds. Goldman Sachs' investment partners manage Allied World, which deals principally in traditional lines of property and casualty insurance, with minimal exposure to natural catastrophe coverage.

Arrow Re, however, is wholly owned by Goldman Sachs, and allows the investment bank to expand its tool kit of products to find solutions for clients' risk problems associated with natural catastrophic events. In its role as a "transformer" of contracts, Arrow Re can write insurance, reinsurance, or financial contracts for its clients and then hedge the risk of such undertakings with further reinsurance or with securitized contracts in the form of cat bonds and options. The cat bond offerings are packaged in tranches with different risk profiles. The more conservative subgroupings put only the interest at risk, while the riskier tranches, which offer a higher yield, put both interest and portions of principal at risk in the event of a catastrophic event. Under Bermuda law, capital requirements for the client and hedging contracts can be offset, thus facilitating risk transfers of this sort.

Goldman Sachs has also taken a leadership position among investment banks in the weather markets, acting in the capacity of both intermediary and trader. The confluence of increased liquidity in the weather futures market with energy companies' desires to hedge weather effects on their revenues has led Goldman Sachs to establish a dedicated weather derivatives desk in the fall of 2001, making it one of the first investment banks to enter the weather derivatives market. The weather-trading desk, which is located in the commodities group adjacent to the energy desk, focuses primarily on temperature-linked contracts for energy companies in the northeastern United States.

Goldman Sachs' involvement with weather derivative products has led to the arrangement of a number of risk transfer deals, including the first and, so far, only weather-linked bond, which the bank structured in 1999 for the energy group Koch Energy Trading. Both swaps and options were used to raise $50 million through bonds that were marketed as private placements to reinsurance companies, hedge funds, and pension funds (Kirby 2001a; Millette 2001).

More recently, Goldman Sachs has created a package of options that brings weather protection for large energy companies to market. This portfolio of volume hedges, called the

Mercury Winter Weather Option Portfolio, allows a large portion of U.S. weather risk to be transferred principally to European investors. In this structured weather portfolio, investors sell the buyer of the needed weather protection five heating-degree-day (HDD) put options, each of which has "seasonal risk periods" for the three consecutive winters from 2001/2002 to 2003/2004. Each period of each option has a payout limit for the investor of $10 million. The total risk-bearing capacity added to the weather market in this undertaking, then, is $150 million (Nicholls 2001e). Buyers of these options include power and utility weather trading desks, reinsurers, and cat bond and other specialized natural hazard fund managers, including hedge funds. This portfolio is viewed as a "capacity-building" undertaking, which injects substantial liquidity into the weather market (Nicholls 2001a). The services of Goldman Sachs are also available to help clients—who want to buy weather protection—think about hedging products.

Most recently, the bank has entered into discussions with a large entertainment conglomerate that is seeking weather protection. According to Michael Millette, vice president of the Risk Management Group at Goldman Sachs, a number of other colorful but minor nonenergy trades have taken place using temperature, precipitation, or snow as the basic measurement vehicle. For example, pubs in England have undertaken a number of highly publicized temperature contracts to hedge against cool summers, which imply the need for fewer pub visits. In addition, Corney & Barrow, a chain of wine bars and restaurants, has hedged against bad weather, which deters customers from relaxing on their outdoor terraces.

TRADING POLLUTION REDUCTION CREDITS

In the previous section on the weather market we saw that some trading was directly motivated by firms that decided to hedge exposure to weather risk, such as energy suppliers and the construction industry. Indirectly the market is driven by changes in the regulatory framework, such as deregulating the energy sector in the United States and mandating the Non-Fossil Fuel Obligation in Britain. The trading of pollution reduction credits is driven more directly by regulation. Targets for pollution reduction are set and enforced by public authorities that also validate the credits. Increasingly these credits are being traded, driven by the need to achieve compliance at the lowest possible cost.

The successful prototype for this approach is the Environmental Protection Agency (EPA)'s Acid Rain Program, introduced in 1990, with Phase 1 reductions of sulfur dioxide coming into force from 1995 to 2000, targeting 263 of the most polluting industrial plants (Cooper 2000e). The program met its 50 percent reduction target at a cost that was only one-fifth of what the EPA itself had estimated!

The success of SO_2 allowance trading in the US has a significant place in the debate surrounding market-based solutions to global warming. The program is the largest successful market of its kind. Acid rain has been dramatically reduced and at a significantly lower cost than experts forecast. . . . The weight of evidence supports the argument that elements of the SO_2 market should be applied to carbon trading. These core elements simultaneously assure environmental integrity, cost reduction, efficient trading and valid price discovery. They include: clear rules on emission monitoring and non-compliance penalties; unimpeded trading; fully fungible trading instruments; public-private partnerships to achieve transparent prices. (Sandor 2000)

Also in the United States, a similar market was established in nitrogen oxide emissions (NO_x) reduction. NO_x is a precursor to ground-level ozone, "which is an irritant to the throat and lungs and aggravates conditions such as chronic lung and heart disease, allergies and asthma, and is especially harmful to children and the elderly" (Chartier 2000).

That is not to say that these results were achieved without any problem. The evolution of the markets has proceeded among a welter of court cases from the various proponents, including the EPA, various state governments, and the utilities themselves. But the successful outcome is widely recognized, and—as Richard Sandor pointed out (quoted above)—it proved that it could be done. A similar scheme is under development in Ontario (DeMarco 2001).

Other pollution reduction credit markets are evolving, especially in the United States. For example, there are watershed-based trading regions for nutrient reduction in streams and lakes in the states of Michigan, Idaho, Pennsylvania, Maryland, and Virginia (Faeth and Greenhalgh 2001). Mandated reductions were established by the 1972 Clean Water Act, based on the total maximum daily load for various pollutants of concern. Offers to buy and sell are posted and matched on a web site hosted by the World Resources Institute at www.nutrientnet.org (Box 9.2). Trading has focused on nitrogen and phosphorous so far, and it is obviously a smaller-scale operation than the SO_2 and NO_x markets. It could be argued, though, that success is equally critical given the poor state of health of waterways throughout the industrialized and developing world. The market includes both point sources (mostly industrial and processing plants) and nonpoint sources (including agricultural and urban runoff). "Trading could include municipalities, irrigation districts, farmers, wastewater treatment plants, food processing plants, and livestock operations" (World Resources Institute 2001).

BOX 9.2   Example of Offers Posted through NutrientNet

Offers to Buy Phosphorous in the Kalamazoo River Watershed
You may also view *offers to sell*. To select other types of offers, please visit the *offer options page*. To post an offer, please visit the *post offers page*.

Details:	Gives you more information on a specific offer.
Respond:	Allows you to bid on the offer or to make questions about the offers.
Edit/Delete:	Allows you to edit or delete your offer.

Quantity	Price	Submitted By	Offer Date	Close Date	Actions
1,000 credits	$3.00	Barker	November 8, 2001	November 12, 2001	Details . . . Respond . . . Edit/Delete . . .
3,000 credits	$10.00	Riter	November 11, 2001	November 19, 2001	Details . . . Respond . . . Edit/Delete . . .
1,000 credits	$6.00	Jones	November 12, 2001	November 12, 2001	Details . . . Respond . . . Edit/Delete . . .

Source: World Resources Institute (www.nutrientnet.org).

CONCLUSION

There is no doubt that an appropriate regulatory framework can create markets that can achieve environmental quality at a lower price than can generally be achieved by the old command-and-control approach. Understanding the interplay between appropriate regulation and the market potential is the key to a company successfully participating in these innovative approaches.

No major company, and few small ones, can afford to ignore the environmental challenge, whether it will simply increase the cost of material inputs and waste disposal or it will change the very basis of the enterprise. The appropriate environmental strategy is highly dependent on the particular circumstances in which a company operates. Most would want to include all the elements identified in this chapter—green housekeeping, environmental reporting, global monitoring, and the exploration of the opportunities for developing new products to improve environmental quality. Not many would need to go to the same lengths as Munich Re to monitor global environmental conditions. Much of the relevant information is available publicly (especially on the World Wide Web) or through trade associations. Not many companies are as deeply embedded in the physical environment as the oil and gas companies (like TransAlta) or water supply and treatment companies (like Wessex Water). Not all may see the need to hedge their exposure to unfavorable weather. However, the great majority of companies will have some need to understand their role in environmental change and how it might affect their operations and profitability. They may see the need to make some changes.

Often the problem for decision makers is one of timing, especially in the development of an entirely new kind of business like weather trading or pollution reduction credit trading. The creation of business infrastructure and marketing tools takes money and effort. Understanding the potential of environmental finance requires a new mind-set. It also requires governments to stay on course to meet the objectives they have identified, but governments are not well known for their resolve. Other serious challenges such as an economic slowdown or a major security issue like global terrorism may distract them. They may not be reelected, and the new government may choose a different course.

Even under this much uncertainty some corporations have set out into the new territory because they believe that environmental change—especially climate change—requires an entirely different approach, one that puts the planet on which we live at the center of their calculations. The Kyoto Protocol has not yet been ratified, but there is already a vibrant community of carbon traders. Although both industrial waste and widespread poverty threaten the integrity of our water supplies, global companies have emerged to deliver water supply and treatment anywhere in the world. These are companies that have put excellence into their core values, along with a competitive product and an acceptable share of the market.

ENDNOTES

1. Article 12.5(c) of the Kyoto Protocol defines certifiable emissions reductions as those "reductions in emissions that are additional to any that would occur in the absence of the certified project activity."

2. Supplementarity refers to the wish by some countries to ensure that there is a limit to a country's reduction efforts through international offsets. This limit would ensure that each country takes responsibility for reducing its own CO_2 emissions before buying projects from another country.
3. Listing by Standard & Poor's, quoted by the Reinsurance Association of America, available at www.reinsurance.org/download/IntPremRank.pdf.
4. Dr. Weizsäcker is a Member of the German Parliament; Founding President of the Wuppertal Institute for Climate, Environment, and Energy; and coauthor of *Factor Four*.

WEB SITES

Black Emerald Group	www.blackemerald.com
Canada's Voluntary Challenge and Registry	www.vcrmvr.ca/vcr-002.cfm
Chicago Climate Exchange (CCX)	www.chicagoclimatex.com
EU ETS	http://europa.eu.int/comm./ environment/climate/ home_en.htm
European Commission climate change initiatives	http://europa.eu.int/comm./ environment/climate/ home_en.htm
GHG Emissions Management Consortium (GEMCo)	www.gemco.org.
Munich Re	www.munichre.com
Netherlands ETS	www.minvrom.nl/minvrom/ pagina.html
Pembina Institute	www.pembina.org
TransAlta Corporation	www.transalta.com
U.K. ETS	www.defra.gov.uk/environment/ climatechange/trading/ index.htm
Voluntary Challenge and Registry (VCR)	www.vcr-mvr.ca
Wessex Water Services	www.wessexwater.co.uk
World Resources Institute, Nutrient Exchange Network	www.nutrientnet.org

CHAPTER 10

The Way Ahead

INTRODUCTION

There is a growing understanding that environmental change poses a serious challenge for all elements of society, including the business community. The problems we face are not a figment of the overheated imagination of environmentalists. They are real physical problems that will require an unprecedented level of cooperation among many countries and different elements of society within each country. However, most national governments have shown deep reluctance to come to terms with this change in our planetary situation. Expressions of concern have not, in general, led to implementation of appropriate policies and regulations. In the meantime, forward-looking companies and organizations have begun their own preparations for the conditions they anticipate they will soon be living in. These conditions include increasing pressure on improperly managed renewable resources (water, soils, forests, and fisheries), contaminated lands, and a changing climate.

BUSINESS AND ENVIRONMENTAL CHANGE: WHAT'S NEW?

What is new about managing this particular kind of environmental change is that the scale of change is now global and some of it is irreversible in the lifetime of anyone alive today. Environmental change on a global scale includes climate change and the attendant injection of a huge amount of uncertainty into our daily affairs. Only recently has the enormity of the implications of this risk factor truly penetrated the minds of the business community.

It is becoming increasingly evident that climate change is going to become one of the most important drivers of economic change over the next 50 years. Vast amounts of shareholder value will be destroyed as companies—and even whole industries—fail to make the necessary adjustments. But even larger amounts of value are likely to be created by the companies and technologies of the post-carbon world. (Hunt and Casamento 2001)

This statement brings together both sides of the environmental change coin: It has both a serious downside and an equally compelling upside. Both aspects have been widely ignored until quite recently. For example, polluting fossil-fuel-based operations will certainly change dramatically and at some significant cost over the next few decades. However, a power supply based on renewable sources and fuel cells will be more decentralized than current systems, and hence less subject to regionwide outages. Uninterrupted power supply will become the norm, rather than a luxury available only to high-tech corporations.

In a broader context, we need to reexamine a number of twentieth century assumptions that brought us to this situation. For example, it is still widely assumed that *policies that protect economy and environment constitute a zero-sum game* and that pollution is an inevitable by-product of businesses in pursuit of profit. Simply by holding this assumption, businesses would oppose any new environmental regulation, using whatever argument came to hand, such as denying any serious health implications or claiming that regulation would put them at a disadvantage compared with foreign competition. Government enforcement agencies might respond with sweeping legislation like Superfund, which expended enormous sums of money for relatively little environmental improvement.

The emergence of the fledgling field of environmental finance has clearly demonstrated the essential complementarity of regulation, production, and trade. Only within the appropriate regulatory framework will an environmentally benign economy evolve. It has become commonplace to speak of "designing markets" by establishing that framework through dialogue between government and business. The old notion that markets somehow emerged spontaneously from chaos is being replaced by a clearer understanding of what will be required to develop more sustainable means of production and exchange. Many emission reduction markets are being designed throughout the industrial world, and the issue of "inter-scheme compatibility" is already on the agenda (Nicholls 2001f, 2001g, 2001h). This level of activity has established an interesting new paradigm for environmental management.

THE NEW PARADIGM

The new paradigm is founded on a recognition of the fact that we are facing a major environmental challenge that is very long-term and yet requires immediate attention. Scientists have been aware of the dangers for some time, but business was resistant because of fear of a command-and-control approach that would make many businesses less profitable and some businesses impossible. The idea that we could make use of markets to ease the transition to a postcarbon world emerged only slowly. Some experiments failed. Environmentalists were skeptical, especially because the collapse of communist economies in central and eastern Europe had already reduced the amount of CO_2 they produced, compared with the Kyoto Protocol's 1990 baseline. Supposedly they would be able to sell these reductions. This Russian and Ukrainian "hot air" was seen as a typical loophole for the backsliders to slip through. The Clean Development Mechanism is regarded by some environmentalists as just a diversion to allow the industrial countries to continue business as usual. Trading emissions reduction credits was seen as little more than a license to pollute.

Gradually these attitudes are changing. Large fossil-fuel companies like BP and Royal Dutch/Shell looked down the road while assuming that the science reviews coming from the Intergovernmental Panel on Climate Change might be correct. They could see that doing nothing could suddenly be replaced by panic, followed by draconian legislation that could undermine their businesses. Their exposure to this risk was huge. They could not afford to ignore it. They left the anti-Kyoto Global Climate Coalition in 1997 and 1998 respectively. They began to invest seriously in renewable energy. In the meantime, the first large-scale emissions reduction trading scheme (for SO_2 and NO_x) was producing some surprisingly good results in the United States (Sandor 2000). Even the proponents of the scheme were surprised how quickly emissions were reduced and how low was the cost of reduction credits in the market. Suddenly it became clear that markets could get the job done, given the right incentive structure and freedom to trade credits.

Carbon reduction will be more difficult than SO_2 and NO_x reduction as it must be undertaken globally to be effective and that will inevitably be more complicated than a regional scheme. But at least we now know that a properly designed market can work.

The paradox is that deregulation and market-driven environmental solutions require more input from the government, not less. Governments may no longer be in the business of running airlines and banks, producing oil and gas, making steel, providing electricity, or even supplying water anymore. But governments are needed to set policy objectives and to develop new regulations for all those operations they now no longer run, but for which they must provide some transparent reassurance to the public. We find a similar situation with climate change and other environmental challenges for which we are turning to the market for help. For example, for emissions reductions trading, governments must set the reduction targets, develop protocols for verifying reductions, and establish the rules for trading the reductions credits. The critical role of regulation can be seen throughout this book, from California's requirement for zero-emission automobiles to Britain's Renewables Obligation.

The simple lesson to be drawn from these experiences is that governments and businesses must work together on this issue. In the view of ICF Consulting:

> *Governments will need to develop domestic policies to meet their emission reduction targets. Companies that emit GHGs will be faced with a new source of business risk and opportunity.*
>
> *In anticipation of Kyoto Protocol ratification, some companies are already taking action. Leading companies are learning by doing while developing more accurate estimates of their internal cost of carbon. There is an increasing recognition that GHG emissions have an explicit financial value. GHG emissions need to be managed like any other strategic asset or liability on the corporate balance sheet. Since 1997, transactions representing more than 100 million metric tonnes of CO_2 equivalent reduction have been conducted.*
>
> *(Document available from ICF Consulting at www.emissionstrategies. com/template.cfm?NavMenuID=9)*

DATA QUALITY

Within the field of environmental finance the business of hedging weather risk is emerging alongside emissions reduction trading as a major opportunity. (See Chapter 9.) This new activity has suddenly increased demand for reliable data in order to price contracts accurately. As noted earlier, the poorer the quality of the data, the greater the uncertainty premium that must be added to the price on the contract, and the more slowly the market will grow—or perhaps it will not grow at all (Harry 2001). The provision of reliable data is clearly a role for government, as few private entities have the right or ability to fulfill this role—unless contracted to do so by the government. The call for better and more available data is obvious, anyway, due to our need to monitor climate change. In Europe the situation is much more complicated than in North America, as there are differences in reporting practices between countries (Dawes 2001; Jewson and Whitehead 2001). Previously, the emphasis on the use of meteorological data was for predicting the weather. With the arrival of the weather derivatives business, there is now a pressing need to ensure the quality of data collected, in order to develop the probability distributions to support the market. Some weather features are easier to measure than others. For example, temperature is relatively tractable, while precipitation and wind are more of a measurement problem due to their greater temporal and spatial variability (Etkin 2001).

The other important data quality issue that has been identified in this book is the lack of standardized reporting procedures for measuring the environmental performance of a company. Although progress is being made on this front, the lack of a broadly accepted standard inhibits the development of the environmental component of socially responsible investment markets.

LEADERSHIP

It has been difficult for the business community to accept that major environmental issues could pose significant risk to their well-being. Environmental preoccupations were considered to be the concern of a minority of the population to which governments paid spasmodic attention if a crisis arose. Even when governments contemplated enacting significant environmental action there was an expectation that business lobbyists could dissuade them or at least water it down. For example, California's requirement for zero-emission automobiles was enacted in 1990 and due to come into force in 2003, with a review every two years along the way. Right to the final review (in January 2001) industry lobbyists worked against the measure. It will, however, go into force.

During the 1990s opinion began to change. The notion that the landscape was configured by two opposing forces—environmental nongovernmental organizations at one end and businesses at the other, with the public and governments somewhere in between—weakened. Change occurred not because of the overwhelming strength and logic of the environmental movement, which could be as self-serving as any other body. Change occurred because members of the business community assessed what data they had and came to the conclusion that some elements of the environmental argument were valid and required some action. Change requires leadership. The following are examples of the many people who provided this crucial quality.

Gerhard Berz (Ph.D. in meteorology and geophysics, University of Cologne) is director of Munich Re's Geoscience Research Unit, described in Chapter 5. The Unit has played a key role in keeping the world informed of the trend in economic and insurance losses due to extreme events. The Unit is staffed by scientists and represents an unusual commitment of resources within the insurance industry. Dr. Berz and his team have published widely and made public the results of their research (Berz 1988, 1993, 1996, 1999; Berz and Conrad 1994; Berz and Loster 2001). The task that Dr. Berz and his team face is to interpret the loss trends and estimate where we might be in the near future, without sounding alarmist. In doing so they have been able to help people at least imagine where we might be heading. In a presentation at the second meeting of COP 6 in Bonn (July 2001), Dr. Berz and his colleague from Munich Re, Thomas Loster, said:

> *If the most probable greenhouse predictions come true, the present problems will be magnified dramatically. Changes in many atmospheric processes will significantly increase the frequency and severity of heat waves, droughts, bush fires, hailstorms, floods and maybe also tropical and extra-tropical cyclones as well as storm surges in many parts of the world. . . . It also stands to reason that the particularly destructive tropical cyclones will advance into regions where they have not appeared in the past because of the temperatures prevailing there. Likewise the extra-tropical storms, the so-called winter storms, will penetrate far into the continents more frequently because the lack of snow will reduce the blocking effect of the cold high-pressure system over eastern Europe. (Berz and Loster 2001, 1)*

From all of this they draw a simple conclusion: "We simply cannot be responsible for leaving future generations on this planet with a climate that is out of balance" (Berz and Loster 2001, 2).

Another important figure in the insurance industry who has worked to bring the evolving scientific knowledge of climate change into the public forum is Dr. Andrew Dlugolecki, retired director of General Insurance Development at CGNU in the United Kingdom. Concern about climate change was first brought home to the U.K. insurance industry by the winter storm of 1987, which, with hurricane-force winds, inflicted £1 billion of insured losses in 24 hours, the first event ever to do so. As one of the few business members of the United Kingdom Climate Change Impacts Review Group (most being from the university or government), he was responsible for the financial sector of the Group's report, *The Potential Effects of Climate Change in the United Kingdom*, to the government (Parry et al. 1991). He went on to develop the financial sector of the IPCC's Working Group II on Impacts, Adaptation and Vulnerability (Watson et al. 1996). He brought the issues back to the U.K. financial services sector in reports on *The Impacts of Changing Weather Patterns on Property Insurance* (Dlugolecki 1994), the *Government Review of the Potential Effects of Climate Change in the United Kingdom* (Dlugolecki 1996b), and *Climate Change and Insurance* (Dlugolecki et al. 2001). At COP 6 at the Hague he warned the conference that an exponential rise in natural disaster losses could bankrupt the global economy, and that the aims of the Kyoto Protocol were merely "tactical" (Dlugolecki 2000).

He advocates the adoption of "Contraction and Convergence" as the best long-term framework to control climate change, and has underlined the key role that investors can play in the move toward a sustainable energy economy (Mansley and Dlugolecki 2001).

In an earlier report he explained how the insurance system might be seriously damaged by climate change:

> *The real threat is probably from a cluster-in-time of extreme events which might exhaust the reinsurance protection and channel back the bulk of later events to the primary insurance market. (Dlugolecki 1996b)*

Dr. Dlugolecki recently retired from CGNU and became a Visiting Fellow in Climate Change and Insurance at the Climatic Research Unit of the University of East Anglia. He is also director of the Carbon Disclosure Project and the Tyndall Research Centre for Climate Change.

Jeremy Leggett, author of *The Carbon War* (1999), began his career as a petroleum geologist at the Royal School of Mines at the Imperial College of Science, Technology, and Medicine in London. But the North American drought of 1988 and the Toronto conference *The Changing Atmosphere* in the same year persuaded him that he was on the wrong side in what he saw as an inevitable conflict between the burning of fossil fuels and the dangers of global warming. He left Imperial College to become the scientific director of Greenpeace International's Climate Campaign (1990–1994) and director of its Solar Initiative (1995–1996). As a geologist and consultant to the oil industry, he was in an unusual position, especially in an NGO with an unrivaled reputation for activism in the struggle for public attention.

Soon after the Earth Summit in Rio de Janeiro (1992) he had realized that the process driving the Framework Convention on Climate Change on its own would make slow progress, at best. What was needed was "a wholly new dynamic." He saw that the Global Climate Coalition (Box 7.1) represented only certain businesses:

> [F]ossil fuels, automobiles and, to a degree, chemicals. They were not the voice of the fishing industry, the agriculture industry, the tourism industry, the water industry, the skiing industry, the medical profession—all sectors that stood to lose in a world making no effort to reduce the enhanced greenhouse risk. They were certainly not the voice of the financial sector, or most especially the insurance industry. (Leggett 1999, 100)

He then identified the insurance industry as his best potential ally in the business community, given the losses they were sustaining (Leggett 1990, 1993, 1995).

> I decided to refocus my efforts, post-Rio, on the financial services sector. We needed to enlist their help if ever we were to undermine the carbon wall. . . . Insurers, along with banks and pension funds, were the primary bankrollers of fossil-fuel profligacy, both in debt and equity. (Leggett 1999, 100)

He left Greenpeace in 1996 and became chief executive of Solar Century, a solar power company. That year he chaired the U.K. Industry Solar Taskforce.

By the mid-1990s the Kyoto ratification COP process had assumed what was to become a painful habit of taking one step forward, followed by one step backward. Although some banks and insurers had signed UNEP's Financial Initiative, few had publicly spoken of withdrawing investments from fossil fuels. "Green Investment" was still considered somewhat quixotic and not something a mainstream asset manager would, or could, champion. However, despite the apparent lack of progress on the climate issue, oil majors BP and Royal Dutch/Shell were at that time mapping out a whole new strategy for their companies. This suddenly became clear when John Browne, CEO for BP, made his well-publicized announcement during a speech at Stanford University, his alma mater, in May 1997 (Box 7.2). He accepted that there were many uncertainties associated with the process of climate change, but there were undeniable risks as well. Every decision balances uncertainty against risk. Speaking for the company, he said:

The time to consider the policy dimensions of climate change is not when the link between greenhouse gases and climate change is conclusively proven, but when the possibility cannot be discounted and is taken seriously by the society of which we are part. We in BP have reached that point. (Browne 1997)

Four years later he confirmed:

We have to accept that the industry of which we're part faces a fundamental challenge—on the environment. . . . Serious scientific work by the IPCC and others has identified the risks as substantial, and a company in the energy business would be foolish to ignore those risks—particularly since so many of our customers believe them to be real. (Browne 2001)

The public process of responding to climate change has been as complex and difficult as was expected, and it is still very far from over. Members of various governments have shown leadership from time to time, but few have been able to chart a steady course through all the other unpredictable events that intrude on their decision-making space. The private sector faces many of the same difficulties, with a commitment to environmental quality often compromised by seemingly more urgent and immediate problems. What is significant is that a number of companies have taken a far more public position than the law or public relations demand, in order to signal a change of course. This is not "greenwash." It is a major strategic realignment. For a major fossil fuel company to have struck out on this path would have been unthinkable a decade ago.

ENVIRONMENTAL CHANGE:
FROM CHALLENGE TO OPPORTUNITY

In his recent speech, quoted in the preceding section, Lord Browne made an unusual comment for a corporate executive:

Giving up the illusion that you can predict the future is a very liberating moment.

And then he went on to say:

All you can do is give yourself the capacity to respond to the only certainty in life—which is uncertainty. The creation of that capacity is the purpose of strategy. Our strategy starts from a view of the world in which we are participants. The world we see is one of growth and opportunity. (Browne 2001)

An essential component of the liberation to which he refers is the acceptance of the notion that creative companies now see themselves as providing services, rather than selling products. People will still need energy, even if we phase out the use of fossil fuels in order to slow down the rate of global warming. The need for energy remains, even though the product line must be replaced. This is the service paradigm to which we referred at the beginning of this book.

If we accept that the world faces significant environmental challenges, and that these challenges are there for the private sector to respond to proactively—rather than fight a rearguard action against government regulation—then human society can draw on *all* of its strength to face the challenge. This is very different from the situation that existed until the early 1990s. Until then a great deal of energy and effort was wasted in conflicts between interests that were operating on vastly outdated assumptions. Earlier we quoted former President Clinton as saying:

There is nothing so dangerous as for a people to be in the grip of a big idea that is no longer true. It was once true that you had to put more greenhouse gases into the atmosphere to grow the economy, to build a middle class, make a country rich. It is not true anymore.

But, despite the willingness of pioneers to chart a new future for the global economy, many people and companies are still—in Clinton's phrase—"in the grip of a big idea that is no longer true." They are still preoccupied with fighting the old battles with the old weapons—they send in the lawyers. For one Superfund trial, 208 law *firms* were retained (Miller 1997). *Firms*, not lawyers. This type of situation is nothing but a colossal waste of resources.

In this book we have focused on the private sector and examined opportunities for companies to evolve in a way that enhances the environmental quality of life, rather than threatens it. However, it is implicit that it is not the private sector alone that needs to change. We have noted that the new paradigm requires a much more active commitment from government to become engaged in environmental change by developing appropriate policies and regulations. It has become very clear that the policy of deregulation and privatization implies the commitment of governments at all levels to *reregulate* the way in which businesses operate, including their impacts on the environment and human health.

Similarly, environmental NGOs need to evolve, too. Confrontation alone will not produce a better world. Again, progressive NGOs are learning to work with the business community, rather than simply boycotting their products. The last century saw the rise of the "eco-warrior," but this new century will probably belong to the "eco-auditor." Even if old adversaries decide to make common cause for the greater good, serious problems remain. For example, there are major challenges for developing affordable mechanisms for transferring risk related to environmental issues and climate change. There are catastrophic risks associated with extreme weather events, and there are risks associated with weather that is simply adverse for business. The probability of various types of adverse weather conditions will change as climate changes, and this will pose challenges for the fledgling business of weather derivatives. As noted earlier in this concluding chapter, one important support in this area could come from much higher-quality and more comparable weather data.

The huge potential market for carbon trading will also pose new challenges. Again, help may be at hand:

> *It is conceivable, for instance, that the insurance industry would provide cover for emissions trading and would help to guarantee its success. (Berz and Loster 2001)*

Although the energy sector faces the greatest challenge—in divesting itself of fossil fuels—it still offers opportunities for the innovative. There will be a more diverse mix of energy sources, and there will be more choices for end users in deregulated markets. We may even arrive at a situation where there is genuine competition among energy suppliers—at which point it may no longer be necessary to set price caps of the kind that disrupted the California energy market in the summer of 2000. Previously, under the big regional monopolies, whether private or public, the consumer had no choice. The energy systems of the future will rely partly on hydrogen derived from renewable sources, solar power, wind power, and other renewables. Power sources will be distributed rather than centralized. Systems will evolve in an incremental way and hence encourage experimentation in design.

It is possible that this type of approach will be applied to other infrastructure and production systems, such as water supply and treatment. For some operations the traditional advantages of large-scale production will apply, such as powering water treatment systems from the combustion of the biosolids recovered from the treatment process itself. We may see systems where the large and the small can usefully coexist, which is what we find in nature. One management consultant thinks that experimental incrementalism may be the hallmark of the leaders of this new century, and that these leaders will "set up little experiments instead of grand transformations" (Chowdury et al. 2000).

THE ENVIRONMENTAL LEARNING CURVE: REDEFINING SUCCESS

The big lesson from the asbestos problem from the 1970s onward was the futility of denial. The companies that stonewalled the claims were the same companies that went bankrupt. We are at a similar point today when considering the future of fossil fuels. As John Browne said:

> *It is clear that the only acceptable way for a company to respond to challenges such as the environment is to offer solutions. We can't live in denial or pretend that air quality and global warming aren't real issues. (Browne 2001)*

The resolution of certain issues requires higher-quality information, that can be shared among the proponents of different approaches to problem resolution. Many of the environmental problems that have arisen over the past 50 years took society by surprise because few people had access to the relevant information. Sometimes—as in the asbestos case—those that did have the information decided to conceal it, for fear of the consequences of disclosure. The basic arithmetic of the carbon cycle—the actual quantities of carbon passing from the burning of fossil fuels and biomass to the atmosphere, and then down to the land and oceans—was not known until the late 1970s and early 1980s. It was at a conference in the 1950s where scientists observed that more carbon dioxide was being emitted from the land than was being absorbed by the oceans. So where, they wondered, was the rest? Measurements of carbon dioxide concentrations in the atmosphere were started in 1957 at a single test site in Hawaii; it took a few years for the accumulation trend to be accepted by scientific opinion. Even Jeremy Leggett recounts:

> *The shameful truth is that I didn't even know the carbon arithmetic figures myself—despite having done a PhD at Oxford on ancient oceans—until the mid-1980s. . . . I had no idea that there was so little*

*carbon in the modern atmosphere, and so much in fossil-fuel reserves.
(Leggett 1999, 62)*

Knowledge and good data are prerequisites for improved environmental management.

Another major lesson from the recent past is that good regulation also is an essential component of a better managed future. Bad regulations—like the initial application of Superfund—do more harm than good. However, the environmental pioneers in the private sector need assurances from government that they are on the right course. Usually this can be guaranteed by regulation that requires that the target being pursued by the pioneers will be imposed on the rest of the field in due course. Timing is crucial. Many environmental issues are urgent; but setting unrealistic time lines will not help. The success of the SO_2 and NO_x markets is partly attributable to the fact that the time lines adopted by the regulators proved to be appropriate.

Not everyone is convinced that we need a paradigm shift in order to manage our environmental liabilities. We may have to wait until the hurricane zone expands a little, enough perhaps to bring in New York and Los Angeles, or until London succumbs to a £10 billion flood. It is sincerely to be hoped that such an event will not be necessary and that consensus will quickly coalesce behind the pioneers. We conclude with an observation made nearly 500 years ago:

It is a common failing of men not to take account of tempests during fair weather.

—Niccolò Machiavelli, The Prince *(1513)*

appendixes

UNEP Statement by Financial Institutions on the Environment and Sustainable Development

List of Signatories to the UNEP Statement by Financial Institutions on the Environment and Sustainable Development

UNEP Statement of Environmental Commitment by the Insurance Industry

Status of the UNEP Statement of Environmental Commitment by the Insurance Industry

UNEP STATEMENT BY FINANCIAL INSTITUTIONS ON THE ENVIRONMENT AND SUSTAINABLE DEVELOPMENT

(As Revised—May 1997)

We members of the financial services industry recognize that sustainable development depends upon a positive interaction between economic and social development, and environmental protection, to balance the interests of this and future generations. We further recognize that sustainable development is the collective responsibility of government, business, and individuals. We are committed to working cooperatively with these sectors within the framework of market mechanisms toward common environmental goals.

1   Commitment to Sustainable Development
1.1 We regard sustainable development as a fundamental aspect of sound business management.
1.2 We believe that sustainable development can best be achieved by allowing markets to work within an appropriate framework of cost-efficient regulations and economic instruments. Governments in all

countries have a leadership role in establishing and enforcing long-term common environmental priorities and values.

1.3 We regard the financial services sector as an important contributor towards sustainable development, in association with other economic sectors.

1.4 We recognize that sustainable development is a corporate commitment and an integral part of our pursuit of good corporate citizenship.

2 Environmental Management and Financial Institutions

2.1 We support the precautionary approach to environmental management, which strives to anticipate and prevent potential environmental degradation.

2.2 We are committed to complying with local, national, and international environmental regulations applicable to our operations and business services. We will work towards integrating environmental considerations into our operations, asset management, and other business decisions, in all markets.

2.3 We recognize that identifying and quantifying environmental risks should be part of the normal process of risk assessment and management, both in domestic and international operations. With regard to our customers, we regard compliance with applicable environmental regulations and the use of sound environmental practices as important factors in demonstrating effective corporate management.

2.4 We will endeavor to pursue the best practice in environmental management, including energy efficiency, recycling, and waste reduction. We will seek to form business relations with partners, suppliers, and subcontractors who follow similarly high environmental standards.

2.5 We intend to update our practices periodically to incorporate relevant developments in environmental management. We encourage the industry to undertake research in these and related areas.

2.6 We recognize the need to conduct internal environmental reviews on a periodic basis, and to measure our activities against our environmental goals.

2.7 We encourage the financial services sector to develop products and services which will promote environmental protection.

3 Public Awareness and Communication

3.1 We recommend that financial institutions develop and publish a statement of their environmental policy and periodically report on the steps they have taken to promote integration of environmental considerations into their operations.

3.2 We will share information with customers, as appropriate, so that they may strengthen their own capacity to reduce environmental risk and promote sustainable development.

3.3 We will foster openness and dialogue relating to environmental matters with relevant audiences, including shareholders, employees, customers, governments, and the public.

3.4 We ask the United Nations Environment Programme (UNEP) to assist the industry to further the principles and goals of this Statement by providing, within its capacity, relevant information relating to sustainable development.

3.5 We will encourage other financial institutions to support this Statement. We are committed to share with them our experiences and knowledge in order to extend best practices.

3.6 We will work with UNEP periodically to review the success in implementing this Statement and will revise it as appropriate.

We, the undersigned, endorse the principles set forth in the above Statement and will endeavor to ensure that our policies and business actions promote the consideration of the environment and sustainable development.

LIST OF SIGNATORIES TO THE UNEP STATEMENT BY FINANCIAL INSTITUTIONS ON THE ENVIRONMENT AND SUSTAINABLE DEVELOPMENT

The list is by company as of October 2001.

Abbey National plc., United Kingdom
Algemene Spaarbank voor Nederland, Netherlands
Arab Bank, PLC, Jordan
Balkanbank Ltd., Bulgaria
Banca Catalana S.A., Spain
Banca Internacional d'Andorra—Banca Mora, Andorra
Banca Monte dei Paschi di Siena S.p.A., Italy
Banco BHIF, Chile
Banco Bilbao Vizcaya S.A., Spain
Banco Bilbao Vizcaya (Portugal) S.A., Portugal
Banco Continental, Peru

Banco del Comercio S.A., Spain
Banco do Estado de São Paulo SA, Brazil
Banco Frances, Argentina
Banco Ganadero, Colombia
Banco Nacional de Angola, Angola
Banco Nacional de Desenvolvimento Economic e Social, Brazil
Banco Portuges do Atlantico SA, Portugal
Banco Provincial, Venezuela
Banesto, Banco Espagnol de Credito, Spain
Bank Austria, Austria
Bank Depozytowo-Kredytowy S.A., Poland
Bank für Tirol und Vorarlberg Aktiengesellschaft, Austria
Bank Gdanski S.A., Poland
Bankhaus Bauer AG, Germany
Bankhaus Carl Spängler & Co. Aktiengesellschaft, Austria
Bankhaus C. L. Seeliger, Germany
Bankhaus Max Flessa & Co., Germany
Bankhaus Neelmeyer AG, Germany
Bank Ochrony Srodowiska, Poland
Bank of Baroda, India
Bank of Cyprus, Cyprus
Bank of Handlowy W. Warszawie SA, Poland
Bank of Ireland Group, Ireland
Bank of Montreal, Canada
Bank of Philippine Islands, Philippines
Bank Polska Kasa Opieki S.A., Poland
Bank Przemystowo-Handlowy S.A., Poland
Bank Rozwoju Eksportu S.A., Poland
Bank Sarasin & Cie, Switzerland
Bank Slakski S.A., Poland
Bank Zachodni S.A., Poland
Bankverein Werther AG, Germany
Banky Fampandrosoana ny Varotra, Madagascar
Banque Cantonale de Genève, Switzerland
Banque Populaire du Haut-Rhin, France
Barclays Group PLC, United Kingdom
Basellandschaftliche Kantonalbank, Switzerland
Bayerische Handelsbank AG, Germany
Bayerische Hypo-und Vereinsbank AG, Germany[1]
Bayerische Landesbank Girozentrale, Germany
BBV Brazil, Brazil

BBV Privanza Banco S.A., Spain
BBV Probursa, Mexico
BBV Puerto Rico, Puerto Rico
Beneficial Bank AG, Germany
Bezirkssparkasse Heidelberg, Germany
BfG Bank AG, Germany
BMCE Bank, Morocco
B. Metzler seel. Sohn & Co. KgaA, Germany
Budapest Bank RT., Hungary
Caisse des Depots, France
Caixa Cataluyna, Spain
Canadian Imperial Bank of Commerce, Canada
Central Hispano, Spain
Citigroup, United States[2]
Commercial Bank of Greece, Greece
Commerzbank AG, Germany
Community Capital Bank, United States
Conrad Hinrich Donner Bank AG, Germany
Co-operative Bank, Manchester, United Kingdom
Corporación Andina de Fomento, Venezuela
Credit Andorra, Andorra
Credit Local de France, France
Credit Suisse Group, Switzerland
Creditanstalt-Bankverein, Austria
Credito Italiano, Italy
DEG—German Investment and Development Company, Germany
Degussa BankGmbH, Germany
Delbrück & Co., Privatbankiers, Germany
Den Danske Bank, A/S, Denmark
Den Norske Bank, ASA, Norway
Deutsche Ausgleichsbank, Germany
Deutsche Bank AG, Germany
Deutsche Bank Saar, Germany
Deutsche Pfandbrief-und Hypothekenbank AG, Germany
Deutsche Postbank AG, Germany
Development Bank of Japan, Japan
Development Bank of the Philippines, Philippines
DG Bank, Germany
Dresdner Bank AG, Germany
EBI Capital Group LLP, United States of America
Econatsbank, Russian Federation

Ekobanken—Din Medlemsbank, Sweden
EPS Finance Ltd., Switzerland
Eurohypo AG, Europäische Hypothekenbank der Deutschen Bank,
    Germany
Export Bank of Africa Ltd., Kenya
Export Development Corporation, Canada
Finanzia, Banca de Credito S.A., Spain
FMO, Netherlands
Friends Ivory & Sime Trust Company, United States
Friends Provident Life Office, United Kingdom
Fürstlich Castellische Bank, Credit-Casse, Germany
Global Business Bank, Philippines
Good Bankers Co. Ltd., Japan
Hamburgische Landesbank Girozentrale, Germany
Hesse Newman Bank (BNL Group), Germany
HKB Hypotheken-und Kommunalkredit Bank, Germany
HSBC Holdings Plc, United Kingdom
Innovest Strategic Value Advisors Inc., United States
Investitionsbank des Landes Brandenburg, Germany
Istituto Nazionale di Credito Agrario S.p.A., Italy
JAK—Jord, Arbete, Kapital, Sweden
Kansallis-Osake-Pankki, Finland
Kenya Commercial Bank Group, Kenya
Kreditanstalt für Wiederaufbau, Germany
Kreditna banka Maribor d.d., Slovenia
Kreissparkasse Düsseldorf, Germany
Kreissparkasse Göppingen, Germany
Land Bank of the Philippines, Philippines
Landesbank Baden-Württemberg, Germany[3]
Landesbank Schleswig-Holstein Girozentrale, Germany
Landsbanki Islands, Iceland
LBS Badische Landesbausparkasse, Germany
Lloyds TSB Bank, United Kingdom
Luzerner Kantonalbank, Switzerland
Merck Finck & Co., Germany
Metropolitan Bank and Trust Company, Philippines
M. M. Warburg & Co., Germany
National Bank of Kuwait SAK, Kuwait
National Fund for Environmental Protection and Water Management,
    Poland
National Savings and Commerical Bank Ltd., Hungary

NatWest Group, United Kingdom
Nikko Asset Management Co. Ltd., Japan
Nikko Securities Co. Ltd., Japan
Österreichische Investitionskredit Aktiengesellschaft, Austria
Österreichische Kommunalkredit Aktiengesellschaft, Austria
Philippine Bank of Communications (PB Com), Philippines
Planters Development Bank, Philippines
Polski Bank Inwestycyjny S.A., Poland
Pomorski Bank Kredytowy S.A., Poland
Powszechna Kasa Oszczednosci—Bank Panstwowy, Poland
Powszechny Bank Gospodarczy S.A. w todzi, Poland
Powszechny Bank Kredytowy S.A., Poland
Prudential plc., United Kingdom
Quelle Bank AG, Germany
Rabobank, Netherlands
Raiffeisen Zentralbank Austria AG, Austria
Republic National Bank, United States
Rizal Commercial Banking Corporation, Philippines
Romanian Commercial Bank SA, Romania
Royal Bank of Canada, Canada
Royal Bank of Scotland PLC, United Kingdom
Sal. Oppenheim Jr. & Cie, Germany
SchmidtBank KGaA, Germany
Schröder Münchmeyer Hengst AG, Germany
Schwäbische Bank AG, Germany
Scotia Bank (Bank of Nova Scotia), Canada
Service Bank GmbH & Co. KG, Germany
Shiga Bank, Japan
Skandinaviska Enskilda Banken, Sweden
Sparkasse Leichlingen, Germany
Sparkasse Staufen, Germany
Stadtsparkasse Hannover, Germany
Stadtsparkasse München, Germany
Stadtsparkasse Wuppertal, Germany
Sustainable Asset Management, Switzerland
Svenska Handelsbanken, Sweden
Swedbank AB, Sweden[4]
Thai Investment and Securities Co. Ltd, Thailand.
Toronto-Dominion Bank, Canada
Triodos Bank, Netherlands
UBS AG, Switzerland[5]

Uganda Commercial Bank, Uganda
UmweltBank AG, Germany
Unibank, Denmark
Vereins-und Westbank AG, Germany
Volksbank Siegen—Netphen eG, Germany
Westpac Banking Corporation, Australia
Woolwich PLC, United Kingdom
Zürcher Kantonalbank, Switzerland

Associate Members

Coopers & Lybrand, United Kingdom
Ecosecurities, United Kingdom

Endnotes

1. Bayerische Hypotheken-und Wechselbank, Germany/Bayerische Vereins-bank AG, Germany (merged 1998).
2. Salomon Inc. formally signed the Statement in 1997, and then Citigroup signed in 2000.
3. Südwestdeutsche Landesbank Girozentrale, Germany/Landesgirokasse Bank, Germany & Landeskreditbank (merged 1998).
4. Föreningsbanken, Sweden/Sparbanken Sverige AB, Sweden (merged 1997).
5. Union Bank of Switzerland/Swiss Bank Corporation (merged 1998).

UNEP STATEMENT OF ENVIRONMENTAL COMMITMENT BY THE INSURANCE INDUSTRY

Preamble

The insurance industry recognizes that economic development needs to be compatible with human welfare and a healthy environment. To ignore this is to risk increasing social, environmental and financial costs. Our Industry plays an important role in managing and reducing environmental risk, in conjunction with governments, individuals and organizations. We are committed to work together to address key issues such as pollution reduction, the efficient use of resources, and climate change. We endeavour to identify realistic, sustainable solutions.

1 General Principles of Sustainable Development

1.1 We regard sustainable development, defined as development that meets the needs of the present without compromising the ability of future generations to meet their own needs, as a fundamental aspect of sound business management.

1.2 We believe that sustainable development is best achieved by allowing markets to work within an appropriate framework of cost efficient regulations and economic instruments. Government has a leadership role in establishing and enforcing long-term priorities and values.

1.3 We regard a strong, proactive insurance industry as an important contributor to sustainable development, through its interaction with other economic sectors and consumers.

1.4 We believe that the existing skills and techniques of our industry in understanding uncertainty, identifying and quantifying risk, and responding to risk are core strengths in managing environmental problems.

1.5 We recognize the precautionary principle, in that it is not possible to quantify some concerns sufficiently, nor indeed to reconcile all impacts in purely financial terms. Research is needed to reduce uncertainty but cannot eliminate it entirely.

2 Environmental Management

2.1 We will reinforce the attention given to environmental risks in our core activities. These activities include risk management, loss prevention, product design, claims handling and asset management.

2.2 We are committed to manage internal operations and physical assets under our control in a manner that reflects environmental considerations.

2.3 We will periodically review our management practices, to integrate relevant developments of environmental management in our planning, marketing, employee communications and training as well as our other core activities.

2.4 We encourage research in these and related issues. Responses to environmental issues can vary in effectiveness and cost. We encourage research that identifies creative and effective solutions.

2.5 We support insurance products and services that promote sound environmental practice through measures such as loss prevention and contract terms and conditions. While satisfying requirements for security and profitability, we will seek to include environmental considerations in our asset management.

2.6 We will conduct regular internal environmental reviews, and will seek to create measurable environmental goals and standards.

2.7 We shall comply with all applicable local, national and international environmental regulations. Beyond compliance, we will strive to develop and adopt best practices in environmental management. We will support our clients, partners and suppliers to do likewise.

3 Public Awareness and Communications

3.1 Bearing in mind commercial confidence, we are committed to share relevant information with our stakeholders, including clients, intermediaries, shareholders, employees and regulators. By doing so we will improve society's response to environmental challenges.

3.2 Through dialogue with public authorities and other bodies we aim to contribute to the creation of a more effective framework for sustainable development.

3.3 We will work with the United Nations Environment Programme to further the principles and goals of this Statement, and look for UNEP's active support.

3.4 We will encourage other insurance institutions to support this Statement. We are committed to share with them our experiences and knowledge in order to extend best practices.

3.5 We will actively communicate our environmental activities to the public, review the success of this Statement periodically, and we expect all signatories to make real progress.

Steering Committee:

General Accident, Perth, United Kingdom
Gerling-Konzern Globale, Cologne, Germany
NPI, London, United Kingdom
Swiss Re, Zurich, Switzerland
Sumitomo Marine & Fire, Tokyo, Japan
Storebrand, Oslo, Norway
United Nations Environment Programme, Geneva, Switzerland

STATUS OF THE UNEP STATEMENT OF ENVIRONMENTAL COMMITMENT BY THE INSURANCE INDUSTRY

The following list of signatories as of October 2001 is sorted by organizations. Members of the Insurance Industry Initiative for the Environment in association with UNEP are indicated by an asterisk.

1. Aachener Rückversicherung (merged with Employers Re), Germany
2. Aachener und Münchener Versicherung, Germany
3. ACE Insurance, Japan[1]
4. Achmea Group, Netherlands
5. AEGIS Insurance Company Ltd., South Africa
6. Bangkok Insurance Public Company Limited, Thailand
7. Basler Versicherungs Gesellschaft, Switzerland
8. Bayerische Beamten Versicherung AG, Germany
9. CGU plc., United Kingdom[2]
10. City Insurance Company, Russia
11. Co-operative Insurance Society ltd., United Kingdom
12. Copenhagen Re, Denmark[3]
13. Daiichi Mutual Fire and Marine Insurance Company, Japan
14. Delvag Luftfahrtversicherungs AG, Germany
15. Dominion of Canada General Insurance Company, Canada
16. Elvia Versicherungen, Switzerland
17. Employers Reinsurance Corporation, United States
18. Energogarant Ltd., Russia
19. Folksam, Sweden
20. La Fondiaria Assicurazioni S.p.A., Italy
21. Gegenseitigkeit Versicherung Oldenburg, Germany*
22. Generali Assicurazioni Generali S.p.A., Italy*
23. Gerling Konzern, Germany*
24. Grupo Fortuna SA, Argentina
25. Helvetia Patria Versicherungen, Switzerland*
26. HSB Group, Inc., United States*
27. Hyundai Marine and Fire Insurance Co. Ltd., South Korea
28. Imperio S.A., Portugal
29. Independent Insurance Company Ltd., United Kingdom*
30. Industrial Insurance Company, Russia
31. Interpolis, Netherlands
32. Iron Trades Insurance Group, United Kingdom
33. Istituto Nazionale delle Assicurazioni, Italy
34. JI Accident & Fire Insurance Co. Ltd., Japan
35. KPA AB, Sweden*
36. Landesschadenhilfe Versicherung VaG, Germany
37. Legal and General Group Plc., United Kingdom*
38. Lider Insurance Company, Russia
39. Mannheimer Versicherungen, Germany
40. MAPFRE Mutualidad de Seguros y Reaseguros a Prima Fija's, Spain
41. Mitsui Sumitomo Insurance Co. Ltd., Japan[4]

42. Muenchener Rückversicherungs Gesellschaft (Munich Re), Germany*
43. MUSINI, Sociedad Mutua de Seguros y Reaseguros a Prima Fija, Spain
44. National Corporation of Tanzania Ltd., Tanzania
45. National Insurance, New Zealand
46. NPI, United Kingdom[5]
47. Nürnberger Allgemeine Versicherung, Germany*
48. Oeco Capital Lebensversicherung AG, Germany[6]
49. Overseas Union Insurance Limited, Singapore
50. Pool Español de Riesgos Medioambientales, Spain
51. QBE Insurance Group Ltd., Australia
52. Rentenanstalt/Swiss Life, Switzerland*
53. Rheinland Versicherungen, Germany*
54. Riunione Adriatica di Sicurata, Italy*
55. Rosno Insurance Company, Russia
56. R&V Versicherungsgruppe, Germany
57. Sampo Group, Finland
58. Schweizerische Mobiliar, Switzerland
59. Sibrosso Insurance Co., Russia
60. Skandia Insurance Company Ltd., Sweden
61. SOGAZ Co. Ltd., Russia
62. SOREMA, France
63. Sovereign Assurance, New Zealand
64. Spasskiye Vorota Insurance Group, Russia
65. SPP Forsakringsbolaget, Sweden
66. Storebrand, Norway*
67. Stuttgarter Allgemeine Versicherung, Germany
68. Stuttgarter Lebensversicherung AG, Germany
69. Sumitomo Marine & Fire Insurance Co. (Europe) Ltd, United Kingdom
70. Sumitomo Marine & Pool Insurance, Indonesia
71. Sumitomo Property & Casualty Insurance Co. (Hong Kong) Ltd, Hong Kong
72. Swiss Reinsurance Company, Switzerland*
73. Swiss Union General Insurance Company, Switzerland
74. Tokio Marine & Fire Insurance Co. Ltd., Japan*
75. Trygg Hansa, Sweden*
76. Vaudoise Générale Compagnie d'Assurances, Switzerland
77. Vereinte Versicherung AG, Germany
78. Victoria Versicherungen, Germany*

79. VJV Volksfürsorge Jupiter Allg. Versicherungs AG, Austria
80. Volksfürsorge Holding AG, Germany
81. WASA Försäkring, Sweden[7]
82. Wiener Städtische Allgemeine, Austria
83. Winterthur Versicherungen, Switzerland*
84. Württembergische Versicherung AG, Germany*
85. Yasuda Fire and Marine Insurance Co. Ltd., Japan*
86. Zurich Insurance Company, Switzerland*

Associate Members

1. Aon Group, United Kingdom
2. Barlow Lyde & Gilbert, United Kingdom
3. DaimlerChrysler—debis Assekuranz Makler GmbH, Germany
4. NatWest Insurance Services, United Kingdom
5. Skogbrand Insurance Company, Norway

Endnotes

1. ACE Insurance, Japan, formerly known as CIGNA Insurance Company—change since October 1, 1999.
2. General Accident Fire and Life Assurance Corporation merged with Commercial Union, June 1998.
3. Copenhagen Re, Denmark, formerly known as Alm. Brand—change October 1, 1999.
4. Mitsui Marine & Fire Insurance Co. Ltd., Japan, merged with Sumitomo Marine & Fire Insurance Co., Japan, in October 2001.
5. NPI is part of AMP Group, Australia (1999).
6. Oeco Capital Lebensversicherung AG is now part of Colonia Insurance, Germany.
7. WASA has merged with Länsförsäkringar Miljö, Sweden (summer 1998).

APPENDIX B

General Motors
GM

Rating: `A` Average sustainability performer.

SustainableValue'21™

Industrial Sector: Automotive   1-Mar-2001

Key Issues for Management

Product Risk: Above average emphasis on large, low-milage vehicles increases regulatory and market risks from climate change concerns.
Reputational Risk: Opposition to California ZEV law weakens efforts to position as sustainable company.
Developing Country Risk: Above average developing country exposure increases image and economic risks.

Strategy and Management

Strategy: Driven partly by pressure from customers and more proactive competitors, GM incorporated the concept of sustainability into its corporate vision in 1999. Its strategy focuses on sustainable mobility, supply chain management, community involvement, philanthropy, H&S and product safety. GM has endorsed the Sullivan Principles and is a signatory of the CERES principles and a WBCSD member. GM sustainability reporting follows the GRI guidelines. **Corporate Governance:** GM has a Public Policy Committee of the Board of Directors which oversees its social commitment worldwide. The General Motors Foundation's Chairman serves as VP of Corporate Relations and Diversity. No known shareholder resolutions involving social/ethical factors.

Current profile of company in public domain

Very Negative	Negative	Average or No profile	Positive	Very Positive

Stakeholder Capital

Stakeholders: As part of its sustainability efforts, GM is working with groups including BSR, CERES, GRI, Habitat for Humanity, WRI, and other research institutes. **Community:** GM has a Community Impact Strategy Team to identify internal and external community issues and reputational risks. Projects include volunteer efforts with charities and local communities. **Philanthropy:** Charitable contributions amounted to $68 million in 1999. GM has implemented an electronic pledge process to allow employee payroll deduction contributions in the US. GM ranked No. 2 on the list of "Top 50 Givers" of Worth Magazine.

Assessment

SRI Negative Screening Risks

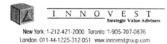

	Low	Moderate	High
Tobacco			
GMOs			
Weapons Production			
Nuclear Power			
Alcohol			
Animal Testing			
Human Rights Abuses			
Gambling			
Contraceptives			
Pornography			
Gender Discrimination			

Human Capital Development

Employee and workplace policies of GM, such as its "Employee Enthusiasm Strategy", are intended to improve employee morale, foster employee development and maximize corporate performance. Its policies are about average relative to competitors. H&S: GM has had a global health and safety initiative in place since 1995. Globally, GM has improved its recordables rate by 63% and its lost workday rate by 78% since 1995. Intellectual Capital: In 1997, GM established the GM University, a global network of education and training to help employees improve their skills. Diversity: GM's employment decisions are based solely on candidates' qualifications. No explicit diversity requirements. A sexual harassment lawsuit filed by a former employee was dismissed on appeal in June 2000.

International

GM is the largest U.S. exporter of cars and trucks, with activities in 190 countries and manufacturing and assembly operations in 30 countries. GM has 25,000 employees in Latin America, Africa and the Mid-East, and 10,000 in Asia Pacific. With substantial operations in developing countries, the company's exposure is high in risk areas including corporate image, regulatory and regional economic. Human rights: As a signatory of the Sullivan Principles, GM has committed to support human rights and to encourage equal opportunity at all levels of employment, including racial and gender diversity, and to train and advance disadvantaged workers for technical, supervisory and management opportunities.

Overview

General Motors Corporation designs, manufactures and markets vehicles in North America under the nameplates Chevrolet, Pontiac, GMC, Oldsmobile, Buick, Cadillac and Saturn and vehicles outside North America under the name plates Opel, Vauxhall, Holden, Isuzu, Saab, Chevrolet, GMC and Cadillac. Other services include vehicle financing, fleet leasing, residential and commercial mortgage services and vehicle and homeowners insurance. GM has operations in the US, Europe, Canada, Mexico, Australia, and Brazil. In 1999, GM sales were $176 billion. Automotive products accounted for 88% of 1999 revenues, and financing and insurance operations, 12%. GM has 388,000 employees worldwide, including 81,000 in Europe, 23,000 in Latin America, and 10,000 in Asia Pacific. In 1999, GM endorsed sustainability as its corporate vision.

Products and Services

Product Safety: The company was the first automotive manufacturer to develop and announce a retrofit trunk anti-entrapment system for children. In March 2000, GM received the National Highway Traffic Safety Administration (NHTSA) Award for Public Service. **Negatives:** GM's overall fuel economy is the 3rd worst among 14 global auto manufacturers, partly because of its significant exposure via SUVs. GM is also the only car company to sue California for its Zero Emission Vehicle mandate. These issues will negatively impact GM's efforts to position itself as a sustainable company.

Supply Chain

Given the breath and depth of GM's supply chain, the company has significant potential to positively or negatively impact sustainability issues. Recognizing the frequent synergies between improved sustainability and financial performance, GM assists its suppliers in implementing new technology, increasing product quality, reducing costs, and improving environmental and social performance. Relative to competitors, the proactivity of GM's supplier policies in areas including compliance, labor and sustainability are about average.

I N N O V E S T
Strategic Value Advisors
New York: 1-212-421-2000 Toronto: 1-905-707-0876
London: 011-44-1225-312-051 www.innovestgroup.com

FIGURE B.1   Innovest SVA Company Profile: General Motors Sustainability^Plus Rating
Source: Innovest SVA. Reprinted with permission.

Sustainability issues, such as those addressed in this report, are having a growing impact on corporate financial performance due to factors including globalization and increasing regulations. Innovest's SustainableValue'21™ ratings (ranging from AAA to CCC) identify sustainability risks, management quality and profit opportunity differentials typically not identified by traditional equity analysts. As a result, SustainabilityValue'21™ ratings indicate a company's ability to effectively address complex management challenges and succeed in the longer-term.

Key Issues for Investors

Product Risk: Above average emphasis on large, low-milage vehicles increases regulatory and market risks.

Image Risk: Opposition to California ZEV law weakens efforts to position as sustainable company.

Dev. Country Risk: Above average developing country exposure increases image and economic risks.

Supply Chain Risk: Average proactivity on implementing sustainability requirements in supply chain yields limited image and regulatory risks.

Financial Performance (change in stock price):

Relative Social Performance:

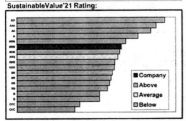

| | Worst | Average | Best |

SustainableValue'21 Rating:

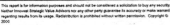

■ Company
▨ Above
☐ Average
■ Below

Overview

General Motors Corporation designs, manufactures and markets vehicles in North America under the nameplates Chevrolet, Pontiac, GMC, Oldsmobile, Buick, Cadillac and Saturn and vehicles outside North America under the name plates Opel, Vauxhall, Holden, Isuzu, Saab, Chevrolet, GMC and Cadillac. Other services include vehicle financing, fleet leasing, residential and commercial mortgage services and vehicle and homeowners insurance. GM has operations in the US, Europe, Canada, Mexico, Australia, and Brazil. In 1999, GM sales were $176 billion. Automotive products accounted for 88% of 1999 revenues, and financing and insurance operations, 12%. GM has 388,000 employees worldwide, including 81,000 in Europe, 23,000 in Latin America, and 10,000 in Asia Pacific. In 1999, GM endorsed sustainability as its corporate vision.

Sustainability Strategy & Management

Strategy: Driven partly by pressure from customers and more proactive competitors, GM incorporated the concept of sustainability into its corporate vision in 1999. Its strategy focuses on sustainable mobility, supply chain, community involvement, philanthropy, H&S and product safety. GM has endorsed the Sullivan Principles and is a signatory of the CERES principles and a WBCSD member. GM sustainability reporting follows the GRI guidelines. **Corporate Governance:** GM has a Public Policy Committee of the Board of Directors which oversees its social commitment worldwide. The General Motors Foundation's Chairman serves as VP of Corporate Relations and Diversity. No known shareholder resolutions involving social/ethical factors.

Stakeholder Capital

Stakeholders: As part of its sustainability efforts, GM is working with groups including BSR, CERES, GRI, Habitat for Humanity, WRI, and other research institutes. **Community:** GM has a Community Impact Strategy Team to identify internal and external community issues and reputational risks. Projects include volunteer efforts with charities and local communities. **Philanthropy:** Charitable contributions amounted to $68 million in 1999. GM has implemented an electronic pledge process to allow employee payroll deduction contributions in the US. GM ranked No. 2 on the list of "Top 50 Givers" of Worth Magazine.

Human Capital Development

Employee and workplace policies of GM, such as its "Employee Enthusiasm Strategy", are intended to improve employee morale, foster employee development and maximize corporate performance. Its policies are about average relative to competitors. **H&S:** GM has had a global health and safety initiative in place since 1995. Globally, GM has improved its recordables rate by 63% and its lost workday rate by 78% since 1995. **Intellectual Capital:** In 1997, GM established the GM University, a global network of education and training to help employees improve their skills. **Diversity:** GM's employment decisions are based solely candidates' qualifications. No diversity requirements.

International

GM is the largest U.S. exporter of cars and trucks, with activities in 190 countries and manufacturing and assembly operations in 30 countries. GM has 25,000 employees in Latin America, Africa and the Mid-East, and 10,000 in Asia Pacific. With substantial operations in developing countries, the company's exposure is high in risk areas including corporate image, regulatory and regional economic. Human rights: As a signatory of the Sullivan Principles, GM has committed to support human rights and to encourage equal opportunity at all levels of employment, including racial and gender diversity, and to train and advance disadvantaged workers for technical, supervisory and management opportunities.

Products / Services

Product Safety: With a relatively low milage fleet and an emphasis on building larger vehicles, GM has higher exposure to involvement in highway fatalities and resulting damage to corporate image. The company was the first automotive manufacturer to develop and announce a retrofit trunk anti-entrapment system for children. In March 2000, GM received the National Highway Traffic Safety Administration (NHTSA) Award for Public Service. Environmental compatibility: GM is the only car company to sue the State of California for its Zero Emission Vehicle mandate. This issue will likely negatively impact GM's efforts to position itself as a sustainable company.

Supply Chain

Given the breath and depth of GM's supply chain, the company has significant potential to positively or negatively impact sustainability issues. Recognizing the frequent synergies between improved sustainability and financial performance, GM assists its suppliers in implementing new technology, increasing product quality, reducing costs, and improving environmental and social performance. Relative to competitors, the proactiveness of GM's supplier policies in areas including compliance, labor and sustainability are about average.

SRI Screens - Involvement Risk Level			
Alcoholic Beverages:	0	Abortifacients:	0
Firearms:	0	Contraceptives:	0
Nuclear Power:	0	Animal testing:	0
Tobacco:	0	Gambling:	0
Weapons Production:	0	Other:	0
Embryo cloning:	0	Other:	0
GMOs:	0	Other:	0

The screening issues displayed above are provided for information purposes only, and do not represent endorsement nor rejection by Innovest on any of the listed items. Innovest SustainableValue'21 score does not reflect the moral content of these items, but estimates the market and reputational risks represented by these issues.

Innovest New York: (212) 421-2000 London: +44 (0) 20 7868 1714 Toronto: (905) 707-0876 www.innovestgroup.com

FIGURE B.1 *(Continued)*

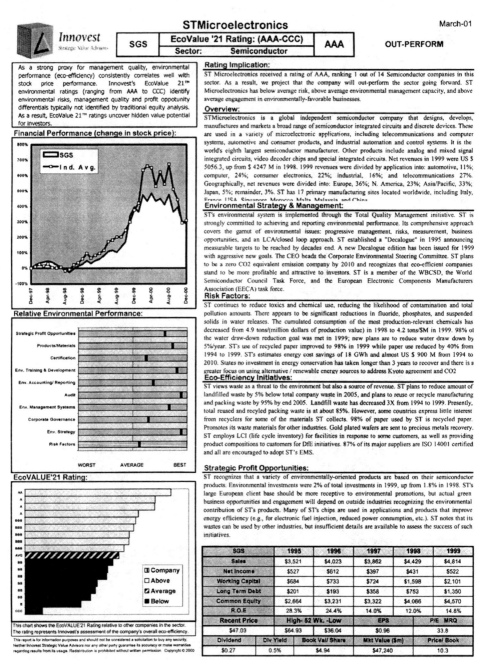

FIGURE B.2 Innovest SVA Company Profile: STMicroelectronics EcoValue '21 Rating. *Source:* Innovest SVA. Reprinted with permission.

THE ANNEX 1 COUNTRIES

Signatories to the Kyoto Protocol

Australia	Liechtenstein
Austria	Lithuania*
Belgium	Luxembourg
Bulgaria*	Monaco
Canada	Netherlands
Croatia*	New Zealand
Czech Republic*	Norway
Denmark	Poland*
Estonia*	Portugal
European Community	Romania*
Finland	Russian Federation*
France	Slovakia*
Germany	Slovenia*
Greece	Spain
Hungary*	Sweden
Iceland	Switzerland
Ireland	Ukraine*
Italy	United Kingdom
Japan	United States
Latvia*	

---

*Signifies a party "undergoing the process of transition to a market economy to which a certain degree of flexibility" will be allowed "in the implementation of their commitments" (Articles 3.5 and 3.6 of the Kyoto Protocol).
Source: Grubb et al. 1999, 284, 301.

acronyms

ABI	Association of British Insurers
ACBE	Advisory Committee on Business and the Environment (United Kingdom)
AsrIA	Association for Sustainable and Responsible Investment in Asia
ATM	Automated teller machine
BASE	Basel Agency for Sustainable Energy (UNEP)
CDM	Clean Development Mechanism
CEP	Council of Economic Priorities
CEPA	Canadian Environmental Protection Act (Canada 1988)
CERCLA	Comprehensive Environmental Response Compensation and Liability Act (United States 1976)
CGL	Commercial general liability
DJSGI	Dow Jones Sustainability Group Index
DSI400	Domini 400 Social Index
EBRD	European Bank for Reconstruction and Development
ECI	Environmental condition indicator
EEER	Energy Efficiency and Emission Reduction Fund
EIRIS	Ethical Investment Research Services
EMAS	Eco-Management and Audit System (European Community)
EMS	Environmental management system
EP	Environmental performance
EPI	Environmental performance indicator
FEE	Fédération des Experts Comptables Européens
FII	Financial Institutions Initiative on the Environment and Sustainable Development (UNEP)
FP	Financial performance
FTSE	Financial Times Stock Exchange (index)
GCL	General comprehensive liability (insurance policies)
GHG	Greenhouse gases
GRI	Global Reporting Initiative
IAPC	International Auditing Practices Committee
IASC	International Accounting Standards Committee

IDW	Institut der Wirtschaftsprüfer in Deutschland
IFAC	International Federation of Accountants
IFC	International Finance Corporation
III	Insurance Industry Initiative on the Environment (UNEP)
IPE	International Petroleum Exchange
IPO	Initial public offering
IRR	Internal rate of return
IRRC	Investor Responsibility Research Center
JI	Joint implementation
JSI	Jantzi Social Index
KLD	Kinder, Lydenberg, Domini & Co.
LIBOR	London Interbank Offered Rate
MJRA	Michael Jantzi Research Associates
MPI	Management performance indicator
NGO	Nongovernmental organization
NPRI	National Pollution Release Inventory
NRTEE	National Round Table on the Environment and the Economy (Canada)
OPI	Operational performance indicator
OSFI	Office of the Superintendent of Financial Institutions (Canada)
PCF	Prototype Carbon Fund (World Bank)
P/E	Price/earnings ratio
PRP	Potentially responsible party
REEF	Renewable Energy Efficiency Fund (World Bank)
ROA	Return on assets
ROE	Return on earnings
SARA	Superfund Amendments and Reauthorization Act (United States 1986)
SFE	Sydney Futures Exchange
SIO	Social investment organization
SME	Small and medium-sized enterprise
S&P	Standard & Poor's
SRI	Socially responsible investment
TRI	Toxic Release Inventory
UNEP	United Nations Environment Program
VfU	Verein fur Umweltmanagment in Banken, Sparkassen und Versicherungen (German Association for Environmental Management in Banks, Savings Banks and Insurance Companies)

references

AAF. (1995) *Environmental Issues in Financial Reporting*. Brussels: European Union Accounting Advisory Forum.

ABN Amro. (1998) *Milieuversag 1994–1997*. Amsterdam: ABN Amro.

ABN Amro. (2001) *Environment Report 1998–2000*. Amsterdam: ABN Amro (available at www.abnamro.com).

ACBE. (1993) *Report of the Financial Sector Working Group, London*. London: Department of the Environment, Advisory Committee on Business and the Environment, Financial Sector Working Group.

Adams, R., M. Houldin, and S. Slomp. (1999) Towards a generally accepted framework for environmental reporting. Pages 314–329 in M. Bennett and P. James (eds.), *Sustainable Measures*. Sheffield, UK: Greenleaf.

Afsah, S., A. Blackman, and D. Ratunanda. (2000) *How Do Public Disclosure Pollution Programs Work? Evidence from Indonesia*. Washington: World Resources Institute.

Afsah, S., and D. Ratunanda. (1999) Environmental performance evaluation and reporting in developing countries. Pages 185–201 in M. Bennett and P. James (eds.), *Sustainable Measures*. Sheffield, UK: Greenleaf.

AIG Environmental. (1997) *Cleanup Cost Cap Program: Remediating Contaminated Real Estate, a Financially Sound Decision*. Information available through http://access.aig.com.

Aldred, C. (1995) Ruling may increase U.K. asbestos claims. *Business Insurance* (November 27): 31.

Allen Consulting Group. (2000) Report prepared for the Ethical Investment Workshop. Melbourne: Allen Consulting Group. www.allenconsult.com.au/reports.html.

Allen Consulting Group. (2000) *Socially Responsible Investment in Australia*. Sydney: Allen Consulting Group.

Andrews, K. E., and R. J. Blong. (1997) March 1990 hailstorm damage in Sydney, Australia. *Natural Hazards* 16: 113–125.

Angel, J., and P. Rivoli. (1997) Does ethical investing impose a cost upon the firm? A theoretical perspective. *Journal of Investing* 6(4): 57–61.

Aon Limited. (2001) *World Trade Center Bulletin, Issue 7, 7th November 2001.* London: Aon Limited.

Aspen Institute. (1998) *Uncovering Value: Integrating Environmental and Financial Performance.* Queenstown, MD: Aspen Institute Publications.

Association of British Insurers. (2000a) *Contaminated Land Report.* London: ABI.

Association of British Insurers. (2000b) Subsidence—a global perspective. *General Insurance—Research Report No. 1.*

Azzone, G., M. Brophy, C. Noci, R. Welford, and W. Yong. (1997) A stakeholder's view of environmental reporting. *Long Range Planning* 30(5): 699–709.

Bahree, B. (2001) BP bid to be environmental inspires activists to want more. *Asian Wall Street Journal* (April 17): N4.

Bakker, K. J. (2000) Privatising water, producing scarcity: The Yorkshire drought of 1996. *Economic Geography* 76(1): 4–27.

Bank Sarasin. (2001) *Sarasin Today,* www.sarasin.ch/sarasin/show/content.

Barnes, A. (2001) Stock funds outperforming index funds. *Globe and Mail* (October 2): B6.

Barth, M., and M. McNichols. (1995) Estimation and market valuation of environmental liabilities relating to Superfund sites. *Journal of Accounting Research* 32, supplement: 177–209.

Barton, D. (2001) McKinsey and Company, Seoul, Korea, personal communications, April 20.

BASE. (2001) *Inventory of Sustainable Energy Funds.* Geneva: UNEP Financial Initiatives and Basel Agency for Sustainable Energy.

Bayon, R. (2001a) Can SRI funds shrug off a rocky year? *Environmental Finance* 2(4): 16.

Bayon, R. (2001b) SRI meets the mainstream. *Environmental Finance.* 2(5): 24–25.

Bayon, R. (2001c) Pension fund giant takes SRI flyer. *Environmental Finance.* 2(10): 20.

Bayon, R. (2002) Reporting goes global. *Environmental Finance* 3(7): 16–18.

Beck, T. (2000) Australia shows the way. *Environmental Finance.* 1(4): 19–21.

Beder, T. (1999) The great risk hunt. *Journal of Portfolio Management, Derivatives and Risk Management.* Special issue: 28–34.

Beets, S., and C. Souther. (1999) Corporate environmental reports: The need for standards and an environmental assurance service. *Accounting Horizons* 13(2): 129–145.

Beloe, S. (2000) Looking to the future of SRI. *Environmental Finance* 1(5): 28–29.

Benston, G. (1996) The origins of and justification for the Glass-Steagall Act. Pages 31–69 in A. Saunders and I. Walter (eds.), *Universal Banking: Financial System Design Reconsidered*. Chicago: Irwin.

Berger, A., R. Demsetz, and P. Strahan. (1999) The consolidation of the financial services industry: Causes, consequences, and implications for the future. *Journal of Banking & Finance* 23(2–4): 135–194.

Berger, A., R. DeYoung, and H. Genay. (2000) The globalization of financial institutions: Evidence from cross-border banking performance. Pages 23–158 in R. Litman and A. Santomero (eds.), *Brookings-Warton Papers on Financial Services*. Washington, DC: Brookings Institution.

Bernstein, P. L. (1996) *Against the Gods: The Remarkable Story of Risk*. New York: John Wiley & Sons.

Bertazzi, P. A. (1991) Long-term effects of chemical disasters: Lesson and results from Seveso. *Science of the Total Environment* 106(1–2): 5–20.

Bertazzi, P. A., I. Bernucci, G. Brambilla, D. Consonni, and A. C. Pesatori. (1998) The Seveso studies on early and long-term effects of Dioxin exposure: a review. *Environmental Health Perspectives* 106, supp. 2 (April).

Berz, G. (1988) Climatic change: Impact on international reinsurance. Pages 579–587 in G. I. Pearman (ed.), *Greenhouse: Preparing for Climate Change*. Clayton South, Victoria: Commonwealth Scientific and Industrial Research Organisation, and Leiden: E. J. Brill.

Berz, G. (1993) Global warming and the insurance industry. *Interdisciplinary Science Reviews* 18(2): 120–125.

Berz, G. (1996) Hurricane Andrew—the most costly natural disaster of all time. Pages 28–32 in *Munich Re Annual Review of Natural Catastrophes 1995*. Munich: Munich Re.

Berz, G. (1999) Population development and urban growth. Pages 70–77 in *Topics 2000: Natural Catastrophes—The Current Position*. Munich: Munich Re.

Berz, G., and K. Conrad. (1994) Stormy weather: The mounting windstorm risk and consequences for the insurance industry. *Ecodecision* (April): 65–68.

Berz, G., and T. Loster. (2001) Climate change—threats and opportunities for the financial sector. Paper presented at the Conference of the Parties (COP 6b), Bonn, July.

Bhatnagar, V. (1999) Evaluating corporate environmental performance in developing countries. Pages 185–220 in M. Bennet and P. James (eds.), *Sustainable Measures*. Sheffield, UK: Greenleaf.

Biello, D. (2002a) A leap in the dark. *Environmental Finance* 3(6): vi.

Biello, D. (2002b) New Hampshire imposes CO_2 cap. *Environmental Finance* 3(7): 11.

Biello, D. (2002c) Bush ties GHG cuts to economic growth. *Environmental Finance* 3(5): 4.

Blacconiere, W., and D. Northcutt. (1997) Environmental information and market reaction to environmental legislation. *Journal of Accounting, Auditing and Finance* 30: 149–178.

Blacconiere, W., and D. Patten. (1994) Environmental disclosures, regulatory costs, and changes in firm value. *Journal of Accounting and Economics* 18(3): 357–377.

Blank, H., and M. Carty. (forthcoming) The eco-efficiency anomaly. *Journal of Investing*.

Blumberg, J., G. Blum, and A. Korsvold. (1997) *Environmental Performance and Shareholder Value*. Geneva: World Business Council for Sustainable Development, www.wbcsd.com/ecoeff1.

Blyth, W. (2001) To trade or not to trade? *Environmental Finance* 2(4): 25–27.

Boot, A., and A. Thakor. (1996) Banking structure and financial innovation. Pages 420–430 in A. Saunders and I. Walter (eds.), *Universal Banking: Financial System Design Reconsidered*. Chicago: Irwin.

Bouma, J., M. Jeucken, and L. Klinkers (eds.). (2001) *Sustainable Banking: The Greening of Finance*. Sheffield, UK: Greenleaf.

Bowen, L., M. Salling, K. Haynes, and E. Cyran. (1995) Toward environmental justice: Spatial equity in Ohio and Cleveland. *Annals of the Association of American Geographers* 85(4): 641–663.

Boyle, G. (ed.). (1996) *Renewable Energy—Power for a Sustainable Future*. Oxford: Oxford University Press in association with The Open University.

Brennan, T. (2001) *The California Experience, an Education or Diversion?* Washington, DC: Resources for the Future.

Browne, J. (1997) Climate change: the new agenda. Presentation made at Stanford University, May 19.

Browne, J. (2001) Marketing strategy. Lecture delivered for Bradford University's Fourth Lord Goold Memorial Lecture, London, November 23, available at www.bp.com/centres/press/s_detail.asp?id=141.

Brun, S. E. (1997) The space-time proposal. *The Review—Worldwide Reinsurance* (October): 49–51.

Brun, S. E., and D. Etkin. (1997) Occurrence definition. Pages 111–199 in S. E. Brun., D. Etkin, D. Gesink-Law, L. Wallace, and R. R. White (eds.), *Coping with Natural Hazards in Canada: Scientific, Government and Insurance Industry Perspectives*. Toronto: Institute for

Environmental Studies, University of Toronto. Available at www.utoronto.ca/env/nh/title.htm.

Brun, S. E., D. Etkin, D. Gesink-Law, L. Wallace, and R. R. White (eds.). (1997) *Coping with Natural Hazards in Canada: Scientific, Government and Industry Perspectives*. Toronto: Institute for Environmental Studies, University of Toronto. Available at: www.utoronto.ca/env/nh/title.htm.

Bryan, L., J. Fraser, J. Oppenheim, and W. Ball. (1999) *Race for the World: Strategies to Build a Great Global Firm*. Boston: Harvard Business School Press.

Bürer, M. (2001) Funds offer carbon "kicker." *Environmental Finance* 3(1): xviii–xx.

Burke, M. (1997) Keeping a lid on hurricane risks. *Risk Management* 44(5), May.

CalPERS. (2000) *The Sacramento Bee* (October 17).

Cameron, J., and R. Ramsay. (1996) Transnational environmental disputes. *Asia Pacific Journal of Environmental Law* 1(1,2): 5–25.

Campbell, K., S. Sefcik, and N. Soderstrom. (1998) Site uncertainty, allocation uncertainty, and superfund liability valuation. *Journal of Accounting and Public Policy* 17(4,5): 331–366.

Canter, M., and J. Cole. (1997) The foundation and evolution of the catastrophe bond market. *Global Reinsurance* (September). Can be viewed at www.hedgefinance.com.

Canter, M., J. Cole, and R. Sandor. (1996) Insurance derivatives: A new class for the capital markets and a new hedging tool for the insurance industry. *Journal of Derivatives* (Winter). Can be viewed at www.hedgefinance.com.

Carleton, W., J. Nelson, and M. Weisbach. (1998) The influence of institutions on corporate governance through private negotiations: Evidence from TIAA-CREF. *Journal of Finance* 53(4): 1335–1362.

Case, P. (1999) *Environmental Risk Management and Corporate Lending: A Global Perspective*. Cambridge, UK: Woodhead Publishing.

CBOT (Chicago Board of Trade). (1995a) *PCS Catastrophe Insurance Options: The New Standardized Alternative to Managing Catastrophic Risk*. Chicago: Chicago Board of Trade.

CBOT. (1995b) *PCS Options: A User's Guide*. Chicago: Chicago Board of Trade.

CFO Publishing Corp. (2002) *Strategic Risk Management: New Disciplines, New Opportunities*. Boston: CFO Publishing Corp.

Chartier, D. (2000) Trading NOx in the north-east USA. *Environmental Finance* 1(3): 23.

Chartier, D., and T. Powers. (2002) Writing the rules in Massachusetts. *Environmental Finance* 3(6): 13.

Chowdury, S., and other contributors. (2000) *Management 21C: New Visions for the New Millennium*. London: Financial Times/Prentice Hall.

CICA. (1990) *Canadian Institute of Chartered Accountants' Handbook*. Toronto: CICA.

Citigroup. (2000) *Lead by Example: 1999 Annual Report*. New York: Citigroup. Available at www.citigroup.com.

Cohen, M., S. Fenn, and J. Naimon. (1995) *Environmental and Financial Performance: Are They Related?* Washington, DC: Investor Responsibility Research Center (IRRC).

Cooper, G. (2000a) Climate change funds exceed target. *Environmental Finance* 1(8): 7.

Cooper, G. (2000b) New funds eye carbon credits. *Environmental Finance* 1(5): 6.

Cooper, G. (2000c) Shell steps off the gas. *Environmental Finance* 1(4): 14–15.

Cooper, G. (2000d) Credit Lyonnais eyes carbon fund. *Environmental Finance* 1(6): 5.

Cooper, G. (2000e) Confusion reigns as SO_2 market expands. *Environmental Finance* 1(3): 22.

Cooper, G. (2001) Back to earth for green funds. *Environmental Finance* 2(4): Comment, 2.

Cooper, G., and M. Nichols. (2000) Trading around the corner. *Environmental Finance* 2(1): xii–xiv.

Co-operative Bank. (2000) *The Partnership Report 2000: Making Our Mark*. Manchester, UK: Co-operative Bank.

Cormier, D., and M. Magnan. (1997) Investors' assessment of implicit environmental liabilities: An empirical investigation. *Journal of Accounting and Public Policy* 16(2): 215–241.

Corten, F., D. Metz, J. van Soest, and R. Vervoordeldonk. (1998) *Environmental Information for Investors*. Amsterdam (Culemborg): VBDO (Vereniging van Beleggers voor Duurzame Ontwikkeling, Association of Investors for Sustainable Development).

Cozijnsen, J. (2002) CO_2 is not the only gas. *Environmental Finance* 3(3): 38–39.

Crane, J. (1999) Vice President, South Shore Bank, Chicago, personal communication, September 10.

Crathorne, B., and A. J. Dobbs. (1990) Chemical pollution of the aquatic environment by priority pollutants and its control. Pages 1–18 in R.

M. Harrison (ed.), *Pollution: Causes, Effects and Control*. Cambridge, UK: Royal Society of Chemistry.

Credit Suisse. (2000) *Environmental Report 2000*. Zurich: Credit Swiss Group.

Cumming Cockburn Ltd. (2000) *Hurricane Hazel and Extreme Rainfall in Southern Ontario*. Research Paper #9. Toronto: Institute for Catastrophic Loss Reduction, Insurance Council of Canada.

Damodaran, A. (2001) *Corporate Finance Theory and Practice*. 2nd ed. New York: John Wiley & Sons.

D'Antonio, L., T. Johnsen, and R. B. Hutton. (1997) Expanding socially screened portfolios: An attribution analysis of bond performance. *Journal of Investing* 6(4): 79–86.

Dasgupta, S., B. Laplante, and N. Mamingi. (1997) *Capital Market Responses to Environmental Performance in Developing Countries*. World Bank Research Group working paper #1909 (October).

Dawes, C. (2001) The data debate. *Environmental Finance* 3(1): 17–18.

Deloitte Touche Tohmatsu International (DTTI), International Institute for Sustainable Development (IISD), and SustainAbility. (1993) *Coming Clean: Corporate Environmental Reporting, Opening Up for Sustainable Development*. London: DTTI.

Delphi and Ecologic. (1997) *The Role of Financial Institutions in Achieving Sustainable Development*. Report to the European Commission by Delphi International Ltd. in association with Ecologic GMBH, Washington, D.C.

DeMarco, E. (2001) Ontario sets out emissions trading plans. *Environmental Finance* 2(7): 22–23.

Dembo, R. S., and A. Freeman. (1998) *Seeing Tomorrow: Rewriting the Rules of Risk*. New York: John Wiley & Sons.

Descano, L., and B. Gentry. (1998) Communicating environmental performance to the capital markets. *Corporate Environmental Strategy: The Journal of Environmental Leadership* (Spring): 22–27.

DeSimone, L., and F. Popoff. (1997) *Eco-efficiency: The Business Link to Sustainable Development*. Cambridge, MA: MIT Press.

Dillon Ltd., Global Risk Management Corporation, and Tecsult. (1996) *The Financial Services Sector and Brownfield Redevelopment*. Prepared for the National Round Table on the Environment and Economy and the Canada Mortgage and Housing Corporation, Ottawa, Canada.

Diltz, D. (1995) Does social screening affect portfolio performance? *Journal of Investing* (Spring): 64–69.

Ditz, D., and J. Ranganathan. (1997) *Measuring Up: Toward a Common*

Framework for Tracking Corporate Environmental Performance. Washington, DC: World Resources Institute.

Dlugolecki, A. (1996a) *Financial Services, Climate Change 1995: Impacts, Adaptations and Mitigation of Climate Change, Scientific-Technical Analysis.* Contribution of Working Group II on the second assessment report of the Intergovernmental Panel on Climate Change. Pages 540–560. Cambridge, U.K.: University Press.

Dlugolecki, A. (1996b) Insurance. Chapter 13, pages 167–176, in *Government Review of Climate Change in the U.K.* London: H.M.S.O.

Dlugolecki, A. (2000) Presentation to the Conference of the Parties (COP 6) at the Hague, November, reported in *The Times,* "Climate changes 'could bankrupt the world'" (November 23).

Dlugolecki, A., and other contributors. (1994) *Task Force on the Impacts of Changing Weather Patterns on Property Insurance.* London: Chartered Insurance Institute.

Dlugolecki, A., et al. (2001) *Climate Change and Insurance.* London: Chartered Insurance Institute.

Döbelli, S. (2001) An environmental fund with the WWF label. Pages 379–389 in J. Bouma, M. Jeucken, and L. Klinkers (eds.), *Sustainable Banking.* Sheffield, UK: Greenleaf.

Doherty, N. (1997) Insurance markets and climate change. *Geneva Papers on Risk and Insurance* 22(83): 223–237.

Donaldson, T., and L. Preston. (1995) The stakeholder theory of the corporation: Concepts, evidence and implications. *Academy of Management Review* 20(1): 65–91.

Dowell, G., S. Hart, and B. Yeung. (2000) Do corporate global environmental standards create or destroy market value? *Management Science* 46(8): 1059–1074.

Dupont, G. (2001) FTSE goes green. *Environmental Finance* 2(6): 9.

Economist. (1995) Trading places. *Economist* (April 15): 26–29.

Economist. (2001a) Unprofitable policies. *Economist* (August 11): 57.

Economist. (2001b) The world's biggest companies. *Economist* (July): 89.

Economist. (2001c) New trends in accounting: Touchy feely. *Economist* (May 19): 68.

Economist. (2002) Outsmarting their country cousins. *Economist* (April 6): 65.

Edwards, D. (1998) *The Link between Environmental and Financial Performance.* London: Earthscan.

Elkington, J., and S. Beloe. (2000) *A Responsible Investment?* London: Centre for Business Performance, Institute of Chartered Accountants of England and Wales (ICAEW); London: SustainAbility.

Ellisthorpe, D., and S. Putnam. (2000) Weather derivatives and their implications for power markets. *Journal of Risk Finance* (Winter): 19–28.

Environment Canada. (1988) *The Changing Atmosphere: Implications for Global Security*. Conference Statement. Ottawa: Environment Canada.

Environmental Finance. (2001a) *Environmental Finance*, Data File: Domini 400 Social Index, 2(4): 31.

Environmental Finance. (2001b) *Environmental Finance*, Data File: Domini 400 Social Index, 2(10): 39.

Environmental Finance. (2001c) Rothschild enters Australian SRI market. *Environmental Finance* 2(7): In Brief, 5.

Environmental Finance. (2001d) Dow Jones Sustainability Indexes. *Environmental Finance* 3(1): 7.

Environmental Finance. (2001e) SAM raises 65M for private equity fund. *Environmental Finance* 2(20): In Brief, 13.

Environmental Financial Products. (2001) The right to make the climate right. Chicago Climate Exchange. Available at www.chicagoclimatex.com.

Environmental Protection Agency (EPA). (1996) *EPA's 33/50 Program, Seventh Progress Report*. Washington, DC: Environmental Protection Agency.

EPA. (2000) *Green Dividends? The Relationship between Firms' Environmental Performance and Financial Performance*. Report by the Environmental Capital Markets Committee to the U.S. EPA National Advisory Council for Environmental Policy and Technology, Washington, DC.

EPA. (2001) Superfund—Clean-up figures and key dates. Available at www.epa.gov/superfund/about.htm.

EPI-Finance. (2000) *Environmental Performance Indicators for Financial Service Providers*. London: EPI-Finance.

Ertel, A. (2001) A broking revolution. *Environmental Finance* 2(6): 32.

Eskeland, G., and A. Harrison. (1997) *Moving to Greener Pastures? Multinationals and the Pollution Haven Hypothesis*. World Bank Policy Research Working Paper #1744. Washington, DC: World Bank.

Etkin, D. (2001) Environment Canada, Adaptation and Impact Research Group, Toronto, personal communication, October 23.

European Commission DG XI—Environment, Nuclear Safety and Civil Protection. (2001) Commission organises "name and shame" seminar on city sewage. Available at www.waternunc.com/gb/dg11en49.htm.

Evans, J. (2002) Manager, Environmental Risk Management, Royal Bank of Canada, Toronto, personal communication, June 6.

Faeth, P., and S. Greenhalgh. (2001) A trading solution for water quality. *Environmental Finance* 2(6): 28–29.

FASB. (1975) *Statement of Financial Accounting Concepts No. 5: Accounting for Contingencies.* Stamford, CT: Financial Accounting Standards Board.

FASB. (1993) *Emerging Issues Task Force No. 93–5: Accounting for Environmental Liabilities.* Norwalk, CT: Financial Accounting Standards Board.

FEE. (1999) *Providing Assurance on Environmental Reporting.* Brussels: FEE Discussion Paper, October. Fédération des Experts Comptables Européens.

FEE. (2000) *Towards a Generally Accepted Framework for Environmental Reporting.* Brussels: Fédération des Experts Comptables Européens.

Feldman, S., P. Soyka, and P. Ameer. (1996) *Does Improving a Firm's Environmental Management System and Environmental Performance Result in a Higher Stock Price?* Fairfax, VA: ICF Kaiser International.

Firor, J. (1990) *The Changing Atmosphere: A Global Challenge.* New Haven: Yale University Press.

Flatz, A., L. Serck-Hanssen, and E. Tucker-Bassin. (2001) The Dow Jones Group Index. Pages 222–233 in J. Bouma, M. Jeucken, and L. Klinkers (eds.), *Sustainable Banking.* Sheffield, UK: Greenleaf.

Flur, D., L. Mendonca, and P. Nakache. (1997) Personal financial services: A question of channels. *McKinsey Quarterly* 3: 116–125.

FöreningsSparbanken. (2000) *Miljöredovisning 1999.* Stockholm: FöreningsSparbanken.

Forge. (2000) *Guidelines on Environmental Management and Reporting for the Financial Services Sector.* London: Forge Group.

Foster, D. (2001) In search of standardisation. *Environmental Finance* 2(8): 20.

Fox, C., and S. Zabel. (1997) Environmental fiduciary liability: The mist clears. *Trusts and Estates* 136(1): 30–32.

Freedman, C. (1996) Financial structure in Canada: The movement towards universal banking. Pages 724–736 in A. Saunders and I. Walter (eds.), *Universal Banking: Financial System Design Reconsidered.* Chicago: Irwin.

Friedman, M. (1970) Social responsibility of business. *New York Times Magazine* (September 13).

Friedman, T. (2000) *The Lexus and the Olive Tree.* New York: Random House.

Friends of the Earth. (2000) *Capital Punishment: UK Insurance Companies and the Global Environment.* London: Friends of the Earth.

Furrer, B., and H. Hugenschmidt. (2000) *Financial Services and ISO 14001: The Challenge of Determining Indirect Environmental Aspects in a Global Certification.* Zurich: UBS AG.

Ganzi, J., and A. DeVries. (1998) *Corporate Environmental Performance as a Factor in Financial Industry Decisions.* Status report prepared for the Office of Cooperative Environmental Management, U.S. EPA reference number K1J078/QT-DC-97-003341.

Ganzi, J., F. Seymour, and S. Buffett. (1998) *Leverage for the Environment: A Guide to the Private Financial Services Industry.* Washington, DC: World Resources Institute.

Ganzi, J., and J. Tanner. (1997) *Global Survey on Environmental Policies and Practices in the Financial Sector.* Chapel Hill, NC: Environment & Finance Enterprise.

Garber, S., and J. Hammitt. (1998) Risk premiums for environmental liability: Does Superfund increase the cost of capital? *Journal of Environmental Economics and Management* 36(3): 267–294.

General Cologne Re. (2002) Asbestos and lead. *Pollution News Review* 2(2) (June–December 2001): 17–26. Available at www.gcr.com.

Gibbs, L. M. (2001) The 20th anniversary of Love Canal. Available at www.chej.org/lcindex.html.

Giddy, I., A. Saunders, and I. Walter. (1996) Alternative models for clearance and settlement: The case of the single European capital market. *Journal of Money, Credit, and Banking* 4(2): 986–1003.

Global Commons Institute. (1999) The detailed ideas and algorithms behind contraction and convergence. Available at www.gci.org.uk.

Global Reporting Initiative (GRI). (2000) *Sustainability Reporting Guidelines on Economic, Environmental and Social Performance.* Boston: Global Reporting Initiative.

Goldman, Sachs & Co. (2001) *Investing in Risk-Linked Securities.* New York: Goldman, Sachs & Co.

Goodfellow, M. (2002) Denmark hopes for Kyoto reprieve. *Environmental Finance* 3(6): 5.

Goodin, R. (1986) The principle of voluntary agreements. *Public Administration* 64: 435–444.

Gottsman, L., and J. Kessler. (1998) Smart screened investments: Environmentally screened equity funds that perform like conventional funds. *Journal of Investing* 7(4): 15–24.

Goveia, T. (1996) Looking for cover. *Canadian Insurance* (July): 14–15, 32.

Gray, J. (1994) Environmental risk management: Royal Bank of Canada. In S. Vaughan (ed.), *Greening Financial Markets*. UNEP Round Table Meeting on Commercial Banks and the Environment, Geneva, September 26–27.

Green Futures. (1998) Money changers. *Green Futures* (January/February): 28–29.

Grice, M. (1999) BP Amoco goes global with emissions trading. *Environmental Finance* 1(1): 5.

Griffin, J., and J. Mahon. (1997) The corporate social performance and corporate financial performance debate. *Business and Society* 36(1): 5–31.

Gros, D., and K. Lannoo. (2000) *The Euro Capital Market*. Chichester, U.K.: John Wiley & Sons.

Grossman, G., and A. Kreuger. (1995) Economic growth and the environment. *Quarterly Journal of Economics* 110(2): 353–377.

Grubb, M., with C. Vrolijk and D. Brack. (1999) *The Kyoto Protocol: A Guide and Assessment*. London: Royal Institute of International Affairs.

Guerard, J. (1997) Additional evidence on the cost of being socially responsible in investing. *Journal of Investing* 6(4): 31–35.

Haggart, B., A. Laurin, G. Kieley, M. Smith, and M. Wrobel. (2001) *Bill C-8: An Act to Establish the Financial Consumer Agency of Canada, and to Amend Certain Acts in Relation to Financial Institutions*. Ottawa: Library of Parliament (February 14).

Hague, K. H. (1996) Derivatives: Bridge to the capital markets. *Canadian Underwriter* (April): 30–33.

Halal, W. (2001) The collaborative enterprise: A stakeholder model uniting profitability and responsibility. *Journal of Corporate Citizenship* 1(2): 27–42.

Hamilton, J. (1995) Pollution as news: Media and stock market reactions to the toxic release inventory data. *Journal of Environmental Economics and Management* 28(1): 98–113.

Hamilton, S., H. Jo, and M. Statman. (1993) Doing well while doing good? The investment portfolio of socially responsible mutual funds. *Financial Analysts Journal* (November/December): 62–66.

Hammond, A., A. Adriaanse, E. Rodenburg, and R. Woodward. (1995) *Environmental Indicators: A Systematic Approach to Measuring and Reporting on Environmental Policy Performance in the Context of Sustainable Development*. Washington, DC: World Resources Institute.

Harrison, R. (2002) Vice president, INVESCO, Toronto, personal communications, April.

Harry, S. (2001) A following wind. *Environmental Finance* 2(7): 28–29.

Hart, S., and G. Ahuja. (1996) Does it pay to be green? An empirical examination of the relationship between emission reduction and firm performance. *Business Strategy and the Environment* 5: 30–37.

Havemann, R., and P. Webster. (1999) *Does Ethical Investment Pay?* London: Ethical Investment Research Services (EIRIS).

Hawken, P., A. B. Lovins, and L. H. Lovins. (1999) *Natural Capitalism: The Next Industrial Revolution.* London: Earthscan.

Hector, G. (1992) A new reason you can't get a loan. *Fortune* 126(6): 107–110.

Helme, N. (2001) *Lessons Learned from National Trading Schemes.* Proceedings from Environmental Finance Carbon Finance Conference, New York, November 28–29.

Henry, E. (1999) *Environmental Responsibility for Financial Institutions: A Risk Management Approach.* UNEP Fifth Annual Round Table Meeting on Finance and the Environment, Evanston, IL, September 9–10, Geneva.

Henry, J. G., and G. W. Heinke (eds.). (1989) *Environmental Science and Engineering.* Englewood Cliffs: Prentice-Hall.

Henshaw, S. (2001) UBS Warburg, personal communication, Toronto, August 15.

Hensler, D., S. Carroll, M. White, and J. Gross. (2001) Asbestos litigation in the U.S.: A new look at an old problem. *Documented Briefing*, DB-362.0-ICJ. Santa Monica: Rand Institute for Social Justice.

Hettige, H., R. Lucas, and D. Wheeler. (1992) The toxic intensity of industrial production: Global patterns, trends, and trade policy. *American Economic Review* 82(2): 478–481.

Higuchi, K., C. W. Yuen, and A. Shabbar. (2000) Ice storm '98 in south-central Canada and northeastern United States: A climatological perspective. *Theoretical and Applied Climatology* 66, 61–79.

Holtom, R. B. (1987) *Underwriting: Principles and Practices.* 3rd ed. Hoboken, NJ: National Underwriter Company.

Hoshi, T. (1996) Back to the future: Universal banking in Japan. Pages 205–239 in A. Saunders and I. Walter (eds.), *Universal Banking: Financial System Design Reconsidered.* Chicago: Irwin.

Howes, R. (2001) Wessex Water puts a price on sustainability. *Environmental Finance* 2(10): 35–37.

Hull, J. (2000) Derivatives: Lessons we have learned. Lecture delivered on the occasion of the inauguration of the Maple Financial Group Chair in Derivatives and Risk Management, Rotman School of Management, University of Toronto, November 30, 2000.

Hunt, E., and R. Casamento. (2001) Investors enter climate debate. *Environmental Finance* 3(2): 24–25.

IASC. (1994) *International Accounting Standards*. London: International Accounting Standards Committee.

ICF Consulting. (2001) Greenhouse gas emission strategies. Available at www.emissionstrategies.com/template.cfm?NavMenuID=9.

IFAC. (1999) *Exposure Draft: Assurance Engagements—Proposed International Standard on Assurance Engagement*. London: International Federation of Accountants.

ING Group. (1999) *Environmental Annual Report*. Amsterdam: ING Group, www.inggroup.com.

Innovest SVA. (2001a) *Uncovering Hidden Value Potential for Strategic Investors*. New York: Innovest.

Innovest SVA. (2001b) Climate change and investment risk. *Research Brief* (August).

Insurance Bureau of Canada. (1994) *Improving the Climate for Insuring Environmental Risk: Report of the Environmental Committee*. Toronto: Insurance Bureau of Canada.

Insurance Information Institute (III). (2000) Environmental pollution: Insurance issues. Available at www.iii.org/media/hottopics/insurance/enviro.

Ip, G. (1996) A catastrophe play. *Globe and Mail,* Report on Business (October 19).

IPCC. (2001a) Summary for Policymakers, Climate Change 2001: The Synthesis Report of the IPCC Third Assessment Report. Available at www.ipcc.ch.

IPCC. (2001b) Summary for Policymakers, Climate Change 2001: Impacts, Adaptation and Vulnerability. A Report of Working Group II of the Intergovernmental Panel on Climate Change. Available at www.ipcc.ch.

IPCC. (2001c) Technical Summary, Climate Change 2001: Impacts, Adaptation and Vulnerability. A Report of Working Group II of the Intergovernmental Panel on Climate Change. Available at www.ipcc.ch.

Irwin, F., and J. Ranganathan. (2000) *Building Bridges: Linking GRI Reporting with Facility Environmental Reporting Initiatives*. Presentation at GRI Conference, Washington, DC, November 2000.

Insurance Services Office. (1997) *The Wildland/Urban Fire Hazard*. New York: Insurance Services Office.

Janssen, J. (2000) Implementing the Kyoto mechanisms: Potential contributions by banks and insurance companies. *Geneva Papers on Risk and Insurance* 25(4): 602–618.

Janssen, J., and U. Springer. (2001) Half a leap forward. *Environmental Finance* 3(1): xvi–xvii.

Jeucken, M. (2001) *Sustainable Finance and Banking: The Financial Sector and the Future of the Planet.* London: Earthscan.

Jeucken, M., and J. Bouma. (1999) The changing environment of banks. Pages 24–38 in J. Bouma, M. Jeucken, and L. Klinkers (eds.), *Sustainable Banking: The Greening of Finance.* Sheffield, UK: Greenleaf.

Jewson, S., and D. Whitehead. (2001) In praise of climate data. *Environmental Finance* 3(2): 22–23.

Joly, C. (2001) International Storebrand Investments, personal communication, Oslo, August 10.

Jones, G. (1999) Alternative reinsurance: Using catastrophe bonds and insurance derivatives as a mechanism for increasing capacity in the insurance markets. *CPCU Journal* 52(1): 50–54.

Jones, K., and J. Walton. (1999) Internet-based environmental reporting: Key components. Pages 412–425 in M. Bennett and P. James (eds.), *Sustainable Measures.* Sheffield, U.K.: Greenleaf.

Kahlenborn, W. (2001) German disclosure rules promise SRI boost. *Environmental Finance* 2(6): 15.

Kaplan, R., and D. Norton. (1992) The balanced scorecard—measures that drive performance. *Harvard Business Review* (January–February): 71–79.

Kashyap, A. (1999) What should regulators do about merger policy? *Journal of Banking and Finance* 23(2–4): 623–627.

Kasouf, J. C. (1996) Lead paint liability costs may increase for insurers. *Business Insurance* (June 17).

Kass, S., and J. McCarroll. (1997) Environmental disclosure in Securities and Exchange Commission filings. *Environment* 39(3): 4–6.

Kearins, K., and G. O'Malley. (1999) International financing institutions and the Three Gorges hydroelectric power scheme. *Sustainable Banking: The Greening of Finance, Greener Management International* 27 (Autumn): 49–64.

Keeling, C. D., and T. P. Whorf. (2001) Atmospheric CO_2 records from sites in the SIO air sampling network. In *Trends: A Compendium of Data on Global Change.* Oak Ridge, TN: Carbon Dioxide Information Analysis Center, Oak Ridge National Laboratory, U.S. Department of Energy.

Kelly, M., and A. Huhtala. (2001) The role of the United Nations environment programme and the financial services sector. Pages 390–400 in J. Bouma, M. Jeucken, and L. Klinkers (eds.), *Sustainable Banking: The Greening of Finance.* Sheffield, UK: Greenleaf.

Kennedy, C. (2001) McDougall, McDougall and McTier, personal communications, Toronto, October 12.

Kennedy, P. (2001) Ballard rally loses power as [share price] targets cut. *Globe and Mail*, Report on Business (October 10).

Kerry, M., G. Kelk, D. Etkin, I. Burton, and S. Kalhok. (1998) Glazed over: Canada copes with the ice storm of 1998. *Environment* 41(1), 6–11, 28–33.

Khanna, M., W. Quimo, and D. Bojilova. (1998) Toxic release information: a policy tool for environmental protection, *Journal of Environmental Economics and Management* 36(2): 243–266.

Kiernan, M. (2001) Innovest Strategic Value Advisors, personal communications, Toronto, July 21.

Kim, S., and R. Singer. (1997) US and Japanese banks: A comparative and evaluative analysis. *Bankers Magazine* (March/April): 56–61.

Kinder, P., and A. Domini. (1997) Social screening: Paradigms old and new. *Journal of Investing* 6(4): 12–19.

Kintner, E. (1993) Politics and deregulation in the Canadian banking industry. *American Review of Canadian Studies* (Summer): 231–246.

Kirby, J. (2001a) Goldman plans weather desk. *Environmental Finance* 2(10): 5.

Kirby, J. (2001b) Shell commits to green trading. *Environmental Finance* 3(1): 8.

Klassen, R., and C. McLaughlin. (1996) The impact of environmental management on a firm's performance. *Management Science* 42(8): 1199–1214.

Knörzer, A. (2001) The transition from environmental funds to sustainable investment. Pages 211–221 in J. Bouma, M. Jeucken, and L. Klinkers (eds.), *Sustainable Banking*. Sheffield, U.K.: Greenleaf.

Koechlin, D., and K. Muller. (1992) Environmental management and investment decisions. Pages 115–127 in D. Koechlin and K. Muller (eds.), *Green Business Opportunities: The Profit Potential*. London: Financial Times Pitman.

Konar, S., and M. Cohen. (1997) Information as regulation: The effect of community right to know laws on toxic emissions. *Journal of Environmental Economics and Management* 32(1): 109–124.

KPMG. (1994) *1993 KPMG International Survey of Environmental Reporting*. London: KPMG.

KPMG. (1997) *KPMG International Survey of Environmental Reporting 1996*. London: KPMG.

KPMG. (1998) *The Supply-Side of Environmental Information*. The Hague: KPMG Consulting.

KPMG. (1999) *KPMG International Survey of Environmental Reporting 1999*. London: KPMG.

Kurtz, L. (1995) No effect or no net effect? Studies on socially responsible investing. *Journal of Investing* 6(4): 37–49.

Kurtz, L., and D. DiBartholomeo. (1996) Socially screened portfolios: An attribution analysis of relative performance. *Journal of Investing* (Fall): 35–41.

Labatt, S., and V. Maclaren. (1998) Voluntary corporate environmental initiatives: A typology and preliminary investigation. *Environment and Planning C: Government and Public Policy* 16(2): 191–209.

Lanoie, P., B. Laplante, and M. Roy. (1997) *Can Capital Markets Create Incentives for Pollution Control?* World Bank Policy Research Department Working Paper #1753, www.worldbank.org/research/workingpapers.

Laplante, B., and P. Lanoie. (1994) The market response to environmental incidents in Canada: A theoretical and empirical analysis. *Southern Economic Journal* 60: 657–672.

Lappen, A. (1999) Think local, act global. *Institutional Investor* 33(5): 71–82.

Lecomte, E. L., A. W. Pang, and J. W. Russell. (1998) *Ice Storm '98.* Toronto: Institute for Catastrophic Loss Reduction, Insurance Council of Canada.

Lecomte, P. (1999) *Polluted Sites: Remediation of Soils and Groundwater.* Rotterdam: A. A. Balkema.

Leggett, J. (1990) *Global Warming: The Greenpeace Report.* Oxford: Oxford University Press.

Leggett, J. (1993) Climate change and the insurance industry: Solidarity among the risk community? *Greenpeace International Special Publication* (February).

Leggett, J. (1995) Climate change and the financial sector. *Journal of the Society of Fellows, Chartered Insurance Institute* 1–23.

Leggett, J. (1999) *The Carbon War: Dispatches from the End of the Oil Century.* New York: Penguin Putnam.

Levin, A., C. Titterton, and J. Sharaf. (1995) CIGNA plays "good bank/bad bank" with insureds. *National Underwriter* 99(43): 21–23.

Levin, A. M. (1996) Environmental liability and the insurance industry. *Standard & Poor's CreditWeek*, Special Report (October 30): 108.

Levy, J. (1992) Landlord and lender liability for hazardous waste clean-up: A review of the evolving Canadian and American case law. *Canadian Business Law Journal* 20: 269–304.

Li, Y., and B. McConomy. (1999) An empirical examination of factors affecting the timing of environmental accounting standard adoption and impact on corporate valuation. *Journal of Accounting, Auditing and Finance* 14(3): 279–321.

Llewellyn, D. (1996) Universal banking and the public interest. Pages 161–204 in A. Saunders and I. Walter (eds.), *Universal Banking: Financial System Design Reconsidered*. Chicago: Irwin.

Lloyd's. (2000) Key dates in Lloyd's history. Available at www.lloyds oflondon.co.uk.

Loss Prevention Council. (1997) *Assessment of Pollution Risk*. Borehamwood, U.K.: Loss Prevention Council.

Mansley, M. (1994) *Long Term Financial Risks to the Carbon Fuel Industry from Climate Change*. London: Delphi Group.

Mansley, M., and A. Dlugolecki. (2001) *Climate Change—A Risk Management Challenge for Institutional Investors*. London: Universities Superannuation Scheme Ltd.

Margolick, M., and D. Russel. (2001) *Corporate Greenhouse Gas Reduction Targets*. Arlington, VA: Pew Center on Global Climate Change.

Marinetto, M. (1998) The shareholders strike back: Issues in the research of shareholder activism. *Environmental Politics* 7(3): 125–133.

Marshall, E. (2001) Socially responsible investment looking east. *Environmental Finance* 2(7): 24.

Mason, P. (1999) Pollution log could be screening tool. *Ethical Performance* 1(3): 5.

Mathias, A. (2002a) Why not cat bonds? *Environmental Finance* 3(5): 22–23.

Mathias, A. (2002b) Dutch shelve domestic trading scheme. *Environmental Finance* 3(7): 6.

McClintick, D. (2000) The decline and fall of Lloyd's of London. *Time* (February 21): 38–58.

McGrath, L. (2002) Director, Fondelec Group, Stamford, CT, personal communications, May 1.

McIntyre, R. (2000). PAR for the weather course. *Environmental Finance* 1(6): 27–29.

Melitz, J. (1990) Financial regulation in France. *European Economic Review* 34(2/3): 394–402.

Merkl, A., and H. Robinson. (1997) Environmental risk management: Take it back from the lawyers and engineers. *McKinsey Quarterly* (3): 150–163.

Meyer, A., and T. Cooper. (2000) Why convergence and contraction are the key. *Environmental Finance* 1(7): 19–21.

Meyer, P., R. Williams, and K. Yount. (1995) *Contaminated Land: Reclamation, Redevelopment and Reuse in the United States and the European Union*. Aldershot, U.K.: Edward Elgar.

Miller, P. (1997) Superfund—Who is cleaning up? Speech delivered at the Insurance Institute of London, February 27.

Millette, M. (2001) Goldman Sachs, VP Risk Management Group, personal communications, November 26.

Mills, E., E. Lecomte, and A. Peara. (2001) *U.S. Insurance Industry Perspectives on Global Climate Change*. Berkeley: Lawrence Berkeley National Laboratory, University of California.

Mittler, E. (1997) A case study of Florida's homeowners' insurance since Hurricane Andrew. Natural Hazards Research Working Paper #96. Institute of Behavioral Science, University of Colorado.

Moffet, J., and D. Saxe. (1996) *Voluntary Compliance Measures in Canada*. Prepared for the North American Commission for Environmental Cooperation, March 29.

Munich Re. (1997) *Flooding and Insurance*. Munich: Munich Re.

Munich Re. (1999) *Topics 2000: Natural Catastrophes—The Current Position*. Munich: Munich Re.

Munich Re. (2001a) *Munich Re Group, Annual Report 2000*. Munich: Munich Re.

Munich Re. (2001b) *Topics: Annual Review of Natural Catastrophes 2000*. Munich: Munich Re.

Munich Re. (2001c) *Perspectives: Today's Ideas for Tomorrow's World*. Munich: Munich Re Environmental Magazine.

Muoghalu, M., I. Robison, H. Daid, and J. Glascock. (1990) Hazardous waste lawsuits, stockholder returns, and deterrence. *Southern Economic Journal* 57(2): 357–370.

Natural Resources Canada. (2000) *Sustainable Development Strategy*. Ottawa: Natural Resources Canada.

Nattrass, B., and M. Altomare. (1999) *The Natural Step for Business*. Gabriola Island, British Columbia, Canada: New Society Press.

Neale, A. (2001) Pension funds and socially responsible investment. *Journal of Corporate Citizenship* 1(2): 43–55.

Negenman, M. (2001) Sustainable banking and the ASN Bank. Pages 66–71 in J. Bouma, M. Jeucken, and L. Klinkers (eds.), *Sustainable Banking*. Sheffield, U.K.: Greenleaf.

Nguyen, L. (2001) Attack puts heat on Talisman. *Globe and Mail* (September 15): B6.

Nguyen, L., and J. Mahoney. (2001) Edmonton Talisman stake ignites controversy. *Globe and Mail* (April 6): B1, B6.

Nicholls, M. (1999) Investors eye new weather structure. *Environmental Finance* 1(1): 4.

Nicholls, M. (1999/2000) City welcomes new rating. *Environmental Finance* 1(3): 18–20.

Nicholls, M. (2000a) The bankers are coming. *Environmental Finance* 1(10): 14–15.

Nicholls, M. (2000b) US firms 'infringing SEC rules' on environmental disclosure. *Environmental Finance* 2(2): 4.

Nicholls, M. (2001a) New Japanese eco-fund bucks market. *Environmental Finance* 2(10): 6.

Nicholls, M. (2001b) New energy firms face tough times. *Environmental Finance* 2(7): 18–20.

Nicholls, M. (2001c) Market eyes Liffe weather indexes. *Environmental Finance* 2(10): 8.

Nicholls, M. (2001d) AGO stamps its approval on carbon neutrality. *Environmental Finance* 3(1): 7.

Nicholls, M. (2001e) Huge weather trade heralds new capacity. *Environmental Finance* 2(7): 4.

Nicholls, M. (2001f) Climate change and cooperation. *Environmental Finance* 3(2): 2.

Nicholls, M. (2001g) Battle looms on EU emissions trading scheme. *Environmental Finance* 3(2): 4.

Nicholls, M. (2001h) US, Canada halfway to cross-border market. *Environmental Finance* 3(2): 5.

Nicholls, M. (2001i) Insurers return . . . but in company. *Environmental Finance* 2(10): 32–33.

Nicholls, M. (2001j) Summer season hots up. *Environmental Finance* 2(5): 13–14.

Nicholls, M. (2001k) Funds add SRI to governance rules. *Environmental Finance* 2(6): 7.

Nicholls, M. (2001l) AGF, SG boost weather capacity. *Environmental Finance* 2(4): 7.

Nicholls, M. (2001m) Never mind the ballots. *Environmental Finance* 2(8): 12–13.

Nicholls, M. (2001n) After Bonn, what price carbon? *Environmental Finance* 2(10): 16–18.

Nicholls, M. (2001o) Deutsche Bank enters emissions market. *Environmental Finance* 2(10): 5.

Nicholls, M. (2001p) "Little thought" given to measuring SRI success. *Environmental Finance* 2(4): 8.

Nicholls, M. (2002a) CDM fears cloud Marrakech success. *Environmental Finance* 3(3): 24–25.

Nicholls, M. (2002b) Relative values. *Environmental Finance* 3(6): xi.

Nicholls, M. (2002c) Not trading but hedging. *Environmental Finance* 3(6): 14–15.

Nicholls, M. (2002d) Trading begins in UK ETS—and across borders. *Environmental Finance* 3(7): 4.

Niedzielski, J. (1996) N.J. okays claim on voluntary pollution cleanup. *National Underwriter* (April 1): 5–6.

NOAA (National Oceanic and Atmospheric Administration). (1999) www.publicaffairs.noaa.gov/storms.

NPRI. (1996) *National Pollution Release Inventory: Summary Report.* Hull, Quebec: Environment Canada.

NRTEE. (1996) *The Financial Services Sector and Brownfield Development.* Ottawa: National Round Table on the Environment and the Economy.

NRTEE. (1999) *Measuring Eco-Efficiency in Business: Feasibility of a Core Set of Indicators.* Ottawa: National Round Table on the Environment and the Economy.

NRTEE. (2001) *Calculating Eco-Efficiency Indicators: A Workbook for Industry.* Ottawa: National Round Table on the Environment and the Economy.

O'Sullivan, N. (2001) UNEP FI, personal communications, Geneva, October 1.

Pacelle, M. (2001) Federal-Mogul to seek protection. *Globe and Mail*, Report on Business (October 1): B6.

Parry, M., and other contributors. (1991) *The Potential Effects of Climate Change on the United Kingdom.* London: H.M.S.O.

Partner Re. (1997) *Floods: Causes, Effects and Risk Assessment.* Pembroke, Bermuda: Partner Reinsurance Co. Ltd.

Partner Re. (1998) *Hurricane Georges, September 15–29, 1998, Partner Research.* Pembroke, Bermuda: Partner Reinsurance Co. Ltd.

Patten, D., and J. Nance. (1998) Regulatory cost effects in a good news environment: The intra-industry reaction to the Alaskan oil spill. *Journal of Accounting and Public Policy* 17(4–5): 409–429.

Patzelt, R. (1995) Presentation to the Insurance Bureau of Canada Symposium on Improving the Climate for Insuring Environmental Risk, Toronto, June 7.

Pava, M., and J. Krausz. (1996) The association between corporate social responsibility and financial performance: The paradox of social costs. *Journal of Business Ethics* 15(3): 321–357.

Pembina. (1998) *Corporate Action on Climate Change 1997: An Independent Review.* Drayton Valley, Alberta, Canada: Pembina Institute for Appropriate Development.

Piesse, J. (1992) Environmental spending and share price performance: The petroleum industry. *Business Strategy and the Environment* 1(1): 45–52.

PIRC. (1998) *Environmental and Social Reporting: A Survey of Current Practice at FTSE350 Companies.* Pension Investment Research Consultants (PIRC) Seminar, London, February 1998.

Plungis, J. (2001) California mandates zero-emission vehicles by 2003. *Detroit News* (January 27).

Porter, M., and C. van der Linde. (1995) Green and competitive: Ending the stalemate. *Harvard Business Review* 73(5): 120–134.

Pritchard, P. (2000) *Environmental Risk Management.* London: Earthscan.

Probst, K. N., and D. M. Konisky. (2001) *Superfund's Future: What Will It Cost?* Washington, DC: Resources for the Future.

Radecki, L., J. Wenninger, and D. Orlow. (1997) Industry structure: Electronic delivery's potential effects on retail banking. *Journal of Retail Banking Services* 19(4): 57–63.

Ranganathan, J., and A. Willis. (1999) *The Global Reporting Initiative: An Emerging Tool for Corporate Accountability.* Washington, DC: World Resources Institute.

Rappaport, E. N. (1993) *Hurricane Andrew, 16–28 August 1992: Preliminary report.* Available at ftp://ftp.nhc.noaa.gov/pub/storm_archives/atlantic/prelimat/atl1992/andrew/.

Rauberger, R., and B. Wagner. (1997) *Environmental Reporting for Financial Service Providers.* Bonn: Verein fur Umweltmanagment in Banken, Sparkassen und Versicherungen (VfU).

Read, A. (1997) Building signposts for the future: Pension fund investment strategy, socially responsible investing, and ERISA. *Journal of Pension Planning and Compliance* 23(3): 39–55.

Reed, D. (1998) *Green Shareholder Value: Hype or Hit?* Washington, DC: World Resources Institute.

Repetto, R., and D. Austin. (2000) *Pure Profit: The Financial Implications of Environmental Performance.* Washington, DC: World Resources Institute.

Rikhardsson, P. (1999) Statutory environmental reporting in Denmark. Pages 344–352 in M. Bennett and P. James (eds.), *Sustainable Measures.* Sheffield, U.K.: Greenleaf.

Robson, D. (2000) Finance firms offered help with reporting. *Environmental Finance* 2(3): 9.

Romm, J. J. (1999) *Cool Companies: How the Best Businesses Boost Profits and Productivity by Cutting Greenhouse Gas Emissions.* London: Earthscan.

Rosenzweig, R., M. Varilek, and J. Janssen. (2002) *The Emerging International Greenhouse Gas Market*. Arlington, VA: Pew Center on Global Climate Change.

Rosewell, B. (2001) GHG trading: Easier than you think. *Environmental Finance* 3(1): xii–xv.

Ross, A., and J. Rowan-Robinson. (1997) It's good to talk! Environmental information and the greening of industry. *Journal of Environmental Planning and Management* 40(1): 111–124.

Ross, A. H. (1997) Kyoto and beyond. *Canadian Insurance* (December, 10): 19, 26.

Russo, M., and P. Fouts. (1997) A resource-based perspective on corporate environmental performance and profitability. *Academy of Management Journal* 40(3): 534–559.

Sandor, R. (2000) SO_2 market exceeds expectations. *Environmental Finance* 1(7): 11.

Sandor, R. (2001) Corporate giants to aid design of US carbon market. *Environmental Finance* 3(4): 14.

Sandor, R. (2002) CCX progress report. *Environmental Finance* 2(8): 11.

Saunders, A., and I. Walter (eds.). (1994) *Universal Banking in the United States*. New York: Oxford University Press.

Saunderson, E. (2000/2001) Equity analysts wake to weather. *Environmental Finance* 2(3): 22.

Saunderson, E. (2001a) Stream flow deals quicken. *Environmental Finance* 3(1): 15–16.

Saunderson, E. (2001b) European firms blow cool on weather derivatives. *Environmental Finance* 2(6): 26–27.

Schaltegger, S. (1997) Information costs, quality of information and stakeholder involvement: The necessity of international standards of ecological accounting. *Eco-Management and Auditing* 4: 87–97.

Schaltegger, S., and R. Burritt (2000) *Contemporary Environmental Accounting: Issues, Concepts and Practice*. Sheffield, UK: Greenleaf.

Schaltegger, S., and A. Sturm. (1998) *Eco-efficiency by Eco-Controlling*. Zurich: Swiss Federal Institute of Technology.

Schmidheiny, S., and Zorraquin, F. (1996) *Financing Change: The Financial Community, Eco-Efficiency and Sustainable Development*. Washington, DC: MIT Press.

Schmid-Schonbein, O., and A. Braunschweig. (2000) *Environmental Performance Indicators for the Financial Industry*. Zurich: E2 Management Consulting AG.

Sclafane, S. (1996) EIL "Black Hole" manageable, Best says. *National Underwriter* (January 22): 1, 6.

Scott, P. (2000) Reporting all over the world. *Environmental Finance* 2(3): 36–37.

Scott-Quinn, B. (1990) US investment banks as multinationals. Pages 268–293 in G. Jones (ed.), *Banks as Multinationals*. London: Routledge.

SEC. (1993) *Accounting and Disclosure Relating to Loss Contingencies*. Staff Accounting Bulletin No. 92. Washington, DC: U.S. Securities and Exchange Commission.

Siddiqui, F., and P. Newman. (2001) Grameen Shakti: Financing renewable energy in Bangladesh. Pages 88–95 in J. Bouma, M. Jeucken, and L. Klinkers (eds.), *Sustainable Banking*. Sheffield, UK: Greenleaf.

Silcoff, S. (2001) Fund giant battles for rights. *Financial Post* (May 21): C1, C8.

Simm, I., and B. Jenkyn-Jones. (2000) Turning green to gold. *Environmental Finance* 2(2): 28–29.

Skillius, Å., and U. Wennberg. (1998) *Continuity, Credibility and Comparability: Corporate Environmental Reporting*. European Environment Agency, Environmental Issues Series No. 9, Lund University, Sweden.

Skinner, D. (1994) Why firms voluntarily disclose bad news. *Journal of Accounting Research* 32(1): 38–60.

Sloan, M. (2001) Renewable energy credits—a success in Texas. *Environmental Finance* 2(6): 23.

Smith, M. (1996) Shareholder activism by institutional investors: Evidence from CalPERS. *Journal of Finance* 51(1): 227–252.

Smithson, C. W. (1998) *Managing Financial Risk: A Guide to Derivatives Products, Financial Engineering and Value Maximization*. 3rd ed. New York: McGraw-Hill.

Social Investment Forum. (1999) *1999 Report on Socially Responsible Investing Trends in the United States*. www.socialinvest.org/areas/research/trends/1999–Trends.htm.

South, S. (2000) *Corporate Leadership on Climate Change*. Arlington, VA: Cutter Information Corp.

Southam, S. F., B. N. Mills, R. J. Moulton, and D. W. Brown. (1999) The potential impact of climate change on Ontario's Grand River Basin: Water supply and demand issues. *Canadian Water Resources Journal* 24(4): 307–330.

Spindle, B. (1998) Japan's brokers meet mutual funds match. *Asia Wall Street Journal Weekly* (November 30): 1, 4.

Stanwick, S., and P. Stanwick. (2000) The relationship between environmental disclosure and financial performance: An empirical study of US firms. *Eco-Management and Auditing* 7: 155–164.

Statistics Canada. (1990a) Road motor vehicles registrations. Catalogue No. 63–223 Annual. Ottawa: Statistics Canada.

Statistics Canada. (1990b) National income and expenditure accounts. Catalogue No. 53–219 Annual. Ottawa: Statistics Canada.

Steinherr, A. (1996) Performance of universal banks: Historical review and appraisal. Pages 2–30 in A. Saunders and I. Walter (eds.), *Universal Banking: Financial System Design Reconsidered*. Chicago: Irwin.

Stetter, T., and K. Böswald. (2002) Lessons from UBS. *Environmental Finance* 3(4): 16.

Storebrand Scudder. (1996) *Storebrand Scudder Environmental Value Fund*. Oslo: Storebrand ASA.

Stratos Inc., Alan Willis and Associates, and SustainAbility Ltd. (2001) *Stepping Forward: Corporate Sustainability Reporting in Canada*. Ottawa: Stratos Inc. Available at www.stratos-sts.com.

Street, P., and P. Monaghan. (2001) Assessing the sustainability of bank service channels: The case of the Co-operative Bank. Pages 72–87 in J. Bouma, M. Jeucken, and L. Klinkers (eds.), *Sustainable Banking*. Sheffield, UK: Greenleaf.

SustainAbility. (2000) *A Responsible Investment?* London: Centre for Business Performance, Institute of Chartered Accountants of England and Wales (ICAEW), SustainAbility Ltd.

SustainAbility/Ketchum/UNEP. (2002) *Good News & Bad: The Media, Corporate Social Responsibility and Sustainable Development*. London: SustainAbility Ltd.

SustainAbility/UNEP. (1999) *The Global Reporter*. London: SustainAbility Ltd.

SustainAbility/UNEP. (2001) *Buried Treasure: Uncovering the Business Case for Corporate Sustainability*. London: SustainAbility Ltd.

Sutton, B. (1991) *The Property and Casualty Insurance Industry*. Ottawa: Conference Board of Canada.

Swiss Re. (1994) *Global Warming: Element of Risk*. Zurich: Swiss Re.

Swiss Re. (1998) *The Global Reinsurance Market in the Midst of Consolidation*. Swiss Reinsurance Company Sigma Report No. 9/98. Zurich: Swiss Re.

Swiss Re. (1999a) *Environmental Report*. Zurich: Swiss Re.

Swiss Re. (1999b) *Insurance-Linked Securities*. Zurich: Swiss Re.

Swiss Re. (2000a) *Japan's Insurance Markets—A Sea Change*. Sigma Report No. 8/2000. Zurich: Swiss Re.

Swiss Re. (2000b) *Europe in Focus: Non-life Markets Undergoing Structural Change*. Sigma Report No. 3/2000. Zurich: Swiss Re.

Swiss Re. (2000c) *The Impact of e-Business on the Insurance Industry: Pressure to Adapt—Chance to Reinvent*. Swiss Reinsurance Company Sigma Report No 5/2000. Zurich: Swiss Re.

Swiss Re. (2000d) *Emerging Markets: The Insurance Industry in the Face of Globalization*. Swiss Reinsurance Company Sigma Report No. 4/2000. Zurich: Swiss Re.

Swiss Re. (2001a) *World Financial Centres: New Horizons in Insurance and Banking*. Swiss Re Sigma Report No. 7/2001. Zurich: Swiss Re.

Swiss Re. (2001b) *Capital Market Innovation in the Insurance Industry*. Swiss Re Sigma Report No. 3/2001. Zurich: Swiss Re.

Tarna, K. (2001) Reporting on the environment: Current practices in the financial services sector. Pages 149–165 in J. Bouma, M. Jeucken, and L. Klinkers (eds.), *Sustainable Banking: The Greening of Finance*. Sheffield, UK: Greenleaf.

Taylor, M. (1995) *What's Wrong with the Chemical Release Inventory? The Fundamental Flaws*. Lutton, UK: Friends of the Earth.

Thomas, E. (2001) Danish power sector squeals. *Environmental Finance* 3(1): xi.

Thomas, W. (2001) Globalisation and its discontents. *Environmental Finance* 2(5): 26–28.

Thompson, G. (1993) The impact of environmental law on the lending industry in Canada. Pages 409–453 in G. Thompson, M. McConnell, and L. Huestis (eds.), *Environmental Law and Business in Canada*. Aurora, Ontario: Canada Law Books.

Thompson, H. (1995) The role of financial institutions in encouraging improved environmental performance. In M. Rogers (ed.), *Business and the Environment*. London: MacMillan Press.

Thompson, M. (1998) *TransAlta's Sustainable Development Efforts, Successes and Challenges—1988–2000*. Geneva: International Academy of the Environment.

Tindale, S. (2001) Confront and engage. *Environmental Finance* 2(7): 32.

Toulson, D. (2000) Pricing the weather—basic strategies. *Environmental Finance* 1(4): 27–29.

Triodos Bank. (2000) *Milieujaarverslag 1999*. Zeist, Netherlands: Triodos Bank.

UBS. (2000) *Environmental Report*. Zurich: Union Bank of Switzerland. www.ubs.com/environment.

U.K. Department of Trade and Industry. (2002) The renewables obligation/ Non-fossil fuel obligation. Available at http://www.dti.gov.uk.

UNEP (United Nations Environment Program). (2000) Statement of Environmental Commitment by the Insurance Industry. Available at http://unepfi.net/iii/index.htm.

UNEP. (2001) *0.618. . . , UNEP FI Quarterly* 1 (June), Geneva.

UNEP FI. (1999) *Financial Institutions Initiative 1998 Survey.* Geneva: UNEP.

UNEP/SustainAbility. (1994) *Company Environmental Reporting: A Measure of the Progress of Business and Industry Towards Sustainable Development.* Technical Report No. 24. Paris: United Nations Environmental Program, Industry and Environment (UNEP IE).

UNEP/SustainAbility. (1996a) *Engaging Stakeholders: The Benchmark Survey—The Second International Progress Report on Company Environmental Reporting.* London: UNEP/SustainAbility Ltd.

UNEP/SustainAbility. (1996b) *Engaging Stakeholders: Twelve Users Respond to Company Environmental Reporting.* London: UNEP/ SustainAbility Ltd.

UNEP/SustainAbility. (1999) *The Internet Reporting Report.* London: UNEP/SustainAbility Ltd.

Valdez, S. (1997) *An Introduction to Global Financial Markets.* 2nd ed. Basingstoke, UK: MacMillan Press Ltd.

van Bellegem, T. (2001) The green fund system in the Netherlands. Pages 234–244 in J. Bouma, M. Jeucken, and L. Klinkers (eds.), *Sustainable Banking.* Sheffield, UK: Greenleaf.

Varilek, M. (2000) What Kyoto can learn from the NOx market. *Environmental Finance* 1(9): 20.

VfU. (1996) *Environmental Reporting of Financial Service Providers: A Guide to Content, Structure, and Performance Ratios of Environmental Reports for Banks and Savings Banks.* Bonn: Verein fur Umweltmanagement in Banken (Association for Environmental Management in Banks, Savings Banks and Insurance Companies).

Victor, D. G. (2001) *The Collapse of the Kyoto Protocol and the Struggle to Slow Global Warming.* Princeton: Princeton University Press.

von Weizsäcker, E., A. B. Lovins, and L. H. Lovins. (1998) *Factor Four: Doubling Wealth, Halving Resource Use.* London: Earthscan.

Waddock, S., and S. Graves. (1997) The corporate social performance–financial performance link. *Strategic Management Journal* 18(4): 303–319.

Wade, S., J. Hossell, M. Hough, and C. Fenn (eds.). (1999) *Rising to the Challenge: Impacts of Climate Change in the South East in the 21st Century.* Epsom: W. S. Atkins.

Walsh, M. J. (2002) Senior Vice President, Environmental Financial Products LLC, Chicago, personal communication, May 30.

Watson, R. T., M. C. Zinyowera, and R. H. Moss, eds. (1996) *Climate Change 1995: Impacts, Adaptations and Mitigation of Climate Change: Scientific-Technical Analyses.* Published for the Intergovernmental Panel on Climate Change. Cambridge: Cambridge University Press.

Weber, J. (1996) Is CIGNA's asbestos plan fireproof? *Business Week* (December 16): 118.

Wessex Water Ltd. (2000) *Striking a Balance.* Bristol, England: Wessex Water.

Wessex Waterservices. (2001) *Tapping into Your Water Source.* Bristol, England: Wessex Water. www.wessexwater.co.uk.

White, A. (2000) *Introductory comments.* GRI Conference, Washington, November 2000.

White, M. (1995) The performance of environmental mutual funds in the United States and Germany. Pages 323–344 in D. Collins and E. Starik (eds.), *Research in Corporate Social Performance and Policy*, Supplement 1. Greenwich, CT: JAI Press.

White, M. (1996) *Investor Response to the Exxon Valdez Spill.* Southern Finance Association Meeting, presentation paper, Sarasota, FL, November.

White, R. R. (2001) Catastrophe options: An experiment in the management of catastrophic risk in the United States. *Journal of Environmental Management* 62(3) (July): 323–326.

White, R. R., and D. Etkin. (1997) Climate change, extreme events and the Canadian insurance industry. *Natural Hazards* 16: 135–163.

White, W. (1998) *The Coming Transformation of Continental European Banking?* Basel: Bank for International Settlement, Monetary and Economic Department.

Whittacker, M. (2001) Innovest Strategic Value Advisors, Inc., personal communications, October 1.

Whittacker, M., and M. Kiernan. (2001) *Environmental Performance in Industry: Hidden Risks and Value Potential for Strategic Investors.* Toronto: Innovest Strategic Advisors Inc.

Willard, R. (2002) *The Sustainability Advantage: Seven Business Case Benefits of a Triple Bottom Line.* Galliano Island, Canada: New Society Publishers.

Williams, M. (2001) Japan's banks pump out cash. *Globe and Mail* (September 27): B13.

Willis, A. (2001) Mum's the word on bank mergers, yet it's still a hot topic. *Globe and Mail* (August 23): B14.

Willis, A., and J. Desjardins. (2001) *Environmental Performance: Measuring and Managing What Matters*. Toronto: Canadian Institute of Chartered Accountants.

Wocjik, J. (1996) Voluntary cleanup covered. *Business Insurance* (April 1): 1, 4.

World Bank. (1999) *Greening Industry: New Roles for Communities, Markets and Governments*. Washington, DC: World Bank Policy Research Report.

World Bank. (2000) *Entering the 21st Century: World Bank Development Report 1999/2000*. Washington, DC: World Bank.

World Resources Institute. (2001) NutrientNet. Available at www.nutrient net.org.

Zeng, L. (2000) Weather derivatives and weather insurance: Concept, application and analysis. *Journal of the American Meteorological Society* 81(9) (September): 2075–2082.

index

CPSIA information can be obtained at www.ICGtesting.com
Printed in the USA
BVOW031030270812

298787BV00005B/1/P